The Joburg Book

Edited by Nechama Brodie

First published 2008
by Pan Macmillan South Africa
Private Bag X19, Northlands 2116
www.panmacmillan.co.za

and

Sharp Sharp Media
48 Rothesay Avenue, Craighall Park 2196

ISBN-13: 9781770100794

Design: Adéle Sherlock and Orange Juice Design
Typesetting and layout: Adéle Sherlock and
Pilgrim Communications
Proofreading: Isabelle Delvare, Valda Strauss, Kirsty von Gogh
Printed and bound in Malaysia

Acknowledgments
The publishers would like to thank the following people for their advice and assistance in conceptualizing and producing The Joburg
Book: Lael Bethlehem, Elsabe Booysens, Jenny Briscoe, Don Briscoe, Branko Brkic, Luli Callinicos, Marie Canin, City of Johannesburg –
Land Use Management, Lucille Davie, Mandy Esterhuysen, Neil Fraser, Sally Gaule, Vance Gray, Phil Harrison, Daryl Howes, Jo'burg
Property Company, Johannesburg Development Agency, Khotso Kekana, Gugu Mazibuko, Sammy Mafu, Kensani Maluleku, Rees
Mann, Revel Mason, John Matshikiza, Alice Moloto, Kamini Pillay, Pier Luigi Porciani – the editor of La Voce, Kobus Potgieter, Lloyd
Ross, Lauren Segal, Francois Smit, Natercia Taylor, Urban Inc, Basil van Rooyen, Naashon Zalk, the staff of The Lenasia Indicator.

Contents

Greater Joburg

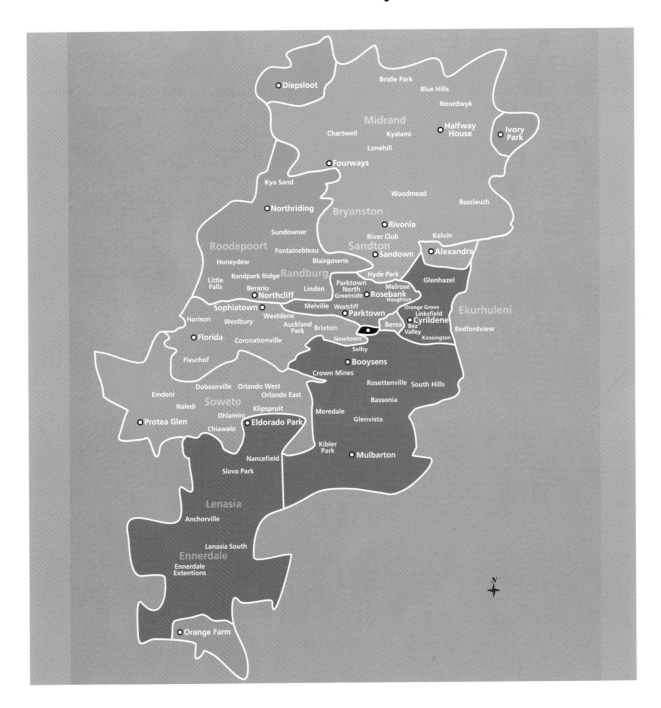

Introduction

Johannesburg covers a geographical area slightly larger than that of Greater London – some 1644 km^2, divided by mine dumps and money, railway tracks and freeways.

A little over twenty years ago – to mark the city's centenary in 1986 – the Johannesburg City Council published a history of the city, called Johannesburg: One Hundred Years. Of the book's 332 pages, just ten mention Soweto; while Alexandra is mentioned on only two pages. Written at the height of the national state of emergency, the book reveals as much by its omissions as by its carefully researched content.

The events of history cannot be changed, but how we recount them does alter: our representations of our past are filtered through our present. The Joburg Book tells the history of Johannesburg from the vantage point of 14 years of democracy, which is to say of equal parts of optimism and frustration. It also explores this history in an unusual way: through space as well as time. Each chapter – with the exception of the first and last – explores a specific urban geography (broadly, the centre, east, west, north and south of the city) by looking at the communities that have inhabited these spaces. Spaces traditionally excluded – such as Soweto, Sophiatown and Fietas – have been specifically included; as have urban areas largely ignored even by contemporary historians: Lenasia, Alexandra, the city's informal settlements, and the 'southern suburbs'.

The content, developed and written over several years by a motley and gifted network of academics, journalists, urban geographers and urban warriors, aims to present an inclusive history of Johannesburg. What this means in practice is that some aspects of Joburg's history have had to be edited out, or reduced to fleeting references, in order to make space for others. Where possible, the book refers the reader to other, more specialised, publications that offer greater insight into some of the themes, topics and events it covers.

Three researchers and writers deserve special mention – not because they have contributed directly to this book (although they are cited many times, and we are fortunate to include extracts from their work), but because they have inspired and paved the way for future readers, writers and students of history.

Social historian, Luli Callinicos, who continues to write great histories, is noted for her early volumes detailing working life on the Rand and how ordinary people survived in the city (in Working Life 1886–1940, published by Ravan but now out of print). Also acknowledged is historian and story-weaver, Charles van Onselen, whose essays contained in New Babylon, New Nineveh (Jonathan Ball) remain the best-researched and undoubtedly best-written accounts of Johannesburg's early years. The third individual singled out is Keith Beavon, a master of an area of knowledge known as 'urban geography', which I had not even heard of before I started to work on this book. Four years ago, Keith published his exceptional Johannesburg: The Making and Shaping of the City (University of South Africa Press). His research has transformed my own understanding of how this city works, and of how it grew. As Keith also trained the wonderful Margot Rubin, one of this book's contributors, I owe him a double debt.

Thanks are owed also to Kathy Brookes, former curator of the unimaginably vast collection of archive images at Museum Africa. Kathy and her colleagues provided this book with most of its visual history. I hope that the archives, and the people who work with them, will one day receive the recognition and resources they deserve.

Nechama Brodie
June 2008

WHAT CAME

Ancient rivers filled with gold, a deep-impact meteor strike and massive swellings of molten magma from the earth's mantle contributed to the formation of the world's richest goldfields — and may have set the scene for the dawn of humankind.

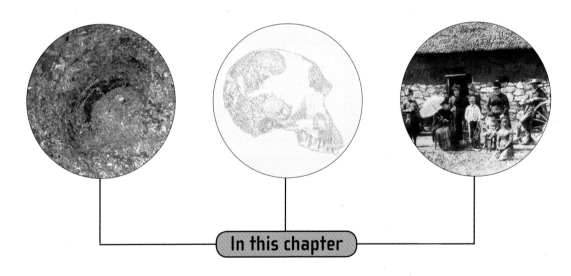

In this chapter

☞ The Origins of Gold

☞ The Cradle of Humankind

☞ Iron Age Johannesburg

☞ Pre-Colonial Johannesburg

☞ The Early Boers

BEFORE

Aerial view of iron age settlements west of Johannesburg

Nine hundred years ago, South Africa's 'city of gold' was home to the most complex society in southern Africa. It was the largest kingdom on the sub-continent; a settlement where the elite lived high on a hill, separated from the commoners and livestock kraals sprawled below. Objects made of iron, copper, gold and ivory were exchanged with traders from as far away as Persia, Egypt, India and China, and royalty was buried with intricately wrought gold ornaments.

Today, the remains of this settlement can be seen on one of the hills within the Mapungubwe National Park, on the border between South Africa and Zimbabwe – more than 550 km away from what would later be revealed as the richest gold deposits in the world, near present-day Johannesburg.

The Mapungubwe ruins yielded several gold artefacts of breathtaking beauty and craftsmanship; but the kingdom's gold probably came from ancient mines at Ngwenya, in modern Swaziland.

At around the time Mapungubwe went into decline (some time in the 14th Century), early groups of seTswana- and seSotho-speaking people began moving into the interior of the Highveld, finding pastures for their crops and their cattle, gradually building extensive stone-walled settlements.

These Iron Age communities co-existed, peacefully for the most part, with the region's hunter-gatherers (Bushmen or San) who had inhabited southern Africa since the Stone Age.

We know that these early Iron Age communities smelted iron ore at furnaces like those uncovered on the Melville Koppies, and in Honeydew, Lonehill and Northcliff. They also built large stone-walled settlements, grew and stored crops and grain, and traded with each other for copper, tin and iron. But – until well into the 19th Century – they had no knowledge of the gold beneath their feet.

In Klipriviersberg, where 19 Iron Age settlements were built, dating back over 500 years, the grave of a teenage girl was found complete with a copper earring, iron anklet and copper beads sewn onto her clothing. She had no gold ornaments, and no gold was found in this or any of the other Iron Age settlements.

While copper was mined at Uitkomst Cave in the Magaliesberg and tin was mined at Rooiberg, the region revealed no ancient gold mines like those further north, towards Zimbabwe, or east, towards Swaziland.

When Mzilikazi's warriors passed through the Highveld in the 1820s, they looted the villages and settlements scattered in the region. If there had been any gold objects hidden in any of these huts, the soldiers would presumably have taken them; yet there is no evidence these invaders found gold.

By the 1830s, early bands of Voortrekkers – rebel Afrikaners who sought freedom from British rule – started arriving in their 'promised land' north of the Orange and Vaal rivers. Many of them were dirt poor, and their first Boer Republics nearly collapsed into bankruptcy several times. They desperately needed wealth to make their independent states viable; yet, until the 1870s, they had no inkling their farms straddled the greatest goldfields on earth.

None of these communities knew about the gold because it was buried deep inside the earth. Where gold occasionally penetrated the surface as an outcrop it was unrecognisable – even to an experienced prospector. The gold was locked in a dense layer of rock conglomerate studded with quartz and pyrite, which would eventually require sophisticated machinery and complex chemical processes to extract it.

This is where the story of 'Joburg' begins.

Stone and Iron Age Settlements in Gauteng

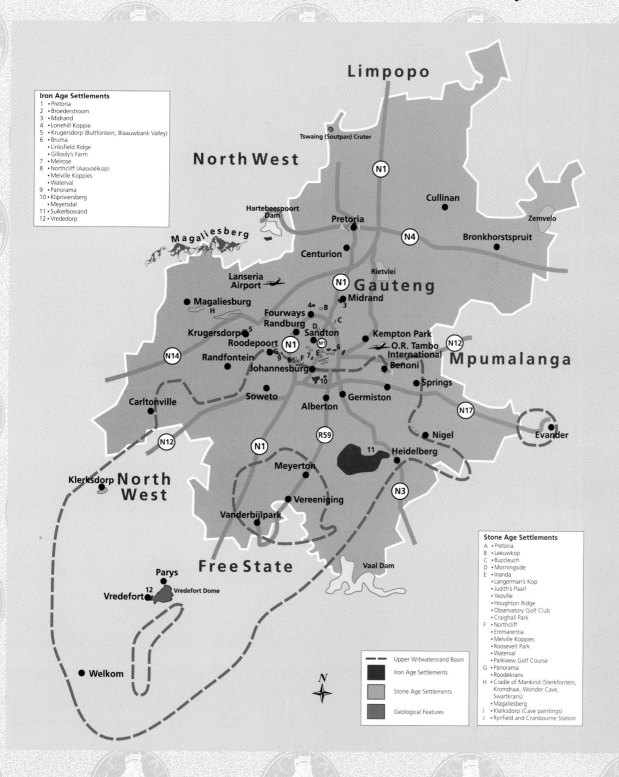

Iron Age Settlements
1 • Pretoria
2 • Broederstroom
3 • Midrand
4 • Lonehill Koppie
5 • Krugersdorp (Bultfontein, Blaauwbank Valley)
6 • Bruma
  • Linksfield Ridge
  • Gillooly's Farm
7 • Melrose
8 • Northcliff (Aasvoëlkop)
  • Melville Koppies
  • Waterval
9 • Panorama
10 • Klipriviersberg
  • Meyersdal
11 • Suikerbosrand
12 • Vrededorp

Stone Age Settlements
A • Pretoria
B • Leeuwkop
C • Buccleuch
D • Morningside
E • Inanda
  • Langerman's Kop
  • Judith's Paarl
  • Yeoville
  • Houghton Ridge
  • Observatory Golf Club
  • Craighall Park
F • Northcliff
  • Emmarentia
  • Melville Koppies
  • Roosevelt Park
  • Waterval
  • Parkview Golf Course
G • Panorama
  • Roodekrans
H • Cradle of Mankind (Sterkfontein, Kromdraai, Wonder Cave, Swartkrans)
  • Magaliesberg
I • Klerksdorp (Cave paintings)
J • Rynfield and Cranbourne Station

- - - Upper Witwatersrand Basin
Iron Age Settlements
Stone Age Settlements
Geological Features

Limpopo

North West

Gauteng

Mpumalanga

Free State

North West

Tswaing (Soutpan) Crater
Cullinan
Zemvelo
Hartebeespoort Dam
Pretoria
Bronkhorstspruit
Magaliesberg
Centurion
Rietvlei
Lanseria Airport
Midrand
Magaliesburg
Fourways
Randburg
Kempton Park
Krugersdorp
Sandton
O.R. Tambo International
Roodepoort
Benoni
Randfontein
Johannesburg
Springs
Carltonville
Soweto
Germiston
Alberton
Nigel
Evander
Heidelberg
Meyerton
Klerksdorp
Vereeniging
Vanderbijlpark
Vaal Dam
Parys
Vredefort
Vredefort Dome
Welkom

N

The Alchemy of Johannesburg

The origin of the Witwatersrand's gold deposits has been described as 'the most disputed issue in the history of economic geography',[1] – a topic scientists and researchers have hotly debated for nearly a century.

Over three billion years ago, during what is known as the Archaean period, the area now occupied by Joburg and its surrounds – the Witwatersrand basin – was covered by a large inland sea or lake. This massive body of water was fed by a system of rivers carrying eroded material from the surrounding highlands. As the rivers fed into the larger body of water, heavier matter (such as large pebbles and heavy minerals) was deposited first; this created gravel-rich deltas near the shoreline. Lighter materials like sand and clay were carried further out. Changes in the sea level – occurring over millennia – affected the position and shape of the shoreline, and the gravel deltas were slowly covered by layers of sand and clay, which were then covered by more gravel and, later, more sand and clay. These sedimentary layers grew several kilometres thick, and were eventually buried under huge eruptions of lava. The weight of these layers provided the heat and pressure needed to transform the separate sediments into what is known as coherent sedimentary rock.[2]

The sea appears to have died about 2,7 billion years ago – the result of lava and ash from the eruptions referred to above.

And it is at this point that the debate begins.

The Origins of Gold

There are two main theories as to how the gold got 'inside' the layers of consolidated rock. The first suggests the gold shares a sedimentary origin and that the rivers feeding the Witwatersrand sea carried small grains of gold into the basin. The higher density of the gold meant that the metal 'fell out' of suspension at the same time as the larger quartz pebbles and rounded pyrite (iron sulphide) pieces, and into the gravel-rich delta. This became the conglomerate that is mined today.

The other school of thought is that the gold has a hydrothermal origin: that the sediment washed into the Witwatersrand basin contained very little or no gold. Instead, 'gold-rich hot fluids emanating from deep within the earth's crust, and travelling along faults and fractures, added gold to the basin long after the sediments consolidated into rock. The gold precipitated from those fluids along chemically favourable horizons within the basin, corresponding to the layers of the conglomerate.'[3]

Each theory has its prominent modern champions: Professor Hartwig E Frimmel, currently at the University of Cape Town's Department of Geological Sciences,

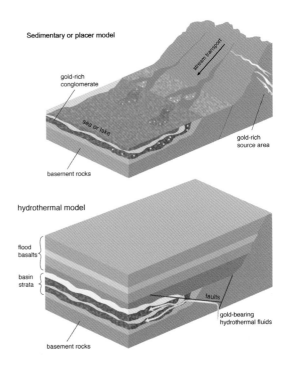

Since the turn of the 20th Century, scientists have argued about the origins of the gold deposits in the Witwatersrand. The two main theories are illustrated above: the sedimentary model (top) and the hydrothermal model (bottom). Illustration from *American Scientist* magazine.

has published numerous papers supporting the sedimentary origin theory – which has recently been updated and presented as the 'modified paleoplacer model'; this modification allows for small levels of hydrothermal gold movement within the conglomerate, not from an external source.

The foremost proponents of the hydrothermal model are Australian-based geologists Neil Phillips and Jonathan Law, of the Commonwealth Scientific and Industrial Research Organisation (CSIRO), Australia's national science agency.

For decades teams of scientists have searched for indisputable evidence that would not only conclusively prove one of the two theories but, simultaneously make it impossible for the opposing theory to be correct.

One study proposed comparing the age of the gold deposits with the age of the rock in which they were found: if the gold were older than its surrounding rock conglomerate, it would prove the sedimentary model – i.e. that river waters had transported the gold from an older source, in the highlands, and deposited the 'old' gold, together with the newer sediments, prior to the formation of the conglomerate. If the gold were younger than its host, it would prove the hydrothermal model: that the gold must have been introduced by hot fluids after the conglomerates had formed.

By dating rocks and other minerals within the Witwatersrand conglomerates, scientists were able to establish the age of the host conglomerates as being between 2,76 and 2,89 billion years old.

Dating the grains of gold contained in the conglomerates, however, was not as simple: geological dating techniques rely on measuring the half-life of unstable elements. Certain elements decay over a known period of time – from a few seconds to billions of years. The time taken for half the atoms to decay in an unstable substance is called its half-life. By measuring the results of this decay, scientists can establish the age of an element – or an object containing the decaying element. Most of the elements found within a grain of gold, however, are relatively stable (even pure gold will contain microscopic amounts of other elements); although one of the reasons gold is such a prized and versatile metal, it made the grains largely unsuitable for isotopic age testing. It would take years before geochemists developed the technology to enable them to work with extremely small amounts of a metal called rhenium, which is found in gold grains together with elements like silver, mercury, bismuth, selenium and platinum.

One of rhenium's isotopes, rhenium-187, decays to osmium-187 over a known period of time (the element has a half-life of about 42 billion years). By measuring the amount of osmium-187 present in the gold grains in the Witwatersrand reef, a research team was able to determine that the gold grains were more than 3,01 billion years old – 120 to 250 million years older than their host rock. The study also asserted that concentrations of rhemium and osmium in the Witwatersrand gold are higher than in rocks and fluids of hydrothermal origin – further proof of the gold's sedimentary origin.

This study, performed in 2002 by a team from the University of Arizona, made a strong case for the sedimentary or 'placer' model; but some research geologists believed it wasn't sufficient to settle the matter. In 2005, following a special meeting of the Society of Economic Geologists which debated the origins of the Witwatersrand gold, an American researcher commented: 'one date from one sample of gold from one reef should not put an end to the debate.'[4] And so the argument continues.

Deep Impact

Two billion years ago, a meteorite the size of Table Mountain came hurtling out of space at a speed of 20 km a second and struck South Africa with the force of hundreds of nuclear weapons. It melted rock over five kilometres deep, ejected debris in the form of a cloud 350 km wide and distributed fine dust that blocked out the sun over

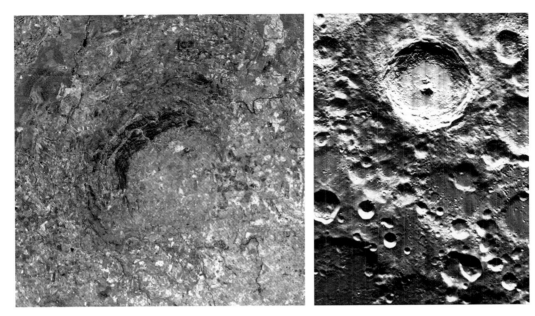

The Vredefort Dome impact site (left), as seen from space. The Tycho impact crater (right) on the lunar surface shows what the dome would have looked like prior to erosion (there is no erosion on the moon because of its low gravity).

the entire globe. The impact crater extended 250 km (it has since grown larger, owing to erosion), covering an area that would have included modern-day Johannesburg and Soweto. At the point of impact, an 'uplift' was created – a geological phenomenon occurring in the centre of impact craters, where the rock 'bounces' back (a similar effect can be seen when an object is dropped into water) and forms a dome.

The Vredefort Dome (the 'bounceback') is now a World Heritage Site, and can be seen near the town of the same name in the Free State province, about 120 km south-west of Johannesburg.

While the crater's walls have eroded, satellite photos confirm it as both the oldest and largest visible impact crater in the world.

The impact of this meteor was the second of two major events that may further explain why the Witwatersrand reef was so rich in gold: the first, an estimated 2,06 billion years ago, occurred when over a million cubic kilometres of magma welled up from the earth's mantle, forming what would later be known as the Bushveld

Igneous Complex (the world's largest source of platinum) to the north. This may have triggered the movement of fluids through the conglomerate in the Witwatersrand basin, further concentrating the gold. Forty million years later, the Vredefort astrobleme (meteorite impact structure) collided with the earth with such tremendous force that it effectively liquidised rock and earth at the very centre of the impact, disrupting the earth's crust and tilting the 'bowl' of the Witwatersrand basin – effectively burying the gold deposits up to several kilometres under the earth.

Without the Vredefort impact, the gold-rich conglomerate would have remained exposed to the surface and the elements, and most likely have eroded until all the gold had been dispersed or washed away.

It is also possible that the impact at Vredefort influenced another, far more important event: the Dome is evidence of the 'world's greatest known single energy release event, which caused devastating global change, including, according to some scientists, major evolutionary changes.'[5] Before the inclusion of the Vredefort Dome as a World Heritage Site, the largest-known impact crater

🦶 PLACES TO VISIT

The Vredefort Dome is 120 km south west of Johannesburg (around an 80-minute drive) in the Free State.

- Specialist full-day guided tours, departing from Johannesburg and hosted by geologist and natural scientist Gavin Whitfield, can be booked by calling Geological Heritage Tours on (011) 886 8722, or by emailing info@geosites.co.za. The website at www.geosites.co.za offers information on the region's geological history, as well as several other fascinating tours.

The Tswaing Crater

- For comprehensive information on the Vredefort Dome area, including accommodation, guided tours and other activities, visit the official Vredefort Dome Conservancy website at www.tvdc.co.za.

Forty kilometres north of Pretoria is the 220 000-year-old **Tswaing Crater** – one of the world's best-preserved meteor impact craters, just 1,4 km wide and 200 m deep. Tswaing's relatively small size makes it easier to see – and to imagine what the Vredefort impact site would have looked like, billions of years ago.

- The Tswaing Meteorite Crater (operated by Gauteng's Northern Flagship Institute) is open every day of the year, except on Christmas and New Year's Day. Visiting hours are between 07h30 and 16h00. Guided tours can be booked by arrangement. For bookings and more information, call (012) 790 2302.

was at Chicxulub, on Mexico's Yucatan Peninsula (the crater is 170 km wide, compared to 380 km at Vredefort). The Chicxulub impact, which occurred 65 million years ago, is almost certainly the deep impact event that triggered the extinction of the dinosaurs. Who is to say that the Vredefort event, with its massive release of cosmic energy, didn't trigger a major evolutionary episode of its own – perhaps stimulating the abundant local organic matter and bacteria (see next page) to make the next great leap forward torwards becoming increasingly complex organisms…

READ MORE

Meteorite Impact! The Danger from Space and South Africa's Mega-impact, the Vredefort Structure
By Uwe Reimold and Roger Gibson
Find out more about the geology of the Vredefort Dome and the research that led to the location being recognised as a World Heritage Site, and learn about past and future meteor impacts on earth. The book also includes a guide to places of interest in the Dome region.

Midas Bugs?

No one knows exactly what the earth's atmosphere was like during the Archaean and subsequent Proterozoic eras – the time when the Witwatersrand goldfields were formed and consolidated. However, much of the reef's gold seams exist in close proximity to bands of carbon and kerogen. This could indicate the presence of large bodies of organic matter – algae, lichen-like organisms, bacteria – which decayed over time into a black sludge that gradually hardened into a rock-like carbon layer. It is further speculated that these primitive organisms played a role in filtering and concentrating gold in the reef...

At the time when ancient rivers were depositing their sediment (and, possibly, gold) into the Witwatersrand basin, there was very little oxygen in the earth's atmosphere. It is believed the vast delta created by the rivers, as they entered the inland sea, was rich with early organic life forms.

Professor Betsey Dyer, of Massachusetts' Wheaton College, speculated that some of the gold particles suspended in the water could have become 'physically trapped' in the filaments of oxygen-producing cyanobacteria. 'At the delta, cyanobacteria would be producing oxygen (a product

PLACES TO VISIT

See what the sky would have looked like millions of years ago – or learn more about South Africa's night skies, our solar system and our satellites. The **Johannesburg Planetarium** (Yale Road, University of the Witwatersrand) offers an annual programme of shows and events suitable for the whole family. For more information contact (011) 717 1392, or go to www.planetarium.co.za.

of photosynthesis) and the sudden increase in oxygen would cause all that gold to come out or precipitate.'[6] Which suggests the Witwatersrand metal deposits could have been assisted by the presence of these primitive organisms. The oxygen generated through photosynthesis may also have helped to make the earth's atmosphere more suitable for other, later, life forms.

In 2006 an Australian scientist, Dr Frank Reith, published research conclusively proving that modern bacteria play a role in the formation of gold nuggets by precipitating gold from solution into solid form. He speculated that bacteria found naturally in Australian mines could have played a crucial role in precipitating the gold deposits found in the Witwatersrand.

The Origins of Man?

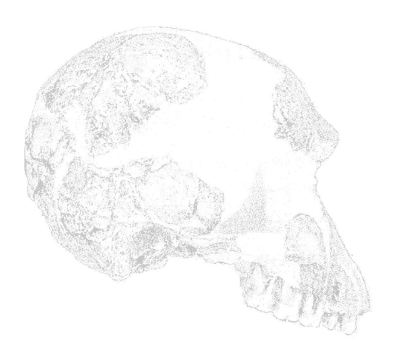

In 1994, a three-million-year-old jigsaw puzzle caught the attention of palaeoanthropologist Dr Ron Clarke. Sifting through a box of miscellaneous bone samples – recovered in the 1970s from Sterkfontein, and believed to be of animal origins – Dr Clarke identified four hominid foot bones. Three years later, in other boxes, Dr Clarke found eight additional leg and foot bones from the same individual. One of the bones appeared to have a very clean break, which Dr Clarke believed might have been caused by miners blasting through stone. He suspected that more bones from the same specimen might still be inside the cave...

The cavern, the Silberberg Grotto, was the size of a large house and accessible only by a wooden ladder through a small hole in its roof.

It was damp, muddy and utterly dark. Dr Clarke's assistants, Stephen Motsumi and Nkwane Molefe, were shown the leg and foot bones of the fossil, and asked to search the cave for the 'owner'. Although it was an almost impossible task, working with small hand-held lamps they found a matching piece of bone in just two days. Further excavations exposed more bones and, amazingly, the left side of a complete skull. It had taken just 48 hours to yield possibly the most important fossil find in the world: the only complete adult Australopithecus skeleton, and also the only complete Australopithecus skull, hand, arm and leg. The specimen – officially known as Stw 573 – was christened 'Little Foot'.

While Johannesburg has been a 'city' for less than a century (it was only officially declared a city in 1928), the region's earliest residents can be traced as far back as three million years – and evidence of their presence has been uniquely preserved in a series of dolomite caves, formed by the decaying skeletons of countless marine creatures (possibly from the same Witwatersrand 'sea' and sedimentary river deposits that created the goldfields).

Less than 50 km west of Joburg is the World Heritage Site known as the Cradle of Humankind. Forty per cent of all human ancestor fossil finds have been made here, including over 500 hominid – or human-like ancestor – fossils. The Cradle area includes the Sterkfontein Caves, and nearby Swartkrans and Kromdraai.

When Little Foot was identified in 1997, it appeared to be the oldest specimen of *Australopithecus africanus* ever found (other well-known *africanus* fossils include the Taung Child, found in the North West province by Professor Raymond Dart in 1924, and Mrs Ples, found by Robert Broom in the Sterkfontein caves in 1947).

Initial datings of Little Foot indicated the fossil was between 3,3 and 4,17 million years old. These

The Skull and arm bone of 'Little Foot'

dates represented a potential breakthrough in the study of human evolution, as it would have meant Little Foot lived at the same time as another famous hominid, 'Lucy', found in Ethiopia in 1972. Lucy belonged to another species called *Australopithecus afarensis*, and her fossilised remains had been dated to just under 3,2 million years ago. The oldest specimens of *africanus* only dated back to around 2,5 million years ago and scientists had long argued that Lucy, as the older hominid, was the 'true ancestor' of modern humans – and that the later *africanus* merely evolved into another species (called *robustus*) before becoming extinct.

If it could be proved that Little Foot was older than Lucy, it could be suggested that Little Foot was the real ancestor of humanity. This would mean that South Africa – and not Ethiopia – was the true 'Cradle of Humankind'.

In 2006, researchers from the University of Liverpool released disappointing test data, claiming Little Foot was a mere 2,2 million years old – making it unlikely *africanus* deserved any space on the human family tree: the date meant Little Foot would have lived after the arrival of *Homo sapiens*' earliest direct ancestor, *Homo habilis*, the 'handy man', named for their tool-making abilities.

These claims were roundly dismissed by Dr Clarke – who said the date of 2,2 million years was 'impossible', as it would have made the deposit in which Little Foot was found (the Liverpool dating was based on the measurements of lead isotopes from the surrounding rock) younger than the rock deposit on top of Little Foot, which had already been dated to well over two million years.

'We're satisfied with 3,3 million [years],' Clarke said in an interview with press agency AFP, adding that Little Foot was 'one of our ancestor's relatives if not a direct ancestor.'

The debate over mankind's true origins has been further fuelled by the recently revealed discovery of the almost complete fossil of an infant *Australopithecus afarensis*, discovered in 2000 by an Ethiopian palaeoanthropologist in the Northern Rift Valley. The three-year-old female has been dated at… 3,3 million years.

The Age of Man

Together with East Africa, South Africa has the longest record of human occupation in the world. We can date early hominid habitation of the region around Johannesburg to over three million years ago, although there are several large gaps in the fossil record of subsequent human and human-like inhabitants. We know that our ancestor *Homo erectus* inhabited the nearby Magaliesberg as long as 500 000 years ago – and that *erectus* harnessed the power of fire, using it to protect himself and his family against predatory leopards; but there is a large fossil gap between the fire-using *erectus* and the next evolutionary leap towards modern humans. The earliest *Homo sapiens* fossils – a group named *Homo sapiens idaltu* – have been found in Ethiopia, and date back nearly 200 000 years. However, the oldest evidence of modern humans (*Homo sapiens sapiens*) was found in South Africa, dating back to 100 000 years ago. Recent studies using human genetics indicate that these first humans – evolutionary Adam and Eve – became the people we know as the Bushmen (or San) some 15 000 to 20 000 years ago.

These Early Stone Age hunter-gatherers (who made tools from stone, but never learned the art of metalwork) proved incredibly adaptable. They appear to have lived through a number of significant climate changes, including the last Ice Age (which ended just

10 000 years ago), successfully preserving their simple nomadic way of life until the much later arrival of early agriculturalist and pastoralist Bantu groups (about 2000 years ago) who were migrating southwards from central Africa.

Evidence from the former Eastern Transvaal (now Mpumalanga) shows that groups of Bushmen peacefully co-existed with these Iron Age groups well into the 19th Century. Bushmen even fought alongside Boer soldiers in the first South African War.

Because of their nomadic hunter-gatherer lifestyle, very little archaeological evidence remains of early humans in the Joburg region, but the nearby Magaliesberg features remains of several rock-art and early hominid settlement sites.

THINGS TO DO
The Johannesburg Hiking Club
offers regular Sunday hikes in the Magaliesberg – where you'll be able to see Stone Age caves, and even rock art (though not on all hiking trails). For more information, go to www.jhbhiking.org.za or call (011) 462 2993.

Hiking in the Magaliesberg

Joburg's Lost History
Johannesburg once boasted a number of Stone Age sites; unfortunately most of these have been destroyed by the city's growth. Aside from the Melville Koppies, evidence of Stone Age sites can still be found in Kensington, at Langermanskop, at the present-day Leeuwkop Prison, and in the suburb of Roosevelt Park. Iron Age sites that were documented but have since been destroyed were to be found in the suburbs of Judith's Paarl, Yeoville, Houghton, Rivonia, Bucchleuch, Inanda, Northcliff, Parkview, Oaklands, Emmarentia and Craighall Park.

The Northcliff Ridge – marked by its distinctive water tower (built in 1939) – was once the site of a Stone Age settlement. Two Iron Age furnaces were discovered just below the ridge.

Visions in Stone: Non-reality in San Rock Art

By Professor David Lewis-Williams

Unlike the popular Western myth of producing art simply for the sake of art, so-called 'primitive' artists have quite specific purposes in mind, and their pictures have specific and often very complex meanings.

Among the San of southern Africa, rock art is associated with the activities of San medicine people, or shamans. These people entered a state of trance at a medicine dance or in more solitary circumstances and, in that condition, cured the sick, went on out-of-body journeys, made rain, and controlled the movements of antelope herds. These activities, and the hallucinations of San medicine people together with symbols of the supernatural potency they activated in order to enter the world of trance experience, are depicted on both rock paintings and rock engravings.

Under certain conditions – such as the trance-like states associated with shamanism – the human mind produces a range of hallucinations. Visual hallucinations are the most widely known, but there are also auditory, physical and olfactory hallucinations. In fact, all the senses – not just vision – can hallucinate.

The conditions that induce an altered state of consciousness in which these hallucinations are experienced are extremely varied. They include the use of hallucinogens, sensory deprivation, intense concentration, rhythmic movement, hyperventilation, hunger, pain and even migraine. San shamans seldom use hallucinogens; they enter trance through hyperventilation, rhythmic movement and music, and intense concentration.

Because much of the trance experience is controlled by the nervous system, and the nervous system is common to all people, it is possible to gain insight into the human nervous system's entrance into, and progression through, trance states – and to assess rock art in these terms. Because the neuropsychological research was conducted without any knowledge of or reference to rock art, it provided an independent line of evidence that the art was associated with altered states of consciousness – in other words, that it was essentially shamanistic.

There are three broad stages in the sequence of mental imagery during altered states of consciousness.

In the first stage subjects experience entoptic (within the eye) phenomena. These are luminous visual percepts that take geometric forms such as grids, zigzags, dots, undulating lines, nested catenary curves and spirals. All these shapes are experienced as incandescent, shimmering, moving, rotating, and sometimes enlarging patterns, and they are independent of light from an external source. They are experienced with the eyes open or closed and tend to be located at reading distance. Sometimes a bright light in the centre of the field of vision obscures the forms, but peripheral images can be observed.

Experiments conducted on a large number of subjects under laboratory conditions identified several common types of shapes (see column 1, opposite) created by the actual physical, neurological structures of the eye, the optic nerve or the cortex. There are striking parallels between these shapes (experienced by modern subjects in the United States) and those taken from ancient rock engravings in two regions of South Africa (columns 2 and 3). Some forms are more common than others, and not all sites have the same range of entoptics. This is because shamanistic societies tend to concentrate on and attach meaning to a limited, standardised range of entoptics and to ignore others, in the same way as they select certain animal species for symbolic purposes and depiction. What is important is that a set of seven distinct forms, the very ones we should expect to find in a shamanistic art, are indeed present.

PLACES TO VISIT

Joburg may have wiped out almost all evidence of its ancient hunter-gatherer inhabitants, but the city still hosts the world's largest museum of rock art at the Origins Centre, University of the Witwatersrand (Wits). The South African Museum of Rock Art explores the origins of rock art, dating back to over 70 000 years ago, taking the visitor all the way through to the contemporary work of South Africa's last rock painter.

The Origins Centre is open from Tuesday to Sunday, from 09h00 on weekdays and 10h00 on weekends. For more information go to www.origins.org.za or call (011) 717 4700/3/4.

• To learn more about rock art, visit Wits University's Rock Art Research Unit online at http://rockart.wits.ac.za. The website also offers links to information about rock-art sites in the Magaliesberg.

In the second stage of the trance experience, subjects try to make sense of their entoptic phenomena by elaborating them into something recognisable. In a normal state of consciousness, the brain decodes sense impressions by matching them to stored experiences.

In altered states the nervous system itself becomes a 'sixth sense' that produces a variety of images, including entoptic phenomena. San shaman-artists who went far enough along the continuum of trance experience elaborated the basic entoptic forms into objects on which their general beliefs about trance experience placed some particular value. In other words, they construed the basic geometric forms as something they hoped or expected to see in the spirit world.

When a [San] shaman enters a trance he or she activates an invisible potency (called *n/um* by the !Kung and *!gi:* by the now-extinct southern /Xam). This potency is named after a range of 'strong' things, such as big game animals. The eland has more *n/um* than any other animal, but also prominent among the powerful animals is the giraffe – which explains why it was common for the entoptic 'grid' form to take the shape of a giraffe rather than, say, a tortoise.

Entoptics	N.W. Cape	Magaliesberg

Entoptic phenomena compared with rock engravings from the north-western Cape, and the Magaliesberg.

More radical changes to entoptic forms are experienced in the third and last stage of altered consciousness. As subjects move from the second stage into the third, marked changes in imagery occur. It is here that subjects experience the first spontaneously produced hallucinations, as entoptics give way to images of people, animals, monsters, houses … These images appear to derive from memory and are often associated with powerful emotional experiences. This shift to iconic imagery is also accompanied by an increase in vividness. Subjects stop using similes to describe their experiences and assert that the images are indeed what they appear to be. Even in this essentially iconic stage, entoptics may persist: iconic imagery is 'often projected against a background of geometric forms'. For example, in a well-known diagram showing 'rain animals', the presence of several zigzag shapes was once through to be a representation of water; it seems more likely, now, that it represents a hallucinatory animal seen through an entoptic haze.

For reasons that are unclear, it seems that San engravers paid more (but not exclusive) attention to the first stage of altered consciousness, and emphasised geometric entoptic phenomena. San painters, on the other hand, concentrated on the second and third stages. The paintings, therefore, have far fewer geometric forms and, when they do occur, have often been construed as objects associated with trance beliefs or intimately integrated with hallucinatory animals and people. The entoptics are there. It is just that they have been obscured by a deeper trance experience.

(Condensed, with permission, from the paper 'Reality and Non-Reality in San Rock Art' by Professor David Lewis-Williams)

Joburg, City of Iron

An early baTswana settlement

'Among the Basutos, the blacksmith, or tribal metallurgist, is held in high esteem; he is ugaka ea tsepe, *the doctor of iron.'[7]*

Of the seven metals known to man in ancient times – mercury, tin, lead, copper, silver, gold and iron – iron was the most difficult to smelt; which is why it was also the last to be discovered, and why its adepts were revered (and, sometimes, reviled) as guardians of a mysterious forge magic.

In much of Africa, the Stone Age segued directly into the Iron Age. There was no Bronze Age – characterised by the use of easier-to-forge copper, and alloyed bronze – south of the Sahara.

Exactly how the craft of iron smelting reached southern Africa is the subject of debate – whether it was introduced through North Africa, from the Mediterranean or Middle East, and spread south with the migrating Bantu; or whether, perhaps, the technique was independently invented in Africa, at around the same time as (or even earlier than) in Europe and Asia.

What is known is that Africa was host to an extraordinary range of iron-producing traditions[8]; by the end of the 19th Century, experts estimate 'there were hundreds if not thousands of different iron-production systems active on the continent.'[9]

The only remaining complete Iron Age furnace in South Africa can be found on the Melville Koppies. Three feet in diameter and over two feet deep, the furnace is described as resembling 'a wide mouthed globular pot' made of 'hard-baked, reddish, clayey soil'. There are also two tuyeres (pipes through which air is forced into the fire) openings[10]; at the end of each pipe a cow's horn would have been attached, and to each horn a large goatskin bellows.

The furnace required intense activity and effort: charcoal for the fire would have been prepared long in advance, using wood from the koppies' trees (it is estimated that two trees were burned for the making of every spearhead). The women would collect lumps of haematite from the nearby shale; the ore was then mixed with the charcoal, in the furnace. The presence of carbon (in the form of charcoal) was essential to successful smelting – not just to achieve the required heat (between 1100°C and 1400°C for iron smelting) but to provide a reducing agent, allowing iron oxides (in rock or clay) to transform into iron metal.

The firing would start early in the morning, possibly accompanied by a magic ritual to ensure its success. Most of the furnace's openings would be sealed with clay, to retain heat; then the men would work all day, in relays, pumping the bellows linked to the tuyere pipes on either side of the furnace. As temperatures rose, the furnace sides would fuse and the clay blowpipe nozzles would melt. Towards sunset, the gasping of the bellows would cease. The men would break the furnace's seals open and rake out a 'bloom', or spongy mass of crude iron, from its base.[11] To consolidate the mass of iron and get rid of unwanted wasted matter (from the fuel, or slag), the bloom would have to be reheated and hammered a number of times before it could be used[12] – to be made into hoes, knives, axes and spears.

Johannesburg's Iron Age people – like those who lived on the Melville Koppies and surrounding hills – lived in the region from about AD 1000, settling in formal villages and building huts and kraals with dry stone walls (although they occasionally used local caves, to hide from marauding bands). They left the area several hundred years ago, not because the iron ore ran out but rather because there were no more trees suitable for charcoal.

The forge at Melville Koppies was discovered in 1963, when then-head of Wits University's Archaeology Department, Dr Revil Mason, was asked to investigate a 'ring' that had been spotted on the top ridge. The uncovered fragments of iron smelting debris were carbon dated to around AD 1600. Further digging on the ridge revealed evidence of a Stone Age camp dating back a possible 40 000 years. Two metres further down, Dr Mason found evidence of additional settlements dating back as far as 100 000 years ago.

Other Iron Age sites have been found on the Linksfield Ridge, and we know that a sizeable Iron Age community once settled on the slopes of Northcliff Hill.

To the south of Johannesburg, in what is now the Klipriviersberg Reserve, aerial photographs revealed 19 stone-walled Iron Age settlements, dating back to AD 1500[13]. A 250-year-old burial site revealed a teenage girl with a copper earring (piercing her upper ear instead of her earlobe), wearing an iron anklet and wrapped in a *kaross* or blanket decorated with iron beads. We know she probably used a glittering iron powder made from haematite mixed with animal fat. This was called *sebilo* and was a form of make-up or facial decoration used by men as well as women. The copper earring was probably obtained from a copper smelting site at Uitkomst Cave near modern-day Krugersdorp, a journey of about three days on foot. Iron was not produced in Klipriviersberg itself and was probably traded for with other groups.

The layout of the houses at Klipriviersberg was similar to that of the baTswana. Individual villages were laid out in a pattern resembling a sunflower, with the animal enclosure in the centre (where herds were closely protected). Each of the 'petals' accommodated an individual household. Smaller enclosures, between the houses, were left for calves, goats and chickens.[14]

Villages and kraals were surrounded by stone walls to protect cattle, and people, against lions. The stone, however, offered no protection from attacks by other, hostile, communities. We know this because a copper necklace has been found hidden under a boulder – so it would not fall into the hands of attackers.

baTswana, Boers and British

baTswana initiates riding oxen, 1934
(Duggan-Cronin collection)

The area now occupied by Johannesburg was once dominated by groups of 'Sotho-Tswana' people – this refers to the inhabitants' closely related group of languages, which include seTswana, seSotho sa Leboa (Northern Sotho), and seSotho.[15]

The Witwatersrand came to be dominated by groups descended from the 'founding fathers' of the baTswana: the chiefs Morolong, Masilo and Mokgatla.

Morolong ruled in about the 13th Century, and his descendants became the baRolong. Masilo dominated the northern Witwatersrand in about the 15th Century; the first offshoot of his followers was the baHurutshe (named after his heir, Mohurutshe). After Masilo's death, there was a further split from the baHurutshe, forming the baKwena (named for Masilo's grandson, Kwena).

In the 15th and 16th centuries, the north-eastern Witwatersrand and Pretoria area was dominated by followers of Mokgatla, who was the founder of the baKgatla lineage. There were several breakaway groups of baKgatla, including the baTlokwa (who moved further north-west, settling in what is now Botswana) and the baPedi.

Early baTswana history was simply passed down orally, from generation to generation – often by speakers more eager to promote their particular group's claim to royalty than to preserve records accurately. As a result, the exact order of Masilo's immediate descendents is a little unclear. The dominant (accepted) view states that Masilo had two sons, Mohurutshe and Malope, and three grandsons (Kwena, Ngwato and Ngwaketse), fathered by Malope. Each of Masilo's grandsons created his own offshoot of followers. Their descendents form the three main baTswana tribes of Botswana.

Other histories, however, claim that Kwena was Masilo's direct son (not grandson), and that Ngwato and Ngwaketse were Kwena's offspring, not siblings. To further confuse matters, there is speculation Mohurutshe was a royal daughter, not a son, and that the baHurutshe – baKwena split was caused by Mohurutshe's gender.[16]

baTswana Culture

Central to baTswana society were its cattle – we can gauge their importance by the location of the kraals: in the centre of the villages, with stone walls for protection. All archaeological remains of baTswana villages and towns show a similar pattern.

Like other cattle-keeping people, the baTswana did not wear woven cloth but made soft leather clothes and sandals from animal hides. They liked to decorate themselves with *sebilo* and wore ornaments made from copper, iron and even tin, which they called 'white iron'. Some baTswana women wore a solid copper ring or necklet around their necks. They also wore hundreds of small discs of ostrich shell threaded onto a waistband. A popular form of jewellery was a bracelet or armband made from twisted iron in a 'barley sugar' pattern. Many baTswana towns had an ironsmith who made metal ornaments like these.

While they lived in large villages, with dwellings built close to one another, the baTswana nonetheless cherished their privacy and built walls around their homes. The chief's family in these larger villages (some settlements were reported to contain as many as 25 000 people) would live secluded to some extent from the rest of the community. Otherwise baTswana communities were tightly knit and strongly communal.

The baTswana buried their dead in three different ways over the centuries. One method was to bury the deceased in a shallow grave for a few years, after which the bones would be dug up and placed in a jar. This burial method was used at Broederstroom over 1500 years ago. A second method was to place the corpse in a sitting position in a deep pit filled with pebbles. In the third method, the body was placed on its side with the knees bent – this was the way the young girl, described previously, was buried at Klipriviersberg.

Ancestor worship was an important element of baTswana beliefs and the chief would be called on to intercede with the ancestors in times of drought or danger. The chief would also protect the baTswana village against the wicked plans of witches. Belief in witchcraft and the healing powers of traditional healers is still common among the baTswana today.

'The Pursuers'

In the 17th Century, an early Nguni-speaking community[17] moved into the north-eastern Highveld regions (possibly from the KwaZulu-Natal area). The Sotho-Tswana people called this group 'Matabele', meaning 'the pursuers'; the Nguni people accepted the name, but altered it to amaNdebele.[18]

These early Nguni were not the same as the later-named 'Matabele' under Mzilikazi, who entered the highveld from KwaZulu-Natal in the early 19th Century.

Despite settling in a predominantly Sotho-Tswana speaking area, the amaNdebele retained their

PLACES TO VISIT
The **Klipriviersberg Nature Reserve** lies to the south of Johannesburg, between Soweto and Alberton. It is a major Iron Age centre, where 160 stone-walled settlements were built between 200 and 600 years ago. Many of these are still visible, and guided tours are provided.
• For more information, including directions on reaching the reserve, go to www.veld.org.za. To find out about guided walks, go to the Klipriviersberg Nature Association at www.knra.co.za.

customs and Nguni language roots (although there is evidence their architecture, settlement patterns and rituals were influenced by the Pedi-Tswana communities they encountered).

The amaNdebele's recorded history begins with the names of their first two kings: Mafana and Mhlanga. By the time Mhlanga's heir, Musi, assumed leadership, the group had moved from the west of Johannesburg and settled immediately north of the future Pretoria, in a place called kwaMnyamana. Succession battles between Musi's sons saw the clan split into a number of smaller groups, the largest two under the leadership of Manala and Ndzundza (typically, groups under each chief were often referred to by the name of their leader's lineage rather than as 'amaNdebele').

Both Manala and Ndzundza appear to have abandoned kwaMnyamana, with the former settling to the north and north-east and the latter moving further east and south-east.

Some histories say that, in the early 1820s, Mzilikazi's forces settled with the Manala group under false pretences before overpowering them through treachery – and co-opting the Manala men into Mzilikazi's main fighting force.

In 1825, Mzilikazi's soldiers attacked the ama-Ndzundza capital at Esikhunjini, burning the settlement and killing the ruler (Magodongo) together with almost all his sons. The remnants of the amaNdzundza fled and re-settled at koNomtjharhelo, near Roossenekal. Subsequently the group's leader, Mabhogo (Magodongo's remaining son) entered into an alliance with a neighbouring baPedi chief, Malewa. This alliance may have been behind the significant baPedi influence on amaNdebele culture.

Boer Encounters

In 1847, Mabhogo was visited by groups of Voortrekkers, who called the amaNdebele either the *Mapog, Mapogga* or *'M'pogga* – terms most modern amaNdebele find derogatory.

From the start there were sporadic fights between the Boers and the amaNdebele-baPedi alliance (this group actively resisted Boer attempts to appropriate land). In 1864, at the Boers' instigation, the alliance was attacked and defeated by an amaSwazi force. Soon after, Mabhogo died, leaving a complex inheritance struggle; as a result, many of his followers dispersed to the surrounding countryside. It took nearly two decades for the amaNdebele to regain structure and power, under the leadership of a chief called Nyabela.

Nyabela established a heavily fortified capital on koNomtjharhelo's mountain slopes. The dwellings were 'built on terraces in front of rocky cliffs intersected with caves. Intertwining stonewalls and parapets snaked round the mountain village, constantly guarded by men armed with assegais and illicit firearms.'[19]

Nyabela's growing strength and independence were perceived as a threat by the British – who had annexed the region in 1877, and systematically set out to break the power of prominent African chiefs including the eventual defeat (after three failed attempts) of legendary baPedi leader Sekhukhune in 1879. They were also seen as a problem by the Boers, who resumed 'rule' of then-Transvaal province in 1881.

Nyabela rejected Boer demands that the amaNdzundza recognise white settlers' ownership of land, provide labour, and pay rent or taxes.

In 1882, the Boers were provided with the perfect 'excuse' to wage a full-scale battle against Nyabela: in August of that year, Chief Sekhukhune (the defeated baPedi ruler who had been captured and resettled) was murdered by his half-brother, Mampuru. Fearing retribution, Mampuru fled and sought refuge with Nyabela.

The Boer government demanded that Nyabela surrender Mampuru for trial on a charge of murder. Nyabela refused. The result was a bitter war and siege, fought in and around the caves of koNomtjhahelo (also known as Mapoch's Caves).

After eight months, the starving ama-Ndzundza capitulated. Nyabela had no choice but to surrender himself and the fugitive Mampuru. After a trial in Pretoria, Nyabela and Mampuru were sentenced to death; Nyabela's sentence was commuted to life imprisonment, but Mampuru was hanged.

This event marked the end of the Transvaal's last remaining independent African Kingdom. As punishment for the amaNdebele, the ama-Ndzundza chiefdom was

A contemporary amaNdebele mural

An amaNdebele woman beading an apron

broken up. All amaNdebele land holdings were confiscated and parcelled out to Boer farmers; the 10 000 amaNdzundza who surrendered were 'distributed' among Boer farmers, as indentured servants who had to work for a period of five years. Family members were scattered between distant farms, and many of the amaNdzundza were not released after the five years had elapsed. Those who were discovered they had no home to return to.

The striking mural art of modern amaNdebele amaNdundza[20] emerged out of this time of forced slavery and displacement – the distinctive graphics and colours became a way for amaNdebele women to assert their presence and identity.

Mzilikazi's Matabele

In the 1820s, amaZulu King Shaka began to feel threatened by the growing strength and reputation of one of his commanders – a young amaZulu chief named Mzilikazi. Rather than face Shaka, the warrior decided to leave Zululand and, together with a few hundred followers, set up his own kingdom.

Mzilikazi moved north and north-west, into the Highveld; along the way, his small force destroyed or absorbed weaker chiefdoms in its path and recruited (or conscripted) the defeated men into its growing army.

The baSotho-baTswana groups Mzilikaze's army encountered referred to him and his followers as 'Matabele' ('the pursuers') – much as they had the Nguni settlers of over a century before.

Although many historical reports make out that Mzilikazi's expansion 'devastated' all the groups he encountered, there is evidence many of the baTswana groups had already been broken and scattered by earlier struggles against local domination by the baPedi. By remaining mobile and avoiding open confrontation, the baTswana settlements were able to incur relatively small human losses.[21] Once Mzilikazi had moved on, 'many of these local communities regrouped and resumed their everyday life as if unscathed by the turmoil.'[22]

Mzilikazi settled for a while in the Magaliesberg, until his defeat in the late 1830s at the hands of the Boers. The Matabele then moved much further north, crossing the Limpopo river and establishing a kingdom which came to be known as Matabeleland. This region was later renamed Southern Rhodesia, the country known today as Zimbabwe.

PLACES TO VISIT

A number of **'cultural villages'** have been developed within an hour's drive from Johannesburg, showcasing pre-colonial African culture. They can be rather cheesy – many are targeted solely at foreign visitors – but they can also be a fun and interactive excursion.

- Lesedi African Lodge (baPedi, amaZulu, amaXhosa, baSotho and amaNdebele homesteads) offers a range of cultural experiences, as well as meals and accommodation within the village complex. For more information, go to www.lesedi.com or call (012) 205 1394.
- The Rainbow Cultural Village (Bushman and amaNdebele exhibits) is eight kilometres west of Hartbeespoort Dam, on the Rustenberg Road. For information, contact (012) 258 0333.
- The Gaabo Motho Cultural Village (pre-colonial baTswana and amaNdebele) is approximately 35 km from Pretoria. For information, you can visit www.hartbeespoortdam.com/gaabomotho/ or call (012) 706 0165.
- The colourful Mapoch Ndebele Village, near the town of Brits, can be contacted on (012) 253 0266.

Zulu dancers at a guest lodge outside Johannesburg

Early Boer Settlements

Early Boer settlement

In the 1830s, a large group of South Africa's Dutch- or Afrikaans-speaking farmers – Boers – became increasingly disgruntled with British rule in the Cape Colony. They were particularly upset with a law abolishing slavery.

Some of the Boers began to make preparations to leave the Colony and head north, beyond the Orange and Vaal rivers, where they hoped to obtain land outside of British rule.

Initially they called themselves 'Boer emigrant farmers', but Afrikaner nationalists later referred to them as the Voortrekkers ('Pioneers').

With all their belongings packed into ox-wagons, the Voortrekkers began an arduous journey northwards. En route they encountered attacks from wild predators, deadly malaria-carrying mosquitoes and tsetse flies, and (of course!) regular clashes with the African people already inhabiting the supposedly 'empty' regions they began to claim as their own.

Although history paints a picture of early Boer settlers as 'subsistence-oriented pastoralists in flight from both modernity and the market',[23] it was exactly the potential of trade in ivory and other hunt-related products through the Portuguese-controlled ports of Mozambique on the East African coast that appealed to many early Trekkers who made the journey northwards.

However, over-hunting of elephants reduced the availability of ivory, while constant troubles with malaria and tsetse flies (on the route to Mozambique) hampered the potential for coastal trade.[24]

It was still possible for certain individuals to make money, but the fledgling Boer states were effectively broke for many of their early years.

One of the biggest assets held by the Boer settlers, and the Zuid Afrikaansche Republiek (the Boer South African Republic) was land.

Farmers and Chiefs

Private property ownership was key to Boer society. The *Volksraad* ('Parliament' or 'Government') 'allowed each registered immigrant burgher two farms. One farm was called an "eiendomsplaats" (freehold farm) for which an annual levy of 10 shillings was payable to the State. The second farm was a "leningsplaats" (loan farm) which cost up to three Pounds per annum.'[25]

The farms were intended to be roughly square-shaped, and varied in size from 1000 ha to 5000 ha. The borders were determined by riding on horseback at a walking pace for 60 minutes in one direction, then for a further 60 minutes in a direction at a right angle to the first. Variances in size and shape would result when the rider had to navigate natural obstacles such as koppies.[26]

Critical to the successful exploitation of this land was a large workforce – and the Boers fully expected that the required labour would be provided by black men (and women and children), who would naturally accept a position subordinate to that of their Boer masters.

Unsurprisingly, the majority of African kingdoms and chiefdoms in the region not only failed to properly acknowledge the Boers' right to the land; they were also disinclined to provide the Boers with a workforce drawn from their own people.

There is little doubt that the Boers and the two Boer Republics beyond the Orange and Vaal rivers in the 1850s displayed a 'deep-seated attitude of racial superiority',[27] but this didn't stop the early Boer settlers from depending on local African communities for trade, assistance with game hunting and, in some cases, treatment from African herbalists.

Many of the chiefs were happy to make alliances with the Boers against rival African groups; and the Boers formed convenient alliances where attempts at dominance failed.[28]

However, the Boer Republic's continued demand for land (the two-farm system was reduced to one farm by 1860, and stopped altogether by 1866 because of land shortages) and its practice of concluding 'recognition agreements' with neighbouring African kingdoms – and then continuing to inspect and parcel out the land to Boer citizens, in complete disregard of the treaty or agreement – meant that conflict was inevitable.

Ultimately, the only way in which the Boers were able to extract the labour they required was by dominating local African communities – through the use of guns (which allowed them to shoot from a distance) and horses (from which to shoot) – and demanding tribute from them, in the form of food, trade items… or people.

Because the Boer Republics had agreed to abandon slavery (in 1857, in return for Britain staying out of the Highveld), they adapted a 'legitimate' system of forced labour first developed by the British in the early Cape Colony.

Ordinance 49 of 1828 criminalised the 'detention' (enslavement) of children – but legalised the apprenticeship of 'abandoned children' until adulthood. It was a distinction that, effectively, encouraged the capture of children and the killing of their parents.

The word used to describe these indentured workers was *inboekeling* – from the Afrikaans verb *inboek* meaning 'register' (the details of 'apprentices' were supposed to be captured in the local Magistrate's or Landdros's register). The apprentices were also sometimes called *inboekselinge*, which referred to the receipt (*inboeksel*) generated as proof of the transaction.

In truth, little if anything was done to monitor the procurement of child apprentices or enforce their release on reaching majority, and the system was frequently abused. The procurement of *inboekelings* remained common practice until the late 19th Century, when a combination of factors (including increased negative public opinion) contributed to its decline.

Of course the demand for 'native' labour had not gone away – it was soon to increase, dramatically, with the discovery of gold on the Witwatersrand.

The labour-intensive mining processes needed to extract the Reef's gold meant that Boer and, later, British governments, would once again have to come up with 'legitimate' ways of compelling black South Africans to work for white masters.

PLACES TO VISIT

Although strongly associated with less-memorable aspects of South Africa's history, the iconic **Voortrekker Monument** outside Pretoria is still worth a visit – although you can expect to encounter strongly nationalist Afrikaner sentiment unless you arrange for an independent tour guide. For further information, go to www.voortrekkermon.org.za or call (012) 326 6770.

The Voortrekker Monument

Joburg's Early Farms

In 1858, under the two-farm deal, burgher Gerrit Bezuidenhout acquired a 3500-hectare farm named Braamfontein – which included the area now known as the Melville Koppies.

Shortly before gold was discovered in the Transvaal, Bezuidenhout sold part of his land to Lourens Geldenhuys who, together with his sons, prospected on the Koppies, blasting rock with dynamite. Fortunately, they did not notice the clay ring in the earth that Dr Revil Mason would examine a century later – and so did not damage the only intact Iron Age furnace in Southern Africa.

Geldenhuys later divided his farm among his three sons, Frans, Dirk and Louw. He then moved onto another of his properties, Elandsfontein (later Bedfordview), where he also prospected for gold. Louw Geldenhuys' original farmhouse can still be seen at No. 14 Greenhill Road, Emmarentia – although it is a private residence, and not open for public viewing. Frans Geldenhuys's neighbouring home was converted to the clubhouse at nearby Marks Park (Judith Road, Emmarentia). The Geldenhuys family cemetery can be seen in Hill Road (also in Emmarentia).

Bezuidenhout farmhouse in 1945

THE DISCOVERY

'My name is George Harrison and I come from the newly discovered goldfields Kliprivier especially from a farm owned by a certain Gert Oosthuizen. I have long experience as an Australian golddigger and I think it a payable goldfield.'

Prospector George Harrison, in an affidavit to Paul Kruger's government, 1886

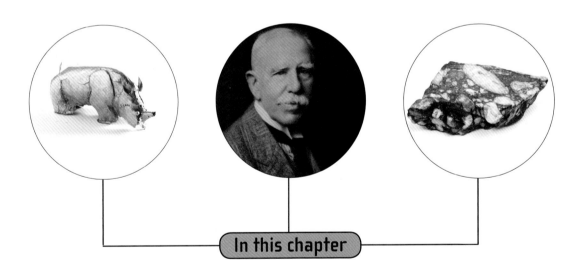

In this chapter

👉 Africa : Place of Gold

👉 The Transvaal Gold Rush

👉 Confidence Reef and the Strubens Brothers

👉 The Three Georges

👉 The MacArthur-Forrest Process

OF GOLD

Godfray Lys (left) and George Honeyball (centre) pointing to the possible site of the original rock outcrop marking the discovery of the Witwatersrand gold reef

Africa: Place of Gold

Golden rhino found at Mapungubwe

'Now the weight of gold that came to Solomon in one year was six hundred threescore and six talents of gold,[1] besides what he had from the merchants, and from the traffic of the spice merchants, and from all the kings of Arabia, and from the governors of the country.

And King Solomon made two hundred bucklers of beaten gold; six hundred shekels of gold went to one buckler. And he made three hundred shields of beaten gold; three pounds of gold went to one shield. And the king put them in the House of the Forest of Lebanon. Moreover the king made a great throne of ivory, and overlaid it with the best gold.

The throne had six steps, and the top of the throne was round behind and there were stays on either side on the place of the seat, and two lions stood beside the stays. And twelve lions stood there on the one side and on the other upon the six steps. There was not the like made in any kingdom.

And all King Solomon's drinking vessels were of gold, and all the vessels of the House of the Forest of Lebanon were of pure gold. None were of silver; it was accounted as nothing in the days of Solomon.

So King Solomon exceeded all the kings of the earth in riches and in wisdom.' (Kings 1: 10)

In the three millennia since the rule of Solomon, explorers, fortune hunters and academics have tried – and failed – to locate the biblical city of Ophir, from which Solomon would receive rich tributes every three years. Whispers and hints circulated that the legendary mines were to be found in deepest, darkest Africa.

Early trade encounters with wealthy African courts and kings gave weight to the idea: from as early as AD 400, Arab merchants from North Africa made the hazardous journey across the Sahara to trade in salt and other goods with the rulers of Mali and Ghana where, it was reported, gold was so abundant that it adorned even the collars of the courtiers' dogs.[2] The locations of the mines were kept secret from Muslim traders – to protect the mineral resources, but also because many of the prospecting and production techniques involved religious and magic practices alien to Islam. Gold remained the primary source of wealth for these two empires – followed by kola nuts, and slaves – for several centuries.

Gold Deposits

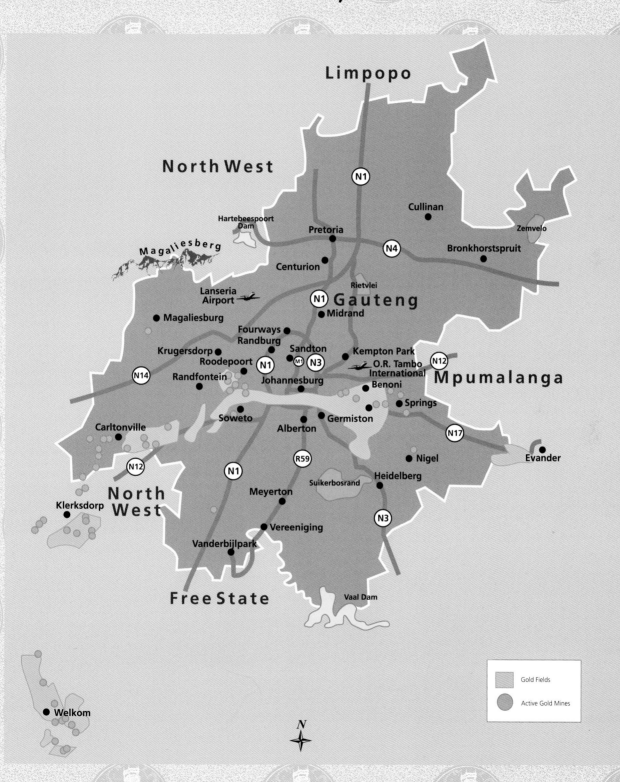

Great Zimbabwe ruins

Gold was also traded along Africa's East Coast from as early as the 11th Century – by the same people who built the famous stone structures of Great Zimbabwe. Merchants from cities in the Arabian and Persian gulfs, or even as far as China and India, sailed to the coastal towns of Kilwa and Moga-dishu to acquire southern African gold. The trade continued right up to the time of the settlement's decline, some time in the 1500s.

Between about AD 970 and AD 1290, the region now known as Mapungubwe, just south of Zimbabwe's modern border and inside South Africa, was inhabited by a wealthy Iron Age community whose skilled goldsmiths left a rich legacy that was only rediscovered in the 1930s – and largely hidden from the public. For six decades, the existence and location of the Kingdom – in the Mapungubwe National Park, in Limpopo Province – was something of an open secret: the site had been the subject of ongoing research by the University of Pretoria since the time of its discovery, but its contents (and significance) were not common public knowledge until recently. It was declared a World Heritage Site in 2003, and opened to the public in 2004.

It has been suggested that the Apartheid government deliberately suppressed information about Mapungubwe, as it provided evidence of a highly evolved,

PLACES TO SEE

There are two ways to experience the Kingdom of Mapungubwe: you can visit the **Mapungubwe National Park**, or go to the **Mapungubwe Museum**, currently housed at the University of Pretoria. The museum contains the largest archaeological gold collection in sub-Saharan Africa, as well as other artefacts from the original site. Noteworthy items include the famous golden rhino (pictured previously), a golden bowl about 10 cm in diameter, a golden sceptre some 15 cm long, and up to 18 000 finely crafted gold beads. The museum and its archive are in Lynnwood Road in Pretoria. Details can be obtained on (012) 420 3146.

• Mapungubwe National Park is located near the town of Musina, in Limpopo Province, and offers a variety of eco-tourism as well as archaeological activities. For information on the park, accommodation and activities go to www.mapungubwe.com or www.sanparks.org.

Mapungubwe Hill in Mapungubwe National Park

distinctly African civilisation existing centuries before the arrival of white men. Reseachers, however, say that the site was kept private in order to control and stabilise the ongoing excavations. Certainly, a degree of caution must have been advisable at Mapungubwe: one burial site alone yielded 2,2 kg of gold.

The Gold Standard

Gold coins were only adopted as currency standards in Europe and Britain around the 14th Century. As the metal assumed a prominent official role, the focus of colonial exploration shifted to new territories in the western hemisphere – with directives from monarchs to explorers to find more gold.

Gold was discovered in Brazil in the mid-16th Century and by 1720 the country was responsible for two-thirds of the world's gold output. A century later, the first gold discovery was documented in the United States (in North Carolina), followed by the country's first gold rush in 1803. By the late 1840s, further discoveries sparked the famous California Gold Rush – notable not just because the gold frenzy attracted an estimated 500 000 people to the state, but because many prospectors cut their teeth on the California goldfields before moving on to new, unexplored and unexploited territories in Australia and South Africa.

In 1851, for example, an Australian prospector returned home from California and made good on his promise to find gold 'within a week' of his return. The discovery, in New South Wales, heralded a rush that not only revealed some of the world's most significant gold deposits but also attracted hundreds of thousands of new immigrants to the island. In 1852 alone, 370 000 people arrived in Australia; within two decades, these immigrants outnumbered the white convicts and criminals who had been deported there in previous years.

The discovery of new goldfields represented wealth, excitement and power, but was also usually accompanied by lawlessness, individual conflicts and larger power struggles – dangers which unstable or fledgling governments were eager to avoid. These aspects applied when early discoveries of gold were made in the Boers' Zuid Afrikaansche Republiek in the 1850s and 1860s.

 PLACES TO SEE

Almost the entire town of **Pilgrim's Rest**, in Mpumalanga, has been declared a national monument – preserving much of the country's early mining history and lifestyle. The town is a great destination for day visits (it's on the Panorama Route

Pilgrim's Rest

along the eastern escarpment), but visitors can also overnight in one of the many hotels and guesthouses. Features include reconstructed diggings, original miners' houses and churches, and a print museum where the local newspaper *Gold News* was published in 1874. For more information, go to www.pilgrims-rest.co.za.

South Africa's First Gold Rush

Several small gold deposits had been found in the northern parts of South Africa by the mid-19th Century. But the country's first 'gold rush' took place in 1873, when alluvial (river) gold was discovered in the Sabie and Pilgrim's Rest regions. Goldfields were officially declared by the Boer government – this meant that the process of staking and mining claims could be monitored by officials – and thousands of diggers arrived in the area to stake and work their claims.

The resulting boom saw the Sabie veld explode into miners' settlements – first ramshackle tents, soon followed by 'civilised' essentials: bars, hotels, theatres and even a racecourse. Confidence in the region was high, and so was investment in the settlement's infrastructure. Pilgrim's Rest became the second town

On the road to Barberton

in South Africa to be electrified (after Kimberley, the country's other mining capital).

By the early 1880s, however, the alluvial gold had started to dwindle. Many of the diggers moved to the nearby Barberton goldfields, where there was reef (rock) and alluvial gold to be found. Years later, archaeological and geological studies would reveal that the Barberton rocks were some of the oldest geological formations in the world (dating back about 3,8 billion years), hinting that the Witwatersrand goldfield deposits may have had their origin in this region.

Mining in the Sabie region continued until well into the 20th Century. Gold production in Pilgrim's Rest declined after 1914, but the last operational mine was only closed in 1971. There are also unmined gold deposits in the region and, recently, new mining rights have been granted.

South Africa's largest gold deposits were still waiting to be discovered several hundred kilometres to the west of Barberton, in the area known as the 'Witwatersrand', the 'white waters ridge' named either for the seasonal waterfalls on the Rand's many ridges or for the deceptive appearance of water on rock created by the presence of reflective quartz and iron pyrite rather than actual water.

Several small discoveries in the Rand area set the stage for what was to follow. In 1874, the first mining operation was set up near the Magaliesberg, after Australian Henry Lewis discovered gold deposits. Four

Unlucky Prospectors

In 1852 a Welsh-born amateur geologist with an interest in mining made his way to the Transvaal (on a prospecting trip) and, happily, found gold in 'considerable quantities' near the present-day municipality of Krugersdorp.[3] John Henry Davis presented his gold sample to then-Boer president Andries Pretorius, who 'immediately realised the danger his people would be in if the occurrence were made known to the world', and 'instructed the treasurer to purchase the gold from Davis and ordered the old man out of the country.'[4]

In 1853 another prospector, Pieter Jacob Marais, decided to try his luck at finding gold in the same region, this time with the consent of the *Volksraad* (government) – although Marais had to sign an agreement in which he solemnly swore to keep his discoveries secret from any other parties. Marais found evidence of some alluvial gold in the Jukskei River, but was unable to recover any significant quantity of the metal – despite the fact that he was working only a few miles from the main Witwatersrand reef. He later moved his search northwards and, having failed to find any further significant deposits, turned his attentions to hunting and trading until his death in 1865.

years later David Wardrop found gold contained in veins of quartz at the Zwartkop Hill north of Krugersdorp. In 1881, Stephanus Minnaar discovered gold on the farm Kromdraai (near today's Cradle of Humankind) and started mining the following year. The farm was declared a public digging in 1885 – the first on the Rand. In 1882, gold was discovered on the farm Tweefontein (five kilometres north of Kromdraai) and a ten-stamp crushing battery (the first in the region) was installed three years later. None of these early mines, however, discovered or worked the main Witwatersrand gold reef.

The Little Reef That Wouldn't

The Struben brothers: Fred (left) and Harry (right)

In 1884 brothers Fred and Harry Struben nearly became the most famous prospectors in the world when they discovered a large quantity of gold in quartz rock outcrops on their farm, Wilgespruit. The brothers optimistically named their site Confidence Reef. The rock that the Strubens began to mine, however, was still not part of the main Witwatersrand conglomerate; rather, it was a smaller reef of quartz, permeated by erratic deposits of gold.

At first, Confidence Reef showed a promising yield: in one sample, recorded in 1885, an incredible 913 ounces (over 25 000 grams) of gold were recovered from one ton of rock[5] (present-day deep-level gold mines may be considered economical or viable when little more than 10 grams of gold are recoverable per ton). The phenomenal result was confirmed by a second assay, drawn from what Fred Struben referred to as a 'chimney' of gold-bearing quartz. After the first discovery, however, 'all trace of it [the chimney] was lost and further prospecting failed to locate its destination.'[6]

The erratic nature of the quartz's gold deposits proved to be Confidence Reef's downfall. After a year, the mine ran dry and had to be abandoned. The reason for Confidence Reef's failure would become evident just a few months later, when large, consistently payable deposits of gold were discovered hidden in the conglomerate rock (not quartz) of the nearby Witwatersrand reef.

Hidden Gold

In the 19th Century, prevailing scientific wisdom held that the world's largest and most important sources of gold were to be found in placer or alluvial deposits – washed down by rivers, from ancient gold-bearing rocks – and, in lesser quantities, in veins of quartz (though it was not yet quite understood how the gold came to be in the rock)[7]. This thinking applied to many of the New World gold rushes at the time – California, New Zealand, Australia, Brazil and Russia all had rich alluvial sources. As a result, many prospectors believed that alluvial gold was the only type worth pursuing.

In the Boer Transvaal Republic, however, the 'prevailing wisdom' clearly did not apply; the variety of reef formations in the region, and conditions under which gold was found, posed puzzling anomalies for geologists, surveyors and prospectors – many of whom missed the presence of the world's largest gold deposit, literally under their feet, simply because it was contained in an unfamiliar form.

On the Witwatersrand reef, gold occurs in an almost-unique conglomerate rock formation known as 'banket' – named after a Dutch confection studded with caramelised almonds (the gold-bearing rock is similarly 'studded', but with quartz pebbles). Some geologists refer to these types of formations as 'pudding stones'.

Although not usually visible to the naked eye, the presence of gold in the banket could easily be confirmed by simple assaying or panning.[8] Initial mining of the Witwatersrand banket was, essentially, a large-scale version of a 400-year-old mining technique: the ore would be mined, crushed to a coarse powder (in this case by large battery stampers), and panned (through water or solution) to reveal the gold.

Conglomerate rock showing gold-containing 'banket' formation

PLACES TO SEE

The remains of the **Confidence Reef Mine** were declared a national monument in 1984, and are to be found in the Kloofendal Nature Reserve in Roodepoort. The diggings – a series of shallow caves and pits in the side of a koppie – can be viewed by appointment. Call the Roodepoort Museum on (011) 761 0225 to arrange a guided tour.

The Three Georges:
Harrison, Walker and Honeyball

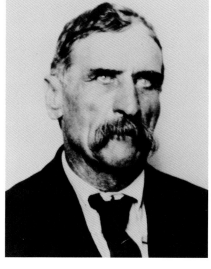

George Honeyball (far left)
George Walker (left)
There are no photographs
of George Harrison.

With the influx of miners, prospectors and explorers coming to and through the central Transvaal (often from the diamond mines of Kimberley), it was only a matter of time before some sharp-eyed prospector would eventually uncover the nature – and location – of the gold deposits hidden in the Witwatersrand reefs.

As it happened, three men – two English, one South African, all named George – share an almost equal claim to being named the 'first' to discover gold on the Witwatersrand. That they all met and knew each other, and discovered gold on the same family farm, has made the issue of who was 'first' secondary to what came next.

The following account summarises the stories of the three Georges, as told by historian Eric Rosenthal in his book, *Gold! Gold! Gold!*[9]:

George Walker was a Lancashire-born coal miner who'd emigrated to South Africa in 1876, to work the Kimberley diamond fields. He'd later (unsuccessfully) tried his luck prospecting for gold at Pilgrim's Rest, Spitzkop and Lydenburg before making his way towards the newly discovered coalfields in Kroonstad, in the Orange Free State. It was at this point Walker encountered another Englishman, George Harrison – who had previously worked as a prospector in Australia, but declined to talk in any further detail about his past. Many suspected his reticence covered up a possible criminal record.

The two Georges decided to leave Kroonstad and head for the Barberton goldfields, in the Eastern Transvaal. On their way, they stopped off in a canteen at Mulder's Drift in the Witwatersrand. Here they heard two brothers – Fred and Harry Struben – were in need of a miner.

The Strubens appointed Walker, as a digger, mason and bricklayer, while Harrison found building work on the neighbouring farm of Langlaagte – a large piece of land, occupied since the 1850s and owned by various members of the Oosthuizen family. Harrison was employed to build additional accommodation for the widow Petronella Oosthuizen, and her son. ☞

Living with Petronella – Auntie Nellie – in a small cottage on the property, was Petronella's nephew George Honeyball, a blacksmith and general handyman.

On Sunday 7 February 1886, George Walker decided to pay a visit to his 'chum' George Harrison. Walking through the long grass, between the farms of Wilgespruit and Langlaagte, Walker stumbled on a projection of bare stone known as an outcrop. According to Walker, he immediately 'recognised' the stone as a banket formation (this, Rosenthal comments, was highly unlikely as the presence of gold in banket conglomerate was not yet known – but that's how Walker's story went). Honeyball recalled that Walker took the sample of rock on to the widow Oosthuizen's house, where he 'borrowed my aunt's frying pan in the kitchen, crushed the conglomerate to a coarse powder on an old ploughshare, and went to a nearby spruit where he panned the stuff. It showed a clear streak of gold.'

Gold or not, Walker didn't seem overly excited by his find and carried on with his regular work at Wilgespruit, until the downturn of the Strubens' fortunes meant he was laid off. He did, however, secure some basic prospecting rights on another part of Langlaagte for a period of three months – spurred into action by the subsequent interest and actions of Petronella Oosthuizen's nephew (Honeyball) – but this does not appear to have yielded anything for Walker himself.

Honeyball, after seeing Walker extract gold from the outcrop, persuaded Walker to show him the site the following morning. From there, Honeyball easily traced the line of the reef until he found another, similar, outcrop and 'knocked a lump off it.'

As Honeyball had very little knowledge or experience of mining, he took the sample to a more experienced person: Fred Struben. Fred, however, thought little of the ore and Honeyball left, disheartened. His spirits changed when he met up with a relative of the Strubens – a man named Godfray Lys, who had recently come from Pretoria and shared accommodation with Fred and Harry. Lys' reaction was the opposite of Fred's. He trembled from sheer excitement, and said: 'By jove, that's gold.'

Lys persuaded Honeyball to show him his outcrop site (for a fee), and the pair also convinced Walker to show Lys his outcrop find.

By April 1886, Walker and Harrison had finished their building work on their respective farms, and entered into a prospecting contract with Petronella's relative Gerhardus Oosthuizen, to look for gold on his portion of Langlaagte (the original farm had been divided up among several family members, including Gerhardus and Petronella). If the Georges discovered payable gold, they would be granted a choice of claims and the rights to work them. If no discovery were made, the agreement would lapse.

Harrison, eager to legitimise his venture, hurried to Pretoria and secured the prescribed prospecting license on May 23, valid for one month.

A little over two weeks later, Oosthuizen wrote to President Kruger to confirm that the reef was payable – and again sent 'Sors Hariezon' to Pretoria, this time with

Petronella Oosthuizen

Langlaagte Farm as it appeared in about 1886

The ruins of the labourer's cottage George Harrison lived in, on the farm Wilgespruit

a sample of the rock as proof.

By October, Gerhardus Oosthuizen had sold his section off to 'Messrs Du Toit and Schoeman', who apparently disregarded Harrison's discoverer's claim staked on the property.

Harrison was forced to submit a petition to Pretoria, in which he stated (or claimed) that he was the 'original prospector' of the quarter on the farm Langlaagte, which legally entitled him to the *zoeker* or discoverer's claim he was fighting for.

After that, Harrison disappeared into obscurity – apparently selling his claim for £10 pounds to a Fred Marsden, before dropping out of the records and into the history books.

George Walker also left the Rand. Years later he returned to lay his own claim to having 'discovered' the main reef. He was given a pension by the Chamber of Mines and lived in a house in Krugersdorp until his death in 1924, at the age of 71.[10]

George Honeyball also disappeared; for more than four decades it was assumed he had passed away, until a storekeeper in Pienaar's River (north of Pretoria) made the connection between the ragged hermit living in a mud hut close to his store and the legendary discoverer of the Reef. Honeyball's reappearance was the subject of intense media interest, and he was even filmed by operators from Metro-Goldwyn (Meyer) in conversation with none other than Godfray Lys (who, unlike the Georges, had established himself

PLACES TO SEE

You can view the two original mining shafts at **George Harrison Park**, Main Reef Road, Langlaagte. The original 10-stamp battery mill used to crush ore has been removed, and is currently on display in the mining district of Main Street, in downtown Johannesburg.

Although George Harrison Park also offers sweeping views of the city, it has been plagued by vandals for several decades and its entrance is now locked. Access can be arranged by phoning (011) 837 7728/4291. It is recommended you visit the park in a group.

Battery stamper on Main Street

THINGS TO DO

The **Parktown and Westcliff Heritage Trust** does frequent tours of the remnants of Joburg's gold prospecting. It takes in the headgear at Langlaagte where the first gold was found, the Crown Mines village south of the city and the Chamber of Mines building in the CBD. Phone (011) 482 3349 for information.

Geologist Gavin Whitfield, of Geological Heritage Tours, also facilitates guided tours exploring the city's mining past. Call him on (011) 886 8722.

Early surface mining in Johannesburg, 1886

as a prominent and wealthy member of new Joburg society). The Chamber of Mines gave Honeyball a pension and he moved to a small cottage on the western outskirts of Johannesburg.[11]

From Prospectors to Investors

Within a few months of the goldfields' discovery, it became clear that the gold deposits in the Witwatersrand were indeed payable and consistent; they were also going to require a different sort of effort, energy, finance and labour to mine.

An early report from state surveyors Johann Rissik and Christiaan Johannes Joubert indicated that the goldfields could not be worked by individual diggers – they required joint undertakings by companies. 'The need for costly machinery calls for a large amount of capital. We do not recommend that the fields should be thrown open to individuals. There is a danger that men who have staked off good claims will be unable to work them, but be forced to leave and, through necessity, take to lawless ways,' they wrote. A claimholder would have needed in excess of £10 000 for the necessary equipment, water rights, claim licenses, dynamite, wages for workers and

other expenses. These economic demands quickly wiped out the smaller companies and individuals.

Within four years, the nature of Reef mining was to change again – permanently removing the prospect of fame and fortune for small-time prospectors, but setting the stage for the industrial barons known as Randlords.

The MacArthur-Forrest Process

The Reef outcrops first exploited by Joburg's early prospectors were weathered and oxidised from centuries of exposure to the elements – which is why they could be mined and treated relatively easily and inexpensively. This surface conglomerate was extracted at such a rapid rate that, within a few years, miners reached depths of 30 m below the surface – where they found the gold ore 'locked' inside sulphur-containing pyrites. This required a much more complex recovery treatment and the chemical technology available at the time meant the recovery rate from ore dropped to below 50 per cent – too low for the mining operations to yield a profit.

For some months it seemed that Johannesburg might turn into another ghost mining town, as profits plummeted and confidence dived. During this time the price of gold shares fell, mines closed down and fledgling companies went out of business.

In 1887, three Glaswegians – two doctors and a chemist – patented a process that would not only save the Witwatersrand goldfields but also shape gold extraction to this very day.

At the end of the 19th Century, with spectacular gold discoveries in the new worlds of South Africa, Australia, New Zealand and North America, there was a race of sorts to discover new chemical methods to sift or leach gold from crushed ore. The primary obstacle was the fact that gold is a very inert metal – which means it fails to react or interact with most chemical solutions. Previously, the accepted method of extracting gold from ore was through the process of amalgamation – treating the ore with mercury, which combined with the gold and made extraction through heating possible. The pyritic Witwatersrand ore, however, was more complex, and the amalgamation method failed to yield high enough recovery rates. Tens of new treatments, involving different chemical compounds, were invented, tested … and rejected. Until JS MacArthur and brothers RW Forrest and W Forrest updated an older process of treating gold ore with cyanide.

To simplify the reactions: crushed ore was added to a weak solution of cyanide, which dissolved the gold, very effectively, into the solution. The remaining rock particles could then be filtered off, leaving the gold-heavy cyanide solution. Adding zinc dust to the cyanide solution initiated a further chemical reaction, causing fine specks of gold to precipitate (condense or separate out) of the cyanide solution; this gold could then be separated and refined and the (highly poisonous) cyanide disposed of.

The 'MacArthur-Forrest' process arrived on the Reef in 1889 or 1890, and proved such a success that avaricious mine and industry owners (in South Africa and around the world) sued to have its potentially costly patent rights removed – on the grounds that the process was based on previously known reactions and was, therefore, not a new invention. The judges sided with the petitioners,

PLACES TO VISIT

The soon-to-be completed **Geological Museum at Museum Africa**, 121 Bree Street, Newtown, will feature South Africa's most extraordinary collection of gems and minerals, across 18 specialist 'zones', including: the cycle of life, Google Earth, a treasure vault, a space area, a spiral of time, a time tunnel and a laboratory area. For information and opening times, contact the Museum on (011) 833 5624.

Rock showing water marks from the Witwatersrand sea

PLACES TO SEE

The **Chamber of Mines** (5 Hollard Street, Marshalltown) is an employer's organisation established in 1887 to represent the interests of the mining houses. The building can be viewed on any walking tour of the pedestrian-friendly Main Street district; you can also contact the Chamber to arrange visits to working gold mines in the region. For more information, contact (011) 498 7100.

leaving the brothers Forrest and Mr MacArthur not just deprived of any future income from their efforts, but also faced with a legal costs bill estimated to be in the region of a million dollars. That the chemical process retained their names was probably scant consolation.

FOUNDATIONS

'They are trying to make Johannesburg respectable. They are trying to make snobs out of us, making us forget who our ancestors were. They are trying to make us lose our sense of pride in the fact that our forebears were a lot of roughnecks who knew nothing about culture and who came here to look for gold.'

Herman Charles Bosman, from *A Cask of Jerepigo*[1]

In this chapter

- 👉 Boom Town – From Mining Camps to City Blocks
- 👉 The Establishment of Joburg's Business District
- 👉 A City of Men
- 👉 Joburg's Illicit Past
- 👉 Migrant Mine Workers
- 👉 Joburg's Bandit King

OF THE CITY

'On the Rand – White, Black and Yellow' (Postcard, early 1900s)

Boom Town

Modern Johannesburg began, effectively, on 20 September 1886, when Paul Kruger, president of the ZAR, declared the area open for public digging.

In July that year, Kimberley's Diamond Fields Advertiser had trumpeted the existence of the newly discovered gold reef, '30 miles long and just 50 miles south of Pretoria' – in a place it called the 'Vetvatterand'. Diggers were, incorrectly, assured the district had a plentiful supply of water.[2] The actual site was treeless, dry and dusty, with little to recommend it except the promise of gold.

Some time between the discovery of gold and the proclamation of the public diggings, the first mining camp was established alongside the area's only water source, known as Fordsburg Dip, on the farm Turffontein. The camp, consisting of tents and wagons, with scattered corrugated iron dwellings, was named after its self-proclaimed leader, Colonel Ignatius Ferreira (a Boer soldier and failed diamond digger). The camp still exists today,

in the form of Ferreirasdorp (Ferreira's town), south of Commissioner street and west of Ferreira Street in the Central Business District.

The Advertiser reported that the population of Ferreirra's Town was 300 persons, and that there were no less than 14 hotels supplying liquor there.

A second mining camp soon sprang up alongside Ferreira's, called Marshall's Town. It was named after the Scotsman Henry Brown (HB) Marshall, who bought the land together with a property syndicate (which included Marshall's brother-in-law William McLaren, Samuel Fox and solicitor WE Hollard).[3]

The previous year, Marshall had married a 'beautiful young [Afrikaans] woman, who attracted a host of eligible suitors.' Her maiden name was Anna Maria Rissik, and she was the only sister of Johann Rissik – who, in August 1886, was appointed as acting surveyor-general for the Witwatersrand.

Ignatius Ferreira

Earliest photograph of Ferreira's Camp, taken in 1886.

Randjeslaagte Triangle

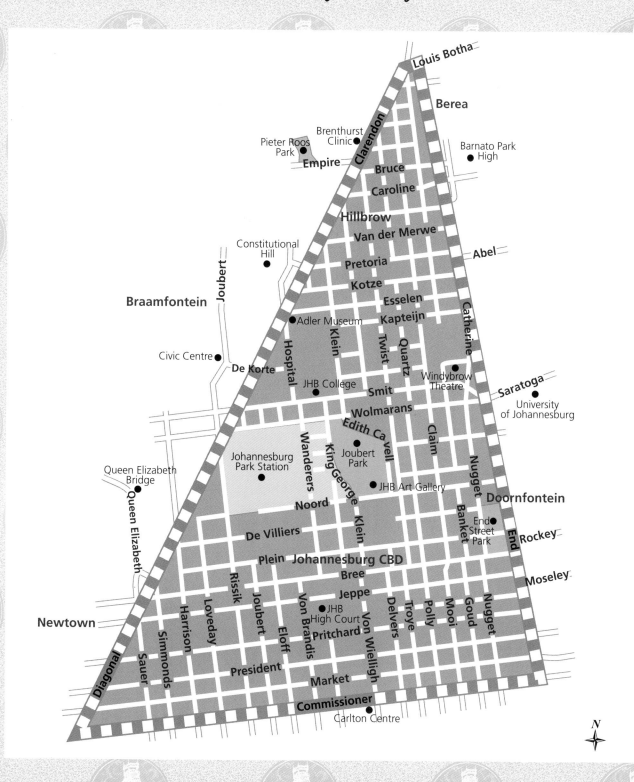

Louis Botha

Berea

Brenthurst
Clinic

Pieter Roos
Park

Barnato Park
High

Clarendon

Empire

Bruce

Caroline

Hillbrow

Van der Merwe

Constitutional
Hill

Abel

Joubert

Pretoria

Kotze

Braamfontein

Esselen

Kapteijn

Adler Museum

Catherine

Civic Centre

De Korte

Hospital

Klein

Twist

Quartz

Windybrow
Theatre

Saratoga

University
of Johannesburg

JHB College

Smit

Wolmarans

Edith Cavell

Claim

Wanderers

Johannesburg
Park Station

King George

Joubert
Park

JHB Art Gallery

Nugget

Doornfontein

Queen Elizabeth
Bridge

Noord

Klein

Banket

End
Street
Park

End

Rockey

Queen Elizabeth

De Villiers

Moseley

Plein

Johannesburg CBD

Bree

Newtown

Rissik

Jeppe

Polly

Mooi

Goud

Nugget

Harrison

Loveday

Joubert

Eloff

Von Brandis

JHB
High Court

Von Wielligh

Pritchard

Troye

Delvers

President

Market

Diagonal

Sauer

Simmonds

Commissioner

Carlton Centre

N

Rissik and a Volksraad member, Christiaan Johannes Joubert, formed the two-man commission established by the Kruger government to settle conflicts in the booming mining camp, over land rights, mining claims and the rights to grazing and water.

This family connection may have proved handy to Marshall when, in late 1886, the proposed sale of stands in Marshall's Town (scheduled for 11 November, a month before the planned sale of the government's own stands a little to the north) was ruled to be illegal. The government eventually conceded to the plots being sold, provided it received 10 per cent of the price.[4]

Marshall's Township Syndicate had its property professionally surveyed and laid out as a township by a draughtsman named Simmonds – who named several of the main streets after his employers, and another after himself. The area, east of Ferreira Street, west of Delvers Street and south of Commissioner Street, is still known today as Marshalltown.[5]

Bolstered by the financial success of his property, Marshall expanded his business interests to include shares in various gold mines and mining houses, a power company, a colliery and a brick manufacturing company. Marshall also started a small brewery on eight stands in Marshall's Township. In 1890, Marshall and his partners – Glass and Welsh – sold the business, including its trademark (a representation of three castles), for £18 000. By 1895, this venture had become known as South African Breweries Limited.

HB Marshall remained one of the city's notable businessmen, living on a country estate in what would later become the suburbs of Melrose and Atholl (Venus Street was named after Marshall's favourite racehorse), until his involvement in the Jameson Raid of 1896 – for which he was imprisoned and sentenced to two years in jail. Marshall negotiated a fine of £25 000 for his early release, and returned to Scotland where he lived until his death in 1948.

Which Johannes?

The exact origin of Johannesburg's name has never been determined – despite the attempts of many historians and commissions and the existence of numerous urban anecdotes.

There is a number of men who, individually or collectively, might lay reasonable claim to having lent their name.

Surveyor-General Johann Rissik and head of the Mines Department, Christiaan Johannes Joubert, were accompanied by Veldkornet Johannes Petrus Meyer, the government official in charge of the area, when they went riding from farm to farm to complete their initial survey. The president of the Zuid Afrikaansche Republiek (ZAR) at the time was also called Stephanus Johannes Paulus Kruger.

Clockwise from top left: Paul Kruger, Johann Rissik, JP Meyer, CJ Joubert

Mapping the City

Rissik and Joubert's commission needed to establish a formal mining village on land that was close to the gold reef – but did not seem to have any likely prospects for gold itself. The Transvaal Surveyor-General, Gideon Retief Von Wielligh, found a barren, stony and unclaimed triangle of land, called Randjeslaagte, tucked between the three major farms of Braamfontein, Doornfontein and Turffontein.

Randjeslaagte existed because of the rough and ready surveying techniques of rural Transvaal, where land was plentiful but qualified surveyors were rare. A system evolved in which each farmer marked out his property with temporary beacons constructed of piles of whitewashed stones (pending the day when some higher and more qualified authority would mark out permanent boundaries).

In some cases, land claims overlapped. In others, there were large gaps between the farm borders, which became known as *uitvalgrond* or 'surplus land', and which was automatically owned by the state. Randjeslaagte was a classic example, a narrow triangle about one-and-a-half kilometres wide at its base in the south, and extending about five kilometres to its apex in the north, covering some 1 100 acres. None of the local farmers had laid claim to it because it was unsuitable for agriculture and had no water.

Yet there were two minor obstacles on Randjeslaagte's route to becoming the centre of the future Johannesburg. The first came in September 1886, when Kruger's newly appointed mining commissioner for the area, a German military man named Captain Carl von Brandis, officially proclaimed public diggings at a long list of local farms – including Randjeslaagte. A Randjeslaagte Syndicate was formed and immediately began diggings

HB Marshall

on 36 claims between today's Bree and Pritchard streets – and even found some gold. By December, the owners realised the ground was not viable for mining, and sold the property to the government.

In October 1886 Rissik appointed a surveyor, Josias Eduard de Villiers, on the basis of De Villiers' previous experience in helping to lay out the diamond-rush town of Kimberley. De Villiers supported the choice of Randjeslaagte for the new village, saying it was centrally placed and the preference of the diggers. De Villiers noted that water was scarce, but said it could be conveyed by pipes from elsewhere once a town was established.

De Villiers completed his task in less than a month. At the instruction of the government (which still, mistakenly, believed the gold would run out – and wanted to make as much quick profit as possible), De Villiers laid out the town with unusually small city blocks and narrower roads, maximising the number of desirable corner stands. Only one stand was set aside to accommodate the mining commissioner, the landdrost and the post office.[6] This design would later prove a major obstacle for the modern, traffic-bound city of Johannesburg, where small blocks meant more intersections and traffic lights.

De Villiers' survey was slightly hampered by Marshall's Town on his southern boundary, where streets (laid out by the aforementioned Mr Simmonds) were already set out in a tight grid that he was obliged to follow. Commissioner Street, for example, at the very south of Randjeslaagte, had already been set out and named by HB Marshall – the name commemorates the fact that it was here that Commissioner Von Brandis proclaimed the mine fields.[7]

Joburg Trivia

The Glenhove offramp, off the M1 freeway, was named after HB Marshall's place of birth.

The Randjeslaagte Triangle

While Ferreira's Town and Marshall's Town remain to this day, the name Randjeslaagte is not commemorated anywhere. But the area's traces are still there to be found, if you know where to look. Its northern point is just off the corner of Boundary Road, Parktown, and Louis Botha Avenue, close to Clarendon Circle. A triangular monument was erected there, now very much the worse for wear, stripped of its surface and looking a little like an oversized water hydrant.

The south-eastern corner is at the intersection of Market and End streets, at the point where the freeway passes overhead. End Street, which runs at a slight angle to other north–south streets, is so named because it marked the eastern boundary of Randjeslaagte. On the eastern side the triangle then runs up a hill along Catherine Avenue (adjacent to Nugget Street), and through Hillbrow, meeting the apex at the corner of Banket Street.

The south-western corner is at the intersection of Commissioner and Diagonal streets. Just off that corner is the start of West Street, thus named because it marks the west side of the triangle.[8]

The Bank Sitting on a Gold Mine

In 1986, during the construction of Standard Bank's head office at No. 5 Simmonds Street, building contractors discovered an old access tunnel or stope leading to mining works three levels below ground.

After investigation it was determined that the stope led to the abandoned Ferreira's Mine, established by Ignatius Ferreira over a century before.

Because of the historic significance of the site, the bank preserved much of the original mine (although certain tunnels had to be filled in and caulked to stabilise the ground) and its surrounding area, and created a public museum. Visitors can still see pick marks on the walls, and look at archived photographs.

Ferreira formed the Ferreira Company syndicate and the Ferreira Gold Mining Company, but lost his shares and eventually retired to a farm in the north of South Africa, near present-day Louis Trichardt.

The Kink in Bree Street

When Randjeslaagte was first surveyed and divided into plots, a small section of the area was occupied by the Randjeslaagte Mining Syndicate, which had set up a mining camp and sunk a shaft between present-day Bree and Pritchard/President streets. De Villiers' original design, therefore, was laid out as two separate entities on either side of this mining area.

When these claims were abandoned and sold back to the government in 1887, a surveyor named Auret Pritchard was appointed to fill the gaps. He started at the south (Pritchard Street) side, and extended the north–south streets northwards. As the streets had never been intended to join up, by the time they reached Bree ('wide') Street, there was a very noticeable displacement or kink at the joints.[9]

Surveyor Auret Pritchard, dressed in prospector's outfit

The Business of Joburg

Early image of Market Square on market day

By 1887 the population of Johannesburg had grown to 3 000 people.

The wagons and mining tents quickly gave way to buildings of wood and iron, and Joburg experienced its first building boom. As a greater sense of permanence developed these structures were again torn down, and replaced with sophisticated brick edifices.

The central focus of the town was Market Square, around which business and financial zones quickly grew. Market Square stretched for six blocks, from Rissik Street in the east to Sauer Street in the west, bordered by President and Market streets. 'Depending on the weather, the Square and streets were either unattended dustbowls or strips of churned-up mud dotted with pools. There were always wagon tracks and horse and ox droppings.'[10]

The eastern portion of the Square became a produce and general dealers' market, while the western half was a cattle market. A market house was built in 1888 – the first building in the space, together with a shelter to house the growing town's first fire-fighting apparatus. By 1895 shops, offices and banks appeared on the Square's perimeter.

Also in 1888, the first government building was established on the Square's eastern edge, on Rissik Street. One wing of the building was occupied by the post office. In 1892, the entire building was taken over by the post office until a still-larger building became necessary several years later (see next page). Gradually, government and municipal buildings took over all of Market Square – the market was eventually relocated several blocks north-west, in what would later be named Newtown – and the original market area was renamed, first Library Gardens and, more recently, Beyers Naude Square.[11]

Between the chains at the Johannesburg Stock Exchange

PLACES TO SEE

The **Rissik Street Post Office**, built in 1897, was designed by Dutch architect Sytze Wierda. At one time it was the tallest building in town. The clock tower was a later addition – in 1905, an additional storey had to be added to the post office because of the rapid growth of the city. The original bell tower was removed and replaced with the clock tower (now under dust covers for protection).

The Post Office was declared a national monument in 1978, but the building has been (very sadly) neglected since the postal services moved out in 1996. Various Joburg development agencies have invested in restoring parts of the building – which is structurally sound, but mostly derelict. It is hoped that, in the next few years, it will return to grace as a multi-use (commercial and other) building. For updates on developments, visit the city's website at www.joburg.org.za.

South of Market Square, on the north-west corner of Commissioner and Simmonds streets, Johannesburg's first Stock Exchange (the JSE) was constructed in 1887. By 1890, the bustling Exchange already required a larger building – and so new premises were built on the same site, adjoining the original building, at a cost of £70 000. The new JSE was considered a 'marvel of progress', boasting electric lights (but, apparently, no telephones).

Trading at the JSE would often continue long after the Exchange had closed; as a result, City Commissioner Von Brandis was asked to close off a section of Simmonds Street specifically for this purpose – between Market and Commissioner streets. Posts were erected, with chains hung between them, giving rise to the expression 'between the chains'; this expression was later used to refer to any dealings at the JSE.[12] As Joburg had no city hall, the area between the chains was also commonly used as a meeting place.

In 1903 the JSE moved to new premises on Hollard Street. A fourth Exchange building was constructed in 1960, on the same site. During construction a temporary

The original Rissik Street Post Office, before the addition of extra floors and its clock tower

home was found for the JSE in Protection House in Fox Street. In 1978 the JSE moved for a fifth time, taking up residence at No. 17 Diagonal Street, where the JSE's stockbrokers, staff and offices were all housed in two buildings next door to each other. In September 2000 the JSE moved premises for the sixth time, to One Exchange Square, corner of Maude Street and Gwen Lane in Sandton.[13]

The Randlords

Abe Bailey, Julius Wernher, JB Robinson, Alfred Beit

Woolf Joel, Lionel Phillips, Barney Barnato, George Albu, George Farrar

Because of the unique nature of the gold ore, mining of the Witwatersrand goldfields required substantial capital investment almost from the start; within two or three years of the diggings being proclaimed, a number of syndicates or joint stock companies had been floated (many of these helmed by businessmen who had made their fortunes from the Kimberley diamond mines, in a similar fashion). By 1889, the Diggers' Committee had given way to the newly formed Chamber of Mines.[14]

During the brief periods of economic depression in Joburg's early years (particularly before the introduction of the MacArthur-Forrest Process), these syndicates took advantage of the slump in property prices, shares and mining equipment and increased their holdings, effectively removing or replacing smaller operators who, with less capital backing, were forced to sell out.

At the front of these syndicates, mining houses and financial institutions were men like George and Leopold Albu, Alfred and Otto Beit, Barney Barnato, Abe Bailey, Hermann Eckstein, George Farrar, Woolf Joel, Lionel Phillips, Cecil John Rhodes, JB Robinson and Julius Wernher – known as the Randlords.

Many of their mining houses and companies formed the basis of the mining interests that still dominate today: Barnato's Johannesburg Consolidated Investment Company became JCI Limited; and the Albu brothers' General Mining and Finance Corporation became Gencor.

As the gold price was internationally fixed, the Randlords were not able to manipulate it in pursuit of profits. Instead, they focused on trying to reduce the extensive costs of underground (and increasingly deep-level) mining, while continuing to increase the volume of gold recovered.

There were several factors influencing profit margins – the price of dynamite, for example. One issue, however, would emerge as central to both the goldfields' viability and the financial and political future of not just Johannesburg but the whole of South Africa: the availability and cost of labour. More specifically, of unskilled black labour.

Working together with the ZAR government – which was almost totally reliant on the profits and revenues generated from the goldfields and had developed close personal ties with many of the Randlords and their colleagues – the mining houses began to develop a series of sytems and processes that would gradually compel rural dwellers to come to work on the mines, for increasingly lower wages.

A Man's World

Early Johannesburg was a town peopled with immigrants and migrants – the population fluctuating according to the demands of the mining industry, which drew workers and fortune seekers from all over southern Africa, Europe, Britain, North America, and even the Middle East and New Zealand.

What most of these early Joburgers did have in common was their gender: for many years the town was overwhelmingly male-dominated, owing to both the expense of transporting and accommodating wives and

families, and its generally unsavoury and uncertain nature.

By the mid-1890s, there were over 100 000 people living in the city – almost half of them black labourers, including 29 000 mine workers living in compounds.

'Even as goldfields went,' explained author Eric Rosenthal in *Gold! Gold! Gold!*, 'the Witwatersrand was notable for its astonishing array of nationalities. Apart

Trading in Market Square

from the scores of African tribes [sic] represented among the black workers, there were migrants from every part of the world.' Men from Britain ('with the Scots even more in evidence than the English'[15]), Germany, Austria, Switzerland, Denmark, France, Belgium, Portugal, Italy, Norway, Sweden, Russia, Greece and Romania were all represented – as were Chinese, Syrians, New Zealanders, Australians and prominent numbers of Americans.

A significant number of Johannesburg's early settlers were Jews who had fled from the *shtetls* (villages) of the 'Pale of Settlement', the western region of Imperial Russia in which Jews were legally allowed to settle – attracted by the promise of religious freedom (or, at least, freedom from persecution) in the ZAR, as well as the gold.

The fact that only Afrikaans (Boer) men were elegible for the franchise – European and other white settlers were referred to as *Uitlanders* or 'foreigners' – and that various ordinances and laws passed by the ZAR government had further restricted the rights of black (and Indian and Chinese) people proved to be no deterrent to optimistic new arrivals.

The promise of busy trade attracted a number of indentured Indians from the Natal sugar plantations (those whose contracts had ended), as well as educated 'free' or 'passenger' Indians. Different groups of Coloured people also moved from the Cape to the Rand, most of them playing a part in the transport industry.

PLACES TO SEE

The **Rand Club** (33 Loveday Street), was established in 1886, by a group including Cecil John Rhodes, Hans Sauer and Hermann Eckstein, and rapidly became the social centre of Joburg's elite – or of most of it: the 'gentleman's' club was widely believed to have a 'no Jews' policy (women and black men were prohibited from joining until the 1990s), despite the fact that the club house served as a makeshift synagogue in Joburg's early years. Undesirable members were further excluded through the time-honoured tradition of blackballing.

The original club house was built on four adjoining stands, two of which were donated to the Club by speculator Ikey Sonnenberg; the remaining stands were purchased from HB Marshall.

The second club house (1890), built on the same location, was a double-storey structure accommodating a bar, billiard room, dining room and various offices.

In 1904, a third version of the Club – designed by Leck & Emley – was constructed (on the same site), and the resulting building remains in use today. The Club, which has been refurbished following a fire in 2005, can be visited by non-members (there is a strict dress code: no jeans, sneakers, leather jackets or shorts are allowed) and boasts an excellent bar – at 103 feet, the longest in the world.

The Rand Club in 1887

The Club as it looks today

Removed from conventional 'family' structures, most of Joburg's working class lived in boarding houses (white men) or compounds (black mine workers) concentrated on and around the actual mining properties themselves – east and west of the city, following the line of the reef. Historian and author Charles van Onselen writes: 'Drinking, gambling and whoring, which would probably have played an important part in the emerging working-class culture of the Rand in any case … thus assumed a central role in the lives of thousands of skilled and unskilled miners. This dependence of black and white workers on alchohol and prostitutes to lend some meaning to an otherwise alienated social existence was swiftly appreciated by the Transvaal ruling classes … .'[16]

Liquid Gold

Mining was thirsty work. Johannesburg's first liquor licence was granted in June 1886[17] – three months before the goldfields were declared public diggings!

The streets of early Johannesburg may have been dusty and unlit, but there was no shortage of bars, music halls and gambling dens – by 1890, the city is said to have boasted no less than 400 bars, one on almost every street corner. These canteens were a welcome haven from the usual wattle-and-daub or tin shacks the miners slept in; also there was usually the added attraction of a welcoming barmaid.

Charles Bain, a member of the Rand Club who arrived in Johannesburg in 1887, gave his account of barroom attractions:

'It was like entering a haven of rest to go into one of these places out of the bitter night and it was cold – much colder than it is now in Johannesburg, because it was a bare windswept ridge in those days, with no houses or buildings or trees to break the wind, and no roads or streets. We just had to stumble along in the dark from one bar to another because there were no lights, and the only illumination was that from the bars. Well,

An old liquor storehouse, now used as a car workshop

we would enter and approach the Presiding Divinity. All bars had women barmaids in those days …'[18]

Some of the better known barmaids included Amanda Acquinza from Kimberley, who came to work at the famous Vienna Café on the corner of Market and Joubert streets in 1886. Within a year, she had moved to the Red Lamp and married the bar owner.[19] Edith Bolster was a barmaid at the Elephant and Castle in Commmissioner Street, and married Ted Sloane, an early pioneer who later became a leading rancher in Texas. Pearl Penrose owned the Pearl Penrose Bar and later married into the British peerage; while her assistant, Del Fincham, married a mining magnate.[20]

Alcohol wasn't just attractive to Joburg's masses (and a few 'gentlemen'); the distillery business proved highly profitable for a handful of the Randlords, who were happy to influence control over their workers through the strategic supply and availability of liquor, as well as for the ZAR government.

In 1881, President Paul Kruger had awarded the concession (in line with a highly criticised ZAR government practice of awarding trade monopolies) for the manufacture of alcohol in the Republic to a Hungarian-born, Pretoria-based Jewish entrepreneur named Alois Hugo Nellmapius. In less than a year, Nellmapius had ceded the concession to a larger partnership (of which he owned 20 per cent). By June 1883 Die Eerste Fabrieken in de Zuid Afrikaansche Republiek Ltd (The First Factory in the ZAR

The men of Johannesburg Fire Brigade – in front of a sign for the Hatherley Distillery

Ltd) opened to much jubilation – distilling spirits from the abundant surplus produce supplied by the region's many Boer farmers.

Initially, the distillery struggled to find a market for the liquor it produced; following the discovery of the Witwatersrand goldfields, however, the Eerste Fabrieken experienced such rapid growth that, even running at full capacity, it failed to keep up with demand. It was decided that the distillery needed more money. In 1892 the concession was handed over (effectively sold) in return for money and shares, and the distillery became a public company – Hatherley Distillery Ltd – which was listed on the London Stock Exchange, attracting local and international investors.

That same year, the number of licensed canteens in Joburg grew to 552[21] – or one bar for every 75 inhabitants. Supplying the canteens with a steady stream of spirits were Hatherley (which undercut most outside suppliers because of the tax-free nature of its concession) and a number of Mozambican distilleries that were able to provide cheap liquor owing to a pre-existing deal between the ZAR and the Portuguese government, which allowed 'Produce of Portugal' to enter the Republic free of duties. Within a couple of years, distillers from Germany and Prussia learned to exploit this loophole by disguising their potato spirits as Portuguese imports.

The spirits sold to the Witwatersrand market were of a crude sort, often containing dangerously high levels of toxic by-products created by the fermentation process. There also high levels of fraud and folly in the marketing and sales of these spirits: many liquor importers and wholesalers would treat and bottle the spirits for resale themselves, using forged or fake labels to pass the bottles off as well-established (better-quality) brand names – or creating all-new (made-up) labels that implied provenance in France or Scotland. The creation of individual brands involved a sometimes terrifying amount of amateur chemistry. Bottlers would use a certain volume of proof spirit, to which they would add water, followed by ingredients such as mashed prunes, tincture of cayenne pepper, sulphuric or nitric acid, glycerine, green tea, acetic acid, creosote, syrup, turpentine, juniper oil, tincture of orange peel, fennel and burnt sugar. From these ingredients entrepreneurs created what they variously labelled as 'brandy', 'whisky' or 'gin' (irrespective of whether the spirit's origin was grain, grape, sugar or potato).[22]

While the distilleries were yielding massive profits and returns for their owners – in 1895 Hatherley declared dividends of 20 per cent and profits of almost £100 000 – mine owners had begun to re-evaluate the effectiveness of their *dop* ('drink') system not long after implementing it. While they knew that migrant miners who were regular consumers of alchohol tended to work underground for longer periods – to compensate for spending their wages on booze – the side-effect of such regular and conspicuous consumption was a severely impaired workforce. Between 15 and 25 per cent of the black labourers were always unfit for work because of drunkenness.[23]

Mine owners' attempts to reduce the ready availability of alcohol to their black workers were, at first, blocked by the Kruger government. Not only was the distillery providing profitable returns for the ZAR, but it also guaranteed a market for surplus grain produced by its Boer citizens; in addition, Kruger was personal friends with several of the distillery shareholders.

Limited concessions were occasionally made to the mine owners, and to increasingly negative (white) public opinion – such as the 1889 law stipulating that a canteen owner could only sell liquor to a black worker on production of a permit signed by a white master. But liquor sales continued to grow, at a rapid rate.

Finally, in 1896, the Chamber of Mines – through a combination of renewed negative public opinion and various political shifts within the ZAR government – succeeded in getting legislation introduced containing a clause for the total prohibition of sales of alcohol to black consumers.

Of course, what the prohibition actually succeeded in doing was to drive the production and sale of alcohol to blacks underground – giving rise to a whole new generation of illegal liquor syndicates and, ultimately, criminal gangs.

A large number of the syndicates was run by legitimate Jewish canteen owners who, not wishing to jeopardise their 'good standing' (or their liquor license), engaged the services of more recently arrived Jewish immigrants (often family members) from eastern Europe. Known as 'Peruvians' – the

READ MORE
The seminal work on Joburg's growth, between 1886 and 1914 – including unmatched writing on the mine owners and the role alcohol played on the Rand – is Charles van Onselen's collection of essays *New Babylon, New Nineveh* (now available as a single volume). Originally published in the early 1980s, it remains the definitive read on early Johannesburg.

 PLACES TO SEE
The **Guildhall Pub** (on the corner  of Market and Harrison streets, opposite Beyers Naude Square and established in 1888) is probably Joburg's oldest remaining drinking spot. The original single-story building housing the pub was demolished and rebuilt before 1900; in about 1913, four stories were added and the building became known as the Meischke Building (after owner Mattheus Meischke). The property was sold to the current owners – the Amoils family – in 1935.

The Guildhall has had a chequered history: until just a few years ago, it was a run-down establishment operating as a local shebeen. It has since been renovated and upgraded, and is a great venue for a pint and a meal. For bookings, call (011) 833 1770.

origins of the name remain a mystery – these lower-class, destitute Jewish 'assistants' were paid to traffic and sell liquor illegally, and take the rap if they got caught.

The family structure of many syndicates contributed to the creation of 'Liquor Kings' (heads of families) and 'Princes' (the heads' sons); and by the turn of the century Joburg boasted at least three notable criminal families: the Nathansons, who 'ruled' Boksburg; the Joffes, in Krugersdorp and Randfontein; and the Friedmans, who controlled central Johannesburg.[24]

Between the blatant corruption of the crime families – who appeared, at one point, to have most of the city's police force in their pay – and the strong prejudice against the Peruvians (who were considered the lowest of the low among immigrants), the illicit liquor trade produced a period of intense anti-Semitic sentiment among the non-Jewish Johannesburg public – Boer and *Uitlander* alike – resulting in more than a few vigilante-style attacks on Jewish-owned premises and individuals.[25]

Pimps and Prostitutes

A census conducted in 1896 reported that Johannesburg's white population consisted of 25 000 men and 14 000 women – just under two males to every female.

In the black population, with 54 000 men and slightly under 3 000 women, the male–female ratio was even more extreme – at 18,5 men to every woman. In the mining areas around Johannesburg this figure rose to 63:1. And, in the case of men aged 25 to 39, there were an astounding 98 men to every woman.[26]

Unsurprisingly, early Johannesburg supported a thriving (but small) population of female prostitutes.

Joburg's first ladies of 'ill repute' were mostly white women, arrived from the country's coastal regions or the Eastern Transvaal's early goldfields. The completion of a rail link between Cape Town and Johannesburg (via Kimberley) in 1892 saw new arrivals from the Cape Colony – including significant numbers of Coloured women, who may have been driven north by the Cape's ongoing imple-

mentation of the Contagious Diseases Act.

At first, these women plied their trade as individuals, working from the city's numerous bars and canteens. By 1895, however, the completion of the railway line from the East African port of Lourenço Marques (Maputo) had opened up the Rand to continental passengers – the German East Africa Shipping Line offered cheap passage from Europe. At almost the same time, regional political pressures saw a number of Russian-American prostitutes, madams and pimps leave North America for Johannesburg.

By 1896, locally born women had been largely replaced by 'continental' women – many of whom were refugees from eastern Europe's economic depression, or victims of the white slave trade – aided and managed by pimps. Brothels were established in houses in the centre of town, catering mostly to white miners (although some accepted black customers).[27]

Joburg's 'red light' district was known as 'Frenchfontein'. Spreading outwards from the centre of town, it lay between Bree Street in the north and Anderson Street in the south, and was bordered by Kruis Street in the east and Sauer Street in the west. The area was a den of canteens, bars and brothels, and the core of Joburg's criminal underworld. It was also, simply, home to many of the city's poorer white immigrants, who either lacked the social clout to complain about the goings on – or were, of necessity, involved in the trade in liquor and women.[28]

Despite numerous complaints from Joburg's righteous citizens about the sordid lifestyles and events in Frenchfontein, the ZAR government adopted a strategy of attempting to control rather than eliminate prostitution. Well-known brothels, with exotic names and staff (Sylvio Villa, on the corner of De Villiers and Rissik streets, offered the services of nine 'French' women) plied their trade under the management of various pimps who, in turn, fitted into a close-knit hierarchy of pimps' clubs and criminal organisations. One of the largest pimps' associations was the 'American Club', headed by Joe

American Club pimp David Krakower and possibly his mistress Sadie Wolff

READ MORE

In 2007, Charles van Onselen released a dramatic follow-up to one of his early essays on prostitution in *New Babylon*: an in-depth look at the life of pimp and crime lord Joseph Silver. While tracing Silver's life from his birthplace in Poland through the slums of Whitechapel in London, South Africa and South America and, finally, back to Europe, Van Onselen became convinced that Silver was the serial killer better known as Jack the Ripper. The book, titled *The Fox & The Flies* (Jonathan Cape), presents a compelling case and makes for fascinating reading.

Silver, a Polish-American Jew and arguably Joburg's most infamous pimp, who worked together with his 'wife' Lizzie Josephs. The American Club was notoriously responsible for 'recruiting' impressionable young women from Britain and Europe with promises of well-paid domestic jobs on the Rand – then forcing these women into the sex trade on their arrival in Johannesburg. No tactic was too low for these traders of flesh: while living in London, Silver and his colleagues would visit newly arrived (eastern European) Jewish immigrant women working in the city's East End. Posing as eligible bachelors, these men would ultimately seduce (or rape) the women – before 'exporting' them to brothels in South Africa and Argentina.[29]

The continued practice of 'white slavery', as well as the fact that many of the continental prostitutes accepted black as well as white clients, saw public opinion continue to build against the presence of legal prostitution in Johan-nesburg. The ZAR government passed a series of laws in 1897, 1898 and 1899 in an apparent attempt to control (if not totally eradicate) the sex trade, but these proved mostly ineffective – the corrupt police were unable or un-willing to take action, and the pimps themselves were too powerful to be frightened off.

The brothel business was eventually disrupted by the outbreak of the South African War, in late 1899 – Cape Town and Durban were apparently flooded with Rand prostitutes (mainly 'continental' women) who were fleeing Johannesburg.[30] But Frenchfontein's principal trade resumed in 1902, despite further immorality legislation passed by the British governing authority, and it was not until 1910 that the last of the European pimps' power was broken – through a combination of police efforts and various legal strategies, including the deportation of hundreds of convicted pimps and prostitutes from the province, under the Transvaal Immigration Restriction acts of 1907 and 1908.

Of course, the sex trade had not disappeared from Joburg. It had simply dispersed – into the city's working-

The AmaWasha

A washing site near Johannesburg

The scarcity of both water and women meant that laundry was a problem for most of the male migrant workers in early Johannesburg. A number of Zulu clansmen – Vilikazi, Mchunu, Buthelezi, Kanyile and Sithole – saw a gap in the market and established a Zulu washermen's guild, known as the AmaWasha. They set up operations at the Braamfontein Spruit (in an area now covered by the German School); by 1896 there were over 1200 washermen operating from 10 sites: Sans Souci, Vrededorp, City and Suburban, Rietvlei, Elandsfontein, George Goch, Booysens, Concordia, Klipspruit and Nancefield Station.

Inspired by Hindu washermen in Durban, the AmaWasha donned turbans and would march to Johannesburg's Market Square in a group once a month to renew their licences.

According to Charles van Onselen in New Babylon, New Nineveh, membership of the guild 'exempted the AmaWasha from carrying passes and got around a local by-law that prevented blacks from carrying weapons. It also allowed them to brew as much beer as they wanted for their own needs.'[31] Entry into the ranks of AmaWasha was restricted through the guild, which also determined the price levied for washing Joburg's laundry.

In October 1895, following a drought and the contamination of water, the washing sites were closed by the city's health inspectors. At the same time, the city's first steam laundry was established in Richmond. In order to undercut the threat to larger capitalist concerns, the municipal authorities insisted the AmaWasha move away from the centre of economic activity – first to Witbank, and then, in 1906, to Klipspruit. Forced to travel long distances to collect and deliver laundry, the AmaWasha were gradually forced out of business. The Rand Steam Laundries continued to operate from Napier Road in Auckland Park until 1962. Until recently, the original steam laundry buildings were still standing, rented by a number of light industrial companies. In January 2008 the Imperial Group demolished the laundry buildings, despite the site being accorded provisional heritage status.

Migrant Labour & Compound Life

MuseuMAfricA, Johannesburg. MA1974/520(22

Migrant workers on their way to the mines

Early Johannesburg's frontier lifestyle appealed to a certain type of character – investors, traders, speculators, exploiters... The prospect of working on the mines apparently appealed to a number of black labourers too: diamond diggers from Kimberley and workers from Natal's sugar cane plantations came to the Rand in search of the (relatively) higher wages on offer. Young men would come in the hope of earning enough to return home and pay the traditional bride price. Most of the black men who came to work at the mines had no intention of staying long: as soon as they'd earned enough money, they returned home.

Four years after the Reef was discovered, there were only 14 000 mineworkers in Johannesburg. By 1899, the Randlords (working together with the Kruger government) had managed to turn this number into 100 000 – a feat which had involved considerable effort and manipulation, requiring the complete undermining of traditional black family systems and social culture.

Early on in both the Boer Republics and the British Cape and Natal colonies, the need for cheap agricultural labour – without actual slavery – had prompted the planning and development of several complex strategies aimed at dividing, conquering and subjugating black peasants. The first was the destruction or dispersion of any remaining strong African chiefs or kingdoms, thus removing political resistance and appropriating arable land.

The black peasant population – many successfully farming on a small or subsistence scale – still exhibited a large degree of economic independence from both English and Boers. Certainly, there was little incentive for them to leave their families to work in distant towns or cities.

In the 1870s the various governments imposed a hut tax on all 'Africans' – ostensibly an attempt to raise revenues for the state, but, in reality, a deliberate strategy aimed at forcing black men into accepting paid work for white settlers.

When this failed to achieve the desired results, the tax law was amended so that taxes had to be paid in cash and not cattle. This too failed to yield the desired mass labour migration, and so an additional (individual) poll tax was levied on every man over the age of 18. In the Cape, then-Prime Minister Rhodes added an extra burden to the tax load, forcing all Africans in his colony to pay an inappropriately named annual 'labour tax' – only men who had not taken on paid work were compelled to pay it.

In 1896, many independent black farmers and herders had their income and livelihood wiped out by the Rinderpest epidemic, and so were also forced into the labour market.

There were limited ways in which black men could earn the cash needed to pay these various taxes. They could sell their farm produce, work on a white-owned farm, take on domestic work in the towns, or work in the mines. Most chose to go to the mines, because the wages were much higher than on the farms.

Mineworkers on a hill

'Native' haircut in the compound (from a postcard)

The taxes may have forced the men to the mines, but they didn't keep them there – most workers would return home as soon as they'd earned enough to cover their debts. The Randlords, keen to secure a more constant workforce, engaged the additional services of special labour recruiters or touts. Often these touts took the form of travelling salesmen, who would encourage black men to get into debt (by purchasing the trader's wares) as a means of recruiting them.

The building and completion of good national and cross-border rail links expanded the recruitment territory. In 1901 the ZAR government entered into an agreement with the Portuguese East African authority, allowing it to source labour from Mozambique. A special recruitment agency – the Witwatersrand Native Labour Association – was formed, and soon set up offices all over the sub-continent. In 1903 the agency entered into a similar agreement with the German governing authority in Namibia.

View of a mining compound – the minedump is to the left

Working Life in the Compounds

South Africa's first mining hostels had been implemented in Kimberley, where mine owners appropriated the Malaysian 'kampong' system (used in Asia, to control potential labour riots) in an attempt to reduce the theft of diamonds by the mine workers. These 'compounds' proved an equally suitable solution for the Randlords a decade and more later: black workers could easily be housed in large buildings on or adjacent to the mine property, reducing transport costs and delays in getting to work; and, while theft of the gold ore was not as big a problem as diamond theft had been in Kimberley, the communal living, eating and sleeping enforced by the compounds translated into significant savings for mine owners, who would deduct money from workers' wages to pay for these 'benefits'. Compound living also meant that it was easier to monitor workers' attendance (absenteeism was greatly reduced by having the workers on site) and to step in with disciplinary measures if the workers got 'out of hand' – walled and fenced compounds could easily be surrounded and controlled by a police or security force.

By providing food and accommodation, mine owners were further able to reduce mine workers' wages – this despite the fact that compound conditions were appalling, unsanitary and, generally, totally unsuitable for human habitation. Typical inspectors' reports would comment on the absence of proper floors, the lack of beds (workers were often forced to sleep on rotten floors or concrete bunks) and the fact that there was no adequate ventilation or heating in the rooms.

There was also no privacy anywhere on the compound. Even the toilets were open – nothing but a long bench with holes where 20 men could relieve themselves at the same time.[32] Because of overcrowding, men slept huddled together in rows – a necessity during the freezing Highveld winter nights but also an opportunity for dangerous infectious diseases to spread.

Meals were supposed to be provided by the compound, but reports from the early 1900s showed that many workers spent as much as half their received wages on buying additional food. Not only were the rations provided at the compound (about two kilograms

Miners at a recruitment office (stripped for their medical examination)

Interior of a mining compound

of mealie meal and less than a kilogram of meat per week) totally inadequate for an adult male doing hard daily labour, but supplies were frequently rotten or of a substandard quality and unfit for human consumption.

Medical care was largely non-existent on the compounds, and the mortality rate from non-mining-related incidents was staggeringly high: in 1903, 5022 black workers died on the mines. More than 59 per cent of these deaths were attributed to pneumonia and meningitis (caused by the crowded and damp conditions, and the sudden changes in temperature as miners emerged from hot and humid deep-level mines to significantly colder surface temperatures); nearly 12 per cent were the result of intestinal infections – caused by the poor food – and a further 5,8 per cent the result (incredibly) of scurvy. Tuberculosis and bacillosis (bacterial infection) each accounted for 5 per cent of the deaths. Only 4 per cent of mining deaths in 1903 were caused by accidents.[33]

Compound workers were subject to a rigid system of control. There was a production hierarchy, with white workers at the top, 'boss boys' (*indunas*) below – appointed by the white compound manager, and usually distrusted by the other compound dwellers – and the mass of workers at the bottom. The compound

Games in the compound

manager also appointed compound policemen, who guarded the entrance and exit to the compound, watched over kitchen and ablution queues and helped the *induna* to settle any arguments. The 'policemen' were allowed to carry knobkerries (sticks) and to search miners' rooms for alcohol, weapons or dagga.

Each room – which could contain anything from 20 to 50 men – would also have a *Sibonda*, who was appointed by his roommates to keep order (delegating cleaning tasks, settling any minor quarrels and speaking up for his colleagues if a problem arose).

Early mine police

The workers were divided further on the basis of their 'ethnic' language group – seSotho, isiXhosa and isiZulu speakers had very little to do with each other at the compound, and ate and slept separately.

Compound life often caused residents to disconnect from the real world; separated from their families and communities, living in single-sex dwellings for months at a stretch with little leisure time and even less money, many men relied on alcohol and dagga to dull the experience.

In an attempt to provide some form of social entertainment, managers started organising dance and singing competitions – heralding the famous gumboot dancing and *isicathamiya* traditions. It was not until the 1940s that black mineworker unions were successfully established.

Another Blanket

A song traditionally sung by Sotho migrants as they crossed the Caledon River (Mohokare) *and came to work on the Rand's mines.*

Mohokare, now I put on another blanket,
Now that I have crossed you,
Wash me from the touch I have had
With women at home.
Here I cross to the other side.
And I do not know what dangers face me.
Perhaps this is the last time I cross you here.
And if ever I have the chance of crossing you again
Wash me clean, Mohokare, and make me a pure man
Make me a man who is fit to go to heaven
Cleanse me from my sins because I am going to
The dangerous place where I may lose my life.

Now if ever I do not come back it will be just
unfortunate.
But now that I have crossed you,
All the evil things I have done
May they move with you and go down.

In crossing the river I become a new man,
Different from the one I was at home.
At home I was secure
But now that I am on this side
I am in a place of danger,
Where I may lose my life at any time.
So prepare me for my death.

Now that I am this side
I assume a different attitude from the one
Where they are soft with other men.
This side they have to be tough to assume manhood
Not be soft like the women at home.[34]

(Published by the Agency for Industrial Mission (AIM) in 1976)

Chinese Indentured Labourers

By Professor Karen Harris

'Greetings from Chowburg', racist postcard 1900s.

In the first decade of the 20th Century 63 659 Chinese were imported to work as unskilled labourers on the Witwatersrand gold mines. Recruited and repatriated within a half dozen years, these labourers were to have an impact on the economic, political and social fibre of the Johannesburg mining and labour world that far outlasted their stay.

The use of Chinese labour was not limited to South Africa. From the mid-19th Century, thousands of Chinese were employed as labourers on plantations, railway lines, road works and mines across five continents. With the colonial abolition of the slave trade in the early 19th Century, Chinese became the preferred labour source, not only because of their numbers and availability, but also because they were regarded as 'industrious and cheap'.

The importation of the Chinese to the Witwatersrand followed in the wake of the South African War (1899–1902), which had interrupted mining operations and contributed to a desperate shortage of unskilled African labour. In order to resume productivity, the Chamber of Mines launched a campaign which was approved and sanctioned by both the British and Chinese authorities. In 35 clearly laid-out sections, the Labour Importation Ordinance of 1904 directed that: the indentured Chinese were to be employed only on the Witwatersrand as unskilled miners and were denied employment in 55 stipulated occupations; they were not allowed to own landed property or engage in trade; they were not issued with a passport; they had to reside on the premises in compounds where they were employed; they could not leave without a permit, which would be granted for periods of less than 48 hours; and transgressions would be punishable by imprisonment and fines.

'4200 Coolies' – Chinese inside a mine compound

All labourers entered a contract of service of three years, which could be extended for a further two, after which they were to be returned to their country of origin. For this reason wives and family were not encouraged. The ordinance also prescribed the conditions for recruitment, the passage to South Africa, compound and ablution facilities and medical and dietary requirements.

The restrictions were created in order to keep the Chinese labourers as a temporary and controlled component of mining society.

The ordinance was dubbed the most unpopular of all unpopular measures as white skilled miners declared it not a sufficient safeguard against Chinese encroachment and competition, while opposition at the other extreme denounced its stringent regulations as a charter of slavery.

In order to defray the costs of importation and

accommodation, the average monthly wage received by the Chinese labourer was lower than that paid to his unskilled African counterpart. It was also agreed that the Emperor of China would appoint a Chinese consul-general to oversee the welfare of the emigrants – hereby establishing the first official link between Imperial China and the South African region.

Despite these detailed regulations as to their conditions and control, Chinese labourers were flagrantly abused. They were subjected to corporal punishment, bad treatment and violent attacks by mine management, Chinese police and fellow white and black miners. They were however not passive victims and often retaliated or committed outrages, which would occasionally also take place beyond the confines of the mining compound as, out of despair, many of them deserted. The latter would be prosecuted for theft or trespassing, while cases of

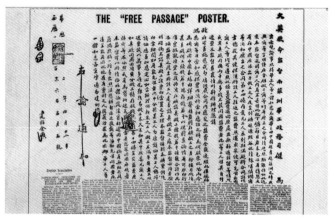

A notice to Chinese labourers on the Rand who wished to return home

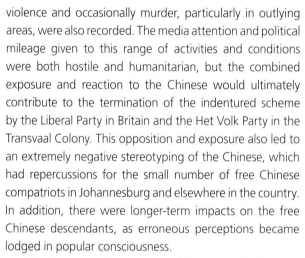

Undated portraits of Chinese miners

violence and occasionally murder, particularly in outlying areas, were also recorded. The media attention and political mileage given to this range of activities and conditions were both hostile and humanitarian, but the combined exposure and reaction to the Chinese would ultimately contribute to the termination of the indentured scheme by the Liberal Party in Britain and the Het Volk Party in the Transvaal Colony. This opposition and exposure also led to an extremely negative stereotyping of the Chinese, which had repercussions for the small number of free Chinese compatriots in Johannesburg and elsewhere in the country. In addition, there were longer-term impacts on the free Chinese descendants, as erroneous perceptions became lodged in popular consciousness.

On the economic front, these labour recruits from the northern regions of China (mainly Chihli, now called Hebei, and Shantung) were primarily responsible for salvaging the gold-mining industry. Within the first two years of importation (1906), the Witwatersrand gold-mining industry was able to recapture its position as the world's largest single producer of gold, surpassing the pre-South-African-War record achieved in 1898. The indentured scheme also inadvertently endorsed the migrant-labour system on the mines, entrenched the all-male compound system and ultimately reinforced the industrial colour bar.

At another level, the Chinese added a new social dimension to the mining landscape of the Witwatersrand.

they created a world of their own, invoking customs and traditions and partaking in other leisure activities within the surrounds of the mines. Chinese festivals were celebrated with feasts and colourful processions; leisure time was occupied with the performance of Chinese theatre and opera in ornate costumes with props and traditional musical instruments; while customary Chinese sports were also practised. On Sundays, on the provision of a pass, the Chinese would visit Cantonese eating houses and general stores run by free Chinese individuals. Some would go to gambling dens and brothels, while others had picnics, strolled in the veld or took cab drives in the surrounding areas. They were also known to have formed secret societies, which, although illegal, gave them a sense of belonging in a foreign land.

Joburg's Bandit King

In the late 19th and early 20th centuries, Johannesburg and its surrounds were plagued by several bands of outlaws. The largest (and most powerful) of these was known as the Ninevites – a group of young black men who had left their rural homes and villages, but refused to work for white bosses in town.

The leader of the Ninevites was Nongoloza Mathebula; born Mzuzephi (sometimes Mzoozepi) Mathebula, he also went by the name of Jan Note (pronounced 'Not').

Nongoloza had grown up in Natal; after a formative few years working as a gardener and groom in Harrismith – Nongoloza's employer tried, unfairly, to make the teenager pay for a runaway horse – he fled to Johannesburg where he found work as a houseboy and, later, as a groom. His employers would, again, influence Nongoloza's path: the then-21-year-old Note discovered that his four 'gentleman' employers were actually highwaymen, and served a brief apprenticeship in the art of relieving travellers of their cash and goods before deciding 'to start a band of robbers of my own.'[34]

Note made contact with a prominent black underworld leader, Nohlopa, who took Note under his wing and formed a small 'gang' based in the caves around the Klipriviersberg hills, south-east of Johannesburg – a place they called *Shabalawawa*. Nohlopa's gang quickly grew in numbers, rising to several hundred members within a few years.

In 1891 or 1892, Nohlopa was arrested and imprisoned; while serving his sentence, he found religion – much to the surprise of his gang of followers – and gave up criminal life to preach the Word of God. This left Note in charge of the group, and he lost no time in shaping his motley crew into a disciplined band, run on military-influenced lines. Note's stronghold was renamed *Madalambane*. It was based in the north-east of Johannesburg, near the one-time Rietfontein Lazaretto, now known as the Sizwe Tropical Disease Hospital but also still performing its original function as an isolation hospital.

Note named his gang *Umkhosi Wezintaba* – the 'Regiment of the Hills'. They were also known as the Ninevites. Note, like Nohlopa, was influenced by the scriptures… although not in the same manner. Deeply affected by his perceptions of white injustice, he hoped his gang would rebel against the government's laws in the same way as the state of Nineveh had 'rebelled against the Lord'.

As the Ninevites became a larger, more structured group, Note became concerned that his warriors were being distracted by trips to town to enjoy the pleasures of female company; he was also worried by their high rate of venereal disease infection (the nearby Lazaretto, which treated syphillis, highlighted this) and instructed his gang members to abstain from all physical contact with members of the opposite sex. Instead, older men in the gang were to take on the younger male initiates as *izinkotshane* ('boy wives'). The practice of homosexuality became closely associated with the Ninevites.

By the mid-1890s, the Ninevites were a regularly reported threat on the Reef. In some circles, Note was viewed as a modern-day Robin Hood.

In reality, however, Note's gang members were just as happy to empty the pockets of (black) migrant workers returning home as they were to waylay white men and women.

At the outbreak of war, in 1899, Note's gang found itself with increasingly fewer victims – black or white – to rob. The 'Regiment' disbanded and many members made their way back to Natal, subsequently forming gangs of brigands in and around the Pietermaritzburg area, and influencing the later formation of male domestic worker *(Amalaita)* 'gangs' in Durban and in Johannesburg.

Note stayed in Johannesburg, eventually attempting to rob a mine workers' compound. He and his few assistants were arrested, convicted and sentenced to five years' hard labour and 25 lashes.

The demands of the war on the Boer forces saw Note released early from his first sentence; but, within a few months, he was arrested again – for firing several rounds of ammunition at a group of 'special constables'. This time, Note was transferred to prison in Pretoria.

Over the next several years, Nongoloza – as he became more commonly known – was transferred between various prisons in Pretoria, the old Fort in Johannesburg and even Volksrust in Natal. These transfers were either attempts to break the control Nongoloza still retained over his criminal empire – both within and without the prison walls – or responses to his numerous escape attempts and subsequent crimes committed 'on the lam'.

Between 1900 and 1912, Nongoloza's incarcerations – and the imprisonment of various members of his gang, at different times – laid the foundation for another type of gang structure: the prison gang. Modern day 26s, 27s and 28s are all criminal descendants of the original Ninevites, and much of Note/Nongoloza's story (including the practice of homosexuality among the 28s) has been transformed into sets of myths and rituals particular to each group.

Nongoloza himself renounced his gang ties in 1912, agreeing to work as a warder for the prison authorities – where he actually participated in suppressing Ninevite activity. Nongoloza briefly

READ MORE

• You can get an in-depth look at the life and times of Nongoloza Mathebula in Charles van Onselen's short book *The Small Matter of a Horse: The Life of 'Nongoloza' Mathebula, 1867–1948. (recently re-issued* by Protea Boekehuis)

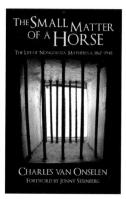

• Jonny Steinberg's acclaimed book, *The Number* (Jonathan Ball), takes a look at the history and mythology of South Africa's present-day prison gangs, many of which were directly shaped by Nongoloza and his 'chiefs'. A paper on the topic, written by Steinberg and preceding his book, called 'Nongoloza's Children', is available on the website of the Centre for the Study of Violence and Reconciliation (www.csvr.org.za)

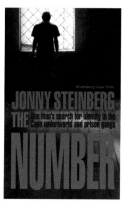

retired to an agricultural plot in Swaziland before returning to the Transvaal to work as an orderly in a mental hospital near Pretoria, then as a compound policeman and watchman at the Premier Diamond Mine. By that stage, Nongoloza (more than 60 years old) was well known for his explosive and anti-social behaviour. In 1930 he was convicted of raping a teenage girl – part of a church group he complained had been making too much noise – and returned to prison a final time. He was released ten years later, in 1940, and died of advanced turberculosis in December 1948. Nongoloza's body was unclaimed, and he was buried in a shared grave in Pretoria's Rebecca Street Cemetery.[35]

THE CITY

'I first saw Johannesburg in my dreams. Oh, the thousands of shiny tall buildings, happy, fast-talking people who had everything they wanted, the fancy cars playing the latest music and, yes, the millions of lights that turned any night into day! At least that is what we heard from those who had been to the mining city of gold, where the hills echo like thunder and delicious meat of every kind is always available, until your teeth can't chew anymore.'

Gcina Mhlope, 'Jozi-Jozi, City of Dreams'[1]

In this chapter

- Tin City to Mini Manhattan
- Religion (and Commerce!)
- Shopping and Recreation
- Segregation in the City
- Braamfontein and Decentralisation
- Student Protests
- The Decline of the CBD

CENTRE

Johannesburg at night

The Tin-clad City

The Clarence Hotel, Fraser Street

By the middle of 1887, most of the original Ferreira's Camp had been abandoned – so that the gold finds beneath it could be prospected – and its buildings moved a few hundred metres to 'Johannesburg proper. Meanwhile open ground on every side was crisscrossed with trenches, from which the miners were removing the surface ore.'²

These early 'buildings' – if they can be classified as such – were made from walls of unbaked clay bricks, taken from the banks of the many springs in the region, the roofs made from reeds. The Highveld storms were so violent that they simply washed away the walls … and the occupants' belongings.

The early miners, learning their lesson, later lined their 'greenbrick' (unbaked, sun-dried brick) houses with new corrugated iron sheets brought up from the coast. The brick walls kept the interior relatively cool, and the corrugated iron prevented them from washing away. When lined with wallpaper, the walls also kept out dust. Ceilings were initially made out of canvas nailed to the rafters. Houses were still vulnerable to heavy downpours, however; as late as 1894, dwellings in Ferreirastown were still collapsing during the rainy season.

Central Joburg

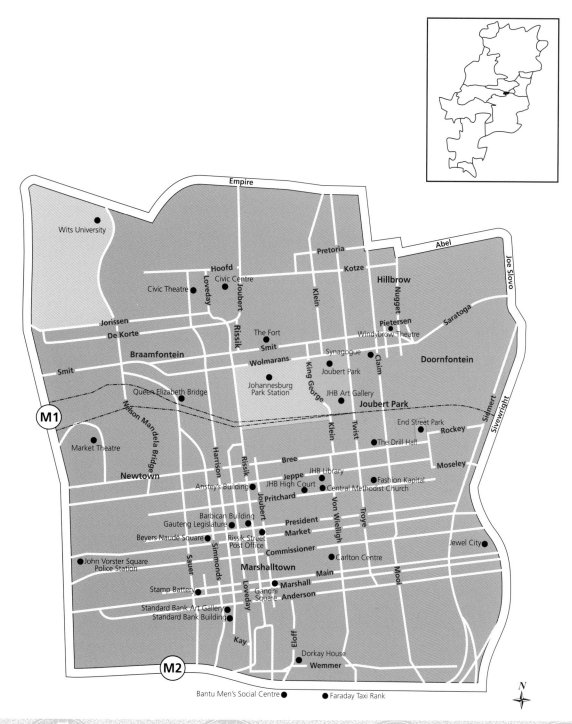

Wits University

Empire

Pretoria

Abel

Joe Slovo

Hoofd
Civic Centre
Loveday
Joubert
Civic Theatre
Kotze
Klein
Hillbrow
Nugget
Saratoga

Jorissen
Pietersen
De Korte
Windybrow Theatre
Braamfontein
Rissik
The Fort
Smit
Wolmarans
Synagogue
Joubert Park
Claim
Doornfontein
Smit
King George
Johannesburg
Park Station
JHB Art Gallery
Joubert Park

M1
Queen Elizabeth Bridge
Nelson Mandela Bridge
Klein
Twist
End Street Park
Rockey
Sidmert
Sivewright

Market Theatre
The Drill Hall
Moseley

Harrison
Rissik
Bree
Newtown
Jeppe
JHB Library
Anstey's Building
Joubert
JHB High Court
Fashion Kapital
Central Methodist Church
Pritchard
Von Wielligh
Barbican Building
President
Gauteng Legislature
Market
Troye
Beyers Naudé Square
Rissik Street
Post Office
Commissioner
Jewel City
John Vorster Square
Police Station
Carlton Centre
Simmonds
Marshalltown
Main
Sauer
Loveday
Marshall
Mool
Stamp Battery
Gandhi
Square
Anderson
Standard Bank Art Gallery
Standard Bank Building
Kay
Eloff
Dorkay House
Wemmer

M2

N

Bantu Men's Social Centre
Faraday Taxi Rank

Commissioner Street in 1910

Commissioner Street today

Joburg's Underworld

Joburg's first mines were worked at relatively shallow depths (compared to later deep-level operations). When these works were abandoned, hundreds of tunnels were left running directly under what would become the city centre.[3]

Many early buildings were built directly on top of the reefs that ran under the town. The Du Preez Reef runs in an easterly direction almost directly under the bench for the judges of the No. 3 Court in the Supreme Court Buildings on Von Brandis Square (in Pritchard Street). Another reef, the West Government runs in a westerly direction and passes under the City Hall. The ground between Bree and Commissioner streets had mineshafts sunk into it, which had to be filled in when Johannesburg was surveyed as a township.

To reduce the risk of subsidence, a number of limitations were placed on development in the old reef area, including whether or not land could be developed

and the height of the building on the stand (in relation to the depth of the mine works underneath). The issue of undermining was a central challenge for the city's engineering department when new motorways were developed in the 1960s. As demand for land in the CBD increased and mine stabilisation methods improved, many of these restrictions were relaxed; occasional earth tremors, however, are still a regular part of life in Johannesburg.

In 2003, a geologist named Jan Arkert warned the *Sunday Times* newspaper that Johannesburg – and its historic buildings – were sinking. Poor drainage beneath several parts of the city (particularly in areas where structures had been built on granite or other rock that had crumbled to sandy soil) had allowed certain areas of ground to become significantly waterlogged. 'Parts of Johannesburg could sink by 270 mm or more in the space of a week,' Arkert warned.[4]

The Central Hotel – in 1888, 1895 and 1955

It wasn't long before Johannesburg began to develop a skyline – of sorts. The first double-storey building was the Golden Mortar Dispensary (it was also the first chemist in town; the regional pharmaceutical association still uses the name for its newsletter) on Commissioner Street. Large numbers of canteens and hotels also sprung up – Height's Hotel (after Sam Height, the American), the Central Hotel (also on Commissioner Street; the building later collapsed and had to be rebuilt), the Grand Hotel …

In the absence of a railway line, raw building materials had to be brought up to Joburg by cart; the Grand Hotel was built out of old corrugated iron transported from Kimberley.

In the late 19th Century, American humorist Charles Godfrey Leland became famous for his 'Breitmann Ballads' – verses written in broken German and English, much as a new immigrant would speak. The style became so popular that an imitation ballad was composed about Joburg:

*If you vill see a vonder
To Africa you go,
And travel to Johannesburg
To see vot's dere on show.
De Strassen ungeplastert
Vill fill you mit amaze,
Till you begin to vonder
Vy dey don't mend their vays*

*Und ach de awful tust clouds
Dat blow mit every vind,
Und choke you zum Ersticken
Und nearly make you blind.
You find de Deutsche Kneipe,
Frau Witte mit a cheer,
Till you fork out a dollar
For every Schoppen beer.*

*Und den de little bedroom
Dat measures eight by ten,
Vot dey tell you you must occupy
Mit several odder men.
Und den dose dreadful gold mines
Vot has more shares dan gold
Und ach de awful prices
At which de shares are sold!*

*Und ven you've lost your money
Clear out so quick you can
Und leave de Rand a viser,
But, ach, a sadder man.
But if you just are lucky,
I tell you alleweil
Make tracks so schnell as Blitzen,
Und sit upon your pile.[5]*

The original Carlton Hotel – the top three floors were a later addition

Taxis outside the Carlton Hotel in 1913

The Carlton

The very grandest of hotels was the original Johannesburg Carlton, opened in 1906; the hotel had been planned since the late 1890s by Barney Barnato (who died in 1897 after falling or deliberately jumping off a ship), and was completed by Barnato's close relative Solly Joel. Linked to the London establishment of the same name, the Carlton was a monument to luxury – and engineering: more than three million bricks were used in its construction; and, although its six floors were somewhat overshadowed by the eight-storeyed JCI building and Cuthbert's shoe store, the nine-storeyed Corner House, or the ten-storeyed Stuttaford & Co department store, for sheer size, 'none could bear comparison' with the new hotel,[6] with frontages on four streets (the main entrance was on Eloff Street).

The Carlton featured all the latest modern conveniences: a form of air conditioning and central heating; vacuum cleaner suction pipes on each floor; and its own waterborne sewerage system. The dining, tea and bar areas quickly attracted large numbers of local patrons too, and became the social centre of Johannesburg's elite. 'Some idea of the scale of operations may be gained from the fact that every three months [the hotel] needed 400 new cases of champagne.'[7]

Despite its success, the hotel never made sufficient profit for its owners; in 1922 it was auctioned off for £250 000 – to a syndicate later revealed to be made up of its original owners, trading under a new name (apparently the sale had tax benefits). Shortly afterwards, the majority shareholding of the new company was bought out by developer and entrepreneur IW Schlesinger, who had been a permanent resident of the Carlton since 1908. On Schlesinger's death, ownership of the hotel went to his son, Johnny. In 1964, the hotel was demolished and replaced by the African Life Building (another Schlesinger business). A new Carlton Centre, complete with hotel and retail premises, was planned for development, several blocks away, on the old South African Breweries site.

In 1967, the foundations were dug for the Carlton Centre: the excavation went five storeys deep, and four city blocks in extent. The foundation blocks, themselves 3,5 m in diameter, descended a further 20 m into bedrock. Special viewer sections were cut out into the surrounding fence to give pedestrians a peek at 'Johannesburg's Big Hole'. Families used to make the journey especially to see it.

The new Carlton under construction, 1971

The Carlton Hotel (foreground) and Centre (behind) today

The basement was meant to hold fourteen acres of shopping outlets and parking for 1 200 cars. New York architects Skidmore, Owings & Merrill designed the Carlton Centre and its neighbouring Carlton Hotel to take up only one third of the site, leaving the rest for gardens and a plaza for public use.[8] When it was completed in 1969, its 50 storeys made it the largest building in Africa and also, apparently, in the Southern Hemisphere at 223 m (although some sources say 220 m). Occupation began in 1971 but construction continued until 1975.

The upside-down Y-shaped Carlton Hotel was, then, the last word in five-star luxury when it was opened. Famous guests included Henry Kissinger, François Mitterand, Whitney Houston and Mick Jagger. Unfortunately the hotel and the adjoining Carlton Centre were completed just at a time when many other businesses (including the Joburg municipality and the South African Broadcasting Corporation [SABC]) were leaving the CBD. By the early 1990s, the city's centre was no longer a prestigious leisure venue. The hotel was mothballed in 1997, and, despite renewed interest in the property, its future remains to be determined. Although mostly abandoned in the late 1990s, the Carlton Centre has turned around and was 98 per cent full by 2001. The top

floor is dedicated to an observation deck, which gives the visitor a wonderful view of the city.

Joburg's Stately Buildings

By the turn of the century, Joburg boasted a number of grand structures. When Winston Churchill visited the town, as a young war correspondent, he remarked:

'One thing showed with sufficient distinctness to attract and astonish all eyes. The whole crest of the Rand ridge was fringed with factory chimneys. We had marched nearly 500 miles through a country which, though full of promise, seemed to European eyes desolate and wild, and now we turned a corner suddenly, and there before us sprang the evidence of wealth, manufacture and bustling civilization.'[9]

A number of impressive public buildings were constructed after the South African War, in what is broadly termed 'Edwardian Classical' style, and can still be seen today – for example, the Johannesburg High Court building (built between 1909 and 1911 by Baker & Associates) in Von Brandis Square in Pritchard Street, and the City Hall on Market, Rissik, President and Harrison streets (built in 1910 by Hawke and McKinlay); today this grand old dame houses the Gauteng Provincial Legislature.

The Barbican Building   **A view of Anstey's, taken in the 1930s**

Manhattan in the Veld

The 1930s saw a remarkable number of Art Deco buildings being constructed in the city. Examples include Arop House (73 Von Brandis Street); the building was designed by Gandhi's close friend Herman Kallenbach (of Kallenbach, Kennedy & Furner) and was used to house the African Russian Oil Products Group, which imported petroleum products from the Soviet Union.

Astor Mansions (corner of Jeppe and Von Brandis streets) was designed by Obel & Obel in 1931. The influence of New York was plain in both its name and its design. In fact, Joburg was often referred to as 'Little Manhattan' during this period.

Probably Joburg's most famous remaining Art Deco building, however, is Anstey's (59 Joubert Street), built in 1937 and now a national monument. The bottom floors housed the Norman Anstey & Company department store, renowned for its large plate-glass windows and flamboyant window displays. The foyer still has floor-to-ceiling mirrors, and several brass frames – with climbing brass monkeys! The actor, playwright and Umkhonto we Sizwe member Cecil Williams, who disguised Nelson Mandela as his chauffeur before his arrest in 1962, once lived there.[10]

The 10-storey Barbican Building in Rissik Street, overlooking the Post Office and Town Hall, was built at roughly the same time. The Barbican has been derelict for years – all its entrances are now bricked up – and it's hoped that proposals to redevelop and restore the building will be embarked upon in the near future.

In Delvers Street is the wonderful Normandie Court, built in 1938, resembling the French ocean liner, the *Normandie*, after which it was named. On the tenth floor is the 'captain's deck' which overhangs the corner of the building. The rounded 'portholes' complete the impression of a stranded ocean liner that somehow ended up in the streets of Johannesburg. The foyer has a framed picture of the Normandie and images of the ship are also sandblasted onto the glass doors.[11]

READ MORE

The definitive – and, sadly, out-of-print – book on Joburg's early architecture is *Johannesburg Style: Architecture and Society, 1880s to 1960s* by Clive Chipkin (David Phillips Publishers). The city's better second-hand bookstores occasionally get copies.

Clive's sequel, *Johannesburg Transition: Architecture and Society 1950 to 2000* (STE Publishers) was released in mid-2008.

THINGS TO DO

The Parktown and Westcliff Heritage Trust conducts occasional **Art Deco tours** of Johannesburg. For more information contact them on (011) 482 3349 or go to www.parktownheritage.co.za.

Houses of Worship

**Police patrol outside the Central Methodist Church
where thousands of foreigners sought shelter after xenophobic violence, May 2008**

Johannesburg's city centre has several remarkable churches, mosques and synagogues that are still standing today even though, in some cases, the nature of the congregants have changed. Most of these are on the north-eastern edge of the CBD running into Joubert Park.

The Central Methodist Church in Pritchard Street and St Mary's Cathedral in Kerk Street are both impressive edifices. An early version of the latter was the red-bricked St Mary's that was erected in Eloff Street by Rev. JT Darragh in 1887, making it one of the town's first permanent buildings.

It was demolished in 1906. Its successor was designed by Sir Herbert Baker and his partners FLH Fleming and Fellows Prynn. It is a beautiful building made from hammer-dressed mountain stone and has a Roman pan-tiled roof.[12] It regularly seats 1500 people but on special occasions can accommodate twice this number.

The Central Methodist Church has long been known as a place of peaceful (but vocal) protest against oppression, and often gave sanctuary to people on the run from apartheid security forces.

The dome of the Wolmarans Street Synagogue

During the apartheid years, the church 'created a candle encircled in barbed wire, modelled after the symbol for the global human rights organisation, Amnesty International. Each week, during worship services, members of the Central Methodist Church lit the candle and listed the names of people who had been harassed, wounded, imprisoned, tortured or killed the previous week for protesting their nation's policy of racial separation. … Then-government leader PW Botha banned the Central Methodist Church's worship services from the radio and TV broadcasts because the congregation refused to skip the readings in services.'[13]

Today, the Central Methodist Church houses a Wellness Centre, assisted by Médecins Sans Frontières, and has become known as a place of refuge for the city's numerous illegal African immigrants – many from Zimbabwe. A police raid on the church premises in February 2008 drew widespread condemnation. In May 2008, the Methodist Church became a temporary place of sanctuary for thousands of foreigners who had fled their homes after weeks of xenophobic violence on the Rand.

The Dutch Reformed Church in End Street, near Saratoga Avenue, is an impressive structure that can be seen today, lying behind the End Street Park. Its predecessor was built in Von Brandis Square in 1890.[14] Visiting congregants from outlying farms would camp there for *Nagmaal* (Communion) because this was forbidden in Market Square.

The Roman Catholic Cathedral of Christ the King, stately and inspiring, is also located here and is worth a visit.

The first cathedral was built in Kerk Street in 1896 but was abandoned when it became too small. Its main entrance is on Saratoga Avenue with a secondary entrance in End Street.[15]

When representatives of Johannesburg's early Jewish community obtained a free stand in order to erect a 'church' (stands were always granted free for this purpose), they considered it too small for a synagogue. When they approached Kruger for a second time for a second stand, he refused and remarked that since they used only half the Bible, they really were only entitled to half a stand![16]

The Witwatersrand Hebrew Congregation eventually bought the land they needed in President Street and erected the Park Synagogue in 1892. President Kruger opened it officially (apocryphally, in the name of Jesus Christ) and it remained there until the railway station expanded and it had to be demolished. In 1913 a much larger synagogue was erected in Wolmarans Street, on the corner of Claim Street, designed by Theo Schaerer. Schaerer had visited Constantinople and was so impressed with Santa Sophia that it influenced him to build an imposing dome for the synagogue. Today, this beautiful building is sadly no longer used for the purposes that it was intended and is surrounded by low-scale shops and hawkers. In 2000, a small-scale replica of the Great Synagogue – known as the Great Park Synagogue – was opened in Oaklands, using many of the fittings from the original temple.

Finally, there is a remarkable mosque, marked by its towering minaret, on Nugget Street between Market and President streets. It is a beautiful building dressed in dark green mosaic tiles. It is called Masjid Himayatil Islam and was established in 1916. It had to be modified to hold over 400 worshippers. A *Mehrab* is carved into one interior wall to indicate the direction to Mecca. Sunlight is let in through the roof since the surrounding buildings were too close and tall to allow sufficient natural light through the windows. Over 400 prayer carpets from Pakistan line the floor. The minaret is 95 feet tall and the Muezzin had to climb it five times a day to call the faithful to prayer until a public address system made this no longer necessary.[17]

Joburg's Financial Zone

The first bank to open a branch in Johannesburg was the Standard Bank – in October 1886. The 'bank' took the form of a tent in Ferreira's Camp, with a piece of paper pinned to the tent flap, indicating the name and the opening 'hours at which the front strings would be untied.'[18] A month or so later, the bank took the step of renting a single room in a cottage – believed to be the first brick building in town – owned by WP Fraser.

The Standard Bank Chambers, on the corners of Commissioner, Fox and Harrison streets, was designed by WH Stucke and WE Bannister, and completed in 1907. It was described by *The Star* as 'very bold and striking in concept … absolutely the finest premises devoted to banking yet erected in South Africa … the surrounding buildings [are] mean and paltry by comparison'.

An interesting story attached to this building is that its steel frame meant that its completion was delayed since all sources of available steel were diverted to San Francisco after its disastrous earthquake in 1906.[19]

Banking was fairly unregulated and many small banks, such as the Robinson Bank, were short lived. The remains of the old Natal Bank (90 Market Street) can be seen next to the Guildhall Pub. Huge old-fashioned bank counters dominate the lobby. Until recently, this building housed the Johannesburg Development Agency (JDA).

In 1921 the South African Reserve Bank was formed to help provide stability to the banking industry, and it held substantial hold reserves to underwrite the banks' liabilities. The original Reserve Bank building (designed by Gordon Leith, built in 1938) on the corner of Fox and Simmonds streets is now known as Matlotlo House, and houses the Gauteng Provincial Government. The new Reserve Bank building (completed in 1996) is in Newtown, on the corner of Ntemi Piliso and Pritchard streets.

Johannesburg's banks were heavily dominated by British capital, even though the *Nederlandsche Bank en Krediet Vereeniging* opened in Pretoria in 1888 (it eventually became known as Nedbank). Afrikaner Nationalist

Standard Bank, Johannesburg, 1886

JBM Hertzog encouraged Afrikaner capitalists to break the British domination of the banking industry. In 1935 Volkskas Bank was launched while Sanlam and Santam propelled Afrikaner capital into the insurance industry. In 1948, with the election of the National Party, *volkskapitalisme*, or Afrikaner capital, became increasingly influential. The Volkskas Building in Market Street dates back to these endeavours, and its external walls are engraved with scenes of the early Voortrekkers. This building narrowly escaped demolition in 2006, when the government announced plans to expand the public space adjoining Beyers Naude Square. The last-minute appeals to the Heritage Resources Agency also spared four other landmark buildings: the Rand Water Board building (also designed by Leith), Custom House, the Art Déco New Library Hotel and the First National Bank building.

By the late 1940s, all the major commercial banks had branches or headquarters in Joburg. There were also branches of several foreign banks: the French Bank of Southern Africa (1949), the South African Bank of Athens (1950) and the First National City Bank of New York (1958). The Bank of Lisbon and South Africa opened in 1965.

In 1955 the Trust Bank was formed and quickly became very popular, requiring the building of the Trust Bank Centre on Fox Street – one of Johannesburg's tallest buildings. It was built on modern lines with a reinforced concrete core and an exterior of heat-reflecting glass and anodised aluminium. It was completed in 1970 and can still be seen today as part of the ABSA complex.[20]

The Standard Bank Chambers

In the mid-1980s Barclay's Bank pulled out of South Africa, in line with international anti-apartheid and sanctions policies. Its operations were taken over by the First National Bank (FNB). Volkskas and Trust Bank later amalgamated with other financial institutions to form ABSA (now owned by Barclays Bank) and are part of the 'Big Four' that dominate the banking industry, along with Nedbank, FNB and Standard Bank. All have their headquarters in Johannesburg's CBD which remains the financial capital of South Africa.

Bank building and building complexes continue to have a strong presence in Johannesburg's CBD. Standard Bank's impressive headquarters sprawl over several city blocks in the south of the city, between Anderson and Frederick streets, the site of the esteemed Standard Bank Art Gallery. Impressive 'skywalks' link the various buildings.

The modern Standard Bank building was built in a highly unusual way: from the top down! The central core was erected first and then each floor, starting with the top floor, was suspended by three cantilevered arms (crossbeams) extending for nine floors. The second and third sections were added for the middle and lower layers, each consisting of nine floors. Another seven floors make up its lowest section. It stands in a square bounded by Fox, Main, Hollard and Simmonds streets and is 139 m high.[21]

In Main Street, in the eastern part of the CBD, ABSA Bank dominates four city blocks and also has a notable art gallery. Finally, in the north-western section of the

PLACES TO SEE

The **Standard Bank Gallery** (corner of Simmonds and Frederick streets) hosts regular exhibitions of contemporary South African artists – from new works, including those of the prestigious Standard Bank Artist of the Year to retrospectives of well-known artists. The gallery has also hosted several notable international exhibitions including works by Marc Chagall, Joan Miro and Pablo Picasso. The gallery is open Monday to Friday from 08h00 to 16h30, and Saturdays from 09h00 to 13h00. For more information go to www.sbgallery.co.za or call 011 631 1889.

Absa Bank's head office in the city centre houses up to 20 000 art works. Group and solo exhibitions are held throughout the year at the **ABSA Art Gallery** (Absa Towers North, 161 Main Street), including the works of finalists in the annual Absa L'Atelier Awards. The gallery is open Monday to Friday from 09h00 to 15h00. For more information call (011) 350 5139.

CBD, centred on Kerk Street, is FNB's 'Bank City'. Parts of the streets have been cordoned off either totally or partially and pedestrianised into walkways. These gentrified spaces are attractive quiet areas provided with ample greenery and fountains, bringing stability to the CBD.

Another pedestrian-friendly area runs along Main Street and parts of Fox Street. It stretches into Gandhi Square and continues east to include the Carlton and Absa centres, ending at Polly Street. Hawkers are banished from this spine and the intention is to create a 24-hour space there. Two blocks in Main Street have been fully closed off and turned into green spaces, and the area boasts a number of coffee shops. The Oppenheimer Fountains, known popularly as the 'Impala Stampede' that used to be displayed in the Rissik Street park behind the Post Office, is restored here.[22] Visitors can also see an original battery stamper and mining headgear.

The Business of Shopping

Joburg Man by Dale Yudelman and Arlene Amaler Raviv

Until the 1970s, the CBD was Joburg's major retail and commercial zone. The most prominent shops were built on Eloff and Pritchard streets – which became the equivalent of London's Saville Row. Going to town was something splendid – an occasion to dress up. Eloff Street was the elite shopping district: it was the most expensive 'street' in South Africa's version of Monopoly when the board game was introduced in the 1960s. In 2002, Eloff Street was dropped entirely from the revised edition of the game, and replaced with Clifton, in Cape Town.

The most famous stores on Eloff Street were Markhams, Stuttafords (originally called Thorne, Stuttaford & Company) and Cuthberts. Their flagship stores still exist, but most of the facades are a little run down and the buildings have long been occupied by new tenants. Other important commercial heritage spots include the first OK Bazaars retail outlet, on the corner of President and Eloff, and Greatermans, on Jeppe Street.

A view of Diagonal Street from above

Diagonal Street

Originally the western border of the Randjeslaagte triangle, Diagonal Street in Marshalltown is one of Johannesburg's most interesting commercial destinations – Indian shops (many owned by the same families since the 1920s) and 'muti' (African medicine) stalls exist in stark contrast with the super-modern glass-covered 'Diamond Building' (11 Diagonal Street), built in 1984 and now owned by ABSA Bank. Until 2000, this was also where the Johannesburg Stock Exchange was based (at No. 17).

More than just a commercial and retail centre, the area surrounding Diagonal Street is rich with history: here, Indian traders and families resisted the apartheid government's attempts to move them; nearby, Walter Sisulu had his estate agent's office; and the legendary Kapitan's Restaurant (11a Kort Street) was where Nelson Mandela had lunch every day in the 1950s. After threatening closure for a number of years, Kapitan's owner Madanjit Ranchod finally closed his doors – his famous meals will not be forgotten.

Today, Diagonal Street's intimate (and odd) trading spaces are again under threat, this time by inner-city upgrades: refurbished office spaces and office-to-residential conversions (like the Franklin building) could see the nature of this unique area undergo its most significant change in over 80 years. Basic 'big city' security precautions should be taken in and around Diagonal Street – no visible cell phones and wallets – but it is relatively safe to walk around the area during weekday and weekend trading hours.

The Fashion District

Based in the eastern part of the city – bounded by Jeppe, End, Commissioner and Von Wielligh streets and centred on developments in Pritchard Street – Johannesburg's 'Fashion District' covers an area of 26 city blocks. Once home to the city's manufacturing fashion industry, the area had fallen into disuse by the 1980s; through the efforts of a few individuals – notably fashion business fundi Rees Mann – working with the city's development agencies, the district has been targeted for significant upgrading and development, and is today home to hundreds of fashion-related businesses including retailers, wholesalers, designers, Cut-Make-Trim (CMT) operations, and the soon-to-be-launched Fashion Kapital Square (41 Pritchard Street).

PLACES TO VISIT

The 66-year-old **KwaZulu Muti 'Museum of Man and Science'** (14 Diagonal Street) is a traditional muti or medicine shop (why it was originally called a museum seems lost in time) described on the board above the door as the 'The King of Muti, Herbal and Homeopathic Remedies'. There are over 1900 dried herbs in the shop, prescribed by inyangas or traditional healers. There are a lot of interesting things to buy: tyre sandals, walking sticks, assegais, knobkerries, bead necklaces, Zulu pots and drums. You can make an appointment with a sangoma, who will throw the bones for you, and give you valuable advice. But even if you don't buy anything, it is just a wonderful experience, with myriad sights and smells.

Open weekdays from 07h30 to 17h00, Saturdays 07h30am to 13h00. Call (011) 836 4470 for information.[23]

PLACES TO VISIT

The **Faraday Muti Market** – near the Faraday Taxi Rank in the south-east of the city – is a striking modern space designed to accommodate up to 280 traditional healers, including sangomas and diviners. It is the second market (the Mai Mai is the other) in Johannesburg dedicated to traditional South African medicine. Visitors are welcome; for security reasons, we recommend travelling to this market as part of a tour group.

PLACES TO VISIT

The **Johannesburg Sewing Centre** (109 Pritchard Street) is the perfect place to stock up on African fabric such as the distinctive ink-heavy original Shweshwe (produced by the DaGama company in King William's town) – the ground-floor store also sells thousands of sewing-related accessories, from buttons and zips to lining and trims. Safe parking is provided for customers, with the parking entrance to the right of the shop front.

PLACES OF INTEREST

Neatly tucked away between the incoming and outgoing M2 highway, **Jewel City** is a precinct covering four city blocks on the eastern edge of the city centre – bordered by Commissioner and Main streets to the north and south, and Berea and Phillip streets in the east and west.

The precinct houses South Africa's only diamond exchange centre, the Diamond Board and Bourse, a training school, several bank branches, the Diamond Merchants' Association, the Rough Diamond Master Cutters' Association and the Jewellery Council as well as specialist diamond couriers. According to the City of Joburg website, Jewel City attracts about 1000 visitors a day, mostly buying cut and polished but unmounted diamonds. For more information go to www.jewellery.org.za.

Sport and Recreation

'In the seventies of the 19th Century, South Africa was full of red-blooded young men and all of them were bored,' reads the opening paragraph of the history of the Wanderers Sports Club. To counteract world-weariness and ennui among Joburg's young (white) males, President Kruger was petitioned for the allocation of substantial land to be used as a sports club. The club's unofficial first name, chosen by the female partners of these young bloods, was *I Zingari* (for the Italian, *Gli Zingari*, meaning 'The Gypsies'). The men didn't appear to like it quite so much, and changed it to The Wanderers, when the venture finally took off in 1888. Sports grounds were laid out on Kruger Park, which was close to today's Joubert Park.

Today this land is taken up by the Johannesburg Railway Station and surrounding buildings. The Union Park, further east, also served as both a cricket and as a football ground.[24]

In the 1930s, the Club was moved to its present location, in Illovo, to make room for the expanding railway services and the planned new Park Station complex.

Joburg Drivers

Johannesburg's urban sprawl has meant that, like Los Angeles, it is a motorised city where cars are more of a necessity than a luxury, even when public transport was better than it is today.

The first motorcar, in 1897, was a 'little Benz' possessing just one-and-a-half horsepower! It was demonstrated in the Wanderers Stadium and President Kruger awarded a medal to its first driver, AE Reno.[26] It was bought by Mr 'Coffee' Jacobs and a large coffee pot replaced its body, to advertise his coffee factory.

IW Schlesinger paid for the first traffic light at the busy intersection of Rissik and President streets in 1927. It caused a sensation. People would travel for miles to see this first 'robot', as South Africans uniquely called it – until a careless motorist crashed into it and damaged it beyond repair.[27]

The Nelson Mandela Bridge

Albert Crowley, who owned a small garage in Eloff Street, opened the first petrol pump in Johannesburg. Up until then motorists bought petrol in gallon tanks from the garages and filled their cars themselves. On the opening day, Crowley himself, dressed in a navy blue suit and white gloves, filled several waiting cars, including a Rolls Royce.[28]

To accommodate increasing traffic, the Queen Elizabeth and Rissik Street bridges were constructed over the railway marshalling grounds in the early 1950s. The latest crossing is the magnificent Nelson Mandela Bridge that links Braamfontein to Newtown. It is 284 m long and 50 m high. Built in 2003, it is the largest cable-stayed bridge in Southern Africa.

Park Station

The first train to arrive in Johannesburg – a light railway, known as the Rand Tram and operated (under the concession system) by the *Nederlandsche Zuid-Afrikaansche Spoorwegmaatskappij* (NZAM – the Netherlands South African Railway Company) – arrived in 1890, carrying coal, from a location to the east of Johannesburg (today Boksburg), to the mines; in its first year, the Rand Tram also carried some 66 000 passengers.[29] By 1894, rail links were completed between Johannesburg and Cape Town.

Although the marshalling yards were north-west

The old Park Station structure, built in 1897 – this can now be seen across the Nelson Mandela Bridge in Newtown

A view over Park Station today

of Newtown, the 'station closest to the centre of Johannesburg was located at the northern end of Eloff Street. Positioned near Kruger Park it was called Park Station.[30] The location of the station also proved a boost for the growing retail areas of Eloff and Pritchard streets.

In 1897 the busy station was 'refurbished with an elaborate and ornate new steel and glass structure 154 m long and 17 m wide.'[31] The structure was imported from Holland, where it had been part of the Amsterdam Exhibition. During the 1913 miners' riots, most of the station's windows and glasswork was smashed.

In 1932 a new station building was completed to accommodate the ever-increasing number of commuters (16 million passengers in 1932); but fast growth soon rendered the facilities inadequate, prompting further expansion and improvements to Park Station – improvements which would necessitate dropping the levels of the railway lines by some four metres, with passenger concourses at street level. Although the plans were delayed by the outbreak of the Second World War, construction resumed in 1946. By 1954 five vehicle bridges (crossing the rail tracks) had been constructed, providing essential additional links between the CBD, Braamfontein and the expanding northern suburbs.

In 1997 Park Station was redeveloped and relaunched, removing all traces of the once-segregated travel classes and systems and linking the station to neighbouring taxi-rank facilities and informal traders. The Station is currently undergoing further development – as one of the key points on the new Gautrain system.

The old Park Station building can still be seen, just a few blocks from Park Station, on an empty lot in Carr Street in Newtown. There are plans to develop the lot, but for the present it remains an occasional concert venue and training ground for learner drivers.

Sure, we have culture

Apart from gambling, drinking and sex, Johannesburg's residents were capable of more refined forms of entertainment. For example, a popular and little-known pastime was ballooning; thousands would flock on Sundays to Johannesburg's surrounding veld to picnic and watch the ballooners. A Miss Cameron made the first female balloon ascent – and parachute descent – in South Africa.

Johannesburg also had 11 booksellers as early as 1890! Juta & Company started business at the corner of Loveday and Pritchard streets, in a small corrugated-iron building in 1887. The Central News Agency established

The façade of the Johannesburg Library

its headquarters on the corner of Commissioner and Rissik streets in 1895. Both institutions expanded rapidly and yet still struggled to keep up with the demand for quality reading material.[32]

A public library was established as early as 1889 and a small room was rented for this purpose in Von Brandis Square in 1891. When it grew too large, it was moved to Kerk Street where it remained until it was demolished in 1929 to make way for the Woolworths building. In 1935 an impressive Public Library was built in what was then the lower part of Market Square (its address is still given as such to this day).[33] The building can be described as a mixture of styles including 'Mediterranean classical, with overtones of Art Deco'. It has three deeply recessed arches with bronze grilles leading down into three separate entrances, set high up from broad steps. Architect John Perry won a nationwide competition with his design. Remarkable sculptured bas-relief decorations depicting the arts and famous philosophers can be seen on its façade.[34]

Johannesburg had a remarkable number of theatres and a taste for refined arts. The Verdi Opera opened at the Theatre Royal as early as 1891 and was very popular. Barney Barnato not only supported the arts but also acted in *A Ticket of Leave Man* at the Globe Theatre. The

money raised went to the building of a synagogue. While most white working-class men preferred drinking and gambling, or had a taste for lewd music-hall entertainment, a substantial number of middle-class and 'respectable' working-class men and women actively patronised the theatre.

The Standard Theatre, built in Georgian style, was very plush and served as the venue for famous American author Mark Twain when he visited Johannesburg and gave four 'at homes' in 1896. These large, beautiful and solidly built structures gave the town a feeling of permanence. Twain later wrote approvingly about Johannesburg: 'the goldfields are wonderful in every way. In seven or eight years they have built up in the desert, a city of 100 000 inhabitants, counting white and black together, and not the ordinary city of wooden shanties, but a city made of lasting material'.[35]

A number of Art Deco 'palaces' devoted to cinema or radio were built (all on Commissioner Street) in the 1930s and 40s, including Broadcast House (1935–37), the Empire (1936), the Colosseum (1933) and His Majesty's (1937–44) all owned by IW Schlesinger.[36]

The Bantu Men's Social Centre

Most of Johannesburg's entertainment venues and cultural facilities were reserved exclusively for white patrons. Even the City Parks were segregated, long before apartheid was introduced. A section of the white ruling elite in Johannesburg, generally referred to as 'liberals', were concerned about the lack of cultural, social and sports facilities for black residents. The Chamber of Mines and various influential church figures also supported the provision of 'healthy' forms of entertainment for the black population. Mining capitalists were concerned about growing radicalism and militancy among black workers as well as serious absenteeism and illness caused by illicit liquor consumption and alleged sexual immorality, associated with *marabi* culture. Black church leaders and other members of the black middle class, such as teachers, lawyers and doctors requested social amenities. As a result of these efforts, a number of initiatives were introduced such as Gamma Sigma Clubs and the building of the Bantu Men's Social Centre, established, according to the foundation stone, in January 1924 at No. 1 Eloff Street in what is Eloff Street Extension today.

One of the founders, Herbert Dhlomo, established a Carnegie Library there in 1929. Famous South African author Peter Abrahams used the library when he worked there in 1937. Eventually the library had over 1000 members and over 3000 books. The Centre had a gymnasium and the Bantu Dramatic Society staged a number of productions during the 1930s. The Centre was run by Richard Victor Selope Thema until 1932 when he left to become editor of *Bantu World,* 'a white-owned newspaper for Africans. Under his leadership, the paper transformed becoming a major force for the politicisation of urban Africans, covering the ups and downs of the African National Congress in detail.'[37]

While designed to distract black people from their grievances and divert them from radical politics, the BMSC was, ironically, used to launch the radical and militant African National Congress Youth League in February 1944, founded by Nelson Mandela, Walter Sisulu, Anton Lembede and Oliver Tambo. When Sisulu married Albertina in the same year, the reception was held in the Centre's hall. In 1956 Father Trevor Huddleston, who actively protested against apartheid and, in particular, objected to the forced removals of Sophiatown, had his farewell party in the Centre after his superiors recalled him to England.

The Centre closed its doors in 1971 and was shortly taken over by the West Rand Administration Board, an

The Manhattan Brothers performing at the Bantu Men's Social Centre

apartheid body dedicated to the implementation of the Group Areas Act. By the 1980s it was located in a run-down part of town blighted by car dealerships and cheap food stores. The Johannesburg Metro Police currently occupy it but there are plans to restore it to its former glory.[38]

Dorkay House

Another important cultural centre for Johannesburg's black residents was neighbouring Dorkay House, a five-storey building which still stands at the corner of Eloff Street and Wemmer Jubilee Road. The Kotzen family built it during the 1940s as a clothing factory. A large rehearsal room and stage was built on the first floor and it was widely used by the cream of Johannesburg's black musicians and performers. The musical greats who rehearsed and jammed there include Miriam Makeba, Kippie Moeketsi, Ntemi Piliso, Hugh Masekela, Abdullah Ibrahim and the African Jazz Pioneers. Sipho 'Hotstix' Mabuse remembers going there during the 1960s for drumming lessons organised by the African Music Drummers Association. John Kani, one of South Africa's most revered actors, remembers it as the place where the internationally acclaimed musical *King Kong* was born.

Today it is a somewhat run-down building where the upper floors are used for residences while the ground floor is allocated to shops. The Dorkay House Trust has been formed to restore the building and musicians still use the small rehearsal room on the first floor. The walls along the staircase leading up to it are decorated with murals depicting musical themes. The floors are red linoleum and the walls are painted a dusty pink. It is a cultural treasure house that deserves recognition.

The Politics of Segregation and Apartheid

Entrance to police headquarters at John Vorster Square

Throughout its history, the centre of Johannesburg was a highly politicised and contested urban space. Protest marches, demonstrations, rioting, even pitched battles and massacres have taken place in the CBD.

The Pass Office, at 80 Albert Street, was a familiar building to Johannesburg's black residents who had to carry a 'pass' (effectively an identity document) on them at all times. Anyone who did not have the required pass could be arrested, jailed in Marshall Square and, in some cases, sent back to some distant rural area that was allegedly their 'homeland'. Today this grim building has been transformed into an upbeat Christian Ministry called Usindiso Ministries, founded in 2003. It has established a nursery school called Little Fish for the children of the local community living in the flats nearby. It also provides shelter for abused women and their children. It is fitting that a building that represented such cruelty and hardship has now become the site of humanitarian care for the needy.

The 12-storey John Vorster building

Marshall Square was the Police Headquarters and was used to incarcerate many of South Africa's most famous political prisoners. It was built in 1899 and completed by the British after the South African War. The British Royal Arms, made by Benjamin Smith, a London sculptor, was erected over its entrance. When white strikers threatened the headquarters during the 1922 Revolt, a trench was built around the building and it was lined with sandbags. Famous ANC activists Arthur Goldreich and Harold Wolpe were imprisoned but Wolpe managed to escape from its walls and eventually made his way to London.

Another famous prisoner was dedicated Fordsburg schoolteacher Frederick John Harris, a member of the African Resistance Movement who planted a time bomb in Johannesburg Railway Station in July 1964. Although he phoned a warning several minutes earlier, the bomb's explosion injured 23 people, one of whom died later from her injuries. He was later sentenced to

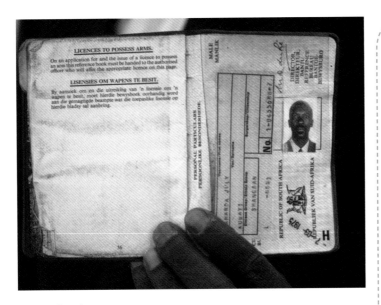

A pass book

Khotso House bombing

On 31 August 1988, agents of the apartheid government placed a series of explosive devices in the basement of Khotso House – the Johannesburg headquarters of the South African Council of Churches (a grouping of several churches opposed to the state's racist policies). The bombing was carried out by a team led by Eugene de Kock of the infamous Vlakplaas Commando; during the Truth and Reconciliation (TRC) hearings, it emerged that former State President PW Botha had given the order to make Khotso House 'unusable'. The resulting explosion demolished the building and injured 21 people.

death and hanged. His young wife, Ann, circulated a petition around Johannesburg pleading for clemency, but to no avail.[39] Harris was remembered as the 'first white martyr in the cause of equality in South Africa'.[40]

Marshall Square was demolished in 1969 and the police headquarters moved to John Vorster Square in Commissioner Street, nicknamed the 'Blue Hotel'. It was opened officially in August 1974, named after the notorious Minister of Police and later Prime Minister. The 12-storey building was located at the end of Commissioner Street near the M2 flyover. It was probably South Africa's most notorious symbol of apartheid. Many ANC and other liberation struggle activists were detained there and tortured during interrogation by the Security Police. In October 1971 Ahmed Timol 'fell' to his death from the tenth floor – his fingernails had been pulled out, his right eye gouged and his testicles crushed. Security Police referred to the technique as 'defenestration' (being dangled or dropped from a high window) and, chillingly, mocked Timol's fate saying: 'Indians can't fly.' In 1982 Dr Neil Aggett, a white physician and labour

activist who was detained for his role in trade union activities, was found hanging in his cell – an inquest revealed that he had died as a result of police torture.

Over 60 people died in detention in John Vorster Square during the worst days of apartheid repression.

After South Africa's first democratic elections were held in 1994, the hated apartheid-era building was not knocked down but was renamed the Johannesburg Central Police Station. The bronze bust of Vorster was removed to the Police Museum in Pretoria. The seventh floor has been painted pink and serves as the communications department where the focus is now on community policing. People working there have rejected the evil connotations of the place and say it is all in the past.[41]

Live at *Jameson's* album cover courtesy Shifty Records

Jameson's

on Commissioner Street, was one of the most vibrant nightspots of the 1980s – due to its possession of a 'Kruger License', granted by the then-president in Joburg's early days; the 'underground bar' was allowed to have a mixed audience, making it one of the few places in the city where a multiracial *jol* could be had (it was also allowed to trade until the small hours of the morning). Many of South Africa's best white rock 'n' roll acts of the time played there but Jameson's was best known for its 'resident' band, the Cherry-Faced Lurchers (known as the Lurchers), fronted by dynamic composer, singer and lead guitarist James Phillips. In sleeve notes to a Lurchers' album, Shaun de Waal described Jameson's as the 'epicentre of a whole new South African culture' – 'this was the unofficial soundtrack to the revolution,' Shaun wrote, 'and it was a revolution we could dance to.' Their signature Jameson's track was called 'Do the Lurch' – however it was Phillips' powerful and emotive lyrics that truly captured audiences. People still recall with awe the Lurchers' seminal 'Shot Down', a powerful condemnation of the State of Emergency. As Phillips evolved his alter ego, Afrikaner troubadour 'Bernoldus Niemand', he wrote his classic 'Hou My Vas, Korporaal' (you can download both these tracks for free by going to the Shifty Records website at www.shifty.co.za). Tragically, Phillips died of complications from a fractured skull following a car accident in 1995.

Braamfontein, early 1900s

Decentralisation

By the 1950s, Johannesburg's CBD – prompted by limited space, and high rentals – began to expand north across the rail tracks, to the working-class area of Braamfontein. Then an area of 'semi-detached cottages, small flats, cheap hotels and canteens',[42] Braamfontein was easily accessible to the white-collar workers of the CBD, many of who lived in suburbs to the north or east of the city centre. At the same time, engineers drew up new plans for the city's traffic, creating the freeway system (the M1 and the M2) that rings the city, linking it with major access roads and arterial routes.

The original farm of Braamfontein extended from the present-day suburbs of Houghton, in the east, to Westdene in the west; and from Parktown in the north to Parkhurst (its southern boundary); the *uitvalground* of Randjeslaagte fell to the south-east of Braamfontein, bordering the farms of Turffontein and Doornfontein. The suburb known as Braamfontein was laid out between 1888 and 1889.

The first major move out of Joburg's CBD came in the mid-1950s, when the Johannesburg City Council announced it would move out of City Hall and relocate to a new complex on Braamfontein Hill (the complex was only completed in 1972); the council also zoned additional stands in Braamfontein for commercial use. A number of other major firms joined the flight from the CBD: in 1954, the energy parastatal Eskom (Escom)

Residential area, Braamfontein in the 1950s

vacated its Art Deco 'ziggurat' in Rissik Street (the build-ing was, sadly, demolished) and moved to Braamfontein, as did South African Breweries (SAB); the SABC set up its new headquarters (incorporating a television centre) in the residential suburb of Auckland Park; the Johan-nesburg Stock Exchange and Standard Bank both moved their offices to just outside the boundaries of the CBD.

The 1960s saw the advent of Joburg's first subur-ban shopping malls – which, gradually, drew consumers away from the established shopping precincts in 'town'. By the mid-1980s, the largest department stores had left the CBD and set up shop in the new malls. Even as of-fice developments mushroomed in Braamfontein, new decentralised business nodes were being developed in Parktown, Rosebank, Sandton and Randburg[43] – follow-ing similar 'patterns of location' to the malls.

Second-hand car showroom, Braamfontein in the 1950s

THINGS TO DO

Joburg's first cemetery was established on a portion of Braamfontein in 1887 – and houses a collection of interesting graves and memorials, dating back to the city's earliest days. The Parktown & Westcliff Heritage Trust conducts occasional tours of the **Braamfontein Cemetery** (corner of Graaf and Smit Streets) – at the cemetery you can see a monument to the victims of the Braamfontein Dynamite Explosion (in 1896); the grave of Enoch Sontonga (who composed our national Anthem, 'Nkosi Sikelel' iAfrika'), and the graves of early martyrs of Mahatma Gandhi's Satyagrahi (passive resisters). For information, call (011) 482 3349 or go to www.parktownheritage.co.za.

PLACES TO SEE

The JDA's 'Braamfontein Precinct Regeneration Plan' has seen millions of rands invested in Braamfontein and its surrounds – creating a 'Cultural Arc' linking the suburb with Newtown and Constitution Hill. Many of the suburb's old office blocks are being converted into contemporary apartments (some of which boast impressive views overlooking the rail lines and the Mandela Bridge), and a mixed community is emerging consisting of students (at nearby Wits University), city-lovers, retail outlets and commercial offices.

Clive van den Berg's Eland

• The City of Johannesburg has used **public art** to create a 'trail' along the arc between Newtown, Braamfontein and Constitution Hill. In Newtown, for example, hundreds of carved wooden heads on concrete stands can be seen at Mary Fitzgerald Square; in Braamfontein, the JDA has partnered with the Trinity Session (a local artists' collective) to create 16 exquisite metal trees (you can see some of the trees as you cross over the Nelson Mandela Bridge). In 2007, a 20-ton concrete eland, designed by Clive van den Berg, was installed at the corner of Bertha and Ameshoff streets.

• The **Civic Theatre** (Loveday Street, Braamfontein) has been operating since 1962, and is one of the best theatre venues in South Africa – it hosts everything from ballet and opera (like William Kentridge's acclaimed *The Magic Flute*) to local productions of Broadway and West End big stage musicals. The theatre complex (there are three theatres, ranging from the 1000-seater Nelson Mandela Theatre to the 176-seater People's Theatre) also includes a late-nite café. For more information, go to www.showbusiness.co.za or call (011) 877-6800.

• Braamfontein's evolving coffee society is a work in progress, but there are a number of little spots worth investigating – particularly the **City Bakery**, at 6 De Beer Street (homemade bread and pastries). Call (011) 339 3932. Open Monday to Friday during the day, and on Saturday mornings.

Above: Wits students protesting against apartheid in the 1960s.
Right: Wits students protesting against all-white elections in the 1980s – under the watchful eye of the police

Higher Learning

In the 1920s, Johannesburg's premier English university – the University of the Witwatersrand (Wits) – moved from Eloff Street to new premises at Milner Park, adjoining Braamfontein. From little more than 1000 students in 1923, by the mid-1980s student numbers had grown to over 16 000, and the campus had expanded into Braamfontein (with the Faculty of Medicine and the Graduate Business School being located in Parktown). In 1984, the university acquired the Milner Park Showgrounds, previously used for the annual Rand Show, to build its 'West Campus' (home to the commerce and engineering faculties).

In addition to being one of the top academic institutes in South Africa – Wits is ranked as one of the top 100 universities in the world, in seven defined fields of research[44] – Wits's staff and students became known for their strong anti-apartheid stance. In 1959, when the government passed the Extension of the University Education Act, barring 'non-whites' from entering white universities, thousands of students and staff stood in silence on campus to 'mourn the passing of academic

freedom'.[45] In the decades that followed, many Wits academics were detained, banned, and even deported for their actions of protest and defiance.

Prominent student organisations (or those with an agenda specifically relevant to students) included the End Conscription Campaign (ECC) – formed in 1983, in protest against compulsory military service for all white males; the National Union of South African Students (NUSAS); and the Azanian Students Organisation (AZASO). Groups like the Johannesburg Democratic Action Committee (JODAC, affiliated with the United Democratic Front or UDF) and the UDF itself were also represented on campus.

A series showing the controlled implosion of a building in Johannesburg

The Fall (and Rise) of the CBD

Premier firms that left the CBD were replaced with second- or third-tier concerns – if the spaces were filled at all; gradually, the vibrant cultural and commercial centre of a century was eroded. Buildings were neglected and, in many cases, simply abandoned.

In the early 1990s, the empty spaces of the inner city began to be reclaimed – not by property owners or well-heeled investors, but by the city's poor, desperate for accommodation and eager to inhabit an area that, for so long, had been denied to them. Thousands of people who lived as (backyard shack) subtenants in the townships sought a new life in the 'city'. In many instances, unscrupulous property owners, looking to profit from buildings long deemed worthless, charged exorbitant rents, creating slum conditions in buildings where facilities and services had not been upgraded – or maintained – in years. In other cases, abandoned buildings were simply invaded by squatters, who took up residence in neglected (and often unsafe) former commercial space. In an effort to combat such invasions, a number of building owners took the step of permanently bricking up the doors and ground-floor windows of their properties.

Since 2000, the Joburg City Council, working with development arms like the JDA, has implemented a number of successful plans and programmes to turn around the declining fortunes of the CBD – office occupancy in the CBD is up; there are tens of new middle-income residential developments across the city centre (in many cases, converting old office space into city apartments); and the inner-city improvement districts have created dynamic commercial and cultural nodes. For updates and information, visit the city's comprehensive website at www.joburg.org.za.

THE EASTERN

Chapter Five

'When we arrived in South Africa we moved into the suburb of Doornfontein, which was the lowest rung of the Jewish residential ladder. Those upon whom fortune smiled trekked northwards via Hillbrow and Yeoville, Bellevue and parts of Observatory. The great leap forward from lower to middle class was symbolised by Orange Grove and Highlands North. In these suburbs seemingly vulgar wrought-iron burglar proofing appeared to cover every square inch of access to the house. Beyond Orange Grove, suburbs like Park Town, Lower Houghton and Dunkeld were legends in the mind of a Doornfontein lad.' – Joe Slovo, *Slovo*, 1995

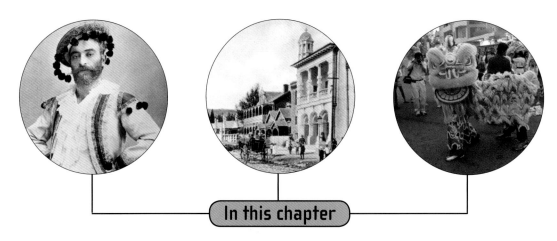

In this chapter

☞ • The 'Swagger' Suburbs

☞ • Joburg's Jews

☞ • Places of Worship

☞ • The City Slumyards

☞ • The Foster Gang

☞ • New Chinatown

SUBURBS

View of Rockey Street, Doornfontein

The 'Swagger' Suburbs

Harrow Road (now Joe Slovo Drive)

Urban geography has as much to do with a settlement's political and social landscapes as it does its geological features. Rivers, ridges and reefs provide one sort of barrier; money and class another. Several years before gold was discovered on the Witwatersrand, the popular British press coined a new term for the overcrowded, immigrant-inhabited working-class London burroughs north of the Thames and east of the city: the East End.

Bounded by the Rivers Lee and Thames, the East End was essentially a collection of one-time villages that fell to the east of London's originial medieval walled city. Because of their riverside location, the eastern settlements were the sites of the docks as well as pungent industries such as the tanneries and fulling mills. The work was menial, and low-paid; the living condititions cramped at best, fatally unsanitary at worst. It was home to the displaced and the poor, rural migrants and foreign immigrants – who came in search of work that wouldn't require a command of the English language – artisans, orphans, revolutionaries and more than a few criminals.

Upwind from the smoke and smells of the crowded city, and close to the royal seat at Westminster, was the West End – enclave of the wealthier classes, and synonymous with money, power and good breeding.

In early Johannesburg, the cardinal points of prestige were reversed.

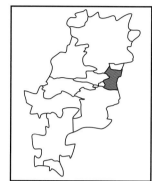

Alexandra
London
Kempton Park

Wynberg
Lombardy East
Modderfontein

Canning
9th
Kew

Corlett
Waverley
Lyndhurst
George
Edenvale Hospital

Athol
M1
Glenhazel
Sizwe Hospital
Club

Glenhove
Louis Botha
Durham
Sandringham
Linksfield

Oaklands
Orange Grove
Huddle Park Golf Club
Sydenham
Royal Johannesburg & Kensington Golf Club
Civin

11th
Ivy
Houghton Estate
Norwood
Linksfield Park Clinic
Club
Linksfield
N1

Houghton Golf Club
Club
Ekurhuleni
O.R. Tambo International Airport

1st
Mountain View
Cooper
Cyrildene
Gillooly's Farm

Houghton
Observatory
New Chinatown
Derrick
Bruma
R24
Van der Linde

Pieter Roos Park
Bellevue
Observatory Golf Club
Marcia
Bruma Lake
Eastgate Shopping Centre

Braamfontein Spruit
Rocky
Bezuidenhout Park
Allum
Bedfordview

Yeoville
Bellevue East
North
Broadway
Queen
Kensington

Barnato Park High School
JHB Observatory
Stiff
Bez Valley
Rhodes Park
Langeman

Claims
Saratoga
Bertrams
Bezuidenhout
Nino
Kitchener
Malvern

Joubert Park
Twist
JHB Stadium
Bertrams
Fosters Caves
Marathon
Geldenhuis
van Buuren

Bree
Doornfontein
Ellis Park Stadium
Standard Bank Arena
Roberts

Troyeville
Fairview

Commissioner
Jeppestown (Belgravia)
Jules
Main Reef (R29)

John Page

N

Less than a year after public diggings had been proclaimed, Johannesburg's centre of gravity shifted from the shanties of Ferreira's Camp to the bustling trade of Market Square and Commissioner Street. Demand for property in 'central' Johannesburg soon exceeded the available space; and the growing presence of 'low-lifes' (from the illicit trade in sex and alcohol in certain sections of the city, like Frenchfontein) prompted better-off residents to seek alternative accommodation.

Mining activity was concentrated to the south of Johannesburg, the gold reefs providing a natural barrier to the expanding urban grid – as well as producing huge clouds of dust (from the mine dumps) and constant noise (from the ore-stamping machines).

The areas immediately west and north-west of Market Square had been designated for small black, coloured and Indian 'locations' – which had caused a dip in neighbouring property prices when the planning information was made known. The western areas were also where Johannesburg's sanitary farms and related services were to be concentrated, and the city's first large cemetery had been marked out directly north-west of the centre, in Braamfontein.

While the working classes shifted to the west, where the land was cheaper, the middle classes moved in the opposite direction: east. And so Johannesburg's wealthier residents gradually migrated to the so-called 'swagger suburb'[1]

◉ PLACES TO SEE

Bezuidenhout Park lies below the Observatory Ridge – which, at 1808 m above sea level, is the city's highest ridge. The land was sold to the city in 1949 by Willem Bezuidenhout (one of Frederick's sons) on condition that it be used as a park, and the family house (in which Willem lived until 1950) was maintained by the City Council.

Today, you can still see the original Bezuidenhout homestead, family burial grounds and some ancient oak trees. The Park is generally safe to visit on weekends and is regularly used by dog walkers most evenings. Access to parking and the farmhouse is via the entrance in Marcia Street.

For more information contact City Parks on (011) 712 6600.

of Doornfontein, today almost indistinguishable from the encroaching city itself but, at the time, the embodiment of the follies, excesses and riches of the City of Gold.

Doornfontein was the first suburb established outside of the central city, named for the farm on which it was situated. The farm Doornfontein was original-

Henri Bettelheim, dressed as a 'Mexican Hidalgo', for a costume ball at the Wanderer's Club (right) The 'Turkish Consulate' in Beit Street (far right)

ly owned by a Voortrekker named Barend Christiaan Viljoen, who named the land 'thorn fountain' (*doorn fontein*) for its thorny acacia trees and freshwater spring.

Viljoen's daughter Judith (after whom the suburb of Judith's Paarl is named) married Frederick Bezuidenhout; their portion of the farm became known as Bezuidenhout's (Bez) Valley. The Bezuidenhout farmhouse was built in 1863, and still stands today in the green space known as Bezuidenhout's Park.

In 1886 a small mining camp was established on Doornfontein. It was known as Meyer's Camp or, more often, Natal Camp because of the large number of diggers from Natal, and had a reputation as a settlement somewhat superior to Ferreira's Camp. A number of prominent figures settled in Natal Camp including HB Marshall, the Jeppe family (who had a raw brick house with a thatch roof) and Mrs Wolhuter, who owned a tennis court.

Initially, Doornfontein was perceived as too far from 'town' and, like other investments, the suburb was a victim of the uncertainty that raged around the gold industry. As a result, many real estate developers were able to buy leases in Doornfontein for £1. However, after 1890 it became a much sought-after suburb by the wealthy and stands went for as much as £500.

From the barren plateau of the Johannesburg veld, a tree-lined suburb with turreted and gabled villas emerged.

Saratoga Avenue, leading from 'town' to the suburb, was established by an American called Sam Height (who also named his house Saratoga). The road became known as 'millionaires' row'; it was where Randlords John Dale Lace, Friederich Eckstein and Theodore Reunert built their mansions. Barney Barnato had a house in nearby End Street; George Albu had a mansion in Pearse Street. The houses were known for ostentation and grandeur – each had its own stable and a coach house; some had

The gates of Belgravia

swimming pools. Henry Bettelheim (the self-appointed 'consul' for the Ottoman Empire, who was better known as 'Beetles') built a complete Turkish palace adorned with 'crescents and other Oriental symbols'.[2]

Buoyed by this growth, investors, most notably the Ford and Jeppe Estate Company, began to develop further eastwards, establishing the middle-class suburb of Jeppestown in 1888 (an equivalent, Fordsburg, was established for the working classes to the west) and neighbouring Belgravia, named after the fashionable London neighbourhood.

Julius Jeppe built a Victorian manor called Friedenheim in the suburb of Belgravia. The house was described as a 'ducal palace',[3] and featured a tollgate (one of Joburg's first gated communities, perhaps) on the tree-lined driveway leading up to his residence.

Friedenheim, which was demolished in the early 1960s after being declared 'unsafe' (right).
Sir Julius Jeppe (far right).

Theodore Reunert

View of Doornfontein with Windybrow in the foreground

Today only Windybrow, built by Theodore Reunert, an importer of mining machinery, remains standing as a reminder of a time and style gone by. Built in 1896 as a family home, its neo-gothic English character reflects only one of a hodge-podge of architectural styles that flourished in Doornfontein at the turn of the century. 'Dilapidated and rotting' in the mid-1980s, it was restored in the 1990s and is now a national monument – and home to a burgeoning arts centre.

 PLACES TO VISIT
Windybrow Centre for the Arts

at 161 Nugget Street (on the corner of Pietersen and Nugget) Falling theatre attendances and the high crime rate in adjoining Hillbrow saw the Windybrow threatened with closure in 2004/5, but the institution was relaunched in 2006 with a strategy focusing on sustainability and relevance.

The Windybrow has three theatres, in which a number of community theatre productions are performed, as well as rehearsal rooms and exhibition space. The centre has become a showcase for work by new and young South African talent, particularly artists who have attended workshops hosted by the Theatre. In 2008, the Windybrow launched a Youth Development Programme aimed at empowering the inner city's residents with acting, dancing and singing skills.

For more information you can visit the centre's website at windybrowarts.co.za – unfortunately the programme information isn't always current – or you can call them on (011) 720 0003/4.

Doornfontein: A Shtetl on the Veld?

By Margot Rubin

Doornfontein after 1906, showing the Lions Shul

Between 1890 and 1896, it is estimated that the population of Johannesburg tripled – almost half lived in the central area of town, in what can only be considered slum conditions. It was during this period that two main enclaves of Jewish settlement came into existence. The fairly well-off (mainly Western European) Jews lived in the 'posh' suburbs of Doornfontein and New Doornfontein – the elite moved even further north, to Parktown and Braamfontein. The majority of Eastern European Jews lived in Marshalltown and Ferreirastown.

The spatial separation was a manifestation of huge cultural, ideological and religious differences. The Western European Jews – the earliest Jewish settlers in South Africa, who had come to the diamond and later goldfields in the 1870s and 1880s – tended to be fairly assimilated and were generally very involved in building the mining industry into the quintessential capitalist dream; the second wave of Jewish immigration, from the Pale of Settlement, particularly Lithuania, were fleeing religious persecution and social instability in Tsarist Russia. The Eastern Europeans spoke Russian, Hebrew and Yiddish, and were generally devout. These two groups existed on very different socio-economic strata: the Anglo-German Jews were predominantly involved in the professions, as stockbrokers, businessmen and financiers. Eastern European Jews were, in general, artisans, craftsmen and wholesalers; they were usually poor, and quite distinct in their manner and dress.

The most impoverished Eastern European Jews were known, curiously, as 'Peruvians' (the origin of the label is unclear) – described by Charles van Onselen as 'perhaps the most visible, dispossessed and unsuccessful group of workers on the Witwatersrand … the unhappy recipients of the most vicious class and race prejudice that society could muster.'[4] They elicited disdain from middle-class Jews, who attempted to distance themselves from any taint. In the non-Jewish press, Peruvians were described as dirty, squalid refugees; even the local *Jewish Chronicle* commented that it would be 'no loss' if the Jewish quarter in Marshalltown was moved.

A third set of Jews, also from Eastern Europe, arrived after the turn of the century and presented a very different face of Judaism. The Jews who came to Johannesburg in the first decade of the new century were better educated, more political (often further left) and certainly more worldly than their co-religionists who had made the same journey just a few years before.

By 1904, there were over 10 000 Jews in Johannesburg – about 12 per cent of the town's white population. The settlement pattern began to shift; the new century saw the Jewish community, or at least those who could afford to, move from the slums of the inner city to the eastern suburbs recently vacated by the wealthier classes (who had moved north). Johannesburg Jewry moved further and further up the economic ranks, moving from artisans and retailers into the professions, and into the suburbs of Doornfontein and New Doornfontein. A synagogue was established in 1903 to serve this community's spiritual needs, and more synagogues, Hebrew schools and community centres were added over the next few decades to keep pace with the demographic growth.

For half a century, the very complexion of Doornfontein and New Doornfontein was transformed – from its start as a sanctuary for the wealthy – into a middle-class, middle-income Jewish enclave comprised of families following an orthodox but consistently evolving

Jewish way of life. Over time the suburbs evolved into a dynamic and bustling Jewish quarter.

Some of the earliest Jewish conveniences within the area required for the continuation of Jewish life was the supply of kosher food. Although starting from humble beginnings with only two kosher restaurants in the area in the 1900s, the number rose to just under a dozen by the 1920s. There was a wide variety of delis and restaurants, each one catering to the necessary tastes of what was still an immigrant community, and imbuing the area with characteristic smells of Jewish cooking.

Food was not the only thing brought from home and the community, at least for the first two decades of the 20th Century, spoke as much Yiddish as English – there was even a Yiddish newspaper in Johannesburg. Most households were bilingual and the first word that came to hand was generally used. Yiddish humour and literature were certainly not forgotten and societies like the Yiddish Literature and Dramatic Society were established. The Dramatic Society put on a number of amateur and professional performances in Yiddish and received much acclaim and popularity within the community. These societies drew people together to socialise and enjoy the dramatists' clever and often bitingly witty performances.

Several Jewish schools were built: the Jewish Government School, and the IH Harris Primary School in Davies Street, which is still in existence (although it's no longer a Jewish school).

By the 1920s the eastern suburbs had achieved something that very few places in the world had accomplished, the 'thrill', for its residents, of being able to '[be] a Jew anywhere and any time'. Doornfontein and neighbouring New Doornfontein provided a Jewish space in which Jews could practise their religion and openly wear their faith both at home and on the streets. The area provided a certain sense of religious spirituality evident on a Sabbath evening, when flickering Sabbath candles could be seen in every house. It also provided a communal identity that many South African Jews

The Lions Shul today

remember fondly. The intensity of the Jewish culture within the area, its limited geographical boundaries and the strong Eastern European flavour of the Judaism practised link the place and its resonance to the shtetls of Eastern Europe, and their beauty and tragedy so eloquently captured in so much of Jewish myth and folklore.

The middle classes of Doornfontein and New Doornfontein, although not particularly wealthy themselves and generally maintaining a middle-class lifestyle, were not unaware of the poverty that existed within the broader Jewish community in other parts of the city. Charitable organisations were established and the good women of the community often held clothing drives and collections for their poorer co-religionists. They distributed the clothes amongst the slums and squalor of the poor living in the inner city.

Many Jews unable to climb the social and economic ladder lived and worked in the south of Johannesburg. Men laboured in 'native' eating-houses (called *'kaffereaters'*) providing cheap food and drink for the black mine workers. Many of the women were not so lucky and the charitable organisations were aware of a number of young Jewish girls and women who had been coerced or co-opted into a life of vice in the inner cities – and did their best to provide sanctuary and help if and when pos-

sible. Many a respectable housewife had not started her life in Johannesburg as a paragon of Jewish virtue.

Rising anti-Semitism in the 1920s and 1930s and the decreasing prices of property in Doornfontein and New Doornfontein (caused by the opening up of new and better-quality middle-class suburbs to the north and further east) meant that Jews who had been living in the south of the city moved into the east, consolidating the community already in residence and replacing the residents who had moved. The Jews coming from the south of the city added a further dimension to the dynamics of the townships. Far more religious and orthodox than their middle-class and aspirant co-religionists, they brought a strong flavour of the old country, with its heavy Yiddish accent, back into an area that was already starting to see the adoption of a more 'South African' identity by many of the younger generation.

From the late 1920s onwards, Doornfontein and New Doornfontein were gradually left to those who could not afford to go elsewhere and for some time remained 'the lowest rung of the Jewish residential ladder'. Many South African Jews who later went on to great prominence were born and raised in this declining suburb, running amongst the slums, and the competing gangs of young boys engaged in various degrees of youthful mischief.

Houses of Worship

Doornfontein and its surrounds are home to many of Johannesburg's oldest places of worship – a number of which are still in use today.

St Mary's the Less (41 Park Street, Jeppestown) is the oldest standing place of worship in the city – built in 1889. It's believed that when St Mary's Cathedral was built in the inner city in 1929, St Mary's bowed to its superior status, and became St Mary's the Less.

The Lions Synagogue (120 Siemert Road, corner of Beit Street), built in 1906, is the only remaining shul in Doornfontein. It takes its name from the two impressive gold-painted cast-iron lions at the entrance. Services are conducted at the shul three times a week. The congregation is largest on Saturday mornings and on high holidays. Many fourth-generation Jews attend services at the shul.

The Greek Orthodox Church (corner of Claim and Wolmarans streets in Hillbrow) was built in 1912 and originally drew its congregation from the Greek immigrants living in Yeoville, Berea and Hillbrow at the turn of the 19th Century. Johannesburg was, at one time, home to a Greek community as large as 70 000 people; today it is estimated at around half that number, as people have emigrated to Australia, America and returned to Greece.

The Middle Class Emerges

New roads and improved public transport encouraged the development of additional suburbs to the east – less expensive than Doornfontein, but equally desirable for individuals and families looking for a permanent home.

The suburb of Morristown (named after Hyman Morris, a 'law man') was established in 1889; just across the rail tracks from the Jumpers Mine, it was home to many of the city's Cornish miners. In 1904, Morristown changed its name to Malvern; the suburb is still dominated by bustling Jules Street (named after Julius Jeppe).

In 1890 the suburb of Yeoville was proclaimed – named after the surveyor, Thomas Yeo Sherwell, who had plotted the streets and stands of Doornfontein. Like

The Greek Orthodox Church on Wolmarans Street

Doornfontein, Yeoville was a largely Jewish suburb and boasted a number of synagogues and Jewish specialty stores. It offered mixed dwellings – freestanding homes, duplex and terraced houses, and apartment blocks – which made it accessible to a wider range of incomes.

In the 1980s Yeoville became one of Joburg's hip spaces – young couples bought old houses with pressed ceilings and wooden floors, or spacious apartments in Art Deco-styled buildings; the central thoroughfare, Rockey Street, became a hot entertainment and hangout spot. As the residents became more cosmopolitan, the suburb became increasingly politicised – it was home to a number of the city's alternative thinkers and activists, and one of the earliest suburbs to integrate black, white, Indian and coloured residents.

By the late 1990s, however, the suburb's proximity to the declining central city had started to show; the middle class moved out as crime and high-density occupancy moved in. Property prices all but collapsed – many people found themselves suddenly unable to sell what had once been desirable dwellings.

Today the suburb is undergoing a series of council-sponsored improvements – to its parks, community centres and community facilities (like the public swimming pool); Joburg's property boom combined with the approaching 2010 World Cup, and the increased demand for centrally located housing, has also seen many estate agents re-enter the Yeoville property market.

Joburg's Little Italy

An Italian family picnic at Modderfontein in 1900

Before the 19th Century, very few Italians had settled in southern Africa; this was largely because of the Protestant Dutch East India Company's policies, which viewed any 'papist' immigration very unfavourably. Religious freedom was finally granted in 1803, however only a handful of Italians made their way from Europe to the tip of Africa, mostly settling in Cape Town – the occasional, daring few trekking north with the Boers, or venturing to Portuguese Mozambique.

The diamond and gold discoveries of the 1870s and 1880s marked a turning point: from that moment, Italians were not to be counted in tens but in hundreds.

South Africa's mining operations saw the country become the largest market for dynamite in the world; and, in Johannesburg, the small Italian community initially took shape around the workers employed in the local explosives manufacturing plant – many of these men and women hailed from the Piedmontese town of Avigliana, near Turin,

which was famous for its large dynamite factory.

The ZAR concession to sell (and, in theory, manufacture) ammunition and explosives was owned by Edouard Lippert, who had formed the Zuid Afrikaansche Maatskappy van Ontplofbare Stoffen Beperk (ZAR Company of Explosive Material Limited) in Leeuwfontein, which in turn had an agreement with the Nobel organisation in France. The dynamite, which was imported in blocks from Europe, was machine-cut into sticks, hand-wrapped in wax paper and then packaged.

When Lippert's concession was revoked, the government decided to build a new dynamite plant closer to the Rand's gold mines, at Modderfontein. At the same time, declining local demand for dynamite in Avigliana prompted unemployed workers to emigrate to the Transvaal to continue working in their particular specialisation. By the time the Modderfontein factory officially opened in 1896, there were over 190 Italians working at the plant.

The closest suburb at the time to the Modderfontein works was that of Orange Grove – coincidentally developed by a prominent Italian landowner Michele Zoccolo (who also owned Bergvlei farm north-west of Johannesburg on the Jukskei River, which he renamed Lombardy Estate).

For several decades, the city's Italian community remained concentrated in this suburb, together with Yeoville and Jeppe.

Italians on the Rand also found work as entrepreneurs, artisans, mechanics, builders, engineers, waiters, chefs and property developers … The Johannesburg suburb of Risidale was named after the Risi family, originally from Salerno, who also developed the suburb of Linmeyer. Luigi Fatti and the Moni family (initially rival importers and retailers in central Johannesburg) became household South African names – as Fatti's and Moni's – when they began manufacturing their own pasta, after the First World War made importation of Italian goods difficult if not impossible.

After reaching a high in the 1910s, Italian immigration slowed down as South Africa became a less 'fashionable' destination (more Italians chose to go to America). The local consul also expressed concerns about regional labour conditions and unemployment: the Johannesburg housing market (in which a number of Italians had found work) was experiencing a crisis; Italian miners (who numbered about 300 in 1907) were not guaranteed of finding jobs, even with the right papers and experience … and, of course, for those who were working, in addition to the daily physical risks of working, digging, drilling and blasting underground, there was the threat of developing miner's phthisis.

Between the First and Second World wars, the Italian community settled and integrated into South African society. A number of Italian cultural and mutual aid societies were established, including Johannesburg's Italian Union and, in 1920, an Italian school. Political, economic and cultural relationships between Italy and South Africa were also consolidated; in the 1930s additional

PLACES TO SEE

Zonderwater (near Cullinan) is today the site of an active prison. Access is restricted (but can be arranged in advance) and the large grounds feature a prisoner of war museum and a cemetery. The wetlands location is also popular with birders. The nearby historic village of Cullinan (named after Thomas Cullinan, who discovered the Cullinan diamond) can be included on your itinerary.

For more information on Zonderwater, call (012) 667 3279 or visit Cullinan's tourism website at www.cullinaneasyfind.co.za.

shipping services were implemented between Genoa and Cape Town, and a three-year course in Italian was introduced at the University of the Witwatersrand.

Threatening this stability, however, were growing political tensions played out among South Africa's immigrant communities: communists jostled with fascist support groups, and a protest against 'Rome's imperialistic aims' was held outside the Italian vice consulate in Johannesburg. Italy's invasion of Abyssinia also prompted widespread anti-Italian sentiment in the Union. Public opposition became more widespread when Rome promulgated a series of anti-Semitic laws in 1938.

When war was declared in September 1939, Italy initially made a declaration of non-belligerence. By June 1940, however, the country had declared hostilities against Britain. South Africa's government, under Jan Smuts, considered itself at war with Rome; Italian citizens were rounded up and sent to internment camps across the country; all assets belonging to private and public Italian bodies were frozen.

Although many of those interned were eventually released – they were not seen as a threat to the war effort, or the country's security – the detainees were deeply affected by their treatment in a 'country to which they had always been loyal, which they had chosen as a second homeland and which, in many cases, was the land of their birth.'[5]

In 1941 the first Italian prisoners of war (POWs) began to reach South Africa after several Allied victories in Italian East Africa. South Africa was considered a strategically good location for the detention of large numbers of enemy prisoners – it was far from the front, and on the route between India and England (sea travel in the Mediterranean had become unsafe for Allied ships).

A large camp, named Zonderwater, was established 45 km east of Pretoria and became the largest Allied POW camp of the Second World War.

Holding as many as 63 000 prisoners at one time (at its peak, in 1942), life for the Zonderwater inmates was 'considered bearable' if not enjoyable. The prisoners were allowed to provide the camps with the necessary infrastructures including hospitals, chapels, sports grounds, schools and theatres.

After the fall of Mussolini and the disbanding of the fascist party in Italy, a number of the young men interned in Zonderwater began to assume a less belligerent and more cooperative attitude towards South African military authorities (this led to tension with the loyal fascist elements within the camps). Cooperative prisoners were moved to so-called external camps or transit centres, where they were given the opportunity to assist with agricultural work and road construction. Before the end of the war, over 20 000 Italian men had gone to work in this fashion. Across South Africa there still exist bridges, roads, churches, chapels and farmhouses bearing the distinction of having been built by these POWs.

After the end of hostilities, many of the Italian POWs chose to remain in South Africa – partly because of the attractive new way of life available outside the camps, and partly because of the miserable state of affairs they knew awaited them in Italy. Among the POWs who chose to remain were renowned artists Edoardo Villa and Carlo Scarpa. The 'non collaborators' were eventually repatriated to Italy in 1947, when the camp ceased operation.

The presence of tens of thousands of Italians in South Africa opened the way to new immigration in the 1950s and 1960s, and Italian names figured prominently in every field of South African life from business to agriculture, the arts and sport.

PLACES TO SEE
Modderfontein Museum
Visit the Modderfontein Museum – Joburg's old dynamite manufacturing plant – where there's a large collection of early artefacts used in the construction and running of the town, as well as a mini laboratory.

The museum is at 2 Main Street, Modderfontein. Hours are Mondays 10h00 to 14h00, Wednesdays 13h30 to 16h30, and Fridays 10h00 to 14h00. Phone (011) 606 3206 for further information.

Barney Barnato and the Braamfontein Spruit

In 1897, mining magnate Barney Barnato (born Barnett Isaacs) built himself a grand mansion in the new suburb of Berea. The estate covered five hectares – now the block surrounded by Park Lane, Beatrice Lane, Barnato Street and Tudhope Avenue. Situated on the property was a spring, the source of the Braamfontein Spruit (Joburg's longest stream). The spring was used to fill a lake Barnato created in front of his mansion – a piece of water large enough for boating, surrounded by a landscaped garden and leafy trees.

Barnato never got to live in his mansion. While travelling to England, he fell off the ship and drowned – some say he committed suicide; others that he was pushed. His body was recovered and he is buried in London.

Today, all that remains of his massive estate are three wrought-iron entrance gates and the original gatehouse, in Barnato Street. The site of Barnato's house is now the location of Barnato Park High School, built in 1970 after the original mansion and an earlier school were demolished (the property was donated to the government in 1910). The school's swimming pool is situated in the area where the lake was originally constructed.

From Berea, the Braamfontein Spruit runs through Pieter Roos Park, down Empire Road to the Frank Brown Park and then on towards the German School in Auckland Park. The stream then flows towards the Parkview Golf Course, exits through Parkhurst, and meets its second small tributary, the Westdene Spruit. The Montgomery Spruit (which has two branches, from Albertville and Albert's Farm, that converge in Roosevelt Park) meets up with the Braamfontein and

Barney Barnato (centre) and friends

Westdene spruits at the bottom of Rustenberg Road, where they flow towards Delta Park.

Decades ago, the Braamfontein Spruit was dammed in the suburb of Craighall, forming what was known as Rattray's Dam (after the owner, William Rattray). Until the dam silted up in the 1930s, the area was a premier leisure spot for Joburg residents. Today, the stone wall still stands (it is visible from the bridge on Conrad Drive) and there is a small cascade of water.

The Braamfontein Spruit eventually merges with the Sandspruit, and flows in the direction of the Hartbeespoort Dam north-west of the city. [5]

For more information on this Spruit and the city's other rivers, you can contact the Voluntary River Rangers group by going to their website at www.riverrangers.org.za.

The Shame of the Slumyards

Doornfontein, 1930s

Sociologist and author Ellen Hellman

A boom town required a legion of workers to keep industry going. By the turn of the century, Johannesburg's black urban population had grown to nearly 60 000; in 1911, this reached over 100 000, less than five per cent of whom were women. The need for black housing and accommodation soon outstripped the meagre supply. The official 'native' location of Klipspruit, well outside the city limits, was only able to accommodate 3000 people; it was also a significant distance from Joburg's business centre and increased transport costs ate away at already meagre wage packets while employers complained about loss of productivity owing to wasted travelling time.

The stated segregationist policies of Joburg's town planners clashed with the demands of employers – for a workforce that was within easy reach of their places of employment. The Johannesburg Town Council was therefore forced to create a system of residence permits, which granted exemption certificates allowing certain black men to reside within the limits of Johannesburg. It did not, however, provide for any suitable accommodation for these residents.

At the same time, landowners and speculators were looking for new ways to make money off previously expensive, now vacant, properties in Doornfontein. With the departure of the wealthy and middle classes, property values plummeted leaving landowners with large but relatively worthless real estate.

Speculators managed to turn declining prices into profitable ventures by rack-renting rooms to black workers who, desparate for central accommodation, were prepared to pay exorbitant rates for the chance to live within Johannesburg's boundaries. Very quickly, Doornfontein became the site of some of the most pitiful slumyards in the inner city of Johannesburg. These slumyards were to dominate the landscape of Doornfontein until the mid-1930s, when they were finally cleared under the Slums Act of 1934.

By 1915 about 3000 men, women and children lived in backyards on properties in Ferreirasdorp, Marshallstown and City and Suburban in increasingly slum-like conditions.

However, it was in Doornfontein – the former 'snob suburb' – where the largest collection of slumyards developed. There were six main yards: Rooiyard, Makapan yard, Molefe yard, Mveyane yard, Magonyanye yard and Brown yard.

Rooiyard was one of the largest slumyards, and was the subject of an intensive study, published in 1948, by a white female sociologist named Ellen Hellman. Hellman spent nearly every day for a year observing and talking with Rooiyard residents, before their eviction and removal to Orlando and other black suburbs outside of the city.

In her book, *Rooiyard: A Sociological Study of an Urban Native Slumyard,*[7] Hellman described Rooiyard as consisting of 107 rooms and a shop, which served as a kind of concession store to the yard. Rooiyard, she explained, was extremely congested – housing as many as 376 people at any one time. Despite the large number of rooms and residents, the yard was serviced by only two garbage bins and just six latrines (three for men and three for women). A single working tap served the drinking and washing water needs of all the yard's residents.

In the rooms themselves, Hellman commented that most of the floorboards were rotten, and the flooring made of bare earth. As the floor level was often below the level of the yard, during the summer rainwater would

Doornfontein Trivia

In the early 1930s, a young Walter Sisulu lived at No. 23 Van Wyk Street, Doornfontein with his mother and stepfather; at first Sisulu worked at the Premier Milling Company, then as a newspaper distribution agent. In 1934, Sisulu and his family were victims of the Slums Clearance Act and were removed to Orlando.

frequently flow into the rooms, carrying dirt and debris from the yard outside.

The rooms were also poorly ventilated, stifling in the summer and freezing in the winter. Smoking coal braziers were used during winter, to create some warmth for the residents – but adding the danger of fire and smoke inhalation.

In contrast to the disorder of the yard outside, the rooms' interiors presented a picture of great care and energy: the spaces were well scrubbed and each family's belongings tidily arranged. The yard's residents took great pride in the purchase and accumulation of Western-style furnishings, starting with a bed (usually curtained off from the rest of the room, so that parents might have some privacy from their children, who would sleep on the floor); two of Rooiyard's families were even noted to have pianos! Almost all things Western were actively embraced, while traditional culture was rejected, removed and left behind.

Urban Brew

The yards were also known as 'skokiaan yards' – after the trade in illegally brewed beer (*skokiaan*), which was central to the yards' social and financial structures.

In the words of the women who lived in the yard (it was the women who brewed the beer), the manufacture and sale of beer was essential for two reasons: firstly, to satisfy the demands of the male and add to his comfort and well-being; the second reason was to supplement his earnings.

Hellman noted 'a good wife would not like her husband to be placed in the position of having to buy his beer from other women', adding that there were 'very few men who, in order to protect their wives from the constant danger of arrest to which they expose themselves by brewing beer, will forgo the pleasure of having their beer in their own homes.' In Rooiyard, a woman who did not participate in the beer-selling business was considered a 'bad wife'.

The beer-brewing business was also the start of what Hellman referred to as a 'stockfair', known today as a 'stokvel' – a 'mutual benefit society', helping the women dispose of surplus beer, and functioning as a rotating savings-benefit scheme. Today, *stokvels* are primarily mutual savings schemes.

The Observatory

The Bezuidenhout family donated 35 ha of land to the government, on which Johannesburg's first meteorological observatory site was built in 1903.

Astronomer Dr Robert Innes moved from the Royal Observatory in Cape Town to become the director, and Herbert Baker designed the structure, built on the hill and opened in 1905. The small, attractive stone building with its cupola still sits on the hill, and offers splendid views over Bellevue and Sandton, and on clear days, the Voortrekker Monument, south of Pretoria.

The Observatory contained a seismograph to record mining tremors, an evaporation pan and a device to record lightning strikes (which are particularly virulent on the Witwatersrand). The first telescope, installed in 1906, was loaned by the Imperial Observatory in Pulkowa in Russia.

One of the observatory's earliest patrons was Theodore Reunert (of Windybrow, in Doornfontein) who took an amateur interest in astronomy, and even had an asteroid named after him.

In 1910, it became known as the Union Observatory. Between 1911 and 1938 the Observatory detected 579 new minor planets. At the time it was a record for any

Observatory in 1909

institution. Among the discoveries was that of Proxima Centauri, the closest known star to our solar system.

In 1961 the Observatory changed its name to the Republic Observatory. In 1972, owing to Johannesburg's bright lights and pollution, it closed as a weather station and the Observatory was moved to Sutherland in the Northern Cape, where it still resides. The site was taken over by the Council for Scientific and Industrial Research for telecommunications research.

The Observatory remains in use, and the main telescope is used by amateur astronomers and members of the public. Every last Friday of the month, a scientific talk-for-the-layperson is given, after which the public is permitted to view the skies through the telescope.[8]

THINGS TO DO
Fridays at the Observatory

On the last Friday of every month the Johannesburg Observatory arranges a talk on scientific matters geared at the general public. The talks normally last about three-quarters of an hour, accompanied by a demonstration, after which the telescope will be opened and available for observing the skies, weather permitting. The talks are informal, kids are welcome, and tea and biscuits are served in the dome afterwards. The Observatory is at 18A Gill Street, Observatory. Phone (011) 487 1512 for more information.

The Foster Gang

Peggy, the baby and Foster

In March 1913, two petty criminals – William Foster and John Maxim (aka John Maxwell) – joined forces to pull off a big heist: the American Swiss Watch Company in Longmarket Street, Cape Town.

Assisted by Foster's brother Jimmy and a friend, Fred Adamson, the gang donned false moustaches and handguns and soon fled with two suitcases filled with jewellery – including 308 diamonds, gold sovereigns and cash. Less than three days later, William Foster was arrested in Cape Town; two of his accomplices were apprehended in Johannesburg, with only Maxim escaping capture (although he was incarcerated a short while later for selling liquor to blacks).

Although William Foster was tried and sentenced to 12 years (with hard labour) at Pretoria Central Prison, the Cape Town robbery heralded the beginning of one of Johannesburg's most notorious criminal partnerships, which

would later be known as the Foster Gang.

Nine months after starting his jail term, William Foster made a daring prison escape (swapping his prison uniform for a suit he had convinced the prison tailors to make for him); by March, Foster had again hooked up with John Maxim and a 22-year-old named Carl Mezar (aka George Smit).

Between April and September 1914, the Foster Gang went on a spree of violent – and, frequently, botched – robberies in and around Johannesburg: in April they targeted the Roodepoort and Vrededorp post offices; in July they hit the National Bank in Boksburg, killing one man and injuring another; in August they attempted to rob a cycle store and a liquor depot; in September more liquor stores were targeted, this time resulting in the death of two policemen.

Eventually, a resident in Regent's Park tipped police off as to where the Gang was staying – in a derelict cottage near Wemmer Pan, together with Foster's wife Peggy and their baby daughter. When detectives tried to approach the house, a shootout ensued leaving one law officer dead; the Gang fled, Foster sending his wife and child to Germiston on a bus.

Foster with his sisters

Foster and Peggy

In the middle of 1914, the Foster Gang had set up an emergency hideaway in an abandoned mining cave in the suburb of Kensington; it was here they fled in September, after police threw up a net of roadblocks around the city to trap the Gang. Within two days, police had found the Foster's hideout and within hours a heavy cordon of police and onlookers surrounded the cave's small entrance, in Juno Street, Kensington. Inside the cave, the three men had decided they would not be taken alive, and wrote farewell notes to loved ones. The first to die was Carl Mezar (not quite able to bring himself to put the gun to his head, he asked Johan Maxim to pull the trigger). At Foster's request, his wife Peggy and baby daughter were brought in to visit him, together with his father, mother and two sisters; an hour later, Foster's family returned – but without Peggy. Moments later, the crowd heard a single shot, followed by two more. Peggy had elected to die with her husband.

It was the end of one of the era's most brutal crime sprees. There had been a number of incidental deaths along the way including two suicides (a postmaster, who had been caught out for an earlier theft after the Foster Gang's robbery, and the policeman who allowed Peggy Foster to enter the cave – he was consumed with guilt);

Police and crowds waiting outside the cave where the Foster Gang hid

and two accidental shootings at the police roadblocks, where officers fired at cars refusing to stop (a doctor, hurrying on his way to surgery; and South African War General Koos de la Rey, who was traveling to Potchefstroom – to start a rebellion against the government).

Chinatown Chronicles
By Darryl Accone

Scenes from New Chinatown

When my great-grandfather and grandfather journeyed from China to Gam Saan, the 'Gold Mountain' of Johannesburg in 1911, they reckoned on staying for a short time, working hard, saving money to send back – and eventually following it – home. My grandfather never set foot on China's soil again. As many others before and since from various parts of China, he settled in Johannesburg. It was from near Canton, now known as Guangzhou, that my forebears came, like the first wave of Chinese immigrants who sailed to South Africa in the 1870s. Many of them settled in the western reaches of the fledgling mining town of Johannesburg and established what others called Chinatown. By 1904 there were almost 180 Chinese businesses in that part of the city. (See page 000 on the first Chinatown.)

Some 90 years later – nobody knows exactly when – a Chinese noodle-bar owner decided to go east from his premises in Rockey Street, Yeoville, towards Bruma Lake. This visionary proprietor had an instinct about his new quarters on Derrick Avenue in Cyrildene, eastern Johannesburg. He was in the midst of businesses catering to altogether different communities: delis selling bagels and lox, kosher butcheries, Portuguese greengrocers, a Video Vampire movie-rental store, barber shops and dry cleaners that had been run by the same families for years. But the location was good and the dynamics of Derrick Avenue were changing with many of the shops in genteel decline and much of their clientele having moved off to other suburbs, cities, countries and indeed continents. The time was ripe for change.

History too was on the side of the unnamed proprietor and founder. In March 1992, South Africa had inaugurated an informal interest office in Beijing, with the People's Republic of China (PRC) following suit in Pretoria under the guise of the Chinese Centre for South African Studies. Representatives in both offices had diplomatic status and executed full consular duties. Soon after, Pretoria's diplomatic relations with the Republic of China/Taiwan were severed, and vigorous bilateral relations and treaties of all kinds were instituted between Pretoria and Beijing. The effects of diplomatic words were soon to become flesh and blood on Derrick Avenue. The old businesses moved on and another Chinatown established itself, seemingly in a few years, brought about by that bridgehead noodle bar and the third wave of Chinese immigrants to South Africa, who followed the pioneering Cantonese and Moiyeanese, and the second-wave Taiwanese of the 1970s and early 1980s.

Today Derrick Avenue is almost wholly Chinese. A walk down the avenue takes you through, if not always into, another world, because language is the final barrier to entry in this second Chinatown. Here Mandarin is the dominant dialect, reflecting the wider base in the PRC of the new immigrants. There is some Cantonese, in places like the Yat Kee supermarket and in establishments run by immigrants from Guangdong and Hong Kong, as well as a smattering of other dialects.

Aside from the hurdle of language, Derrick Avenue is wonderfully accessible to other senses – sight, smell, taste and touch – all of which are more than delighted by a leisurely visit to the area. On each side of the street are restaurants, dumpling shops, noodle bars, teashops, Chinese greengrocers and general dealers, herbalists, beauty salons and video-rental shops. Signs of change are often pointed and amusing. Yesteryear's barber shops are today's hairdressers and beauty salons, the jaunty barber poles of yore still adorning the outside of new, somewhat related ventures such as the Flora Beauty Salon.

Change within Chinatown itself is frequent and rapid. This month's superb dumpling shop may turn out to be less so in a few months given change of ownership, and vice versa. Liang Wen (Wen Liang in Western-style naming) from Guangxi province, Guangdong's south-western neighbour, has observed the constant ebb and flow of the street. He was chef and owner of one of the area's anchor institutions, Happy Man restaurant, until 2002 when he sold because he wanted to return to China. At the time he also felt the environment was not suitable for the non-Chinese market: 'Now I'm starting my career here over again,' he says.

Liang says enthusiastically of his new restaurant, Long Men (long=dragon; men=gate), on the northern side of Derrick Avenue. 'Everyone has dreams. Who knows where they'll lead us? I enjoy restaurants.'

He believes that the ambience of the area has changed markedly: 'There are many more people. There are great changes in safety and security. While Long Men patrons are still mainly Chinese, the Western market will take off.' Long Men is one of the few Cantonese eateries along the street. It offers *dim sum*, Cantonese speciality snacks, every day, but has particularly varied snacks on weekends. At the other end of Derrick, Southern Flavour and Sun Fat offer Cantonese standards such as roast duck and pork; Cantonese and Hong Kong fare are available at Mei Sin ('delicious') and Mongkok (another good *dim sum* place). But this second Chinatown is more a place for northern Shanghainese and Fujian cuisine. At the very fine Northern Dumpling Shop, at the southern end of Derrick, between the Shanghai Supermarket and Da Sung Hung, you can sample a wide range of steamed dumplings.

Across the road is Yat Kee (literally 'diary' and hence has connotations of daily shopping), arguably the best-stocked grocer along the strip (though the newish Tang Ren Wan Jia wholesaler at the other end of the street has lovely displays of spices, condiments and grains). On the pavement near Yat Kee, at an ubiquitous street food stall, you can try rice-flour puff cakes and *yow char gwai* – devil's tails – which taste a bit like vetkoek, but come shaped like thin baguettes.

Moving northwards at the intersection with Lionel Street you'll come across more open-air vegetable sellers, seafood shops, the Xian Ying Meat Shop, a credit bureau, Chinese medicine store and Xiang Wai, which specialises in that very saline Shanghai delicacy, fish balls. Directly across the road is the famed Fisherman's Plate, among the best purveyors of seafood in the country.

Beyond Lionel the shops thin out, but as you continue to drift northwards and cross Janelia and Hettie streets, you'll come across hairdressers, travel agents and medical clinics, some based in houses. Just after Hettie, on the left-hand side going north, are a pastry shop and a breakfast place, neither with English signage. If you're in the mood for a traditional, salty southern Chinese breakfast of *congee*, stop in at the latter.

While on the subject of signs in English: treat these with caution. Some (not those named in this article) have no bearing whatsoever on the business conducted within: they have simply been left over from a previous tenant. This applies also to some of the Chinese signage in the area.

The most beautiful calligraphy in Derrick Avenue is without doubt that which graces the Ching In dumpling shop. The work of a real master, it aptly advertises an excellent eatery. Ching In ('Forever Peaceful') is the old name for Xi'an, site of the 2000-year-old, life-size terracotta warriors. You can't miss this dumpling emporium: it is in the large, somewhat misshapen white building that dominates the northern end of the avenue, and is between Tang Ren Wan Jia and the sign for an internet café (whose denizens frequent the dumpling shop during breaks from their screen lives).

Over the road from Ching In is my favourite sign in a street blessed, and cursed, with many. Alien Financial Management is really a forex bureau, but you'd be forgiven for coming up with other interpretations because any journey down Derrick Avenue transports you to a world far removed from Joburg and South Africa. Second Chinatown is not quite the world of China in one street, but it provides fine samples of many aspects of the vast Middle Kingdom.

Darryl Accone is the author of *All Under Heaven: The Story of a Chinese Family in South Africa* (David Philip).

The suburb of Cyrildene was originally owned by the Bezuidenhout family, which applied to establish a township named Northcrest (the name was rejected because it was too similar to that of Northcliff). In 1937 the area was purchased by Finbourough Estates and named after a land speculator named Cyril Cooper. Cyrildene's streets were named after relatives and friends of the township owners – such as Hettie Street, named after Hettie Finger, the wife of Mr WH Finger (of Finborough Estates).[8]

Stands in Troyeville (named after surveyor Gustav Arthur Troye) were advertised in the August 1889 issue of *The Digger's News*. The sale notice read: 'with an abundant supply of water and good available soil each standholder competing with the other in horticulture, this placed will bloom like a Garden of Eden'.[9] Mahatma Gandhi lived in Troyeville in the early 1900s; decades later, the suburb retained its cosmopolitan, bohemian identity, attracting artists and activists of all races. Like any intended Eden, there were occasional poisonous intruders to be reckoned with: on May Day in 1989, Troyeville resident David Webster, an academic and activist, was gunned down in front of his house on Eleanor Street; Webster's partner, Maggie Friedman, later helped create a beautiful memorial mosaic on the property's front walls. Webster's killer, a covert government operative named Ferdi Barnard, was sentenced to life imprisonment for the assassination in 1999.

In recent years, Troyeville's close proximity to spreading inner-city slums and so-called 'red line' districts (areas where banks would no longer grant mortgages – prompting further disinvestment and decay) has seen many of its picturesque Victorian semis and villas lose their lustre; but it is hoped district improvements for the 2010 World Cup (Troyeville is up the hill from Ellis Park and the Johannesburg Athletics Stadium) will have a positive knock-on effect on this much-loved suburb.

One of Troyeville's beautiful old houses

Ellis Park Lake

PLACES TO VISIT

Ron's House. In the early 1960s, Scientology founder L Ron Hubbard spent several months living in Johannesburg – during which time he developed much of the structural and organisational aspects of Scientology today. Hubbard's house, on the Linksfield Ridge in Cyrildene, has been carefully restored to exactly the way it was it was when Ron was there, including the original bust of Ron sculpted by artist Coert Steynberg, the same bust that today stands in every Scientology organisation. For information, go to www.lronhubbard.org.

PLACES TO VISIT

• The atmospheric **Troyeville Hotel** (25 Bezuidenhout Avenue) offers traditional Portuguese fare, and is famous for its prawns – and its great views across the city (from the outside pub). Call (011) 402 7709 or go to www.troyevillehotel.co.za.
• The **Spaza Art Gallery** (19 Wilhelmina Street) is a venue for art, music, poetry, theatre and dance – and a very special Sunday Lunch (cooked by 'our very own local celeb cooks'), served every Sunday at 14h00. For information go to www.spazaart.co.za or call (011) 614 9354.

Ellis Park

Cricket had the Wanderer's Club; but it wasn't until the late 1920s that rugby had its own home in Johannesburg – Ellis Park, named after the City Council's JD Ellis.

The sports ground was built in just eight months, on an old quarry and garbage dump in Doornfontein. The first test match was played in June 1928, against the All Blacks; significantly, even in these pre-apartheid years, the New Zealand team's two Maori players were not included in the line-up – a practice that continued until 1970, when a boycott (by the New Zealand Rugby Union) forced the South African government to treat Maori players as 'honourary whites'.

In 1979 the original stadium was demolished and a larger, more modern stadium was constructed in its place – the one which stands today. Ellis Park was the venue when South Africa won its first Rugby World Cup final in June 1995. Today Ellis Park is the home ground of the Lions and the Orlando Pirates Football Club, and is also the premier venue for concert events in South Africa.

Ellis Park (Coca Cola Park), is currently undergoing major renovations in preparation for the 2010 World Cup – the upgrading is also being extended to the surrounding suburbs, including Doornfontein.

THE WORKING

'Let no one attempt a midnight exploration of the Brickfields without a lantern which is guaranteed to throw a light for yards distant, otherwise the chances are that he will not leave that district alive...'[1]

Newspaper report in *The Star*, 10 February 1890

In this chapter

☞ The Mineral Revolution

☞ The Melting Pot that Became a Frying Pan

☞ Joburg's Poor Whites

☞ The Birth of Newtown

☞ Fietas, Vrededorp and Pageview

☞ Gandhi's Johannesburg

☞ Sophiatown and the Freehold Suburbs

CLASS WEST

A shopkeeper in Vrededorp, 1967

Museum Africa, Johannesburg. PH2006.

The Mineral Revolution

The discovery of minerals in the latter part of the 19th Century reshaped the social, economic and political landscape of post-colonial South Africa. Kimberley, the site of alluvial diamond discoveries in 1867, became Africa's first industrial hub – in 1882 it became the first town in the southern hemisphere to install electric street lighting. To service the busy diamond fields, new networks of railways were created across the interior; and port facilities in Cape Town, Durban, Port Elizabeth and East London were upgraded to cope with increased traffic and trade.

The 'mineral revolution' transformed South Africa's largely agricultural economy, as black labourers deserted farms in search of work on the mines and 'agrarian capitalism' (prompted by the growing urban areas' demands for fresh produce) saw the consolidation of larger commercial farms, replacing subsistence-level smallholdings.

In the same year as gold was discovered on the Rand, the Dutch Reformed Church called for a conference to investigate what it referred to as the growing armeblanke or 'poor white' problem.

Almost without exception, these poor whites were Afrikaans-speaking; many were unskilled farm workers – bywoners or tenant farmers (sharecroppers) – who had been evicted, and had migrated to urban areas in search of work.

While white poverty was 'not unheard of during the first two centuries of white colonisation in South Africa'[2] the 'severe poverty' of poor white Afrikaners had become a problematic issue by the 1880s – and continued to be so until the 1930s and beyond, ultimately contributing to the rise of Afrikaner nationalism and the election to power of the Herenigde Nasionale Party – the National Party – in 1948.

Several factors contributed to the sudden prominence of poor whites in South Africa. The first was the concept of 'relative poverty' among the white Afrikaner population. Urbanisation and industrialisation meant that certain sectors of white society had begun to earn money and advance, socially and financially, in a short period of time. This highlighted the inequality between the growing middle class and the always-poor rural or lower classes. 'Relative poverty' asserted that, while actual living conditions had not worsened, the improvement in living conditions of other white people created the perception of increased poverty by comparison.

The turn of the century also saw a real increase in absolute poverty – with greater numbers of white families earning less money or with less access to income, food and housing. Poor whites at the time 'tended to find scapegoats for their situation and thereby implicated the "capitalists, the Jews, the locusts and the droughts."'[3] Afrikaner nationalists also blamed (variously) the British, the South African War and the Rinderpest epidemic of 1896.

Boer (or Afrikaner) education was another factor limiting prospects of employment or advancement. The Boers' strong Christian faith and knowledge of the Bible meant many men were literate, but any formal education was almost solely religious in nature, and they lacked practical and industrial skills. Until 1910, the state also made it mandatory for lessons to be conducted in High Dutch. This was a disadvantage in Johannesburg, where the language of commerce was English.

Working Class West

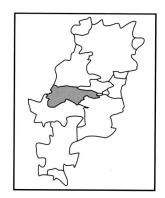

Walter Sisulu
Botanical Gardens

Little Falls

Kloofendal
Nature Reserve
Kloofendal

Northcliff

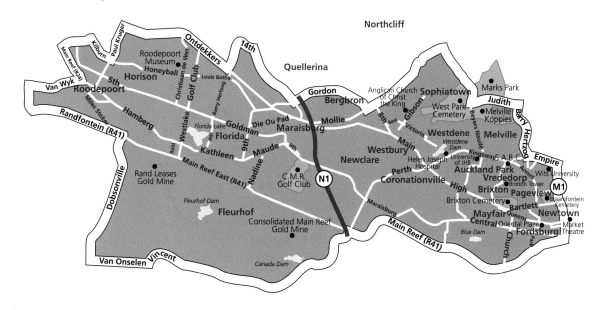

Quellerina

Roodepoort
Museum
Honeyball
Horison
Roodepoort
Louis Botha
Hamberg
Randfontein (R41)
Dobsonville

Rand Leases
Gold Mine
Fleurhof Dam
Fleurhof
Consolidated Main Reef
Gold Mine
Main Reef East (R41)
C.M.R.
Golf Club
N1
Canada Dam
Van Onselen **Vincent**

Goldman
Florida
Kathleen
Maude
Nadine
Florida Lake

Gordon
Bergbron
Maraisburg
Mollie
Die Ou Pad
Newclare
Maraisburg
Main Reef (R41)

Westbury
Perth
Coronationville
High
Helen Joseph
Hospital

Anglican Church
of Christ
the King
Sophiatown
West Park
Cemetery
Westdene
Westdene Dam
University
of JHB
Auckland Park
Vrededorp
Brixton
Brixton Cemetery
Mayfair
Central
Blue Dam

Marks Park
Judith
Melville
Koppies
Melville
S.A.B.C.
Empire
Brixton Tower
Wits University
M1
Braamfontein
Cemetery
Pageview
Bartlett
Queens
Oriental Plaza
Newtown
Market
Theatre
Fordsburg

125

Brickfields in 1889

Poor education may also have contributed to the continued implementation of outdated and unsuccessful farming practices, which meant that the effects of the country's droughts, locust swarms and later the Rinderpest epidemic (in which an estimated 2,5 million head of cattle were lost) were poorly managed and more keenly felt. The viability of many rural farms was further hampered by Roman Dutch inheritance laws, which frequently saw sustainable large farms divided among male heirs, into unsustainable smaller plots.

For all these reasons, the city of Johannesburg in particular saw a rapid increase in poor, unskilled and unemployed Afrikaner residents in the last decade of the 19th Century.

The problem was worsened by the poor whites' unwillingness to take on 'kaffir work' – manual, menial low-paid jobs that many of the inherently racist white community felt were suitable only for black workers. This extended to work on the mines: most of the skilled labour was undertaken by British or European miners with experience gained in their countries of birth. The unskilled Afrikaner workforce was largely unwilling to take on the remaining positions available, above and below ground – or, alternately, was unwilling to do so for the low wages the mine owners were able to pay similarly unskilled black labourers.

The poor whites may have been without income, but they were not without access to political resources: from the very early days of Johannesburg, groups of indigent and unemployed Afrikaners successfully lobbied their government (as citizens, they were entitled to vote) for various concessions, aid and assistance.

In 1887, a number of poor whites petitioned Paul Kruger for the right to settle in the marshy area west of what is now Harrison Street, in a section next to the Fordsburg Spruit. The Spruit area (part of the original farm of Braamfontein which had been purchased by the ZAR government, and was used as a source of water for the mining camps) had no gold deposits; but the muddy soil yielded clay, and the former bywoners saw the opportunity to apply their limited skills and earn an income by producing bricks for the rapidly growing settlement of Johannesburg.[4]

The area soon acquired the name Brickfields. Poor burghers (Afrikaner citizens) could purchase a brickmaker's licence from the government for just five shillings a month. The same concessions were not available to non-whites.

By 1895 the number of new buildings erected in Joburg had reached an all-time high and brickmaking was rated the third-largest industry in the Transvaal, after mining and farming. Brickmaking became an easy entry point for other unskilled workers – black Africans, Europeans, Indians, Chinese and Cape Malays – who flocked to the area, working under white bosses. By the late 19th Century, sizeable locations – the 'Coolie Location' (Indian or Asian location), 'Malay Location' (referring to the mostly Muslim Cape Malay people living there) and an adjoining 'Kaffir Location' (black location) – existed alongside the 'white' Brickfields.

The marshy ground on which Brickfields was situated was not the ideal location for a bustling, congested settlement: the clay digging pits often filled with pools of stagnant water, building and housing were unregulated and haphazard, and health inspectors began expressing concerns about the area's poor sanitation and hygiene. The area attracted the nickname 'Poverty Point'.

The land around the Brickfields attracted the authorities' attention for another reason: Joburg's growing population and the demands of the mining industry had made it necessary to expand the city's existing railway capacity – and the city needed the Brickfields land for a marshalling yard, and other railway facilities. Despite protests and objections from the suburb's Afrikaner residents, between 1892 and 1898 most of the original Brickfields area was appropriated by the government and handed over to the Netherlands Railway Company.

White burghers were resettled in an adjoining section of land named Burgersdorp ('citizens' village') – which was also known as Veldskoendorp after the Afrikaner style of footwear. This was situated in between the original farm of Randjeslaagte, the suburb of Fordsburg (established in 1887 for white miners) and the existing 'Coolie Location'.[5]

Although alternate brickmaking venues were found (in particular on the farm Waterval, 15 km north-west of the city) the move, with its increased transport costs, and followed by the general economic downturn caused by the South African War in 1899, effectively heralded the end of small-scale Afrikaner brickmaking in Johannesburg.

PLACES TO SEE

In 2005 the City of Johannesburg launched the **Brickfields Housing Project**, a mixed-income residential housing development at the foot of the Nelson Mandela Bridge and on the site of the original suburb of Brickfields.

A joint venture between the Gauteng government and the private sector, was the project the first such development in the inner city in 30 years.

The new Brickfields housing development

Sheltered Employment

Poor white children living in a garage in Vrededorp in the 1950s

In addition to the allocation of designated poor white areas like the Brickfields, Burgersdorp, Fordsburg and Vrededorp (where Afrikaners were given substantial discounts or allowances on rental and, later, on home purchase), the ZAR government made several attempts to allocate work to its poorer constitutents: the early ZAR police force (known as the Zarps) only employed burghers; other Afrikaner men were able to find jobs within the civil service – although low levels of literacy and poor education hampered both the placement and the advancement of poor whites.

Before the extension and completion of railway services to and within the Rand, many Afrikaners found work as transport riders (using their oxen and a wagon to transport goods, food, and even coal between towns) while others worked within the urban limits as horse-drawn cab drivers. However, in the face of improved technology and outside competition, neither trade proved sustainable. The first to fall away were the transport riders, made largely redundant by the completion of Joburg's rail links with the rest of the country and the East African Coast. Although Joburg's first electrical tramway was not introduced until 1906, the cab drivers too faced uncertain income prospects – driven by the city's own recessions and booms, as well as attempts by the government to fix or reduce transport prices at various times.

According to the historian, Charles van Onselen, 'In the end the demands of an expanding capitalist economy assured the economic demise of transport riders, cab drivers and brickmakers alike.' The years 1986–7 were key in the movement of Afrikaners into the urban working class and the start of large-scale Afrikaner unemployment in the urban areas. Afrikaners strongly resisted being pushed down the urban road into the working-class'. Though 'militant demonstrations … The poor of Vrededorp extracted concessions in the form of charity, relief work or white labour experiments from the mine owners, the municipality and the state.' One example of relief work was the digging and building of the Main Reef Road (1898–9), built with white labour from poor suburbs. Afrikaners lobbied for, and obtained, better wages on relief work projects, a fact which explains why many did not remain for long in the 500 unskilled mining jobs reserved for poor white men by the mining industry in 1897.[6]

Out of a combination of fear and compassion, businessmen and philanthropists set up the Rand Relief Committee specifically to supply charity aid to poor whites. Tensions cooled – briefly – until the outbreak of war in 1899. Almost overnight, businesses shut down and many of the Afrikaner men left the city to join their commando units. Women and families were left behind without income and, importantly, without even the support of the aid organisations, which had stopped operating due to the War. The Afrikaner suburbs' residents were barely able to contain their anger and resentment at their situation – a fact of which the British were very aware. Before the War had ended, the British had succeeded in either imprisoning or deporting several hundred of the poor white areas' 'undesirable' residents. The new governing authority had also identified the poor white suburbs as a potential troublespot that needed to be defused, with its residents redistributed.

After the end of the War, the needs and demands of poor whites continued to play a formative role in the

PLACES TO SEE

The **James Hall Museum of Transport** (at Pioneer's Park, Rosettenville Road, La Rochelle) is South Africa's largest land transport museum – the exhibits run from animal-drawn carriages and carts through to the country's early trams, motor cars, buses and trains.

The museum is open on Tuesday to Sunday, from 09h00 to 17h00. Entrance is free.

For more information, you can call (011) 435 9718 or (011) 435 9485/6/7, or go to the website at www.jhmt.org.za.

development of Joburg's (and South Africa's) political and economic policies. The provincial and municipal authorities regularly made attempts to create employment opportunities – including, at one point, retrenching hundreds of black city council labourers and replacing them with unemployed white workers… who were paid up to three times the same wage for doing exactly the same task. As one commentator noted:

'The economic interests of the white workers who could vote triumphed over the economic interests of the country as a whole.'[7]

Aid organisations – many of which are still in existence today – under various names and with various functions, also continued to provide handouts and assistance to whites.

By the 1930s and 1940s, the poor white problem appeared to have lessened – not, historians note, because of any government or aid strategies but, more likely, because of South Africa's continued economic growth and strength.

Poor whites, however, continued to play an important political role – from the miners' strikes of 1907 and 1922, to the foundations of various political movements that ultimately resulted in the success of the National Party in the country's 1948 elections.

The Rand Revolt

THROUGH
THE RED REVOLT
ON THE RAND

TWO SHILLINGS & SIX PENCE   PUBLISHED BY 𝕿𝖍𝖊★Star

Because of the large number of miners and working men living in and around Fordsburg, (white) trade unions had become active in Johannesburg's central western suburbs. A number of the unionists were attracted to the spirit and ideals of socialism and communism – with those espousing the latter referring to themselves as 'Reds'. In the early 1920s, these trade unions led an ultimately violent strike campaign against the government, known as the Rand Revolt (or the Red Revolt), which culminated in a series of pitched battles and sieges across the emerging suburbs of Johannesburg.

In 1920 a sharp drop in the gold price led to mine owners announcing their intention to not only lay off thousands of workers (white and black), but also to remove the colour bar – allowing (lower-paid) black workers to assume some of the skilled positions previously reserved for whites.

By the end of 1921 sporadic strikes had become commonplace, but there had been no coordinated mass action by the unions. In January 1922, however, a strike in the Transvaal's coal mines spread to the Rand's gold mines and, subsequently, to allied trades such as foundries and electrical workers. By February talks between the various parties had broken down, resulting in violent mob action through the streets of Johannesburg. A general strike was called for Monday 6 March. By the Wednesday, the strike had turned into an open revolution in a 'bid to capture the city',[8] with white workers attempting to capture Joburg's post office and power station.

At the same time, the 'Red' commandos appropriated weapons from other miners and planned their advance against the police and government defence force.

On Friday 10 March, Johannesburg was shaken by the sounds of explosions signalling the advance of the Red commandos. 'Brakpan was already in the hands of the rebels, and pitched battles were raging between the strikers and the police for control of Benoni and Springs.'[9] In Brixton, 1500 rebels surrounded 183 policemen and laid siege to them for 48 hours. The Union Defence Force was called out, as well as the fledgling South African Air Force. Planes flew over the suburbs, dropping supplies for the besieged forces in Brixton, and bombing the rebels surrounding them.

Martial law was proclaimed, but battles continued to be fought across the Rand – from Doornfontein, where a detachment of the Imperial Light Horse was attacked at Ellis Park, all the way to the East Rand.

Between 12 and 14 March the government's military forces regained control of the city – attacking and imprisoning over 2000 rebels on Brixton ridge, relieving besieged police garrisons, and finally bombarding the strikers' stronghold at Fordsburg Square. The Revolt's two communist leaders, Percy Fisher and Henry Spendiff, committed suicide.

On midnight of 18 March, the revolt was declared over – with the Defence Department issuing a statement that it had been a 'social revolution' organised by 'Bolshevists, international socialists and communists'.[10] More than 200 people had been killed, and as many as 1000 injured.[11]

After the Revolt, white miners went back to work – at wages 25 to 50 per cent lower than before. Black workers were allowed to take on semi-skilled positions, under white supervision.

In the next general election, the white workers voted against Prime Minister Jan Smuts's government, ushering in a Nationalist-Labour joint government, which proceeded to entrench job reservation for white workers, formalising the colour bar.

Witbank platoon in the trenches at Kazerne

 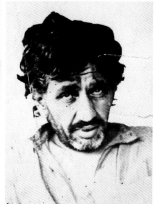

The burnt-out Fordsburg Police Station (left) and an unnamed strike leader (right), believed to be a Russian Jew

READ MORE

The Rand Revolt: The 1922 Insurrection and Racial Killing in South Africa by historian Jeremy Krikler (Jonathan Ball Publishers) offers a thorough appraisal of the Revolt, and the events leading up to it. It also explores the previously little-researched role of racism; and the part played by women in the action.

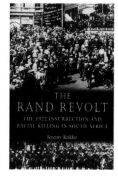

The crater left by the blast in Braamfontein. In the background are up-lifted train tracks.

The Braamfontein Blast

The high-density population the western suburbs turned out to be a liability for a very different reason in 1896: on 19 February, ten railway trucks loaded with a reported 55 to 80 tons of blasting gelatine (used in dynamite) exploded in the Braamfontein railway area. The blast – leaving a crater nine metres deep and 61 metres wide – was heard up to 40 km away, and killed as many as 130 people, injuring hundreds more. President Paul Kruger, who came from Pretoria immediately on hearing of the disaster, apparently wept when shown the bodies of the unidentified adults and children.[12] 1500 homes were destroyed and windows all over town were shattered. Casualties were greatest in the nearby Malay Location and Brickfields areas. A commission of enquiry was subsequently unable to conclusively establish the reason for the explosion – it was suggested, but never proved, that the dynamite had either spontaneously exploded after being left in the sun for too long, or that a collision with a shunting engine had caused a spark that ignited the load.

The Birth of Newtown

By the early 1900s the British governing authority – not unlike the preceding ZAR government – had identified Brickfields, Burgersdorp and part of Fordsburg for demolition and redevelopment. A survey of the area, carried out in August 1902, revealed that 5651 people lived within the 172 acres under consideration. This was 'made up of 2206 kaffirs, 636 Cape Natives [Cape Malays] and 1001 Dutch and other Whites'.[13]

Bordered by a refuse site on one side, and 'night soil' collecting sumps on the other, the area was intensely crowded and poorly drained. Combined with the extreme poverty of its inhabitants, these conditions led to the development of slums. There was also the perceived danger of 'racial intermingling' – clearly, the cause of no small alarm to governing authorities – and the threat of what Joburg's Randlords and ruling classes thought of as the growing mass of unemployed, disgruntled poor whites.

In accordance with the widely held desire to redevelop the land and redistribute its population, the council-appointed 'Insanitary Area Improvement Commission' recommended that the whole area be demolished and re-built – for health reasons.

The recommendation was not effected immediately. White landlords were making a profitable existence through high rentals and sub-lets (often to black, Indian, Malay and Chinese tenants), and objected to the suburbs' destruction. Even after the landlords had been bought off, the remaining poor white residents objected to being resettled.

In 1904 the council was finally provided with the excuse to act – with an (alleged, but never proved) outbreak of bubonic plague. Overnight, the residents of Brickfields and the 'Coolie Location' were removed; the entire area was fenced off, buildings were doused with paraffin and torched by the city's fire department. The blaze reportedly burned for three days.

The locations' black inhabitants were moved to a 'temporary camp' next to the sewerage farm of Klipspruit, about 19 km from Johannesburg. For many, unable to secure work permits or find alternate accommodation closer to town, the relocation turned out not to be temporary after all; the site become known as Nancefield

Burning the 'Coolie Location', 1904

Butchers at the market, Newtown

and, later, Pimville (named after Councillor James Howard Pim for his 'work among the Native population'[14]). It would become one of the first suburbs of Soweto.

Many of the Indian evacuees did return successfully, moving into the Malay Location which appeared not to have been affected by the plague – and was one of the few central suburban areas 'non-whites' were legally allowed to occupy.

Burgersdorp's white Afrikaner residents resettled in the neighbouring suburb of Vrededorp ('Peace Village'), land initially used as a black location before poor Afrikaners petitioned President Kruger to set it aside for their use, at a special price.[15]

In place of Brickfields and the 'Coolie Location' rose Newtown – perhaps the first example of urban regeneration in Joburg. Developed to house a variety of trades and light industry, Newtown gradually became home to the town's fresh produce and livestock markets, relocated from the original Market Square in 1913.

The new market building was divided into two sections – 'out-of-hand' sales on the top level and municipal auctions on the lower one, together with a further 40 to 50 shops on the hall's sides, doing business in 'fresh meat, fish, dried fruits, dairy produce, greengrocery, tobacco and many other lines'.[16] Crowds of more than 8000 people attended the market on a busy Saturday morning.

In addition to the market, the city's first coal-fired power station, turbine hall and cooling towers (these were demolished in 1985), the electric workshop (built to house the turbines for the city's tram systems), and a shed to house and repair the city's trams, were constructed in Newtown.

In the early 1960s the volume of business began to become too large for the Newtown market; a new site was found five kilometres to the south of the CBD, at City Deep, from where it continues to operate.

 'The cry of "wildy" – meaning a stampeding ox – will generally cause the crowd to rush off in a panic, in the course of which its members are likely to do far more damage to each other than the animal at its worst.'
– Allister Macmillan, *The Golden City*

The Newtown Cultural District

In the 1980s, much of the Newtown area fell into decline – including the popular Market Theatre (see below). However the area is now the subject of a major urban renewal scheme, with Newtown designated as the city's official 'Cultural Precinct'; today, Newtown is home to a growing number of cultural, office and residential developments.

In 1976 two visionaries – Barney Simon and Mannie

Manim – converted the old Indian market buildings into the legendary Market Theatre complex (at 56 Margaret Mcingana, formerly Wolhuter, Street). Funded entirely by donations from the private sector (until the 1990s), the independent Market Theatre openly defied the Group Areas Act, welcoming actors and audiences of all races. It became known as South Africa's 'Theatre of the Struggle', showing the works of playwrights like Athol Fugard, Mbongeni Ngema, Welcome Msomi, Zakes Mda, Percy Ntwa, Gibson Kente, Pieter-Dirk Uys, Paul Slabolepzy and Deon Opperman, among others.

Like that of many other developments in and around the CBD, the Theatre's future seemed uncertain in the mid-1990s; luckily, it survived the inner city slump and – with a little financial help from the Arts and Culture Trust, the Rockefeller Foundation, the Swedish/South Africa Culture Fund and the National Lottery – continues to develop and showcase powerful, South African theatre. The Market Theatre has three theatres and a gallery as well as the Market Theatre Laboratory and Photo Workshop. Two restaurants – the acclaimed Gramadoelas and the funky African-inspired chain, Moyo – are on the premises, and there is a small flea market and retail area in front of the Theatre's main entrance.

For more information, go to www.markettheatre. co.za or call (011) 832 1641.

Some of South Africa's most astonishing collections of historical images, artefacts and oddities are housed in the archives of Joburg's Museum Africa (at 121 Bree Street). Unfortunately, many of the exhibits never make it out of storage and onto display – freezes on hiring new personnel and lack of funding mean that only a small portion of the museum's massive display space is used at any given time, while some displays have been left unchanged for years. History buffs and knowledge-seekers should try to contact the museum's curators directly, as certain collections not on display can be viewed by appointment. There is also a small but interesting craft shop on the premises.

For more information, contact (011) 833 5624.

The former wagon site in front of the old market buildings was renamed Mary Fitzgerald Square in 1939, in honour of the first woman trade unionist in South Africa who played a key role in the miners' strike of 1910. The Square boasts the biggest outdoor LED screen in Africa, and hosts a number of major cultural events in Newtown, including the annual Joy of Jazz Festival and the city's official Diwali (Indian festival of lights) celebrations.

The carved heads, visible throughout the Square and surrounding blocks, were manufactured from disused railway sleepers by Newtown artists.

Built in 1927, Turbine Hall originally housed Johannesburg's first coal-fed power station; although declared a heritage site, the distinctive industrial buildings gradually fell into disuse and became derelict and run-down – the central building was used as housing for a number of squatters – until the early 2000s, when the property was earmarked for a new tenant: AngloGold Ashanti. After significant construction and development, and some sensitive demolition, AngloGold moved in to its new premises in 2007.

The Sci-Bono Centre (on Miriam Makeba Street, between President and Jeppe) is the largest science centre in Africa, housed in the building previously known as the Electric Workshop. The 6000 m^2 space – exhibitions are aimed at learners of all ages – includes interactive displays, an education centre and science and technology hubs.

For more information, visit www.sci-bono.co.za or call (011) 639 8400.

Launched in 1995 to mark the centenary of South African Breweries, the World of Beer recently received a R20-million upgrade – not suprisingly, the affordable tour through '6000 years of brewing history' (the admission price includes two free beers) is a popular Newtown attraction, going back in time to a turn-of-the-century pub in Joburg's mining camp and a traditional shebeen in Soweto. For bookings and information, go to www.worldofbeer.co.za.

Once a parking garage for the city's trams and buses – it operated from the late 1930s until the 1990s – the recently renovated Bus Factory (at 3 President Street) is now home to the Johannesburg Development Agency, as well as a handful of private office tenants. The striking space also features a craft shop and a gallery.

A previous compound for black municipal workers who served the city's electricity department, the Worker's Museum and Library now houses a museum commemorating the experience of the compound dwellers and the history of African migrant workers, and a library boasting an impressive collection of labour-related materials. Access to the museum is from the Sci-Bono Centre parking area.

Opened in 2003, the Metro Mall (between Simmonds, Sauer, Ntemi Piliso and Gwigwi Mrwebi streets) is a striking transport and retail hub developed around Joburg's public transport users – more than 150 000 commuters go through the space each day. The Mall has an integrated transport facility for about 3000 vehicles, and operates over three levels; facilities include a food court, and over 600 informal trader stalls; there is also public art on display, from sculptures to murals. The volume of human traffic, combined with the sometimes

The new Market Square and market buildings in Newtown, 1914

Mary Fitzgerald Square today

volatile taxi industry, make this a destination to be approached with some caution. Group visits with a guide are recommended.

Newtown's New Street Names

In October 2004, ten of Newtown's streets were renamed.

- Becker Street became Gerard Sekoto Street, after the world-famous artist.
- Minaar Street was changed to Mahlathini Street – named after Joseph 'Mahlathini' Nkabinde, who is perhaps best known for his work with the Mahotella Queens.
- West Street became Ntemi Piliso Street, after the 1950s jazz musician Bra Ntemi, who started the Alexandra All Star Band.
- Park Road was renamed Barney Simon Road, in honour of the late co-founder of the Market Theatre.

- Bezuidenhout Street was renamed Miriam Makeba Street, after the legendary singer.
- Avenue Road was renamed Dolly Rathebe Road, after the leading jazz vocalist and actress.
- Sydenham Street became Noria Mabasa Street, after the renowned Venda sculptress.
- Pim Street was renamed Gwigwi Mrwebi Street, after the 1950s alto sax player known as Bra Gwigwi.
- Goch Street was renamed after iconic news reporter, 'Mr Drum' Henry Nxumalo.
- Wolhuter Street was renamed after another songstress, Margaret Mcingana, whom many South Africans will remember as the voice behind the haunting theme to the epic television series, *Shaka Zulu*.

Fietas, Vrededorp and Pageview

Vrededorp (Fietas), 1967

Colonial and pre-apartheid South Africa invented and appropriated a variety of (often confusing) racial and ethnic classifications.

Whites were divided into Uitlanders (foreigners) and burghers.

'Malays' generally referred to 'Cape Malays', people descended from South Africa's earliest Muslim immigrants (who were brought to the Cape, initially as slaves, by the Dutch East India Company in the mid to late 17th Century). Today there is much debate as to whether or not to use the designation 'Malay', and many people of Malay origin prefer to be known simply as Cape Muslims.

Blacks were referred to, variously, as 'Africans', 'Natives' or 'Kaffirs'.

The term 'Coolie' was loosely applied to almost every other 'non-white' person – including coloureds (people of mixed race, distinct from black 'Africans' and 'Malays'), Indians (Hindu and Muslim immigrants from India, as opposed to those from Malaysia or the East Indies) and Joburg's early Chinese and Japanese residents (the latter were considered honourary whites, the former were not).

Although the arrival of Johannesburg's earliest Indian and 'Malay' settlers is less documented than that of their white counterparts, their presence is noted almost from the very start of the city. The first 'Malay Camp' was set up in 1886, in the locale of Ferreirastown; where a tent was reportedly pitched, solely for the purpose of daily prayers.

In 1894, repulsed by the wild and 'ungodly' ways of early Johannesburg, the Malay community send a deputation to President Paul Kruger asking for a new settlement 'far away from Ferreirasdorp and far away from pig-eaters, liquor drinkers, brothels and shebeens,' where they could develop spiritually and morally.[17] 'Oom Paul', as he was known, allocated a large piece of ground next to Vrededorp. This became known as the 'Malay Location'.

Distinct from the Muslim 'Malays' from the Cape, Joburg's early Indian community included former indentured workers (mainly Hindus, originally brought in to work on the Natal sugar plantations) who had travelled to Kimberley and, subsequently, the gold reefs in search of new opportunities; as well as the later 'passenger' or free Indians (mostly Muslims, particularly from Gujarat) who had paid for their own passage from India. The latter group consisted of many traders who had come to South Africa with the express intention of taking advantage of the country's rich business opportunities.[18]

Although Indians were prevented from owning land in the city centre (these plots were reserved for whites), permission was given them to purchase plots on the city's less-desirable outskirts – this later became known as the 'Diagonal Street area', a mixed commercial and residential district.

After the plague scare of 1904, the original 'Malay Location' became home to many of the city's working-class coloureds, Indians, blacks and Chinese. The area was known as 'Fietas' (the origins of the name have never been determined) – and was home to a vibrant, diverse community.

Fietas 'comprised twenty-six parallel streets and 352 residential stands, on almost all of which were erected four cottages. Each comprised two rooms, a kitchen and a communal toilet and bathroom.'[19] 14th Street was known for its bustling trade. Mixed-use buildings, with stores on the ground floor and residences above, were a common feature of Fietas architecture, and contributed to the busy commercial and communal lifestyle.

Whites lived in the area north of 11th Street, in the section of Vrededorp sandwiched between the Braamfontein and Brixton cemeteries; as these poor Afrikaner residents became increasingly politically active, they began to lobby for the removal of their 'non-white' neighbours. The co-mingling of Indians, coloureds and black people in Fietas was also a source of concern to the government's urban planners who, in line with ruling party policies, wished to see clear residential segregation in place – not just between black and white, but between the defined different racial groups (which had collapsed into the more streamlined designations of 'black', 'Indian' and 'coloured').

In the end, the Johannesburg Municipality determined that the Fietas area should be set aside for the exclusive use of Indians. Fietas' coloured residents were moved to the suburbs of Coronationville (Coronation Township) and Albertville.

In 1943 the area was renamed Pageview, after then-mayor Mr JJ Page.

Following the National Party's 1948 election victory, the government renewed its attempts to relocate Fietas' Indian community. After the Group Areas Act was passed in 1950, new land – situated 25 km south-west of the city – was purchased and zoned as an 'Indian' area. This area, originally called Lenz, was renamed 'Lenasia'.

Between 1957 and 1970, Pageview's non-white residents were issued with eviction orders. Most often, the people living in Pageview simply ignored the notices and carried on with their lives. In 1976, however, following over a decade of unsuccessful eviction attempts, the government began with forced removals from the area. By 1978 almost all trace of Fietas had been erased – with the exception of a small group of Indian families who refused to move. In 1981 just 67 Indian families remained in the area, illegally. The following year, the first white families were given leases in Pageview. Nevertheless, it was not until as late as 1984 that Pageview's last Indian trader (a butcher, Baba Saheb)[20] was successfully evicted.

Although the council's intention was to develop Pageview into an exclusively white area, the planned demolition and redevelopment of the suburb (as happened in nearby Sophiatown, and District Six in Cape Town) was never completed. The drawn-out decades of forced re-movals and residents' resistance left the suburb pitted with empty plots, half-demolished buildings and several original structures (including two mosques, on 15th and 25th streets, and a church – all of which are still in use). As a result, only a small portion of the suburb was habitable.

In the late 1990s, over 300 land claims were submit-ted for the area – the resolution of which inevitably held up any redevelopment plans. A Fietas Heritage Trust was also established to monitor proposed developments in Pageview and neighbouring Vrededorp.

❝❞ BEING THERE

'We have a variety of people living here – from Pakistan, Bangladesh, Syria and now even from other parts of Africa. The lovely thing about all this is that everyone brings a bit of their culture, and it's all blended and works well together here in Fordsburg. We have what we call the "the square", which is the hub of commercial activity. Here you will find different shops owned by people of different nationalities. Fordsburg was always multilayered and very cosmopolitan, and in that sense it hasn't changed much. It's a very mixed culture, and it makes you see a different side to South Africa.'
–Essop Bahana

👁 PLACES TO SEE

The **Oriental Plaza** in Fordsburg was first envisioned in the late 1960s – as an 'Indian Commercial Centre' designed to offer an alternative retail venue to the shops and traders located on Fietas's 14th Street. Opened in 1974, it was initially boycotted by Indian shop owners who did not want to move their businesses from Fietas.

It was not until 1977, after several clashes between Fietas traders and the police, followed by legal battles and damages claims against the Johannesburg City Council, that the traders reluctantly agreed to give up their premises and move to Forsdburg.[21]

Today, the Plaza retains much of its originally intended 'bazaar' quality: it's a thriving centre populated by hundreds of stores, selling everything from traditional Indian clothing and spices to designer-label fashion and footwear, homeware, luggage and fabric.

The Plaza complex is situated in Fordsburg, near the Market Theatre precinct and Mary Fitzgerald Square. Pay-parking is available at the Plaza, and trading hours are 08h00 to 17h00 during the week and 08h30 to 14h00 on Saturdays. Most stores shut down for prayers on Fridays, between 12h00 and 13h00.

For more information, view www. orientalplaza-fordsburg.co.za or call (011) 838 6752.

The Oriental Plaza

Gandhi's Johannesburg

Gandhi recuperating after being attacked, 1908

Mohandas K Gandhi, Indian-born and English-trained barrister, arrived in South Africa in 1893 – hired by a Durban trader, named Abdulla Haji Adam Jhavery, to represent his interests in a court case against a rival businessman in Pretoria.

Still in his early twenties, young Gandhi was apparently unaware of South Africa's existing racial prejudices and discriminatory legislation. His unexpected (and unpleasant) early encounters with state-sanctioned racism were to transform and shape the rest of his life. As a new arrival, Gandhi was thrown off a train between Durban and Pretoria (he refused to leave the 'whites only' first class carriage); denied lodgings at Johannesburg's Grand National Hotel; and, on another occasion, was assaulted for walking on a footpath reserved for whites.[22]

After concluding his court case, Gandhi elected to remain in South Africa for a time – pressed into providing legal advice and assistance for the Indian community in Natal – and eventually forming the Natal Indian Congress in 1894.

In 1896 Gandhi travelled to India to fetch his family; on his return to South Africa, his published exposé of the conditions under which South African Indians were forced to live attracted significant negative sentiment from Natal's white population.

Such feelings ran high in the rest of the country too, particularly in the Transvaal where a combination of 'traditional' racism together with the perceived threat of economic competition (to white business, from successful Indian traders) resulted in an almost farcical number of anti-Indian laws. As British subjects, Indians were initially entitled to possess property in the Zuid Afrikaansche Republiek's Transvaal. By 1885, however, laws were put in place prohibiting Indians from owning land or trading outside locations specifically set aside for that purpose. In addition, a 9 p.m. curfew was introduced (Indians required a pass to walk on the streets after such time), and they were not allowed to sit next to white people on the city's trams.[23]

The ZAR government also, at various times, imposed immigration restrictions and quotas specifically aimed at preventing the entry of Indians into the Transvaal.

During the South African War, Gandhi – a loyal British subject – organised and led the Indian Ambulance Corps, working as a stretcher-bearer and administering help to the injured. He was awarded a medal for his services.

In 1902 Gandhi travelled to India again, returning to South Africa in 1903 and settling in Johannesburg, where he established a small law office at Court Chambers, No. 15 Rissik Street (between Marshall and Anderson streets).

**Henry Polak, Gandhi and Sonja
Schlesin (front row)**

For a short time Gandhi lived in a room behind his offices, before moving to a family home in the suburb of Troyeville with his wife and children.[24] This house can still be seen today, at 11 Albermarle Street.

1906 saw the publication of the Draft Transvaal Asiatic Law Amendment Ordinance, which would add new conditions to the original Law of 1885. The Ordinance required all 'Asians' (Indians and Chinese persons) 'to obey three rules: those of eight years or older had to carry passes for which they had to give their fingerprints; they would be segregated as to where they could live and work; new Asian immigration into the Transvaal would be disallowed, even for those who had left the town when the South African War broke out in 1899 and were returning.'[25]

On 11 September 1906 over 3000 people attended a meeting, chaired by Gandhi, at the Empire Theatre on the corner of Commissioner and Ferreira streets (the theatre, sadly, no longer exists), to discuss the Ordinance. Gandhi called on all of those present to agree to a policy of non-cooperation with the Ordinance – whatever the penalties might be.

'The meeting heard me word by word in perfect quiet,' Gandhi wrote, years later, recalling that night. 'Other leaders too spoke. All dwelt upon their own responsibility and the responsibility of the audience… and at last all present, standing with upraised hands, took an oath with God as witness not to submit to the Ordinance if it became law. I can never forget the scene, which is present before my mind's eye as I write.'[26]

The Indian community's campaign of resistance became known as *Satyagraha* – more than simply 'passive resistance' (which, the community felt, failed to convey the active and vital nature of their methods). The Hindu phrase literally meant 'clinging to truth'; 'opposing falsehood'; and 'good versus evil'.

The benevolent force of *Satyagraha* would influence Gandhi in the work he later undertook in his birth country of India.

The campaign was joined by most of the Transvaal's Chinese community; and, by the end of the compulsory registration period (after which, the Ordinance implied, non-registered Asians would be expelled or imprisoned) only 511 out of a population of over 13 000 had registered.[27] Some of those who had registered had done so in ignorance rather than defiance – like the Chinese labourer, Chow Kwai For, who, only recently arrived in Johannesburg, registered almost immediately. When he

The mass meeting at the Hamidia Mosque, Newtown

**Martyrs Valliamma Munusamy Mudaliar (left)
and Nagappen Padayachee**

realised what he had done, he committed suicide. His grave, with his letter of apology (written in Chinese) engraved on the headstone, stands in the Chinese section of the Braamfontein Cemetery.[28]

The Transvaal government tried numerous ways of stopping the campaign – Gandhi and others were arrested and jailed in what is now Constitution Hill; many *Satyagrahis* were deported back to India.

In the end, compliance was secured only through deceit: the Transvaal Secretary, Jan Smuts (who would later become prime minister) entered into negotiations with Gandhi while he was in prison, offering to repeal the law… if the Indian and Chinese communities registered voluntarily. Gandhi, perhaps naively, agreed (an action that

was unpopular with many of his colleagues – and resulted in Gandhi being beaten up on his way to register).

In the end, Gandhi's optimism proved unfounded: the act was passed, despite the willing registration of thousands of Indian and Chinese persons.

In response, Gandhi called on people to burn their passes and registration papers – which they did, in front of the Hamidia Mosque in Newtown.

The anti-registration campaign, however, had already lost momentum and by 1909, most of the Transvaal Indians had begun submitting to the humiliating process of being fingerprinted.

Gandhi, aware that a sustainable resistance campaign would benefit from some sort of base or headquarters – for training and as a retreat – secured the use of a large piece of land to the south-west of Johannesburg. Named Tolstoy Farm after the writer Leo Tolstoy (an advocate of non-violent resistance), the property was purchased from the city by an architect named Herman Kallenbach, an ardent follower of Gandhi's who placed the land at the disposal of the *Satyagrahis* in 1910. The Farm was run on similar communal principles as Gandhi's Phoenix Settlement in Natal, and daily activities were divided between lessons and farm labour. It was also a place of refuge for the victims of the *Satyagraha* campaign (such as those who had been imprisoned, or lost the ability to make an income as a result of their participation in the campaign) and their families.

After 1910 the *Satyagraha* campaign had largely come to a halt – not because of any improvement in the circumstances of the Transvaal Indians, but rather owing to a sort of inertia caused by months of fruitless negotiations combined with a resigned acceptance of the way things were. This changed in March 1913, when a decision was handed down by the Cape Supreme Court that had devastating consequences for Indian women: the Searle Judgment declared that all marriages conducted under Indian religious law (rather than South African civil law) were invalid. This meant that thousands of women were

Settlers at Tolstoy Farm (left), 1910 and Herman Kallenbach (above)

suddenly no longer considered their husbands' wives, nor were their children entitled to any inheritance.

In one stroke, the South African government had not only given the *Satyagraha* movement the impetus it was lacking – it also meant that, for the first time, women became prominent and active participants in the resistance campaign. One of the most prominent female protesters was Gandhi's wife, Kasturba, who declared she would go to prison rather than be declared an unlawful wife.

Gandhi, supportive of his wife and delighted by the women's involvement, 'pledged that he and the other men would take care of the children and all the household chores if the women went to prison as a result of protesting.'[29]

In September 1913 Kasturba Gandhi, together with three other women and 12 men, defied provincial immigration law (preventing Indians from crossing the border from Natal into the Transvaal without a permit) by catching the train from Durban to the town of Volksrust. The police, at first, made no attempt to arrest the protesters; but after a stalemate of several days, eventually 'deported' all 16 people (by pushing them across a bridge). The entire group immediately made their way back into the Transvaal. This time they were arrested, and sentenced to three months' imprisonment in Pietermaritzburg.

The original group of 16 were soon joined by a contingent of Transvaal *Satyagrahi* men and women – including several women with children and a 16-year-old named Valliama Mudaliar – who deliberately crossed the border into Natal in order to get arrested. The goal was to 'fill the prisons with *Satyagrahis*'.

The arrest of women particularly angered the Indian community. In October 1913, miners in the coal town of Newcastle went on strike – officially in protest over the £3 poll tax imposed on all formerly indentured Indians, but undoubtedly bolstered by the imprisonment of the *Satyagrahi*s. By the month's end, between 4000 and 5000 workers had downed tools.

READ MORE

Eric Itzkin's *Gandhi's Johannesburg: Birthplace of Satyagraha* provides a detailed account of Gandhi's years in Johannesburg – giving insight into how Gandhi's time in South Africa shaped the city, and how his experiences in Johannesburg shaped the rest of his life.

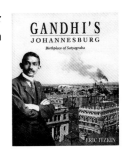

To spread the protest, Gandhi planned a grand march leading the strikers from Natal across the border into the Transvaal. Beginning at 6 a.m. on 6 November 1913, Gandhi was joined by 2037 men, 127 women and 57 children.

During the march Gandhi was arrested and let out on bail three times, but the march continued. Later other leaders were arrested, but still the people marched on.

When they arrived at the town of Balfour, they were greeted by three trains waiting to deport them back to Natal. They were given the choice of getting on the train, or going to prison. The marchers chose prison.

Conditions in the prisons were terrible, and many of the original *Satyagrahi* women who had been arrested suffered badly. Valliamma Mudaliar died of a fever she contracted while incarcerated; another protester, Veer-ammal Naidoo, gave birth to a son the day after she was released from her three-month sentence.

However their sacrifice was not in vain: their imprisonment, the miners' strikes and the cross-border march sparked off further strikes and protest action in Natal (some of it, unfortunately, becoming violent), which ultimately forced the government to negotiate. The poll tax was abolished, and Hindu and Muslim marriages were again recognised. The struggle against discrimination had just begun – but the early *Satyagraha* campaign provided a foundation for later national protests.

Gandhi returned to India in 1914.

👁 PLACES TO SEE

Little remains of 'Gandhi's Johannesburg', but it is still possible to see traces of Gandhi and the *Satyagraha* movement if you know where to look.

- The law courts where Gandhi used to work were demolished in the 1940s, replaced by a large bus terminus named Van Der Byl Square. In 1999 the area was refurbished and renamed Gandhi Square (on Rissik Street); there is a statue of Gandhi in the square.
- Gandhi's original house can be found at 11 Albermarle Street, Troyeville. Further down the same street, at No. 19 Albermarle, is a beautifully renovated Art Deco building that was mistakenly thought to be Gandhi's residence and was even granted national monument status.
- All that's left of Kallenbach's Tolstoy Farm are the foundations, marked by a plaque; the site, about 35 km from Johannesburg, is now privately owned by brick manufacturer Corobrik, which has granted permission for the farm to be developed and used as a heritage site. The construction of a museum and a community centre was approved in 2001, but there are no indications as to when the planned development will take place. For more information, go to www.tolstoyfarm.com.
- In 1914 Gandhi unveiled two memorial tablets in Braamfontein Cemetery, to mark two *Satyagraha* martyrs: Valliamma Mudaliar and Sammy Nagappen Padayachee. During the apartheid years, the gravestones were removed or defaced, and it wasn't until the mid-1990s that the sites were rediscovered and restored.
- Lenasia hosts an annual Gandhi Walk in April each year; this community event attracts up to 4000 walkers, including a host of prominent local and Indian dignitaries. The walk is used to generate funds for charities, as well as promote peace and unity. For more information, go to www.gandhiwalk.org.za.
- The Parktown and Westcliff Heritage Trust conduct tours of Gandhi's Johannesburg. Visit www.parktownheritage.co.za or call 011 482 3349.

Sophiatown and the Western Freehold Suburbs

Dancing at the Ritz (1952). Portrait by Jurgen Schadeberg.

In 1897, a businessman named Herman Tobiansky purchased a 237-acre portion of the farm Waterval, to the west of Johannesburg. He named the proposed suburb 'Sophia' after his wife and several of the streets after his children: Edith, Gerty, Bertha, Toby and Sol. The freehold township (suburb) that would become known as Sophiatown was proclaimed in about 1903. Tobiansky planned to sell plots in the 'charmingly located' settlement to Joburg's aspirant working classes – whatever their colour.

In a newspaper advert in *The Star* in February 1904, Tobiansky advertised that Sophiatown was 'freehold' (stands purchased from the city were often subject to 99-year leases; privately owned land was not); that the stands were 'within reach of the means of one and all'; and that the suburb was near Brixton and Auckland Park, and an easy 30 minutes' bicycle ride from the city centre. The ad also promised good soil, 'magnificent view sites' and 'an abundance of water'.

Payment terms were a £10 deposit, with the balance in three, six or nine months – without interest. Upfront cash buyers would receive a discount of five per cent.[30]

But there was a small hitch to the suburb's desirability: Joburg's expanding sewerage works.

By the turn of the century, new 'sanitary deposit sites' had been established in what would later become the Western Native Township (established in 1919, after the sewerage works had been moved and the land filled; today the suburb of Westbury). Polluted run-off from the sewerage pipes also leached into the stream flowing through the centre of nearby Newclare. Both suburbs (also freehold, but earmarked for coloured residents) were within smelling distance of Sophiatown, which meant that the number of white purchasers (who were able to buy or rent in other suburbs) quickly dropped off. As a result, Tobiansky began to sell erven to black, coloured and Indian buyers whose purchase and residential options were far more limited.

The fact that the city's fortunes were largely dependent on the availability of a cheap black workforce didn't make the city's planners and politicians any more comfortable with the idea of so many black, Indian and coloured persons living in such close proximity to Joburg's white suburbs. The planning, placement and existence of black locations within the city limits was frequently challenged – by individuals, by statesmen, by 'concerned' (white) communities… Their objections were outweighed, first by the operational needs of the early mining companies (which required their workforce to be on site, not several kilome-tres away); and, later, by the lack of existing alternative land and housing options (for the growing numbers of black workers – and consumers – that Joburg's economy relied on).

As transport systems improved, from horses and carts to trains and trams, the idea of establishing and maintaining a large black workforce outside the immediate city environment became more economically feasible – and appealing – to the politicians, if not the people.

Three years after the Union of South Africa (1910) and one year after the formation of a new political party – what would become the African National Congress – the South African government passed the Natives Land Act, which effectively allocated just under eight per cent of the entire country for legal black ownership and tenure (on designated Native Homelands). This meant black people were no longer allowed to own (or rent) land outside of these allocated areas, although at first exemption was granted for black persons who had purchased freehold land prior to the Act. As Sol Plaatje later wrote: 'On 20 June 1913 every Native woke up to find himself a pariah in the land of his birth.'[31]

The Native Trust and Land Act, which increased the allocated land to around 13 per cent of the whole of South Africa followed in 1936. The remaining land – over 80 per cent – was for the use of whites, who made up less than 20 per cent of the country's population.

One of the effects of the land acts allocating unsustainable and undesirable amounts and portions of lands for 'Native' use was to drive greater numbers of black labourers to the cities.

By 1934 it was estimated that 26 000 people were living in Joburg's western freehold suburbs alone. The Slums Act of the same year saw the demolition of many of Johannesburg's illegal (and overcrowded) black residential compounds (see the chapter on the eastern suburbs for information on Doornfontein's slums), forcing hundreds of additional workers to seek accommodation in Sophiatown and its surrounds.

Newclare in 1941

Vibrant, cosmopolitan and – most importantly – freehold, early Sophiatown was not necessarily a great improvement on the crowded slumyards of Doornfontein: although stand owners (about two-fifths of whom were black) paid rates for their properties, there was very little real service from the Joburg Municipality. There were no tarred roads, street lighting or municipal water – residents dug and used open wells. Sewerage collection, always a problem for the city, was reportedly haphazard.[32]

Unsanitary conditions were compounded by overcrowding. This was a not just a result of the shortage of available alternative land or locations for black residents, but was also caused by struggling working-class home owners taking in too-large numbers of paying tenants to cover their mortgages.

Yet the proliferation of backyard shacks and huts, the shared toilet and water facilities and the resulting communal washing, cooking and fighting, also served to create a community that was close-knit and caring. Slum or not, from its earliest days Sophiatown became associated with an artistic, cultural and social freedom that would be romanticised by the press, authors and historians over the years.

What the suburb's early residents could not have known was that, within a couple of decades, the South African government would ensure that Sophiatown's entire community – and much, but not all, of its spirit – were dismantled, dispersed or relocated.

Sophiatown had long been a thorn in the government's side – a 'black spot' (as such areas were officially referred to) nestled alongside a number of 'white' suburbs (such as Westdene and Auckland Park). As early as 1944, the Joburg City Council passed a formal resolution to remove the black residents from Sophiatown, Newclare and Martindale, and relocate them to the Orlando-Pimville area, in what would later become Soweto. The intention was to zone Sophiatown for 'Europeans' and Martindale for light industry.

At the time, there was a large backlog in the construction and availability of black housing, together with a lack of suitable transport facilities (to shuttle workers from outlying areas into the city). These factors, combined with the opposition of the Western Areas' black residents to compulsory resettlement, meant that, despite the resolution, the Council took no immediate action.[33]

In 1948 the National Party was voted into power, and quickly made good on its election promises – with a

> **❝❞** *'Whatever else Sophiatown was, it was home; we made the desert bloom; made alterations, converted half-verandas into kitchens, decorated the houses and filled them with music. We were house-proud. We took the ugliness of life in a slum and wove a kind of beauty; we established bonds of human relationships, which set a pattern of communal living, far richer and more satisfying – materially and spiritually – than any model housing could substitute.'*
> *–Excerpt from* Blame Me on History *by Bloke Modisane*

Forced removals, 1955

rapid series of segregationist legislation. In 1949 it passed the Prohibition of Mixed Marriages Act (making it illegal for whites to marry people of other races). This was followed by the Immorality Act in 1950 – which made any sexual relations between the races illegal. 1950 also saw the introduction of the Population Registration Act and the Group Areas Act. The former led to the creation of a national register in which each person's race was officially recorded; the latter simply formalised what the ruling powers had been working towards all along: the right of the state not only to determine which races should live where but also to forcibly move residents from one area to another.

In 1950 a middle-aged, Dutch-born Afrikaner nationalist named Hendrik Verwoerd had been appointed minister of native affairs. Known as the 'architect of grand apartheid', Verwoerd was a firm believer in both the 'superior' qualities of his white race and the enforced separate development (and habitation) of different racial groups. Under his tenure more than 13 additional segregationist acts were passed and implemented. These included acts which removed coloured people from the voter's roll; restricted trained black artisans in the building trade to using their skills in designated 'black' areas only; allowed the Minister to remove black people from public or private land and establish resettlement camps for displaced people; made it compulsory for all black people to carry a 'pass book' (permitting only some to live and work in the city) at all times; implemented a system of 'Bantu education' that ensured sub-standard education for black people; and segregated public facilities and amenities on the basis of race (also stating that facilities provided for the different races need not be equal).

In 1954 Verwoerd also instituted the Natives Resettlement Act. This granted powers to the government to remove black people from any area within and next to the magisterial district of Johannesburg. In effect, the act was aimed at facilitating the removal of black people from Sophiatown to Soweto.[34]

In 1952 the Joburg City Council had began to construct a plan for the removal and resettlement of Sophiatown's residents. The government had purchased land in Meadowlands for this purpose and begun to develop the site for settlement, constructing houses with access to waterborne sewerage facilities and individual taps.

Various black ratepayers' and housing associations in

Resistance, followed by defeat. Photographs by Jurgen Schadeberg.

Western Areas put forward alternate proposals – such as the building of light industrial buffer strips between black and white residential suburbs. But these were ignored.

In early 1955, sixty black families received notice that they were going to have to leave their houses in Sophiatown and relocate to the new location of Meadowlands. The date given for the move was 12 February. Western Areas residents and organisations including the African National Congress issued statements rejecting the notices – and notifying the government of their intention to resist the planned evictions.

Anticipating possible clashes, the government moved its removal programme forward. At 6 p.m. on 8 February, the first group of families were informed that they had just 12 hours to pack their belongings; the removals would begin at 6 a.m. the next day. The notice was accompanied by a ban on all public gatherings, political or religious, of 12 people or more. In defiance, Sophiatown's Father Trevor Huddleston

held his regular church services.

On the morning of 9 February, before dawn, over 2000 policemen arrived, with 80 removal trucks. Any intended resistance was quickly dampened by the sight of the police force's rifles and Sten guns.

PLACES TO SEE

In 2006 Sophiatown's community launched the **Sophiatown Heritage Experience** – which coordinates a mini-museum, and is responsible for collecting historical material about Sophiatown. The museum (situated on the corner of Good and Herman streets, Sophiatown) is open from 09h00 to 12h00, Mondays to Saturdays. The Heritage Experience also has a small number of trained guides who can arrange historical tours of the suburb. For further information, call (011) 673 1271.

The February 21 issue of *Time* magazine carried the following report:

'By noon it was raining heavily. Mattresses, tables and clothing piled high on army trucks got drenched alongside their owners. But the rain dampened resistance, and by 6 p.m. 700 Sophiatowners – many from Toby Street – were lining up at Meadowlands to be issued a garbage can, a loaf of bread and six bottles of soda pop.

'Back in Sophiatown, the armed cops retired, and squads of workmen moved in to tear down the empty houses. All night the sledge hammers pounded while other Sophiatowners watched, knowing that soon it would be their turn, too.'[35]

Between 1955 and 1968, the Resettlement Board moved more than 22 516 families and 6469 single people – some 65 000 people in total – to Meadowlands and nearby Diepkloof.[36]

'After the relocations and demolitions all that remained of Sophiatown were the street layout, the street names, the Christ the King Anglican Church in Ray Street, former ANC president Dr Alfred Bitini Xuma's house in 85 Toby Street (now 73 Toby Street), 33 Toby Street ... and St Joseph's Home in Good Street, now a national monument.'[37]

The suburb was rebuilt and re-named Triomf ('Triumph'). For the next four decades, it housed working-class Afrikaners – a surburb in sharp contrast to the cultured, aspirational and vibrant community of Sophiatown.

Fifty years after the first forced removals, in February 2005, the suburb was officially renamed Sophiatown.

Sof'town Culture and *Drum*

Nowhere is Sophiatown's extraordinary culture better embodied – and documented – than in the pages of the early *Drum* magazine. The title, founded by Jim Bailey in 1951, became the benchmark of compelling, provocative and independent black journalism in Africa. As 'Mr Drum', writer Henry Nxumalo, wrote as follows in January 1956: 'From the coffee plantations of the Gold Coast to the jazz-stung nightspots of Nigeria, from the slow pomp of Uganda's royal ceremonies to the livid frenzy of Kenya's turmoils; in the dreaming hamlets of Zululand; among Cape Town's fun-filled coon life, and Johannesburg's teeming, thrilling thousands – everywhere, every month *Drum* is read and relished.'

The staff writers at *Drum* read like an honours list of young black talent of the era: Todd Matshikiza; Arthur Maimane; Can Themba; Casey Motsisi; Es'kia Mphahlele; Bloke Modisane; Lewis Nkosi; and Nat Nakasa. A young German immigrant, Jurgen Schadeberg, became *Drum*'s staff photographer, instructing and working with future photographic legends like Peter Magubane while simultaneously building up his own remarkable photographic portfolio.

Drum magazine continues to be published in South and East Africa today. The modern editions, however – which were sold to media giant Naspers (Media24) in the 1980s – bear little resemblance to the original product.

Singer Miriam Makeba on the cover of *Drum*, 1957

Archbishop Trevor Huddleston

English-born Anglican Father (later Archbishop) Trevor Huddleston worked in South Africa as a priest and educator for over 12 years (between 1943 and 1956), most of which time was spent serving the community of Sophiatown from the Church of Christ the King. During his time in Johannesburg, Huddleston became one of the most influential white anti-apartheid activists. Prominent in his support for South Africa's fledgling black freedom movements, and outspoken in his criticism of the National Party government's racist policies, Huddleston was an active participant in numerous protest meetings and marches, including the famous Kliptown Conference where the Freedom Charter was signed. In 1956 he published a blunt account of forced removals in apartheid South Africa, called *Naught For Your Comfort*. He was recalled to Britain shortly afterwards.

Abroad, Huddleston continued to rally support for the anti-apartheid movement, a role he maintained until the eventual collapse of apartheid and the release of Nelson Mandela in the early 1990s.

In 1998, Archbishop Huddleston received the Knight Commander of the Order of St Michael and St George on the Queen's New Year Honours list. He chose the designation 'Bishop Trevor of Sophiatown'. Huddlestone died less than a month later. According with his wishes, he was buried at the church in his beloved Sophiatown – his ashes are interred under a large slab of sandstone alongside the church.

Father Trevor Huddleston (top) and the Church of Christ the King

PLACES TO SEE

The **Church of Christ the King** (49 Ray Street, Sophiatown) still operates today – its distinctive tower (now a national monument) one of the few remnants of the 'first' Sophiatown. Many of Sophiatown's original residents now make the journey from Soweto to Sophiatown for the Sunday service.

The nearby St Joseph's Home (once an orphanage) – another historic building saved from the bulldozers – has been renamed the Trevor Huddlestone Memorial Centre (on the corner of Good and Herman streets), and houses a community education and outreach centre. For more information, go to www.trevorhuddlestone.org or call (011) 673 1271.

The Gangs of Sophiatown

From the mid-1940s until the suburb's demolition, Sophiatown became the 'nucleus of organised crime on the Reef'[38] – playing home to a variety of colourful gangs with names like the 'Americans', the 'Russians', the 'Berliners' and the 'Vultures' (the last-mentioned a child gang started by poet Don Mattera). Each gang had its own turf and usually adopted a very specific style of dress – for example, the Americans wore flashy and expensive American styles; the Russians 'wore Basotho blankets over their smart city pants, and smart hats with an ostrich feather.'[39] Each gang also usually worked a specific crime 'niche': the Americans were sometimes called the 'African Robin Hoods' because they commonly stole goods from (rich) whites and re-sold them in the locations at much cheaper prices. The Berliners were known to be well armed, and specialised in crime such as extortion, robbing and raping.[40]

South Africa's prohibition laws – restricting the sale of alchohol to black people – also saw a number of illicit shebeens (drinking places) spring up in Sophiatown. According to the suburb's former residents there were different grades of shebeens, based on the 'quality' of the drinker – there were rough shebeens; shebeens meant only for the suburb's journalists and cultural elite; private shebeens for intellectuals (at Can Themba's House of Truth)… Some of the most famous 'joints' were the 39 Steps, in Good Street, run by Fatty Phyllis Petersen; and the Back of the Moon in Gold Street, immortalised in the song of the same name.

The Western Area gangs gradually developed and used their own 'patois' – a loose mix of English, Afrikaans and South African languages that came to be known as *Tsotsitaal*. The word 'Tsotsi' (which also means a gangster) was apparently derived from a popular style of narrow-bottomed trouser worn by young black men in the 1940s. In time, this style was used to refer to young, black working-class urban men in general – and was increasingly associated with the growing thug and gang

Sophiatown's artists

If *Drum* was what Sophiatown read, jazz was what it listened to. Heavily influenced by the American music and culture of the late 1940s and early

Gideon Nxumalo

1950s, Sophiatown's jazz clubs saw the birth of sensational groups, whose early members included musicians like Dollar Brand (Abdullah Ibrahim), Kippie Moeketsi (Newtown's famous Kippies Club is named after him), Hugh Masekela and Jonas Gwangwa; nurtured the talents of composers Todd Matshikiza (*King Kong*) and Gideon Nxumalo (*African Fantasia*); and featured iconic performers like Dolly Rathebe and Miriam Makeba.

Sophiatown's streetlife also inspired one of South Africa's first prominent modern black artists: painter Gerard Sekoto, who lived in Sophiatown for several years before going into exile (in Paris) in 1947.

cultures on the Witwatersrand. The word '*taal*' is the Afrikaans word for 'language'.

In *Tsotsitaal*, Sophiatown was known as *Kofifi*, Western Native Township was called *Die Kas*, and Newclare *Maglera*.

Tsotsitaal is still spoken today. Commonly known (and used) words include *babalaas* (meaning a hangover); *cherie* (pronounced 'cherry', referring to a girlfriend); *heita* (hello); *mahala* (obtained without having to be paid for); *mampara* and *moegoe* (variously, a fool or person who is not streetwise).

For an in-depth look at the language and its uses, you can read Louis Molamu's *Tsotsitaal: A dictionary of the language of Sophiatown* (University of South Africa Press, 2003).

The gates to the Hindu crematorium in Brixton

Mining headgear in Roodepoort

How the West was Won

Brixton, named after the suburb in London, was apparently recommended to the government for purchase – to provide grazing for the cattle of Johannesburg. About 500 stands on 'Brixton Estate' went on sale in January 1903, boasting a number of 'Charming View Sites … equal to, if not surpassing, the picked View Sites of Parktown'. The Brixton Ridge, overlooking the gasworks, was once the site of a monument to Irish soldiers who fought on the side of the Boers in the South African War (the Second Anglo-Boer War). The dilapidated monument was apparently relocated to the Afrikaner town of Orania. During the 1922 strike, Fordsburg was shelled by guns from the Brixton Ridge.[41]

The Brixton Cemetery (entry on Krause Street, Vrededorp), facing the headquarters of Johannesburg's Police Flying Squad, is the final resting place of a number of high-profile Johannesburgers, including: miner Samuel 'Taffy' Long, who was executed (wrongly, many believe) after the 1922 Rand Revolt; Randlords George Albu and Lionel Phillips; and trade unionist and city councillor Mary Fitzgerald, after whom Mary Fitzgerald Square in Newtown is named. Joburg's first Hindu Crematorium was also built on the grounds of the Brixton Cemetery in 1918. In 1956 the wood-burning crematorium was eplaced with a gas-fired crematorium, which is still in use today.

Roodepoort
by Carolina Geldenhuys

The Struben brothers weren't the only prospectors working in the west. In 1885, a year before the main reef was discovered, a prospector named Jan Bantjies secured prospecting rights on the farm Roodepoort (named 'Red Valley', after the red colour of its soil); he discovered gold on the farm in 1886. Gold was also discovered on Abraham Petrus Marais' farm of Paardekraal in the same year. In the Staats Courant (Government Gazette) of 15 September 1886, along with the farms that became Johannesburg, the farms Paardekraal, Vogelstruisfontein and Roodepoort were proclaimed a goldfield. Between 1886 and 1888 four mining towns, Roodepoort, Florida, Hamberg and Maraisburg, developed on the three farms. The population there increased rapidly and the mining industry continued to progress.

The first form of local government in the area was the Goldfields Diggers Committee, formed in 1886 to represent the farmers' interests. Dr Hans Sauer was elected as representative for the area of Roodepoort-Maraisburg.

In 1902, after the South African War, a health board was appointed by government; and in 1903 the Roodepoort-Maraisburg Urban District Board was established. In 1904, the District Board was made a municipality. In 1925 the Town Council bought Florida Lake from the Bantjies Gold Mining Company. It is still a favourite picnic spot.

On 1 October 1977 Roodepoort was granted city status and 'Maraisburg' was dropped from its name.

Today Roodepoort is part of the city of Joburg and is known primarily as a residential area with suburb names such as Kloofendal ('Cliff and Valley'), Helderkruin ('Clear Summit'), and Ruimsig ('Wide view'), all inspired by the hills and valleys typical of the area. Mining pioneers are honoured in street and suburb names such as Fredenharry Street in Strubens Valley and Honeyball Avenue in Discovery; and, of course, Ontdekkers Road ('Pioneers' Road'), extending all the way from Johannesburg to Mogale City.

PLACES TO SEE

- **The Old Gaol and Warder House** (Seventh Avenue, Florida) was built towards the end of the 19th Century and is believed to be the only remaining building in Roodepoort that was used for government purposes during the ZAR period. The gaol now houses the offices of the local Red Cross Society.
- Roodepoort's **Old Municipal Offices** (Berlandina Street) were the first permanent offices of the Municipality of Roodepoort-Maraisburg, built in 1906 and used for this purpose till 1936.
- The **Walter Sisulu Botanical Gardens** (Malcolm Road, Poortview) are one of South Africa's eight botanical gardens and consist of almost 300 hectares of both landscaped and natural veld areas. The Witpoortjie Falls in the middle of the Garden has been a favourite picnic spot since the late 1800s. In addition to the botanical life, the gardens are also home to over 230 species of birds, including majestic Verreaux's (Black) Eagles, reptiles and small mammals. The gardens are open daily from 08h00 to 18h00 (no entry after 17h00). Entrance is free on Tuesdays for senior citizens. For more information call (011) 958 1750 or go to www.sanbi.org/sisulu/mainpage.
- In 1972 the **Kloofendal Nature Reserve** was created by the City Council, who set aside 150 hectares in the suburb of Kloofendal as a

protected wilderness area. In 2004 the city reintroduced small game into the park, including mountain reedbucks, duikers, small antelopes and hyraxes (dassies) – the last-mentioned partly for the Verreaux's Eagles nesting in the Walter Sisulu Botanical Gardens. The Reserve is open daily from sunrise to sunset, between the months of September

The Witpoortjie Falls, Walter Sisulu Botanical Gardens

and April. To book for a guided walk of the Reserve, call (011) 674 2980.

- The **Roodepoort Museum** (Civic Centre Building, Christiaan de Wet Road) was closed in April 2006 as a cost-cutting measure – but the community fought against the closure and the museum was re-opened in November 2007. There are over 1500 items on display at the Museum, including a complete early Voortrekker house, a Victorian parlour, a 1920s lounge, and artworks by Jackson Hlungwane, Irma Stern and Walter Battiss. The museum is open by appointment only. Call (011) 761 0225 for information.

JOBURG'S

Chapter Seven

'Jo'burg City
That is the time when I come to you,
When your neon flowers flaunt from your electrical wind,
That is the time when I leave you,
When your neon flowers flaunt their way through the falling darkness
On your cement trees.'

Mongane Wally Serote, *City Johannesburg*

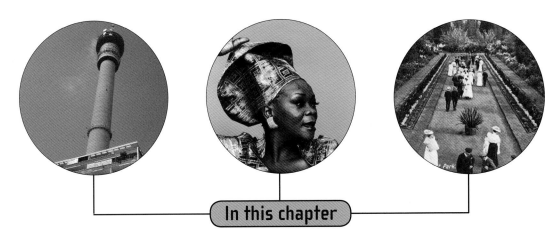

In this chapter

☞ High Rise, High Density

☞ Transition: Modernism to Bohemian

☞ The 'Greying' of Hillbrow

☞ Brenda Fassie's Hillbrow

☞ Joubert Park

☞ Joburg's Hollywood

FLATLANDS

Children playing in a park overlooking Hillbrow

High Rise, High Density

Aerial view of Hillbrow in the 1950s

It's almost impossible to truly conceive the millions upon millions of individuals who live in today's urban sprawls: 11,1 million people in Cairo; 12,6 million people in Buenos Aires; nearly 20 million people in Mexico City ... Tokyo is the most populous city, with an urban residence of over 35 million people.[1]

Johannesburg, with its comparatively modest 3,3 million inhabitants, still ranks among the 100 largest cities in the world. Its population is about the same size as that of Ankara, Athens, Berlin, Milan or Rome. Except, of course, that Johannesburg is a mere 120-odd years old while Berlin dates back to the 12th Century; Athens and Ankara have been inhabited for over 3000 years; Rome and Milan only marginally less (they were founded in 750 BC and 400 BC respectively).

Close on a million of Joburg's residents are crammed into the greater Soweto area, to the south-west; around half that number fill the wider spaces of the city's ever-expanding northern suburbs. And an estimated 250 000 people live in apartment buildings (or 'flats', as they're colloquially known) in Joburg's central high-density zones: Bellevue, Berea,

Braamfontein, Hillbrow and Joubert Park, as well as the fancier suburbs of Rosebank and Killarney.

Hillbrow, Berea and Joubert Park form a virtually contiguous zone that stretches from De Villiers Street in Johannesburg's CBD to the Randjeslaagte Beacon in the north, and Joe Slovo Drive in the east.

Once desirable, cosmopolitan suburbs, Joburg's inner-city flatlands are now considered little better than urban slums – dirty, neglected and heavily populated by African immigrants. Urban renewal projects are slowly changing this; but while suburbs like Braamfontein have become favourites with property developers and urban hipsters, Hillbrow and its surrounds are still considered no-go areas by most outsiders.

In contrast, Killarney and Rosebank have remained (mostly) upmarket. In the past, these suburbs were considered the domain of blue-rinsed grannies; today they're the residences of choice for wealthy young couples and singles (of all ages and races) who love the proximity to the city combined with the apartments' relatively large spaces.

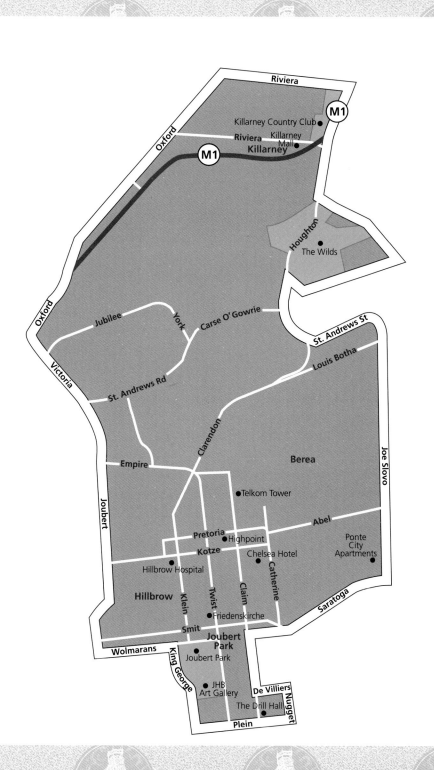

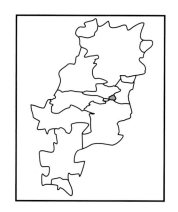

Riviera

M1

Killarney Country Club

Oxford

Riviera

Killarney Mall

Killarney

M1

Houghton

The Wilds

Oxford

Jubilee

York

Carse O' Gowrie

St. Andrews St

Victoria

Louis Botha

St. Andrews Rd

Clarendon

Berea

Empire

Joe Slovo

Joubert

Telkom Tower

Abel

Pretoria

Highpoint

Ponte City Apartments

Kotze

Chelsea Hotel

Hillbrow Hospital

Hillbrow

Klein

Twist

Claim

Catherine

Saratoga

Friedenskirche

Smit

Joubert Park

Wolmarans

Joubert Park

King George

JHB Art Gallery

De Villiers

Nugget

The Drill Hall

Plein

N

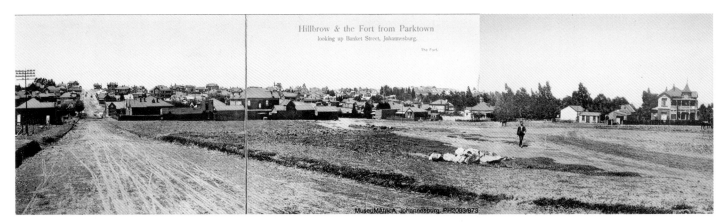

Hillbrow and the Fort, seen from Parktown, 1890s

Hillbrow – An Elite Suburb

At 10 a.m. on 24 July 1895 a crowd of eager buyers stood in the warm winter sun, bidding for what the newspapers referred to as 'Johannesburg's chief and most fashionable suburb in the near future': the Hillbrow Residential Estate, situated on the top (the 'brow') of a hill at the apex of the portion of land once known as Randjeslaagte.

The auction had been advertised for some weeks in the *Standard & Diggers' News* (a paper part-owned by one Emanuel Mendelssohn who, coincidentally, was also involved in the company that owned the land), and attendance was good – prospective purchasers had been visiting the site for weeks, admiring Hillbrow's grand views of the Golden City.

With land selling at a premium in the 'older' residential suburbs of Doornfontein and Jeppestown, Hillbrow, situated between the planned Berea Estate and increasingly wealthy Parktown, proved to be both affordable and desirable. The area was also described as the 'healthiest … suburb of Johannesburg', a statement one must assume was at least partly true: it was, after all, located close to Hospital Hill, the site of the original Johannesburg General Hospital (which later became known as the Hillbrow Hospital).

The limited number of stands were sold without reserve, and under the strict condition that no store, canteen or any other business be conducted out on the grounds – with the exception of one set of stands reserved for an hotel.

By one o'clock, 210 stands had been snapped up for a record £32 000.

Transition Zone

In the early decades, Hillbrow was considered a semi-rural suburb – residents had their own horses and stables on their properties. But between World Wars, as the demand for housing increased, the Johannesburg Council gradually allowed a few multi-storey apartment blocks to be erected.

In December 1932, after much debate and strong resistance, South Africa abandoned the gold standard (a system whereby printed currency was matched by real gold reserves); although the currency fell in value, the overall effect on South Africa – and particularly Johannesburg – was to initiate a major economic boom.

In the centre of the city, a significant number of Art Deco-style buildings had already gone up. Hillbrow, however, took its cue from the reactionary work of a French modernist named Charles le Corbusier – whose concept of the house as a 'machine for living in' contrasted strongly with the decorative elements of Art Deco.

The champions of Le Corbusier, and modernism, were a collective of architects known as the Transvaal

Duchess Court, Berea

Group (or 'Le Groupe Transvaal', as Le Corbusier named them), led by an architect and academic named Rex Martienssen.

Martienssen and his colleagues (including Gordon McIntosh and Norman Hansen) had been introduced to the ideas of modernism by their lecturer at Wits University, Stanley Furner. In the early 1930s, Martienssen made several tours to Europe – eventually meeting with Le Corbusier himself – bringing concepts, ideas and designs back to Africa, where they implemented several fine examples in the changing suburb of Hillbrow.

Guided by Le Corbusier's principles, the Traansvaal Group created distinctive buildings – the style became known as the Hillbrow vernacular, and typically included: '… freestanding rounded, cylindrical or kidney-shaped pilotis at marbled entrances; large projecting sun-trap balconies; extensive north-facing fenestration with framed inset windows in the facebrick end-walls; beam and column construction in reinforced concrete; and, at rooftop level, the dormitory slums of the black proletariat.'[2]

The Group's design work was so successful that its members won international acclaim, including acknowledgment from Le Corbusier himself.

Although many of the pre-war buildings have been demolished or significantly renovated, the use of pilotis can still be seen on buildings in Bruce Street and Paul Nel Street, and at Marlene Mansions in Abel Road (designed by one of Martienssen's students, Harold le Roith). Reading Court (1936–37) on Louis Botha Avenue is raised on pilotis and has verandas so large as to compete with traditional South African stoeps.

In 1946, the Johannesburg Council removed restrictions on building heights. This paved the way for an explosion of high-rises – between 1945 and 1965, the number of apartment buildings increased by 250 per cent.

After the Second World War, Le Corbusier's modernism was gradually supplanted by the increasingly popular designs of Brazil's Oscar Niemeyer and France's Auguste Perret.

Both men were known for working in reinforced concrete; both had connections with Le Corbusier – who had worked in Perret's studio, and consulted with Niemeyer on a government construction in Brazil.

Many of Hillbrow's buildings adopted Brazil's style of *brise-soleil* (sun shades) – vertical or horizontal louvres attached externally to windows to shade the house from the tropical sun. Santa Barbera in Ockerse Street and Brow Hill in Pietersen Street are good examples.

Niemeyer and Perret were important architectural figures in that they designed far more than iconic buildings: they conceived cityscapes. Niemeyer designed structures for Brazil's incredible capital Brasilia; Perret completely refigured the French port city of Le Havre, following its destruction during the War. Both cities are UNESCO World Heritage sites today.

For a brief period, the skyline of Hillbrow was considered equally impressive: 'nowhere in England, … Europe or North America, can such a consistently up-to-to-date neighbourhood be seen,' gushed the *Architectural Review.*[3]

Modern buildings in Hillbrow   **A view of the Telkom Tower**

Swinging Hillbrow

In the 1960s, South Africa enjoyed an economic boom. Despite the withdrawal of foreign investors after the Sharpeville protests (in 1960), the apartheid government took strong measures to rebuild confidence in investments and the stability of the state. Attracted by high returns on capital, foreign investment in South Africa more than doubled between 1963 and 1972. During the same period, large numbers of white professionals were recruited from all over Europe: France, Germany, Britain … The country's white population increased by more than 50 per cent in the same period – drawn by the healthy economic conditions, and the need for skilled labour (which, as a result of the Bantu Education System, black South Africans were largely unable to fill).

Hillbrow, with its cheap rents, short leases and proximity to the airport, became a transit point for the new wave of migrants.

As large numbers of foreigners settled in Hillbrow, it acquired a cosmopolitan Bohemian character. European-style corner cafés and 'Continental' coffee shops were established – Café Kranzler, Café de Paris and Café Wien. A speciality news agency and book shop, Estoril, opened

at the corner of Pretoria and Abel streets, carrying a wide range of German and French magazines. This combination of Continental tolerance and contemporary politics nurtured a subculture that incorporated elements of 'swinging London' and America's hippie culture. Hillbrow's clothing stores sold bell-bottom jeans, winklepicker shoes, platform heels and shirts in psychedelic colours.

Hillbrow Records – at the time, South Africa's largest record store – kept the latest acid rock, and it was possible to spend an afternoon listening on earphones to Bob Dylan or Jimi Hendrix.

Hillbrow became South Africa's answer to New York's Greenwich Village, London's Soho District and California's San Francisco. Hippies established South Africa's first indoor fleamarket in the basement of a Hillbrow building, selling everything from lovebeads to tie-dyed T-shirts and incense.

By the early 1970s, all traces of 'rural Hillbrow' had been removed – the last detached residences were replaced with high rises in 1973. A new building style had also become popular: gigantism. In a relatively short space of time, a number of very tall buildings were constructed including Highpoint (30 storeys), Ponte (54 storeys – or 173 m) and the dramatic cliff-face buildings Tygerberg and Highrise.[4] Highpoint had its own 24-hour supermarket, 333 flats, 64 shops and 81 offices, while Ponte once boasted a ten-pin bowling alley. The tallest of them all was the JG Strydom Tower (the Hillbrow Tower), standing at 270 m – making it the tallest structure in South Africa.

The Hillbrow Tower (officially known as the Telkom Tower), located on the corner of Goldreich and Banket streets, is possibly the most distinctive feature of Joburg's central city skyline – next to Ponte.

Built as a telecommunications signal tower, the building was completed in April 1971 at a cost of about R2 million. At the time, it was a massive engineering project: a laser beam was used to ensure that the tower went up perfectly vertically; construction went on six days a week, 24 hours a day. The first 178 m of the tower went up at an average of 18 cm each hour …

At the top of the tower, visitors could explore six public floors – including a revolving restaurant called Heinrich's, which could seat 108 people. The floor revolved anti-clockwise, at between one and three turns an hour. If the restaurant was full, there was an alternative Grill Room with its own bar and lounge. The tower also featured an exclusive VIP room, decorated in a Louis XVI style, available for special private functions.

Finally, there was a public observation deck that could accommodate 200 people, providing a 360-degree view of the city through 24 large windows.

Special structural techniques (including a 42 m-deep foundation) reduced sway at the building's apex from several metres to just 41 cm; the signal mast, which had been lowered into place by helicopter, had a sway of 86 cm.

The Hillbrow Tower was closed to the public in 1981, for security reasons, and is now used only by Telkom employees.[5]

The nearby Sentech Tower, in Brixton, is slightly shorter – at just 240 m.

The distinctive Ponte building (entrance on Lilly

Base jumping off Ponte

Avenue, Hillbrow) was completed in 1975, costing a cool R11 million. The architect, Rodney Grosskopff, said that Ponte was originally built to provide low-cost housing – but the building's location, height and distinctive hollow structure made it a highly desirable address at the time. Each of its 470 apartments (including 6 penthouses) came furnished, and the views were unparalleled.

Because of its size – Ponte rises 173 m into the sky, and consists of 54 storeys – the architect and construction crew had to overcome several challenges in designing and completing the building. Ponte is built into the ground rock (some of which is still visible at its base); owing to a fault, the rock had to be plugged with concrete and reinforced with steel girders – one of which slipped, killing a construction worker.

Each of Ponte's floors took two weeks to complete, and the entire building took around two years to construct. To combat the great gusts of wind travelling up and down the building, all the windows had to have special seals and only sliding windows were used. The open inner core ensured each room had access to natural light, a building requirement at the time.

As Hillbrow declined in popularity, so did Ponte; the

A church group prays on a hilltop overlooking Ponte

Ponte's interior

building gradually became overcrowded and untidy. In the 1990s, it became synonymous with Hillbrow's criminal elements – hitting its lowest point in 1998, when it was suggested that Ponte be turned into a massive prison (the proposal was rejected).

In 2007 Ponte was bought by a pair of private investors and an ambitious renovation project has been planned for the entire building including converting the existing accommodation into a number of luxury apartments. The centre will also include a gym and entertainment complex. For more information, go to www.new-ponte.co.za.

A Grey Area

In the 1960s, South Africa's overall economic growth rivalled that of Japan's. In the decade that followed, internal and international events conspired to create a very different scenario. The two oil 'shocks' – in 1973 and 1979 – together with generally high (and volatile) oil prices prompted a worldwide recession. In South Africa

this was coupled with an over-reliance on gold exports to strengthen the economy, and increased international condemnation of the country's apartheid policies. The latter led to a number of notable global concerns divesting themselves of their South African business interests.

The Soweto Uprising in June 1976 prompted further capital flight, and an even sharper decline in foreign investment. Immigration from Europe dried up, and many foreign residents opted to return to their home countries; young white South Africans – no longer assured of immediate financial 'good times' – were choosing to live at home for longer. In 1977 military conscription (compulsory for white men over the age of 18) was increased from a period of 12 months to two years, taking even more young men out of circulation.

The combination of these factors created a surplus of accommodation in the flatlands of Hillbrow.[6]

At the same time, conditions in Joburg's designated coloured and Indian areas were becoming uncomfortably overcrowded. The solution was obvious, and only slightly

Street scenes from Hillbrow photographed by Jurgen Schadeberg

hampered by the Group Areas Act legislation restricting Hillbrow to 'whites only'. Frequently making use of white 'fronts' to legally rent the properties, Indian and coloured tenants began moving into the suburb.

While the government was not prepared to grant legal status to 'non-white' residents, it was apparently willing to turn a blind eye to what was gradually termed the 'greying' of Hillbrow. Periodically, there would be arrests, fines and evictions – an attempt to reassure the white electorate that things were still being managed. But the transition continued. The most notable effect of the apartheid laws was to drive up the price of rentals: Indian, coloured or black families living illegally in the suburb would have to pay up to twice the monthly amount landlords were asking from white residents in the same block. Initially, the added cost of living was absorbed by the relatively affluent middle classes who moved into the suburb – and enjoyed the prestige of cosmopolitan Hillbrow and its proximity to the CBD, where many of them worked. Later, the exorbitant rentals would lay the foundation for what would quickly deteriorate into slum conditions – as tenants took in additional sub-tenants in order to share the cost. But that possibility was far from the minds of the model Indian, coloured and black tenants who arrived first.

By 1979 several community organisations had been established to oppose evictions solely on the premises of the Group Areas Act. By 1981 there were an estimated 4000 Indian families living in Hillbrow.[7] By 1983 Actstop (the Action Committee to Stop Evictions) reported there were between 8000 and 12 000 'illegal' residents in Joburg's inner city, the majority in the Hillbrow area.[8]

For Hillbrow, the turning point had already been reached.

Up to 1982, the majority of people of colour who moved into the white spaces of Johannesburg were middle class;[9] by 1985 and 1986 – the height of the States of Emergency – it was black working classes who, driven by acute housing shortages and political turmoil in the townships, 'felt they had no choice but to move into the relative calm and "better" accommodation to be had in the inner city'.[10]

At the same time, a number of businesses (including the Joburg City Council) had decentralised, moving away from the heart of the CBD to its fringes – in Braamfontein, or close to Newtown – or to the new business districts of Sandton, Eastgate and Randburg.

Urban geographer and author, Keith Beavon, explains that 'the overwhelming majority of the African people who came to live in the central city area were either low-income earners, under-employed, or even unemployed people. They sought out the cheapest possible accommodation that was available, and found it in a variety of places. For some it was in the oldest and already deteriorating apartment houses; others found shelter in vacant office space that could no longer be let as such, in empty factory buildings, in the cramped old servants' quarters on the rooftops of tall buildings, and in a number of other nooks and crannies. In the wake of the new arrivals came the hawkers, who set up virtually permanent stalls on adjacent pavements, from where they sold small punnets of fruit and vegetables and other low-cost items needed for everyday living by the new residents.'[11]

With lower-income tenants, landlords either stopped maintaining their buildings – many actively engaged in looting or stripping their own premises – or were unable to afford routine maintenance. The once proud façades of African modernism became worn and broken; services were cut off for non-payment; lifts would stop working – sometimes leaving pensioners trapped in their high-rise apartments.

In 1985, 70 per cent of Hillbrow residents were white. By 1991, this figure was a little over 30 per cent. In the same year, a survey revealed that 35 per cent of Hillbrow's population was living in overcrowded or slum conditions. Banks and lending institutions began to 'redline' Hillbrow and adjacent inner-city properties, meaning that even when buildings or apartments came up for sale, they were excluded from financing.

The Group Areas Act was finally lifted in 1991, but it was too late to salvage any of Hillbrow's swinging past.

After South Africa's first democratic elections, a substantial number of West Africans and immigrants from the Democratic Republic of the Congo poured into the suburb, fleeing persecution and poverty in their own countries. Many of these immigrants could not find legitimate work and became involved in crime. Soon northern Hillbrow became known as 'Little Nigeria'. Hillbrow became renowned for its crime, grime and deteriorated conditions.

As Hillbrow became populated by large numbers of working-class and economically marginalised people, most of the upmarket businesses closed down. These were then either bricked up or were replaced by shops dealing in cheap goods and services. Landmark venues such as Café de Paris closed down while others, such as Exclusive Books, moved into the suburban shopping malls. The clubs and striptease joints survived but became sleazier. By the late 1990s, an estimated 1000 sex workers lived in Hillbow and this, together with its large, transient immigrant population, ensured that Hillbrow had relatively high levels of HIV/AIDS.

Today, Hillbrow is one of the most densely populated areas in the world – with more people per square kilometre than Hong Kong! Hillbrow's reputation as a slum, however, is not entirely accurate. The suburb is characterised by extremes: there are well-managed buildings, where tenants pay their rent on time, send their children off to school each morning, and keep their apartments spick and span. There are also a number of prominent 'bad buildings' where slumlords encourage the practice of room sharing or sub-letting to extremes, where basic services (such as bathrooms and kitchens) are either not provided (in many cases because the Council has cut off services owing to non-payment) or are in disrepair. The extremely poor state of these 'bad' buildings – which, in many cases, is perpetuated by an inability to locate the actual building's owners – has a knock-on effect on its neighbours (through things like overflowing sewerage pipes, or criminal activity).

The Hillbrow community, together with the city and various property development agencies, is attempting to clamp down on bad buildings (and bad residents – drug dealing and prostitution are rife in certain buildings), but it is a long process hampered not only by bureaucratic requirements but also by the fact that upgrading the Hillbrow area will require thousands of alternative accommodation options for many of its current residents.

Brenda Fassie's Hillbrow

By 1989, Hillbrow had shed its 1960s white bohemian and 1970s superfly character. Five years after it was declared a 'grey' area, Hillbrow was anything but. A collage of pink, pitch-black, yellow and brown people from the Cape to Kuala Lumpur had made it their home. Large residential blocks were taken over by streams of black middle-class people, artists, fashion and hair stylists, fresh-out-of-the-closet black gays and township intellectuals. Although she owned a mansion in Fleurhof, MaBrrr also owned an apartment in Century Plaza, then one of Hillbrow's most happening spots.

Meanwhile, back in the townships, Brenda's new single, 'Ngiya Kusaba' ('My Friend U Dangerous') – a slick rip-off of a US disco hit – beckoned all hedonists and clubbers to come get down. In tacky, groovy, California-black polyester bell-bottoms, knee-length boots, a red Afro wig and a rainbow of sequins, Brenda cultivated an empty image consistent with her hot single. On the outside, the party girl was having a blast. She had just left an abusive marriage to Nhlanhla Mbambo, son of a Durban tycoon, and once again she was ready to rock.

Century Plaza was known not only for the musicians who lived there, but also as the epicentre of free expression, style, upward mobility and Jozi's black gays. Jenny Mkhize, now living in Paris, was there at the time: 'It was a combination of 1970s Soweto and designer-obsessed Paris, right in Africa. The exhibitionist gay brigade dripped charm, ruled the style wars, partied hard and ventured deep into the unknown.

'There was a lot of incestuous bonking going on, y'know? Wine, big guys, cross-gender orgies and more orgies. At the same time, there was a beautiful sisterhood there, shared dreams, bashed dreams … we were all connected by that inexplicable glue: the artists' desire to live freely, as if every day is the last. Lesbians were bedding gay boys, gay boys were stealing each other's partners. …

'Through it all, I remember Fassie as the rock goddess: the loudest and most stylish of the bunch. Even if we didn't see eye to eye, I admired how selfless she was. She was many things in one – a very possessive lover and a giving person. At the time, she was seeing my friend Victoria Sihlahla (Poppy), the most beautiful woman in the gang. Naturally, Queen Bee was jealous as hell.'

'Both women and men vied for Queen Bee's attention,' remembers Oscar Tyumre, a musician and one of Brenda's closest friends. 'Once, while she was dating a woman called Buli Arosi, she was also seeing one of her dancers Ludwe Maki – though not in public. It wasn't that she was promiscuous. She dated Ludwe because her girlfriend had double-crossed her with him. So she says, "Aha? Well, let's play this game. By my rules." She had both of them.'

From Hot Type *by Bongani Madondo*[12]

Joubert Park, 1908

Joubert Park

The region of Joubert Park forms part of Johannesburg's inner city and is located around a major park of the same name. Many people, including residents, confuse it with Hillbrow. The Joubert Park area is probably about half the size of Hillbrow, but it shares the same north-south streets and street names as Hillbrow and a similar historical trajectory from small dwellings to high-rise apartments and a transition from a white region to one dominated by black residents. Joubert Park today is a major transit point for commuter traffic. Park Station to the west is used by approximately 800 000 commuters every day while the Jack Mincer parking garage was converted into a taxi rank and holding facility for hundreds of minibus taxis. In 1999 a deck was built over a portion of the railway line adjacent to Park Station to accommodate another taxi rank while both Noord and Wanderers streets now serve as informal taxi ranks, making this an extremely congested transport node. This congestion has degraded the area into a noisy, polluted area with a relatively high crime rate.

Joburg's First Public Space

In 1887 the Diggers' Committee, an early version of local government in Johannesburg (and forerunner to the Chamber of Mines), appealed to Paul Kruger's government to provide a 'public park or garden to be planted with trees'.[13] The land set aside was originally called Joubert's Plein; it was laid out as a botanical garden in 1893, named after General Joubert, who was the commander-in-chief of the Boer forces in the Transvaal.

By 1895 it was a beautiful, green oasis, popular at night with courting couples. One newspaper suggested that the City Fathers change the name of the park to 'Cupid's Garden' because the 'benches are always occupied with engrossed couples who go to study astronomy on cloudless nights'.[14]

In the 1980s Joubert Park and its surrounds experienced a similar decline to that of neighbouring Hillbrow; while it remains a bustling, central hub, the park and surrounding areas share a reputation for housing criminals and the unemployed. It's not recommended tourists visit the park alone, or after hours – one of the reasons is, simply, that while the park grounds and art gallery might be relatively safe, getting to (and from) them can be risky if you're unfamiliar with the area.

Joubert Park remains one of the city's largest parks and has a number of community facilities. It has a large open-air concrete chessboard where enthusiasts gather to play or to watch. About 20 000 people make use of the park or pass through it every day as a shortcut to Hillbrow and Berea.

Joubert Park currently houses a Child and Family Resource called 'Lapeng' (Tswana for 'at home'), established in 1997, and a Neighbourhood Centre, established in 1999. The park's Victorian Conservatory has been renovated, and numerous exotic plants are kept in its hothouse.

Probably the most remarkable feature of the park is the Greenhouse Project, situated in its north-west corner – an old potting shed, refurbished in the 1990s. Local residents and schoolchildren visit the Project to learn about environmentally sustainable practices including organic farming, and medicinal plants are grown in the open space nearby.

Joburg's Hollywood

In April 1895, the very first Kinetescopes (Thomas Edison's boxes that showed moving pictures) were opened to the public in an arcade on the corners of Pritchard and President streets. A year later, an Englishman named Carl Hertz brought a projector and screened the first production at the Empire Palace of *Varieties* in Commissioner Street.

By the time the South African War was declared in 1899, the local film industry was sufficiently established to record the War on film – and use the footage for propaganda purposes.

In the same year as Carl Hertz's 'Cinematicographe' premiered in the new city, a young American called Isidore William Schlesinger (he preferred to be known by his initials, IW) landed in Cape Town, in search of adventure and profit. For Schlesinger, the money was to be found above the ground – he starting by selling life insurance to gold miners and Swazi chiefs.

Schlesinger used his commissions to set up his own insurance company before turning his hand to real estate (graduating to a finance office to assist his clients with their mortgages and loans). Wherever he saw opportunity, Schlesinger took it – including setting up a bus line to get his tenants to their homes![15]

By 1913, west-coast Hollywood had just overtaken east-coast New York as the hub of the American film industry; and, all over the globe, motion pictures were moving out of small-time arcades and part-time venues into luxurious movie houses of their own.

That year, Schlesinger bought out Joburg's Empire Theatre, Africa's Amalgamated Theatres and several other South African companies, to form the African Theatres Trust. Within a month, Schlesinger's theatres were screening the iconic *African Mirror* – South Africa's first newsreel. Schlesinger also formed the African Films Trust, to import and distribute motion-picture material throughout South and East Africa. Not content with simply owning all the major foreign material distribution rights, he

PLACES TO SEE
Johannesburg Art Gallery

(corner of Klein and King George streets) is Joubert Park's pearl. Its founding is as romantic as the building itself. In 1909, Lady Florence Phillips (wife of Randlord, Lionel) had a vision for an art gallery for Johannesburg – and was so determined to achieve it that she sold her diamond ring that her husband had given her and used the proceeds to buy the first three paintings.

The gallery, which offers secure parking on site, features one of the best collections of contemporary South African art, as well as a small collection of old masters – JAG (as it's referred to) houses an impressive collection of 17th Century Dutch paintings and many examples of British 18th and 19th century art. On a given day, the visitor is likely to see artwork by Rembrandt, Lichtenstein, Hockney and Sekoto, each one a masterpiece. There are also works from Rodin, Picasso and Henry Moore.

The Johannesburg Art Gallery in the 1920s (above) and in the 1980s (below)

PLACES TO SEE

Built in 1904, the **Drill Hall** (corner of Plein and Twist streets) was originally the headquarters of the Transvaal Volunteers – as well as the site of the mobilisation of troops who went from the Transvaal to aid colonial forces in Natal in putting down South Africa's last black military uprising: the Bambatha Rebellion of 1906.

During both World Wars, troops would gather at the Drill Hall before being assigned. Between the wars, in the 1930s, it became a popular dance hall. Its most famous moment, however, came in 1956 when it was briefly selected as a site for the court that heard the famous Treason Trial of 156 anti-apartheid activists, including Nelson Mandela, Oliver Tambo, Walter Sisulu and Albert Luthuli.

The prisoners were housed in the Fort (at what is now Constitutional Hill) and brought in to the court by bus. The trial was later moved to Pretoria, for security reasons.

A verdict was finally reached over four and a half years after the initial arrests – finding all the remaining accused not guilty.

In 1964 Mandela, Sisulu and six others were sentenced to life imprisonment for treason at what is known as the Rivonia Treason Trial.

The Drill Hall retained its military function until 1992 when, along with a rapid decline in the numbers of the South African armed forces, it was abandoned. It has recently been refurbished, at a cost of R10 million, and now houses several community groups including Johannesburg Child Welfare, the Johannesburg Community Chest, the Joubert Park Project – and the Rand Light Infantry.

To read more about the Drill Hall and see what events and exhibitions are currently on, go to www.jda.co.za/drillhall.

The Drill Hall in 1906

Bus containing prisoners en route to the Drill Hall, 1956

Protestors outside the Drill Hall, 1956

set up Africa's first motion picture studio, African Film Productions, in 1915, in the residential suburb of Killarney (which Schlesinger owned and lived in).

Between 1916 and 1922, the Killarney Film Studios made an impressive 43 movies. Production of local feature-length films slowed down after that, largely because of the lack of interest in South African movies by foreign markets. African Film Productions, however, continued to grow. By the 1930s, it was producing early sound films, making film advertisements and creating the country's first tourism films. In July 1939, the *African Mirror* newsreel finally got sound – just in time for the events of the Second World War to make it to the big screen.

In 1949, IW died and left his company to his son, Johnny. A decade later, Johnny sold African Film Productions to 20th Century Fox. A short while later, the Killarney Film Studios were demolished to make way for another big idea (this time, that of IW's son Johnny): the shopping mall. In 1961, the Killarney Mall opened its doors.

Killarney

The suburb of Killarney was originally known as Cook's Farm – owner JO Cook, an Irishman, named his farm after Killarney in Ireland, where his wife Jessie Olive Scrooby was born. IW Schlesinger acquired Cook's Farm and surrounding land in 1905.

Killarney became a favoured picnic spot for Johannesburg's young couples. The *Transvaal Critic* issue of 20 November 1908 described it as: 'A garden, an orchard, a vineyard, an orangery, a shrubbery, a pinery, a paradise, a picnic spot, a health resort, a township and a home'.[17]

Schlesinger also established the Killarney Golf Course (now in Riviera) and Transvaal Automobile Club (which now forms part of Lower Houghton). Both institutions welcomed Jews and Schlesinger's own background encouraged many Jewish people to move to the area, especially after the Oxford Synagogue was established in the neighbouring suburb of Riviera after the Second World War.

 ## Places to See

• **Whitehall Court** (4th Street Killarney) is a provisional national monument. Built in 1923, it is a wonderful example of the type of American-in-

fluenced buildings that were erected in the 1920s and has large Art Deco glass and brass doors. It is believed to be the only remaining example of architect John Moffat's work (after whom the architecture building located in the University of the Witwatersrand is named).

• The **Killarney Library** is situated inside the Killarney Mall. In the library you will see wonderful black-and-white photographs of IW Schlesinger's original film studios in Killarney and his 'Metro' Cinema.

• Another attraction for these early residents was **The Wilds**, a nature sanctuary established in the area in 1924. The land, which was bought by the Johannesburg Consolidated Investment Company (JCI) as part of the Houghton Estate, was donated to the citizens of Johannesburg. Right from the start, the intention was to leave this area wild. In 1936 many of the plants displayed in the rock gardens exhibit at the Empire Exhibition that commemorated Johannesburg's 50th anniversary were transferred to The Wilds. The Wilds were later dedicated to Jan Smuts' memory in 1950.

Today, although The Wilds remains an interesting, beautiful and unspoilt patch of veld in the central part of the city, it is not considered safe to visit – even in small groups. A local hiking group does occasionally organise walks in The Wilds – for information go to www.veld.org.za.

THE SOUTHERN

'But I have seen momentarily, the golden sand of the mine-dumps crossed by grey and purple shadows in the evening, transformed into a real beauty — a thing impossible to the slag-heaps of industrial England. And I have come to love the rolling country of the highveld round the city, stretching away to the Magaliesberg mountains and giving to Johannesburg a setting which belongs to few cities in the world.'

Trevor Huddleston, *Naught for your Comfort*

In this chapter

☞ • Joburg's Gold Mines

☞ • The Disappearing Mine Dumps

☞ • The Turf Club

☞ • Suburbs of the South

☞ • Little Portugal

☞ • Soccer – Where Joburg Meets Soweto

SUBURBS

Mining headgear in Crown Mines, 1980s. It was removed in 1988.

Johannesburg has no significant distinguishing natural features – above ground, at any rate. There are scattered koppies and ridges and plains, but no rushing tidal river, no flat-topped mountain, no circle of seven hills… Despite this, the city is easily divided into geographical segments: the garden suburbs of the north, beyond the ridges, looking towards the Magaliesberg; the south-sloping surfaces of Hospital Hill, Berea, Doornfontein and Ellis Park; the city centre, with its east-west railway line following the natural location for a river bed; and the southern suburbs – separated from the commercial district by a broad band of mining properties. The distinctions are not arbitrary: Rosettenville (in the south) has a measurably different rainfall and climate from that of Rosebank (in the north).[1]

The city is also divided – invisibly – by a continental watershed. Streams to the north of Johannesburg flow into the Crocodile River, then into the Limpopo, which makes its way until it reaches the warm Indian Ocean on South Africa's east coast. Water flowing on the southern side of the city will end up in the Vaal River, joining to the Orange River before travelling a thousand kilometres downstream to reach the icy Atlantic Ocean, on the west coast.

Below ground, the city is further defined by sweeping stretches of quartzite, shale and granite, many with names evocative of Joburg itself – like Orange Grove Quartzite, Hospital Hill Shale, Jeppestown Series, Booysens Formation and the Turffontein Subgroup.

The presence of gold, in the reefs south of the city centre, dictated not only the locations of the early mines, but also Johannesburg's initial white residential development: until the early 1940s, most of the city's white townships were established east, west and north of the original Randjeslaagte boundaries. Although a handful of (white) suburbs were established south of the mines in the period between 1886 and 1910, the real development of this region occurred in the years between 1941 and 1976.[2]

The southern suburbs are not as green as those in the north, with its urban forest; they also lack the north's distinctive ridges – instead, the flat south is broken by another kind of koppie: mine dumps. People from the northern suburbs almost never go down south, except perhaps to visit the funfair and casino at Gold Reef City, or to send visitors to the Apartheid Museum. And, while the northern suburbs have become characterised by high walls topped with electric fencing, the southern suburbs still have low garden walls, with only occasional electric fencing, indicative of its lower middle-class and working-class nature.

When, in the late 1980s and early 1990s, the city centre experienced a decline as businesses moved north, to places like Sandton, the southern suburbs experienced a slump too, epitomised by the decline in the use of recreational facilities such as Wemmer Pan and Santarama Miniland, in La Rochelle.

In recent years, however, Joburg's southern suburbs have benefited from the city's property boom – house prices in the south comfortably compete with those of residences in the north.

With their proximity and easy access to the CBD, these suburbs have also become desirable residential areas for black buyers moving out of the townships and into former whites-only areas. As one resident explained, the southern suburbs have 'become the northern suburbs of Soweto'.

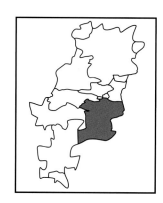

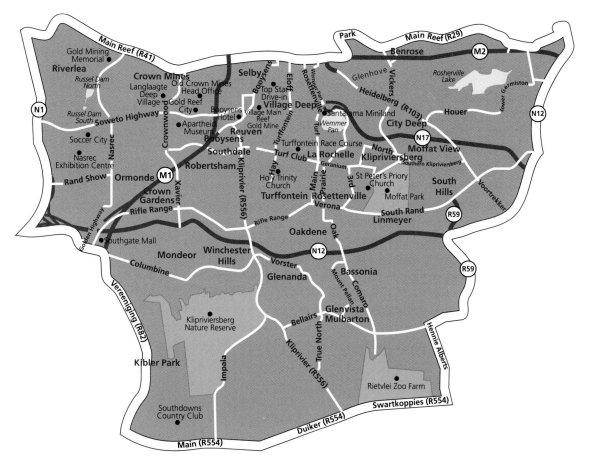

Main Reef (R41)
Park
Main Reef (R29)
Benrose
M2
Gold Mining Memorial
Rosherville Lake
Riverlea
Glenhove
Vickers
Lower Germiston
Russel Dam North
Crown Mines
Selby
Heidelberg (R103)
Houer
Langlaagte Deep Village
Old Crown Mines Head Office
Top Star Drive-in
Booysens
Eloff
Rosettenville
Glenhove
N1
Russel Dam South
Gold Reef City
Booysens Hotel
Village Deep
Santarama Miniland
City Deep
N12
Soweto Highway
Crownwood
Apartheid Museum
Village Main Reef Gold Mine
Wemmer Pan
Reuven
Turffontein
Turffontein Race Course
N17
Moffat View
Soccer City
Nasrec
Booysens
Southdale
Turf Club
La Rochelle
North Klipriviersberg
Nasrec Exhibition Centre
Robertsham
Hay
Geranium
Southern Klipriviersberg
South Hills
Rand Show
Ormonde
M1
3rd
St Peter's Priory Church
Voortrekker
Crown Gardens
Xavier
Kliprivier (R556)
Holy Trinity Church
Turffontein
Rosettenville
Main Prairie
Moffat Park
South Rand
R59
Rifle Range
Verona
Linmeyer
Golden Highway
Southgate Mall
Rifle Range
Oakdene
Oak
R59
Mondeor
Winchester Hills
Vorster
N12
Bassonia
Columbine
Glenanda
Mount Pellan
Conaro
Vereeniging (R82)
Kliprivier (R556)
Bellairs
True North
Glenvista
Mulbarton
Klipriv50ersberg Nature Reserve
Hennie Alberts
Kibler Park
Impala
Rietvlei Zoo Farm
Southdowns Country Club
Swartkoppies (R554)
Main (R554)
Duiker (R554)

N

An early mining trench in Johannesburg

Miners going on shift at Langlaagte Deep

Joburg's Gold Mines

The earliest method of large-scale gold mining in Johannesburg was by open cuts or trenches dug along the outcrops of the reef – some of which went down 18 m or more. The ore was thrown up from level to level by black miners; 'as the depth increased, it was hoisted by means of bullock whims and whips.'[3]

By 1887, underground mining was already being explored – four inclined shafts were sunk at Langlaagte. In 1889, a mining engineer named Hennen Jennings arrived and refined the sinking practice so that one or two main shafts were sunk at each mine (instead of numerous small ones). Boreholes were sent down to test the continuity of the reef, first to 200 m, then to 350 m, steadily increasing until they reached depths of over 1500 m.

By 1906 the Robinson Deep Mine just off Eloff Street in Johannesburg had become, at 800 m, the deepest producing mine in the world. At the lowest level of the deep mine, rock temperatures were nearly 37°C – a problem compounded by the large amounts of water used underground to dampen the potentially silicosis-producing dust (the water reduced the cooling effect of the air). Large ventilation systems were developed and installed to introduce fresh air and cool the temperature to a more manageable 29°C.

As the mines got deeper, more and more labourers were employed in construction of supports – timber, concrete pillars or sand filling used to secure the workings against the frequent earth tremors and 'rockbursts' or phases of subsidence.

Miners would drill underground shafts and stopes using large jackhammer drills that could be operated by one person, drilling on average 24 m a shift.

By the 1970s, most of the mines in Johannesburg had ceased to operate – not because the gold reserves were depleted, but because a drop in gold prices, a combination of old mining technologies (limiting the yield) and political unrest in the area made the mines uneconomic. Although most mining companies retained their headquarters in Johannesburg, gold operations moved outside the city, to the east and west rands as well as south-west of Joburg, clustered near the town of Carletonville – along the 400 km stretch of the ore-bearing Witwatersrand Basin, which extends into the neighbouring Mpumalanga and Free State provinces.

Far left: An underground mining support made of wood
Left: Miner drilling at Crown Mines
Bottom left: Village Main Reef mining operation
Bottom right: Miners coming off their shift

There are indications that new technology could make Johannesburg's old mining operations viable once more. Information released by Central Rand Gold Ltd shows gold of between 7,4 and 8,9 grams per ton in the 11 contiguous mines where the company has secured prospecting rights. The company will not be re-mining old stopes or faces; instead, they plan to use old mine workings to access new mining areas – and then mine these using modern techniques. If the venture gets funding and approval, Joburg could become a true mining town once again.

The Man-made Mountain

There are approximately 200 mine dumps in and around Joburg – many of them 50 m in height, often covered in grass, shrubs and eucalyptus trees in an attempt at urban camouflage. The yellow-sand mountains are made up of finely crushed rock, waste from the city's early mines. In the city's early years, the dumps caused severe air-pollution problems particularly during the dry winter months. The mining industry tried various means of stabilising the surfaces of the dumps, experimenting with things like resin, plastic, cement and bitumen. The ideal natural solution was to encourage the establishment of vegetation on the dumps – the challenge was to get plants to take root and grow in such a hostile and often toxic environment. Interestingly, it was not the presence of cyanide in the sand that created a problem (the cyanide would naturally break down after being exposed to sunlight and air) but rather the low pH levels, very fine quality of the sand and a high rate of erosion. To encourage plant growth, lime was added to increase the pH and mist sprays were used to bring down acidity. Reed windbreaks were planted to control the movement of the sand.

No.2 Shaft and East Plant, Geldenhuis Deep

Environmental mine dump, 2006

Depending on the age of the dump and the gold extraction process used, many dumps contain sufficients traces of gold to be reclaimed by sophisticated modern processes.

There are two kinds of dumps: sand dumps and slimes dams. The latter consist of finer sand, from which more gold was extracted, and are therefore less likely to yield much gold now.

A dump is considered viable for reclamation when 0,4 grams of gold can be obtained from every ton. But some dumps yield more: Menell's Dump, south-east of the city, has produced 0,65 grams a ton. So long as the gold price remains above R80 000 a kilogram, the mine dumps will continue to be reclaimed. Some 170 million tons have already been processed, and the plan is to eventually remove all the dumps – which will, in the process, change the face of south Joburg.

As the dumps are flattened, the sand is going to three new dumps being created alongside Nasrec, which are huge … and growing.

The land that remains once the dumps have been removed can be built on with no fear of subsidence – the ground underneath the original mine dumps was not tunnelled.[4]

The Top Star

One of the city's most striking mine dump landmarks is that of the Top Star Drive-In – the mine dump is over 100 years old, and was originally known as the Ferreira Dump. The area (originally part of the farm Turffontein) was owned and worked by the Ferreira Deep Gold Mine until 1939. In early 1950 the property was transferred to a development corporation, which applied for permission to establish a township (suburb) in the area, which was declined. Permission was then sought for construction of a (European) drive-in movie theatre on top of the dump; this was granted, and the Top Star Drive-In opened in the early 1960s – operating for over 40 years before it finally closed down.

In 2006 the Top Star dump was bought by a mining group hoping to mine the landmark and reclaim the gold it contains – at an estimated 0,7 grams per ton. The move has encountered opposition from heritage groups who want the mine dump to be declared a historical landmark.

Pioneers in the South

Colonel Ignatius Ferreira 'outspanned his wagon and erected his reed hut near the outcrop on Turffontein'[5] (what would later become Ferreira's Camp, and then Ferreirastown) in June 1886. He was soon joined by his friend Samuel Wemmer – whom Ferreira had met in Kimberley – and Mr Wemmer's wife.

Sam Wemmer went on to found the Wemmer Gold Mining Company, together with George Goch (who later became the Mayor of Joburg); the two men erected the new goldfield's first stamp battery – a two-stamper. In 1888, this was replaced by a five-stamp battery.

Hermann Eckstein's company acquired holdings in the Wemmer Mine in the 1890s, and the operation was absorbed into the Village Main Reef Company by 1906 – Wemmer received little profit, and apparently died in poverty.

These days Wemmer is associated with Wemmer Pan, the large lake that is part of present-day Pioneers' Park, north of La Rochelle.

The Wemmer Pan Park was renamed Pioneers' Park in 1924; an area of 70 acres was purchased by the city from various mining houses. The Pan was given free for use by sailing clubs, to be joined later by canoeists in the form of the Johannesburg Canoe Club. A football field, a cricket ground and a swimming pool were built by 'relief labour', probably prisoners. 'Natives' were strictly excluded from the facilities.[6]

Until the late 1980s, one of Wemmer Pan's major attractions was its musical fountains, where (white) Johannesburgers could sit on the grass surrounding the water works and, with gasps of delight, enjoy the varying heights the fountains would attain, accompanied by music, and illuminated, by different colours but the copper piping was stolen and the fountains have never been restored.

Above: The battery stamper at the Wemmer and Goch mine

Sam Wemmer (far left) and George Goch (left)

In the 1990s Wemmer Pan experienced a downturn, linked to rampant crime and vandalism. The notorious serial killer Cedric Maake, convicted of killing at least 27 people before his arrest in 1997, used the Wemmer Pan area to target his victims.

Wemmer Pan is slowly recovering. In 2001 the Wemmer Pan Forum, a section 21 company made up of local community members, was formed and granted a 10-year mandate to rehabilitate and manage the park. New facilities, including a new playground and skateboard park, have been installed, security in the park has been improved, and the lake now plays host to the city's annual Chinese Dragon Boat Spring Festival at the start of September each year.

Santarama Miniland (Rosettenville Road) is part of the Wemmer Pan complex. It features a miniature town, with a large figure of Jan van Riebeeck positioned at its entrance, and his replica *Dromedaris* ship inside the town. Recent additions include a scale miniature of Robben Island. It gets its name from the South African National Tuberculosis Association, and all proceeds go towards the association. Santarama is open Mondays to Sundays from 08h30 to 17h30. Tickets include a boat ride on Wemmer Pan, a mini-train ride, a game of putt-putt, entrance to the play centre, jumping castles and jungle gyms. There is also a restaurant on the site. For more information contact (011) 435 0543 or go to www.miniland. co.za.

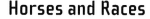

Horses and Races

Within three months of public diggings being proclaimed, Johannesburg held its first horse race – games of chance considered equally if not more appealing than the risky and sometimes boring business of claims and mining – possibly on the site of Ferreira's Mine, or in Twist Street, near the present-day Drill Hall.

The meeting was 'not reckoned a huge success, being poorly organised and attended',[7] but support for the sport was strong enough to warrant a second meeting, fixed for June the following year. In early 1887 the Johannesburg Turf Club was formed; its president was the commissioner Captain Von Brandis, and the executive

A day at the races – Turffontein in the late 1880s

committee included Ignatius Ferreira, Samuel Fox, JS Harrison (after whom Harrison Street was named) and George Farrar. Two years later, after lengthy negotiations, the Turf Club had established permanent premises at the Turffontein Race Course, to the south of the town (where it still operates).

While many people believed the suburb's name sprung from its association with the race course, Turffontein ('clay fountain') was in fact one of the original farms that would later make up greater Johannesburg; it was owned by Abraham Smit, who had lived on the farm since 1857 and died there in 1884, at the age of 73.

Part of the farm was bought by Paul Andries Ras in 1886; after lengthy negotiations Ras eventually consented to a 99-year lease with the Turf Club.[8] In 1892, Ras sold the freehold title to the Club – Joburg was still in the grip of depression, following the discovery of pyritic ores, and it is possible Ras needed the money.

Another portion of the farm was bought by Walter Casey. In 1889 his section of Turffontein was surveyed and laid out, complete with a circular park – the Rotunda Park – and a rectangular one, originally called Turffontein West Gardens (later changed to Christopherson Park). Casey obviously hoped to turn Turffontein into a wealthy area; when stands eventually went on sale, in 1896 or 1897, Casey's Township (or Turffontein) was advertised as the 'most charming' suburb in Johannes-

Aerial view of the tracks at Turffontein

PLACES TO SEE
The **Turffontein Race Club** (Turf Club Street, Turffontein) hosts around 58 races each year, including the R1-million annual Summer Cup. The elegant original buildings still exist, in red brick with white fascias, red tiled roofs and long verandas, although a large modern stand has been added. In recent years, Turffontein has also become available as a conference and wedding venue. For more information call (011) 681 1500.

burg. But the dust and noise and rapidly growing mine dumps appear to have stifled such plans. Over time, Turffontein became a sub-economic suburb, housing mostly miners. Today it's still seen as a working-class suburb, dominated by the race course and a fast-growing landfill site in Turffontein Road, growing on the main mine dump of the defunct Village Main Reef gold mine. The two parks still exist, but Rotunda Park is a little untidy and Christopherson Park has been turned into a sports ground.

The Turffontein Race Course has a rich and unusual history – rich in particular: in late 1897, the Turf Club raced to peg the entire course (mark it out for mining) to prevent any claim jumping (claiming occupied land for mining purposes). As it turned out, there was significant 'gold beneath their hooves' … several kilometres down. The development of effective deep-level techniques saw the Club able to sell off its mining interests without touching a blade of grass on the course itself: all the exploration and digging were in tunnels over 1,5 km underground.

The race course also has a more sinister past.

Femme Fatale

From 1909 to 1922, South Africa's most famous female murderer, Daisy de Melker, lived in Turffontein, at 22 Tulley Street. De Melker poisoned two husbands and her 20-year-old son. She poisoned her first husband by putting strychnine in his Epsom Salts. She gave strychnine to her second husband in a glass of beer. She gave arsenic in coffee to her son. Her third husband, a plumber, was spared a poisonous drink, not because she had stopped murdering, but because she was caught before she could murder again. Her trial took just 30 days, and she was given the death sentence.[9]

In the South African War of 1899 to 1902, it was taken over by the British and used as a concentration camp for Boer women and children. The Johannesburg Camp originally started at the Mayfair School, but soon ran out of space and moved down south, where tents were

179

set beyond the boundary fence of the course. From here the women and children used to watch the British military's 'pony and galloway races', which were ongoing throughout the war.[10]

Some 5000 people were held in the camps, of whom 700 died and were buried in Maluti Street, Winchester Hills, on Piet Meyer's farm, Kliprivierberg. This cemetery was vandalised by an anti-Ossewa Brandwag group during the Second World War, and was overhauled and re-opened in 1961 by then Minister of Justice BJ Vorster. It now consists of a number of coffin-shaped terraces, with a memorial structure listing the names of the dead.[11]

👁 PLACES TO SEE

The original **Turffontein Fire Station** (corner Turf Club and Hay) was constructed in 1910, just opposite the race track. The original 'viewing platform' – allowing firemen to spot smoke and fires from a distance – comprised two exceptionally tall gum trees, 30 m tall. Conveniently, the platform also offered a good view of the race track and the horses (a fact the firemen used to good advantage, when bets were still being accepted after the horses had left the stalls).

Although no longer used as the station base, and superseded by a new building built in the late 1980s, the old red-brick building retains its charm, its interior walls covered in fire department emblems from around the world, shiny brass helmets and other fire-fighting memorabilia. It still has its wood-slatted ceilings, large wooden windows and wooden floor.[12]

A number of old houses of worship can be seen along Hay Street – including the Herbert Baker-designed Holy Trinity Church at 136 Hay Street.

Turffontein Fire Station

Old church on Hay Street (left) and the infamous lookout tower in 1912 (right)

Suburbs of the South

The township of Booysens was proclaimed in 1887, named after the farmer (Jan Booysen) who had a mill on his farm, a portion of Turffontein. The Booysens Hotel (corner of Booysens Road and Fraser Street), built in 1887 and still in operation, was the last staging post for the Zeederburg Coach Company before reaching the town of Johannesburg. The hotel came to be situated where it is now because there is a stream nearby, and it became the last stop for travellers from Kimberley before entering the gold-rush town, around 10 km away. In 1890 a bridge was built across the stream, and soon stores and a police station were built along Main Road, now Booysens Road.[13]

Leo (or Levin) Rosettenstein (after whom Rosettenville was named) came to South Africa from East Prussia in 1876, and was on the Witwatersrand before gold was discovered. He leased some land from Paul Ras in 1886, and had it surveyed in 1889. The stands went on sale the same year, overlooking the race course to the north-west of the new suburb. On 26 July 1889

The Star *reported that the suburb was to become a 'paradise of flowers', judging by the names given to its streets: Bouquet, Rose, Lily, Petunia, Zinnia, Violet and Daisy. Other streets were given Rosettenstein family names: Mabel, Albert, Hugo, Morris, Philip and George.*

In June 1895 the Standard and Diggers' News *noted that trees had been planted, with a blue gum plantation dividing Rosettenville from Turffontein. Some 40 buildings, mostly houses, were in place by then, including a brewery, a distillery, a butchery and a tiny store. Properties had been fenced, with well-maintained kitchen gardens supplied by water from the local spruit, which had been dammed. Dairy farming was thriving. There was even transport from town to Rosettenville. On the suburb's southern border Rosettenstein had two mine claims, still to be worked. Rosettenville was described as a pleasant place to live, a suburb free of 'dust storms, business traffic, and objectionable canteens'. It was a place that was 'very rustic and retired'.*

Undated street scene, Booysens

Daisy Street today

The Booysens Hotel

La Rochelle was originally owned by surveyor JE de Villiers, who advertised 578 stands for sale in 1895. Land was to be sold on a 99-year freehold basis, and included the promise (from de Villiers) that he would sink two wells, and fit them with pumps, order two 'handsome and comfortable Omnibuses', and build stables. Other attractions of the suburb were the charming view, taking in Jeppestown, Doornfontein, Fordsburg and the main reef, with its noisy stamp batteries, and buildings, from Robinson Mine to Boksburg. Of course this was before that view was obscured by the tall mine dumps. And before the dust from the dumps was to make life very unpleasant down south when the wind blew.

To help new homeowners get going, De Villiers offered

PLACES TO SEE

One of Rosettenville's unique heritage spots is on the grounds of St Peter's Priory Church on Victoria Street (built in 1903), and the adjoining St Martin's Preparatory School and secondary school. St Martin's originally functioned as a missionary school, offering education for black students; in 1956 it was closed by the apartheid government, re-opening a year later as a whites-only school. St Martin's alumni include the late ANC President Oliver Tambo and musician Hugh Masekela. Trevor Huddleston and Desmond Tutu, both later archbishops, also spent time at the school – Huddleston as superintendent, Tutu as a student at the Priory. Today St Martin's is a top-class private school for all races.

to make available – free of charge – a sandstone quarry, and a piece of ground for brickmaking. It was a hard sell. The long advert ended by saying: 'This is positively the last chance to secure stands in the immediate vicinity of Johannesburg.' As it happened, the suburb (apparently named after the French town where De Villiers' ancestor came from) was only registered in 1903.[14]

An official's house at the Crown Reef Gold Mining Co., built in 1897

Ophirton in 1967

Selby, located on the site of the old Ferreira mine, was named after Paul Selby, the American mine manager, from 1926 to 1927. It was originally to be called Ferreira Industrial. The suburb's streets were all named after Ferreira Deep officials'[19]: Richards, Rogers, Webber, Pirow, Hans, Ignatius.

City Deep takes its name from the gold mine in the area, and is now the location of the city's fresh produce and flower market, and Spoornet's huge container terminal – referred to as the country's biggest inland port.

Crown Mines, proclaimed in 1928, was named by Godfray Lys, the first general manager of the old Crown Reef Company. The suburb lay on the crown of a koppie, of what was considered to be the central portion of the main reef.

The suburb was the first in which Nelson Mandela stayed in when he arrived in Joburg in 1941. While expecting to see a 'grand building', he was surprised to see 'rusted tin shanties' at the mine.

These days the suburb is much more than tin shanties – factories and warehouses dominate the streets but traces of its early history still remain. Distinguished architect Herbert Baker was commissioned to design a small village of single-quarter houses for white mine workers, and they still exist. There's a scout hall and the mine manager's house, in brick, red tin roofs and quaint verandas, just off Main Reef Road.

The Langlaagte Deep Village Mandela described still stands, but in sad condition. It consists of three rows of Victorian iron-roofed houses, now occupied by squatters – although the buildings have been declared a national monument. The metal headgear of No. 5 Crown Mines still stands starkly against the sky in the suburb, close to the Langlaagte Station, and surrounded by open ground and tall gum trees that dot the suburb, a reminder of how the area would have looked 100 years ago when miners nuzzled the gold out of the earth.

The Parktown & Westcliff Heritage Trust runs annual bus tours of the early gold mining areas. For more information, phone (011) 482 3349.

Ormonde was originally the name of the farm in the area. In 1886 the Duke of Westminster's Derby winner was called Ormonde, and it's believed the farm got its name from the horse. Mondeor is an anagram of Ormonde, the farm on which the 350-ha suburb was developed in 1958.[21]

Ophirton was laid out in 1887, one of the town's earliest residential areas. It was probably named after the Paarl Ophir Gold Mining Company, an early mine owner. 'Ophir' refers to the biblical land, famous for its gold, referred to in the book of Kings. At various times in its history it was called Height's Township (after Sam Height) and Mewettsville. Some of the street names are derived from officials of Rand Mines.

Little Portugal

The Portuguese community first settled in Johannesburg at the turn of the 19th Century, a third of them coming from Madeira. They were mostly market gardeners and greengrocers, but also builders and other artisans.

Between 1924 and 1972 census figures indicate there were over 50 000 Portuguese residents. More than half were from Portugal, some 10 000 from Madeira (leaving Madeira shortly before the Second World War) and 2500 from Mozambique. They settled in La Rochelle and Rosettenville, where cheap housing was available.[15]

The number of Mozambican immigrants grew after that country gained independence in 1976. Most Mozambican Portuguese settled in the southern suburbs of Rosettenville, Regent's Park and La Rochelle, and the eastern suburbs of Judith's Paarl, Belgravia, Kensington and Malvern.[16]

In the 1960s, La Rochelle became known as Little Portugal – evidence of Portuguese tilework is still visible, in the beautiful blue and white tiles of the Dias Mall in Johannesburg Road, but also on the bandstand and fountain wall in Boyland Park in the suburb. At one time the suburb was buzzing with Portuguese businesses, restaurants, taverns and bars. One or two restaurants still exist, and are well patronised by Portuguese people who, these days, come from middle-class southern suburbs like Glenvista, Glenanda, Oakdene, Bassonia, or middle-class eastern suburbs like Bedfordview and Edenvale.

In the past two years there has been a noticeable move to renovate the small homes in La Rochelle, possibly as a result of the rebuilding of the Rand Stadium in preparation for the 2010 Soccer World Cup.[17]

Figures for the Portuguese community vary, but the 1989 census reveals that around 80 000 Portuguese were living in South Africa, with possibly some 20 000 living in Johannesburg. Nevertheless, the community was sufficiently large to warrant its own telephone directory, a part-time radio station, Parelelo 27, and a weekly newspaper, O Seculo. The Bank of Lisbon helped establish a Portuguese TV channel, still running on M-Net. There were a number of Portuguese social clubs, and the Portuguese Welfare Society was established with the flood of immigrants from Angola and Mozambique. Cardosa cigarettes were created by local Portuguese businessmen.[18]

Tiles in Boyland Park, La Rochelle

A Portuguese presence is evident in the Vasco da Gama Shopping Mall in Bassonia, where a statue of the explorer welcomes visitors to the mall.

Portuguese can still be heard in the traditional Portuguese suburbs of La Rochelle, Turffontein and Rosettenville, but it's mostly spoken by black immigrants from Mozambique and Angola, both former Portuguese colonies.

PLACES TO SEE
The **St Anthony's Catholic Church** in Church Street, Crown Mines, is a typical Portuguese church. It was built in 1965, and has beautiful tilework on its entrance walls and stunning stained glass inside the church.

PLACES TO VISIT
Situated inside the old La Rochelle Police Station – the bars of the holding cells are still visible in the covered courtyard – the **Parreirinha Restaurant** (No. 9 Sixth Street, La Rochelle) is one of Joburg's favourite Portuguese eateries. Ask for a seat in the smoking section, where you can see hundreds of ties (donated by guests) hanging from the ceiling. To make a booking, contact (011) 435 3809.

THINGS TO DO
The annual **Lusitoland Festival** takes place in April each year, and has grown into a 13-day eat, drink and be merry occasion – with the highlight being its dozens of Portuguese restaurants, bars and cafés, offering fresh traditional Portuguese (as well as Mozambican, Brazilian and Angolan-influenced) foods – from peri-peri chicken, through *caldo verde*, *chouriço* sausage and sardines, to heady Caiparinha cocktails, cold Portuguese beer and traditional sweet treats such as *farturas* and *Pasteis de Nata*. There is also an amusement park, over 100 flea-market stalls (some of which are actually worth a visit) and a stage where live bands, dancers and entertainers perform (expect this to be very cheesy, and you will be fine). The Festival tends to get crowded over weekends and public holidays, but is a great family destination. Entrance fees go to the Lusito School, a school for mentally and physically handicapped children, based in Regent's Park. For more information, go to www.lusitoland.co.za.

The small suburb of Glenesk (1931) sits just above the Turffontein Race Course. The intention was to call the suburb Glen or Glen Township but it never happened. The source of the eventual name is unclear. The town planner, F Strugnell, lettered in Greek numbers the cul-de-sacs of the suburb, on the plan, and was surprised to find they'd been adopted as street names. So the suburb has Alpha, Beta, Gamma, Delta, Epsillon and Zeta as street names.[24]

In 1951 Rand Stadium, seating 15 000, was built in Hector Norris Park in Glenesk. Some of the world's top teams played in the stadium: Motherwell, Wolverhampton Wanderers, Newcastle United, Ajax, Tottenham Hotspurs, Real Madrid and Arsenal. The old stadium was demolished in 2006 and a new stadium will rise from the rubble. Because of the stadium's age, it has been recommended that the scoreboard be retained for heritage purposes. A photographic display will trace its history. The Rand Stadium is to be a training venue for the 2010 Soccer Cup.[25]

PLACES TO VISIT

Six kilometres south of the city centre is **Gold Reef City**, a recreated turn-of-the-century mining town, complete with charming Victorian buildings – and a 73-roomed, Victorian-themed hotel and casino.

Gold Reef City is Joburg's amusement park, and it provides a fun day for every member of the family. You can watch a gold-pouring demonstration, or you can go on one of 28 rides including the ferris wheel, the Earthquake Tunnel, Miner's Revenge, the Tower of Terror (going up and racing down Shaft 15 headgear) and the River Rapids. Or, you can take a penny-farthing ride around the village.

If you're feeling you need to get off your feet, you can take the train that runs around the perimeter of the town. Or hop on one of several horse-drawn carriages that canter around the place. There is a farmyard, stables and funfair for the younger kids.

One of the biggest adventures at Gold Reef City is a ride down Shaft 14, the original mine that was opened in 1897 on the site, part of the farm Langlaagte. The mine is part of the 100-km reef stretching from Boksburg in the east to Randfontein in the west, and visible from a distance with its impressive headgear protruding above the surrounding mine dumps. The mine goes down 57 levels or 3500 m, and over its 90-year lifespan produced some 1,4 million kilograms of gold, blasted out of the ground by 30 000 miners.

When the mine was opened, there was no electricity in the town and lighting underground was by means of candles, which posed a risk for explosions caused by methane gas. Combined with the darkness, the damp, the heat, the closeness and the ear-shattering noise of the drills, it was a tough way to earn a living.

There is a pub underground on level 5 of Shaft 14, only open for functions. The pub used to be where 300 donkeys were kept for three months. Their job was to pull cocopans filled with gold-laden rocks for removal above ground. The donkeys were invariably blind by the time their three months was up.[20]

Gold Reef City is open Tuesdays to Sundays. Go to www.goldreefcity.co.za for more information.

PLACES TO VISIT
The Apartheid Museum

(Northern Parkway and Gold Reef Road, Ormonde) occupies approximately 6000 square metres on a seven-hectare site which consists of natural recreated veld and indigenous bush habitat containing a lake, alongside its stark but stunning building. A multi-discipliniary team of curators, film-makers, historians, museologists and designers was assembled to develop the exhibition narrative which sets out by means of large blown-up photographs, artefacts, newspaper clippings, and some extraordinary and previously unseen film footage, to graphically tell the apartheid story.

Tickets for the Museum are plastic credit-card-size cards indicating either 'Non-white' or 'White' and indicate the beginning of a harrowing journey. Tall cages greet you on entering; inside the cages are blown-up copies of the racially-tagged identity cards, identity books and the despised pass books or *dompasse*. Numerous monitors display continuous re-runs of apartheid scenes, set in a double-volume ceiling, with concrete and red brick walls and grey concrete floor.

Other features of the Museum are graphic reminders of the horrors of apartheid: a large yellow and blue Casspir in which you can sit and watch footage taken from inside the vehicle driving through the townships; 121 nooses dangling from the roof of the Museum, representing the political prisoners hanged during apartheid; a cage full of dreadful weapons that were used by the security forces to enforce apartheid policies; footage of a remarkable 1961 BBC interview with Nelson Mandela when he was in hiding from the authorities; footage of Prime Minister Hendrik Verwoerd addressing a crowd in English, explaining how the country could be happily ruled only when the races were separated.

And just when you feel you can't tolerate the bombardment of your senses any longer, you reach a quiet space, where you can express your solidarity with the victims of apartheid by picking up a pebble and throwing it on a pile on the other side of the room.

The multimedia displays are not static: visitors can interact with them by adding their contributions. There are blown-up monolithic figures in transparent cases of the descendants of the first people who came to the Witwatersrand, with their artefacts in cabinets on the wall beside them – you can leave your own historical artefacts and have your photograph put in one of these cases. There is a recording studio in which you can leave your experiences under apartheid for others to hear.

The displays in the Museum are ongoing – in 2007, the history of the Truth and Reconciliation Commission was portrayed; the contribution of whites to the downfall of apartheid has been expanded.

An architectural consortium consisting of five leading architectural teams was assembled to design the museum. Mostly in bare concrete, with rounded walls, small claustrophobic rooms, tall ceilings, with an outer wall of stone packed into rusted wiring, the architecture captures a symbolic rawness.

The Apartheid Museum changes its temporary exhibitions twice a year. The museum is open Tuesdays to Sundays from 10h00 to 17h00.[22] For information go to www.apartheidmuseum.org or call (011) 309 4700.

Soccer: Where Joburg Meets Soweto

The police monitor a match between Orlando Pirates and Dynamos FC.

About eight kilometres south of Johannesburg's city centre, in the barren land between the old mines of the south and the border of Soweto, is the 420 ha suburb known as Nasrec. In the mid-1980s, Johannesburg's annual Rand Easter Show – established in 1895, as an agricultural fair – was moved from Milner Park (now the west campus of the University of the Witwatersrand) to Nasrec's custom-built facilities; the expo centre is now one of the largest such sites in Africa, and the Rand Show attracts over 500 000 visitors during its two-week run.

In 1987, an 80 000-seater soccer stadium was opened in Nasrec – conceived by black soccer officials (and funded without government assistance) as a home for Soweto's hugely popular (black) professional football league. Although the branding rights to the stadium were owned for many years by First National Bank (FNB), the stadium is better known simply as Soccer City. In addition to hosting fierce derbies between local teams, particularly Kaizer Chiefs and Orlando Pirates, Soccer City was the venue for the welcome-home rallies for released anti-apartheid leaders – Walter Sisulu, Govan Mbeki, Ahmed Kathrada and others in 1989, and Nelson Mandela in 1990 – as well as a mass funeral for assassinated Chris Hani in 1993.

Soccer City is currently undergoing a multi-million-rand renovation to upgrade its facilities for the 2010 World Cup, which will see the stadium's seating capacity grow to over 94 000 places.

Pirates and Chiefs

Organised football in South Africa originated in Natal, and was soon exported to other provinces. The first documented soccer matches in Johannesburg (in 1888) were all-white affairs – the Wanderers played the Rangers for the Transvaal Challenge Cup (by the Seventies, most of the white soccer leagues had ended as the game moved towards integration).

Gradually, migrant labourers coming from Natal to work on the mines introduced the game in the mining compounds; the sport 'provided valuable entertainment and granted temporary relief from police harassment and grinding poverty.'[26]

In the 1930s and 40s, as increasing numbers of black people migrated to the cities to find work, football became part of daily life among the township youth – 'the principle of "advancement by merit" that underlies sport helped transform football into a field … where black South Africans could seek greater social visibility, status and prestige than was afforded in the segregated South African society. Male-dominated football teams, contests and organisations enabled those who were denied basic human rights to adapt to industrial conditions, to cope with urban migration, and to build alternative networks on a local, regional and national scale.'[27]

Soweto's oldest soccer team is the Orlando Pirates; the club dates back to 1934, when a small band of teenagers formed a soccer club at the Orlando Boys' Club. By 1937, the youngsters – barefoot, and without colours or a kit – were competing in a minor division of the Johannesburg Bantu Football Association (JBFA), playing most of their games at the Waterval grounds in Sophiatown. Two years later, they broke away from the Boys' Club and reconvened at the house of one of the Club's boxing instructors, Andries 'Pele Pele' Mkhwanazi, who dubbed them 'amaPirate'; inspired by this and the popular pirate movies of the time, they adopted the name 'Pirates' (the team is also known as the Buccaneers).

Armed with a name, but still without colours, the young club made rapid progress in the Saturday League Division Two of the JBFA, playing at the Wemmer Parking Grounds in the city.

In 1940, the boys were presented with their first kit – provided by another influential figure, Bethuel Mokgosinyana, who had played for a soccer team called Phiri Phiri in his early days. Bethuel gave the team the old Phiri's jersey, which had a big 'P' inscribed in front (the team's skull-and-crossbones logo only appeared a decade later). Bethuel also built a room in his backyard in Orlando, which became the Pirates' clubhouse. On Friday nights, before matches, the boys would camp there, sleeping on the floor.

By the end of 1944, the team had been promoted to Division One of the JBFA – to do so, they had to beat the African Morning Stars, a strong, predominantly coloured side from Sophiatown (that included a member of the notorious Americans gang). The first match was remembered as a brutal goalless draw; Pirates won the replay 2-1. After the game, the young players were attacked and beaten, and the team lodged a complaint.

In 1945, Pirates arrived in the JBFA's Sunday League, the city's most elite division and the one with the most spectators. However, their intense rivalry with the Morning Stars – culminating in another 'battle' between the teams, and another unheeded complaint – saw them quit the JBFA. Pirates then helped establish the Orlando African Football Association, at what is today the Orlando Stadium; but, finding the opposition weak, they returned to the JBFA leaving their second team, the Sea Robbers, to represent their interests in Orlando. Their stay with the JBFA was again short, and for several years they 'freelanced' as an unaffiliated club, competing with other clubs on a friendly basis. Pirates also interacted with the JBFA's rival: the Johannesburg African Football Association (JAFB), an independent organisation (the JBFA was controlled by the City Council) run by Dan Twala.

In 1950, Pirates won the country's top competition, the SA Robertson Cup, beating their old rivals Morning

ANC and SACP leaders arrive for a rally at Soccer City, 1990

MK cadres carrying the coffin of assassinated SACP leader Chris Hani at Soccer City, April 1993

Stars 3-2 in a replay in front of a crowd 10 000 strong. The following year Pirates retained the Cup, repeating the feat in 1952 – together with a clean sweep of all the competitions they entered, including the JBFA League and the Transvaal Challenge Cup. The powerful Pirates beat all the top teams, like the Moonlight Darkies from Alexandra and the Naughty Boys. By 1954, the original Pirates line-up was growing old and newer players were becoming stars; they were not invincible however – in 1955 Moroka Swallows (also then known as Corrugated Rovers – see 'The Birds' for more on this team) trounced Pirates 5–0 in the Transvaal Challenge Cup Final.

In 1961, a strong-willed sponsor named David 'Oom Day' Motsamai, a successful bootlegger, joined the Pirates as their 'patron' – he provided kit and transport for the team. Oom Day had come from the Free State to Sophiatown in the 1940s, later marrying a shebeen queen known as Elizabeth 'Babes' Shub; during the forced removals from Sophiatown, Oom Day and his family had relocated to Dube in Soweto.

Under Oom Day – who was also a boxing promoter – Pirates' fame spread far and wide; his aspirations (of purchasing a soccer club outright), and strong personality, however, soon saw the patron and his charges on a collision course. By the end of 1961, Oom Day and the

Pirates had parted ways. In the late 1960s, the two most powerful clubs in the country were Orlando Pirates and Highlands Park (the latter then campaigning as Highlands Power, in the white National Football League).

Across the Atlantic, one of Pirates' favourite sons, Kaizer Motaung, was setting the North American Soccer League alight – he was the leading goal scorer for his club in 1968, and was chosen as Rookie of the Year.

In the same year, the neighbouring Kingdom of Swaziland had just completed building its new national stadium – and it was suggested (by Prince Dlamini, a staunch Pirates supporter) that a game between Orlando Pirates and Highlanders be staged as part of the opening celebrations. The teams were approached and were intrigued by the idea; the fans were enthusiastic – thousands of them arranged to travel to Swaziland to see the match, for which each club would receive a handsome appearance fee plus basic costs, and would be accommodated in one of Swaziland's best hotels.

However, approval had not been obtained – or even sought – from the South African Bantu Football Association (SABFA), which adopted the petty standpoint that Pirates should not be permitted to play. The game was abandoned, leaving soccer followers disappointed … and the two teams deprived of substantial revenue.

A Kaizer Chiefs supporter

Soccer and Apartheid

South Africa's apartheid policies saw the country's 'official' (white) Football Association (FASA) expelled from FIFA (the world Football governing body) in 1961. Two years later, the ban was lifted and FASA announced it would send an all-white team to the 1966 World Cup … and an all-black team to the 1970 Cup! FASA was suspended again in 1964 and expelled in 1976. In 1991, the non-racial South African Football Association (SAFA) was formed; seven months later SAFA was re-admitted to FIFA to a standing ovation.

The Clever Boys

The oldest Joburg soccer team is that of Wits University – dating back to 1922. Originally established as a university soccer team, it began playing semi-professional soccer in 1961, moving up to the white National Football League's (NFL) first division in 1976. In 1978 it was one of the first NFL teams to join the non-racial National Professional Soccer League.

SABFA then began to put pressure on Pirates to abandon its non-black players – under threat of disciplinary action from the government and Joburg's Sports and Recreation section, Pirates was forced to comply with certain provisions of the apartheid law, and the multiracial 'Bhakabhaka' squad of 1966 to 1968 came to a sad end.

Internal politics at Pirates also had far-reaching effects on the soccer landscape: a number of Pirates players had received invitations from leading soccer clubs in Swaziland and Botswana – the latter without prior approval from the club. It was voted that the players involved would be excluded from the club.

At the same time, Kaizer Motaung was due to return to South Africa on holiday – and offered to share his knowledge of professional football overseas with any soccer player willing to learn. The result was that many players approached Kaizer, and the nucleus of a new team – the Kaizer Motaung International XI – was formed. Despite some opposition, it wasn't long before Kaizer's team played invitation games at Orlando Stadium and other venues throughout the country. Kaizer's reputation grew, and calls were made to establish a permanent club (a call Kaizer initially resisted, believing it would be a betrayal of his former club); the pressure on Kaizer,

however, became too much. When he returned to South Africa at the end of his contract with Atlanta Chiefs, he severed all relations with Pirates. To avoid red tape – and membership of the Johannesburg Bantu Football Association – Kaizer Chiefs FC was affiliated to the Football Association in Nigel. A number of former Buccaneers became owners of the new club, and players were drawn from both Pirates and Moroka Swallows. Chiefs are also known as 'Amakhosi'.

In a later interview with Kaizer Motaung, he recalled: 'Kaizer Chiefs was formed, I guess, at the right time. We were living through a politically repressive and violent era. For instance, if you defeated Pirates at Orlando

Eric 'Scara' Sono, play-ing for Pirates (undated)

Ezenkosi

In 1982 Ephraim 'Jomo' Sono (son of famous Pirates midfielder Eric 'Scara' Sono) bought out the Highlands Park FC and renamed it Jomo Cosmos. The club's training grounds are in Turffontein, near the race track. Somo, a skilled player and legendary coach, is known by a string of nicknames including Black Prince, King of African Soccer and 'Thata-machans' (take a chance).

Stadium, chances were that it would be difficult to leave the stadium unharmed.

'Then along came Chiefs. Our dress code was such that it appealed to a lot of people. Maybe that is why, when we started, we had such a large number of women supporters [laughs]. But seriously though, we promoted the concept of love and peace, and incorporated it into our slogan. We emphasised through words and deeds, both on and off the field, that soccer was about comradeship, about friendship, sportsmanship.'[28]

To this day, Chiefs and Pirates are arch rivals on the sports field.

The Birds

The third big Soweto team is Moroka Swallows – or the Birds – founded in 1947 in the Moroka Emergency Camp. The exact early history is not clear, but soccer journalist Walter Mbeba credits Lawrence 'Rhee' Mbanya with establishing the soccer team, playing in the alleyways of the then-shanty town. A separate history, on the Swallows website, credits Johnny 'Walker' Kubeka, Ishmael

Lesolang and Strike Makgatho as the club's founding fathers who handpicked young boys they saw playing soccer on the streets to form a new club – the name suggested for the group was the Moroka Sweepers, but one of the players argued (convincingly) that swallows flew higher than sweepers, and so the name Moroka Swallows was adopted.

Having dispatched local opposition such as Rockville Hungry Lions, Mighty Greens, Rangers and Moroka Naughty Boys, the young Moroka Swallows team joined the Orlando Football Association.

After a number of Cup victories in the late 1950s, Moroka Swallows became the first club to have an official supporters' club, established by Mr Maswidi Gumede. Swallows also saw one its own prominent players head-hunted to play abroad: Joseph 'Carlton' Moloi joined Cardiff City in 1959 – he took his own coloured blanket with him to the United Kingdom.

In the early 1960s, Swallows became a professional club and joined the South African Soccer League (SASL), an organisation born from a merger between the SA African Football Association, the SA Indian Football Association and the SA Coloured Football Association.

By 1964, a National Professional Soccer League (NPSL) was launched – headed by president Bethuel Morolo, who followed government instructions that all races should play separately, at grounds allocated to them.

The existence of the two leagues caused a rift within the Swallows team – as different players campaigned to belong to different leagues. The division nearly saw the end of Swallows as a team – some left, later joining Kaizer Motaung's XI. Carlton Moloi formed a new group within Swallows, known as Swallows Big XV; a rival group became known as Moroka Swallows Babes. The former became the Moroka Swallows in existence today; the latter disappeared in the 1980s.

In 1985, the NPSL was sidelined by the new National Soccer League (NSL). In 1996 this body became known as the PSL (Premier Soccer League), which still operates today.

The Klipriviersberg

The unspoilt 680-ha Klipriviersberg Nature Reserve remains largely as it was when people first settled in the Johannesburg area around 1000 years ago. Hikes around the reserve will reveal some of the 150 species of birds, and around 650 indigenous plants and trees, with the pleasant Bloubosspruit flowing idly through it. And, with the recent reintroduction of grazing animals, the reserve is probably closer to its natural state than it has been in over 100 years.

In around 1850, a Voortrekker named Sarel Marais settled just above the Bloubosspruit with his family, in the southern part of what is now the reserve. Marais built the five elements of what characterised a typical 1850s farmstead: a farmhouse, a *waenhuis* or wagonhouse, an orchard, an irrigation furrow and a cemetery. A diary from the time indicates that lion, caracal, lynx and genet were found on the farm. Today, only the walls of the farmhouse remain; the roof and interior structures were destroyed by fire. The orchard – which once grew peach, pear, fig and pomegranate trees – is also gone; the peaches, it is said, were used by Marais to make Witblitz, the high-proof white spirit.

The family cemetery still exists, some 500 m north of the house, now overgrown and vandalised. Sarel Marais' grave is in the cemetery. He died in 1897, aged 83.

Marais' son Jakob took over the property, but sold it in 1917 to the Quilliam family who developed the land, successfully farming dairy, 10 000 pigs, and growing lucerne, barley, and maize.

The City Council bought the farm around 1950, after most of the Quilliam family had left and grandfather Quilliam had died. His wife remained on the farm until it became unsafe for her to stay on her own.

In 1984 Klipriviersberg was proclaimed as a nature reserve; it belongs to the city, but is monitored by the Klipriviersberg Nature Reserve Association. In 2003 game was reintroduced to Klipriviersberg. There are now 12 springbok, 15 black wildebeest, 22 blesbok, 8 zebra, 5 red hartebeest, and some 24 mountain reedbuck. Other smaller animals spotted at Klipriviersberg include porcupine, duiker, genet, civet, black-backed jackal, scrub hare and mongoose. The reserve is fenced. For information go to www.knra.co.za.

PLACES TO VISIT

There are several access points for the **Klipriviersberg Nature Reserve**: from the Recreation Centre on Peggy Vera Road; and the most popular one, via Frandaph Drive in Mondeor, where the old dam wall is located. There is a guard stationed here.

The reserve has a network of trails running through it, the two longest ranging from 5,8 km to 9 km. Organised walks take place every second and fourth Sunday of the month, from the Frandaph Drive entrance. Further information can be obtained from the website at www.footprint.co.za/klipriviersberg.htm.

There are 10 horses in the reserve, used for patrols but also for leisurely trots, by arrangement with Greg Martin. He also has a wagon that is pulled by four donkeys, especially for young children, the disabled or the elderly. Trips by schools or corporates can be arranged with Greg by calling him on 082 645 0248.[29]

Klipriviersberg Nature Reserve

THE NORTHERN

'Mrs. Eckstein wore Eau de Nil silk, the bodice veiled in Brussels lace. Mrs. Fitzpatrick, white silk beautifully trimmed with bands of pearl passementerie and chiffon. Miss Fitzpatrick wore a pretty frock of pink satin trimmed with pink Gase de Soie.'
Johannesburg Mademoiselle, 1898
(on a dinner party hosted by Mrs Dalrymple)

In this chapter

☞ The Braamfontein Estate Company

☞ The Jameson Raid and the South African War

☞ Parktown and Westcliff's Grand Houses

☞ The Joburg Zoo and Zoo Lake

☞ Gay Johannesburg

SUBURBS

The Zoo Lake. Photograph by Jurgen Schadeberg.

Economic Geography

View from Munro Drive under construction, 1919

In 1890, Johannesburg hit its first slump. A little over three years after digging had started in earnest on the Reef, the exposed outcroppings of ore (which were crushed in stamp batteries, with the gold extracted using a mercury amalgam process) had been exhausted. That there was more gold to be found was not in doubt; the problem lay in the fact that the Reef continued deep underground – and that the unexposed (unoxidised) pyritic ore was much less responsive to the mercury treatment than the surface ore had been.

Between 1886 and 1889, Johannesburg – and its 300 listed mining companies – had produced over 630 000 ounces of gold, at not inconsiderable expense. Now, it looked uncertain as to whether it would be possible (or affordable) to mine any gold at all.

The share market collapsed and banks and lending houses called in their loans, prompting many debtors to simply flee the scene. Houses and stores were left unoccupied and boarded up.

A young Percy Fitzpatrick, already a veteran of the collapsed Barberton gold rush, despondently predicted that 'grass will grow in the streets of Johannesburg within a year'.

Amidst such uncertainty, even the town's booming suburban real estate market seemed – momentarily – to stall, particularly in the planning or proclamation of suburbs (townships) in the wealthier regions to the east and north-east.

The insecurity lasted several months, until June 1890 – when ore tailings (ores which had already been through the standard crushing and amalgam treatment processes) were subjected to the new MacArthur-Forrest process, which used cyanide instead of mercury and produced spectacular results.

The fortuitous intervention of science saw the slump turn into a new boom – bolstered by bigger investments and newly consolidated mining houses, led or managed by Joburg's ruling moneyed class: the Randlords.

The revival of fortunes saw a rash of new residential property developments; specifically, a number of suburbs were proclaimed to the north of Johannesburg, far away from the mining lands in the south.

The newly fashionable north was considered to be out 'in the country'. There were deliberately no tram or train links beyond the urban border of Braamfontein; this, in addition to the premium-priced larger stands, put the land decidedly out of reach of the pockets of the pedestrian working class.

By 1895 it was evident that 'the homes of the really wealthy would not only lie in the northern suburbs, but they would face north, and the prize location would be the Parktown Ridge',[1] with its views stretching to the Magaliesberg, and its ridge conveniently hiding almost all evidence of the sprawling mining camp to its south.

The Braamfontein Estate Company

Of all the original farmlands making up what is now Johannesburg, the portion known as Braamfontein was referred to as the unluckiest. 'Its southern boundary fell short of the outcrop of the Main Reef by approximately 1,000 yards. Beyond it lay Turffontein and the various portions of Langlaagte. … But Braamfontein, though it was prospected more thoroughly than any other farm on the Witwatersrand before the dip of the reefs was understood, produced no gold. All it had was an abundant supply of water in the hollow that someone had named "Sans Souci".'[2]

Hermann Eckstein and his wife   **Edouard Lippert**

In 1887 Edouard Lippert – a close friend of Paul Kruger's who had been given the concession to produce dynamite in the ZAR – was given a freehold lease on a large section of the northern portion of Braamfontein. He called it Sachsenwald (anglicised to Saxonwold during the First World War), built his home Onderkopjes at the foot of the Parktown Ridge, and planted thousands of trees.[3]

In 1892 Hermann Eckstein took over the water rights at Sans Souci and purchased the Natal Mining Company's lease of the southern portion of the farm. Eckstein formed the Braamfontein Estate Company, and persuaded Lippert to contribute his land in Sachsenwald in return for shares.

In March 1893 the directors of the Braamfontein Company decreed the new township was to be called Park Town. As the area fell beyond the city limits, it would be administered as essentially a private estate until 1904. The Company provided services – a horse-and-cart sanitation service, roads, electric street lights and water.[4]

From the start, steps were taken to ensure it would be a truly elite suburb: commercial use was prohibited, only one dwelling was allowed per property, and all building plans had to be submitted to and approved by the Company. In an effort to retain the 'country' feel, the streets were laid out along the natural contours of the ridge and surrounding land instead of the city's geometric grid system.[5]

Parktown was a private suburb and had to provide its own amenities, including its water supply. This had to be pumped from Sans Souci; two tall water towers were erected at the highest part of the ridge near the spot where Milpark Hospital stands today. A pasture was retained for cows in the centre of the suburb and was called 'The Oval'. The Wits Business School in St Andrews Road now occupies this land.

The first residence erected in Parktown was that of Corner House executive Lionel (later Sir Lionel) Phillips – who, as the story goes, was petitioned to move out of the city by his wife Florence, who had fallen in love with the Parktown Ridge and its views while out riding one day. The Phillipses had, until that point, lived in Hermann Eckstein's former house in town, which was named Hohenheim after the German town where Eckstein was born.

In 1892 Phillips commissioned architect Frank Emley to design a new 40-room mansion – also to be called Hohenheim – on a 20-acre site on the Parktown Ridge. Florence, who suffered from ill health and was in England, recuperating, directed the finishings and furnishings of her new residence through a series of long letters.

Returning to South Africa with numerous staff members and household items, Florence soon helped to turn Hohenheim into the centre of sophisticated entertainment in Johannesburg, hosting a Baron Rothschild and various members of the British aristocracy in a series of lavish dinners, garden parties, afternoon teas and formal dances. In less than two years, Hohenheim had become too small for its owners' requirements. Florence departed for England as the renovations were about to start; little could she know how the city's landscape would have changed on her return.[6]

Lady Phillips.
Inset: Lionel Phillips

The first Hohenheim in Parktown

The second Hohenheim, later the Otto Beit Convalescent Home

PLACES TO SEE

Later, Hohenheim became the residence of Sir Percy Fitzpatrick. This, famously, is where he told the fireside tales that would later become the classic, *Jock of the Bushveld*.

Hohenheim was taken over by Julius Friedlander in 1912 and was subsequently bought by Sir Otto Beit. In 1915 Beit presented the property to the Johannesburg Hospital, which turned it into the Otto Beit Convalescent Home. In the 1970s it was demolished to make way for the Johannesburg General Hospital. Its original position is marked by a plaque.

Sir Percy Fitzpatrick

The Jameson Raid

Dr Leander Starr Jameson

On 29 December 1895 a regiment of 600 men, led by Dr Leander Starr Jameson, crossed into the Transvaal from Matabeleland (today Zimbabwe), heading for Johannesburg. Jameson's goal was to provoke an uprising in the Golden City, where foreigners – Uitlanders – significantly outnumbered the Boers but did not have the franchise; and, ultimately, to initiate a revolt against the Boer government itself.

The original idea had been for Jameson to storm the Transvaal after Johannesburg had risen in (pre-planned) rebellion; Jameson would then, conveniently, arrive to 'restore order' in the Boer republics. The plan even included a pre-fabricated letter (written a month earlier) containing a formal request of help, imploring:

'Thousands of unarmed men, women, and children of our race will be at the mercy of well-armed boers; while property of enormous value will be in the greatest peril.'

Jameson's Joburg counterparts – known as the Reform Committee – were, however, struggling to agree on exactly what would happen after the coup: would the Transvaal become a British Colony, for instance, or remain independent? The rebellion seemed increasingly unlikely, a victim of inertia and lack of consensus.

Jameson, however, was restless; he believed his presence alone would be enough to spur the Reformers into action. He telegraphed his intention – to invade the Transvaal, unless he heard 'definitely to the contrary' – to Cecil Rhodes, co-conspirator and chief facilitator of the Raid (also Prime Minister of the Cape Colony and proprietor of the British South Africa Company, which owned the portion of Matabeleland where Jameson was based). By the time the messages reached Rhodes, Jameson's men had already cut the telegraph wire to the Cape and no reply was possible. Not only was there no 'rebellion' ready and waiting on the goldfields; as Jameson would discover, there was to be no help at all.

At dawn on 2 January, just 30 km from Johannesburg, with very little sleep and having fought intermittent skirmishes en route, Jameson and his men were forced to pitch a hopeless last stand against a substantial Boer force – which had been warned of Jameson's incursion (owing to the Raiders' failure to correctly cut the telegraph line to Pretoria). Within hours, Jameson's men had surrendered, and he was being led away to a Pretoria jail, weeping.[7]

CJ Rhodes

In the tin trunk of one of Jameson's men was found a set of coded telegraphs, discussing preparations for the Raid; and the accompanying cipher book.[8]

On hearing of the defeat of 'Dr Jim' (Jameson was a medical doctor), the 'gentlemen of Parktown' – the city's leading business and social figures – rode into town to await arrest at the premises of the Rand Club.[9] Among them were the Reform Committee's leaders: Lionel Phillips; John Hays Hammond, an American; Frank Rhodes (Cecil's brother); and George Farrar. Co-conspirators included John Dale Lace, Solly Joel (Barney Barnato's nephew), Percy Fitzpatrick, Abe Bailey, Dr Hans Sauer, Henri Bettelheim, HB Marshall and Max Langermann.

Lionel and the Reform leaders were all sentenced to death; the others were fined £2000 each, plus two years' imprisonment to be followed by a three-year banishment.

The death sentences were later commuted, first to 15 years' imprisonment, then to fines of £25 000 each, together with an undertaking not to interfere in the country's politics for a period of 15 years. The Phillipses left immediately for London, not to return until after the war.[10]

Jameson (who, together with his commanding officers, was tried in London) was sentenced to 15 months' imprisonment without hard labour. After serving a portion of his term in Holloway Prison, he returned to South Africa and later served as Prime Minister of the Cape. Jameson was subsequently appointed a baronet and retired to the UK in 1912.

For Cecil John Rhodes, it was a disaster. He was acquitted of responsibility for the invasion; after all, he had never signed an actual order for Jameson to proceed. However, his involvement in the plot was undoubted – and the same investigating committee found that he had acted irresponsibly in his roles as Prime Minister and head of the British South Africa Company. Rhodes had to resign both posts.

PLACES TO SEE

The View (18 Ridge Road, Parktown) is the only Parktown house constructed before the South African War to retain its original style and form.[11] Not only did the structure survive intact (narrowly escaping demolition during construction of the Joburg highway), but many of the interior fixtures and fittings have also been preserved. The house was designed in 1896, by Aburrow & Treeby, for Thomas Major Cullinan, a businessman and building contractor whose ventures into diamond prospecting later yielded the discovery of the Cullinan Diamond – at the time, the largest diamond ever found. The Cullinan Diamond was cut into nine gems, the largest of which (the 'Star of Africa') was set into the Sceptre of the British Royal Crown Jewels.

Today, The View serves as the headquarters of the Transvaal Scottish Regiment and can be hired for conferences. Call (011) 643 2961.

A Thin Gold Fuse

The tensions leading up to the Jameson Raid were not quite as simple as the matter of a franchise for the region's large Uitlander community – although the vote certainly was an issue: at the time, foreigners were required to give up their previous citizenship and live in the Transvaal for 14 years before becoming naturalised.

Joburg's economic recovery had come at a price. Deep-level mining was considerably more expensive than surface prospecting had been. It required large amounts of dynamite for blasting mine shafts – and explosives were sold exclusively through Kruger's concession to Edouard Lippert, at an exorbitant mark-up; it needed significantly more manpower (which meant more had to be spent on salaries); and the state taxes reduced profits even further. Despite not being citizens, Uitlanders made a significant contribution to the ZAR treasury (over £1 500 000 in 1889[12]).

The mining bosses and their advisors determined that, 'with efficient government in the Transvaal', they would be able to reduce these onerous costs to such an extent that the 'costs of production on the Rand could quickly fall by maybe 15 or 20 per cent'.[13]

The idea of increased profits was appealing to Cecil Rhodes, as was the possibility of expanding his personal (and the Imperial) Empire. Which explains, in part, why the Jameson Raid – what statesman Jan Smuts later referred to as the 'real declaration of war'[14] – was originally planned.

Many prominent historians have attributed the start of the South African War (also referred to as the Anglo-Boer War) three years later to one principal factor: gold.

Other students of history dispute such claims. They point out that the mine owners may have desired a more benevolent dispensation, but certainly didn't want a war that would bring mining production to a halt and threaten their hefty investments in machinery and infrastructure.

The British government also seemed to shy away from to the idea of outright hostilities, preferring to negotiate where possible. Milner, the British High Commissioner, had managed to convince Kruger to reduce the franchise requirement to seven, then five, years, a concession he initially viewed as a triumph.

Although threatening war was something of an accepted diplomatic technique at the time, it was usually reserved for harder-to-negotiate circumstances or stubborn opponents.

Public British sentiment, however, seemed very pro-Empire and anti-Boer. The English public still remembered the humiliation of their country's defeat at the hands of Boer forces at Majuba in 1881; there was also strong support for securing Britain's position as the 'paramount power in South Africa'.[15] In short, many Britons did not only look to the riches the Transvaal (or any colony) had to offer: they also wanted to put the Transvaalers in their place. There was, moreover, a generally held assumption that any war between the Imperial might and the backward Boers would be a short one – over 'before tea time'...

Stores boarded up in town

Boer Commando leaving Jeppe

Not surprisingly, Boer sentiment was becoming strongly anti-British as the political concessions ate away at the pillars of Afrikaner communities – the Transvaal Boers 'saw themselves as fighting for national independence and the preservation of a distinctive native Afrikaner culture'.[16] This, perhaps more than any other material or Imperial goal, led to the eventual outbreak of war in 1899; which, as historians point out with interest, was initiated by the eventual loser.

Even before the outbreak of hostilities, Johannesburg made ready for war: tens of thousands of *Uitlanders* fled the city – trains were filled to capacity, and 'every other means of transport' was utilised. The Chamber of Mines decamped to Cape Town, as did most of the mining houses.

Once the first shots were fired (in October 1899), able-bodied Afrikaans men left town to join their commando units.

Johannesburg suffered very little actual military action – skeleton crews kept basic services running, although 'the streets were unswept and grass began to grow in the roads'; many business were boarded up – although some institutions like the Rand Club remained open, admitting principal Republican officials as honorary members. Gradually, food stocks began to run low and food prices started

to rise. The Boers imposed martial law; all bars were closed, and no one was allowed to go out at night without a permit. An improvised police force, made up of 'neutrals' (all the regular force had gone to the front), policed the relatively quiet town; mining companies recruited similar forces to guard and protect their properties – the Boer government worked several of the mines on a small scale, and also commandeered Begbie's iron foundry, converting it into a factory for the manufacturing of shells. On 25 April 1900 a large explosion destroyed the foundry, killing 12 men (mostly Italian immigrants) and wounding 56 others; foul play was suspected and Begbie's son, William, was arrested – but later discharged for lack of evidence.

Rumours that the explosion had been caused by British sympathisers prompted an order expelling most of the remaining British subjects; only about 60 English men and 'a few women and children' were allowed to remain. The British forces, however, were fast approaching the mining town: on 20 April, three thousand Boer commandos retreated through town; and trenches were dug in Parktown to defend Johannesburg. By the end of May, the sound of British guns were being heard. Realising that Johannesburg could not be held, Dr FET Krause, the governor, went to meet the British and agreed to surrender the town uncon-

Lord Roberts arrives in Johannesburg. In the centre (in black hat) is Dr FET Krause.

A market pass issued during the British occupation of Joburg, June 1900.

ditionally. 'He asked the British not to come in until May 31 so that there might be time for the armed burghers to get away and to avoid street fighting, and in return he undertook to safeguard the mines.'[17] On the agreed date, lines of khaki-clad men advanced over the Kensington hills; the Boer flag was lowered and a silken Union Jack was run up in its place. Johannesburg became, for a time, a great military camp.

Less than a year after the first shots were fired, both the Transvaal and the Orange Free State were under British control – following the fall of Kroonstad, the surrender of Johannesburg and the capture of Pretoria. The war, however, continued for another two years – through the efforts of small groups of Boer 'guerrilla' soldiers.

The last of the Boer fighters surrendered in May 1902. The 'tea-time' war had cost as many as 75 000 lives: 22 000 British soldiers (an astonishing 65 per cent of deaths were caused by disease, and not as a result of battle); between 6000 and 7000 Boer soldiers, together with as many as 28 000 Boer civilians (many of these lost in the terrible conditions of the concentration camps), and an estimated 24 000 black South Africans – who died in battle and in internment camps.

PLACES TO VISIT
The South African National Museum of Military History

Built in 1914, the Edward Lutyens-designed Rand Regiment's Memorial commemorates the deaths of volunteers who fought on Britain's side during the 1899–1902 war. The memorial is on the grounds of the Museum of Military History (Erlswold Way, Saxonwold), adjoining the Joburg Zoo.

Opened in 1947, the Museum houses a collection of military items, including weapons, aircraft, tanks and even a submarine, as well as a collection of paintings completed by official war artists appointed during the Second World War. After 1994, the collections were expanded to include artefacts from Umkhonto we Sizwe, the ANC's military wing. The Museum facilities include a small café, offering light meals, and a shop selling military artefacts and memorabilia. For more information, go to www.militarymuseum.co.za.

Milner's Kindergarten

Milner and friends. He is seated in front, on the right.

By March 1901 the British High Commissioner, Sir Alfred (later Lord) Milner, had taken official residence at the Parktown home known as Sunnyside – built in 1895 for an American engineer named Hennen Jennings (who had not only been instrumental in bringing the MacArthur-Forrest process to the Rand but had also been a member of the Reform Committee and spent several months in jail, along with most of his neighbours[18]). Although English Prime Minister Joe Chamberlain disapproved of Milner choosing Joburg rather than Pretoria for his headquarters, Milner appeared to particularly like the city, saying: '… it would be a strange failure indeed if this did not become a city to live in, a city to be proud of, one of the great cities of the world.'[19] Sunnyside remained the Official British Residence until Union in 1910, and was occupied by Milner's successors, including Lord Selborne and Lord Gladstone.

Milner's tenure at Sunnyside became strongly associated with what became known as 'Milner's Kindergarten' – an 'informal club of colonial administrators and political activists in southern Africa that comprised a number of young Oxford graduates'[18] who were specially recruited by Milner and his successor to fill various administrative posts after the war. Members of the 'Kindergarten' went on to become prominent international players in politics, business, finance and journalism.

Parktown's 'New Look'

While Sir Milner may have enjoyed the view from Sunnyside – where he could look out over 'miles of rolling veldt to the great mountain barrier of the Magaliesberg' with Pretoria's forts just 'specks' in the distance[21] – he was less than impressed with Joburg's elaborate and somewhat pretentious buildings.

In 1902, Milner sought the services of an architect – a Briton named Herbert Baker, a protégé of Rhodes – 'to establish a new and more permanent order of architecture' in Johannesburg.

Baker initially experimented with sun-dried bricks, corrugated iron and roof timbers imported from the Cape. 'Necessity forced him to look for indigenous material that was more easily obtainable. He began quarrying quartzite from the ridges and found it to be hard, durable and attractive. The combination of natural stone walls and timber roofing gave rise to a … style of architecture that blended with the ridge environment and soon characterised the Parktown area.'[22]

Sir Herbert Baker

Herbert Baker travelled to the Cape from England in 1892, at the age of 30, to join a younger brother who had embarked on a farming venture.

After working on the restoration of Cecil Rhodes' residence, Groote Schuur, and travelling to Europe to study architectural monuments, Baker became the most fashionable architect of South Africa's post-war colonial set. He became part of Milner's famed 'Kindergarten' and built his own house – The Stonehouse – on land provided by another member, Lionel Curtis. Baker worked with several partners: Massey, taken on in Cape Town in 1899; Kendal, in Bloemfontein; and Sloper in Johannesburg (later replaced by Fleming).

Some of Baker's more famous public buildings include the Rhodes Memorial in Cape Town, the Union Buildings in Pretoria, and the South African Institute for Medical Research in Johannesburg.

Baker left South Africa for India in 1913, but many of his pupils – Pearse, Leith and Solomon, to name a few – continued to dominate the local architectural scene. He returned to South Africa in 1927 to work on the Reserve Bank in Pretoria, and designed South Africa House in Trafalgar Square, London, in 1935. He was knighted in 1923, and died in 1946 at his family home in Kent. He is buried in Westminster Abbey.

Better Homes & Gardens

Hazeldene Hall, 20 Ridge Road, Parktown (1902)

Hazeldene Hall was built by coal magnate and entrepreneur Charles J Jerome, after he purchased a stand adjacent to that of his friend Thomas Cullinan (The View). Both men had met in Barberton and had come to the Rand together to try their luck. The grand home was designed by the partnership of Aburrow & Treeby in 1902 but was only completed in 1907.

Today, Hazeldene Hall is headquarters to one of Joburg's favourite catering companies – By Word of Mouth – and is also rented out as a function venue. For more information, go to www.hazeldenehall.co.za or call (011) 544 1600.

Northwards, 21 Rockridge Road, Parktown (1904)

One of the first post-war mansions was Northwards, built by Herbert Baker for John Dale Lace, a mining magnate. Dale Lace was essentially a speculator who gambled on mining shares, and he lost and won his fortune several times. Clearly when he built Northwards, his fortunes were on the rise.

It is made of rough, quartzite *kopje* stone quarried from the site so that it appeared to grow out of the ridge – one of Baker's signature touches. John's wife, Josie Dale Lace, held famous parties there and notoriously arranged for zebras (housed in stables on the property, since knocked down) to pull her coach.

In 1908 the Dale Laces lost all their wealth. They seem to have been abandoned by their former friends and associates; John Dale Lace spent his twilight years in poverty in a semi-detached house in Rosettenville, while Josie lived in greatly reduced circumstances in Rondebosch in the Cape, where she was known as the 'rag woman'.

George Albu, another mining magnate, acquired Northwards. It burnt down in 1912 but Albu decided to rebuild it, hiring Baker to do the job. The stone walls had survived but the interior had to be completely rebuilt.

Northwards now houses the South African Institute of Architects – as well as the headquarters of the Parktown and Westcliff Heritage Trust – and is a national monument. Much of the house's original grounds were destroyed when the M1 freeway was built in the 1970s, and Northwards itself narrowly escaped demolition when the city's television signal tower was constructed in Auckland Park.

Hazeldene Hall

Northwards

John and Josie Dale Lace

Dolobran in the 1950s **Interior of Dolobran**

Dolobran, 16 Victoria Avenue, Parktown (1906)
Situated on the corner of Victoria Avenue and Oxford Road, Dolobran was built in 1906 for Sir Llewellyn Andersson, an accountant who made a fortune as a speculator. Andersson played a key role during the Jameson Raid, operating a searchlight from Auckland Park in an attempt to guide Jameson and his men to Johannesburg.

Andersson originally hired Herbert Baker to design his home, but disliked his plans as he felt that the windows were too small and allowed in too little light. The new plans, by English architect JA Cope-Christie, produced what is generally regarded as the most 'romantic' mansion in Johannesburg – with splendid turrets (since removed as they began to crumble in later years), distinctive cupola and weathervane.

Dolobran is still owned and occupied by the Andersson family and is not open to public viewing.

Villa Arcadia, 22 Oxford Road, Parktown (1909/10)
In 1906, the Lionel Phillipses made a return to Johannesburg society, purchasing a Swiss chalet-style property not far from their original residence.

The existing house, called Arcadia, proved too small for their significant social and entertaining requirements; however, as the site was suitable they simply knocked down the existing structure and commissioned Herbert Baker to design a new residence.

Baker's design combined elements of an English country house with Mediterranean influences – such as terracotta tiles (made in Vereeniging), black and white marble in the entrance hall and 'the double columns and arches of the loggias'.[23] The interior also features rococo fanlights, carved by Anton van Wouw.

The Phillipses remained owners of Villa Arcadia – where their first grandson was born – until 1922, when it was sold to the South African Jewish Orphanage. Lady Phillips' last reception at Arcadia was in 1923, when she was nearly 60 years old.

Arcadia remained Joburg's Jewish orphanage for over 80 years; in 2003 the house and property were sold to Hollard Insurance, which has redeveloped the land, adding additional office blocks – specially designed not to compete with the mansion – and restored aspects of the original house. Today the beautiful Arcadia villa – still with exceptional views – houses Hollard's art collection (well worth a visit in itself), including changing exhibitions and art for sale, and is also used as a corporate and private function venue.

For information, go to www.hollard.co.za/arcadia. asp and click on the link to the villa.

Glenshiel, 19 Woolston Road, Westcliff (1910)
Built from stone quarried on the spot, with a commanding position at the top of the Westcliff ridge, Glenshiel was designed by Herbert Baker for Scottish immigrant William (later Sir) Dalrymple, a key player in the mining industry. He and his wife Isabel (later Lady) Dalrymple were famous for their civic involvement, as well as for entertaining guests on Glenshiel's extensive grounds.

The present owner, Mr Haggie, lives in a converted cottage in what were once the mansion's stables; the main building (now a national monument) houses the order of St John's Priory – an arrangement made after the Second World War, during which time Glenshiel served as a military hospital.

Tours and visits are usually arranged through the Parktown and Westcliff Heritage Trust, and Glenshiel offers wheelchair-friendly access.

Emoyeni, 25 Queens Road, Parktown (1905)
Built in 1905 for The Honourable Henry Hull, Emoyeni was the work of architects Leck and Emley, who had just completed the new Rand Club building, the Corner House and the second Johannesburg Stock Exchange. The design was influenced by what was known as the 'Wrenaissance' – a revival of interest in English Renaissance architecture, particularly the work of Sir Christopher Wren.

Although the house has been known by several names – Highfield Manor, Brynrywen, Braemar and Rothley – it is best known as Emoyeni, meaning 'Place in the Air' in Zulu. Today Emoyeni retains much of its original exterior and some unusual interior features – all of the original fireplaces are intact, and chandeliers of Venetian glass still hang from the ceilings. The building is used as a conference and function venue. For more information go to www.emoyeniestate.co.za or call 011 484 0146.

The first Villa Arcadia

The reconstructed Villa Arcadia

Lady Dalrymple in Parktown

Kitchen Politics

'It was common knowledge within the circle of gardeners, usually passed on from elders who were themselves gardeners or domestic servants, that the red binding which edged the short sleeves and trousers of the "kitchen-suits" indicated up to where on the body of the madam or daughters of the house one could look; we were told that violation would result in one's arms or legs being amputated, as indicated by the red stripes.'[24]
Mxolisi Mchunu, 'The Advent of the Kitchen Suit: Understanding Zulu Male Initiation'

An 1896 census, taken within a three-mile radius of Market Square, showed Johannesburg had a population of 102 078, of whom 50 907 were whites.[25] While mining was the chief industry and employer, a little over eight per cent of the community provided domestic support services. There were: '3253 domestic servants (largely black), 3054 servants (white and Coloured), 402 cooks (white), 345 laundresses (Coloured), 341 waiters (white), 235 housekeepers (white), 219 nurses, 165 grooms, 146 'houseboys', 84 coachmen (black and white), 8 stable-keepers, 5 charwomen, 5 stewards, 4 mother's helpers, 3 valets and 1 page.'[26]

By far the largest group of servants in the early Witwatersrand was made up of black men. For various reasons, many of the male domestic workers were Zulu speakers, often from KwaZulu-Natal – so much so that 'the words "houseboy" and "Zulu" [became] almost synonymous on the Rand labour market.'[27]

Because of the high level of demand for domestic service, a 'houseboy' could command a considerable wage – up to £4 monthly, compared with just £2.9s.6d for a black miner[28] in 1899. Domestic wages usually incorporated a number of payments in kind, such as food, lodging and clothing, but were high enough for employers to make regular, often public, complaints about the cost of servants.

When, in 1896, the Chamber of Mines implemented a wage cut for black mine workers, domestic employers toyed with similar ideas – reducing their servants' wages, through the formation of a Housekeepers' Protection Association[29] – but were insufficiently organised to effect any mass cuts. The result of the mining wage cut was to induce greater numbers of men to look for less risky and better paid domestic positions. Despite the increase in available domestic labour, demand was so strong (particularly in a city still dominated by men) that servants' wages remained at the same high levels.

Before the outbreak of the South African War in 1899, the 'intersectoral competition' for black labour posed little problem for Johannesburg's mining industry: the domestic market was relatively small, and there was sufficient inflow of labour to the Rand to meet its needs.[30] After 1902, however, the labour market underwent a shift. Johannesburg continued to grow at a rapid rate, and its appetite for cheap labour intensified. Labour, however, was in increasingly short supply. This was aggravated by newly introduced permit systems that slowed the movements of Zulu workers – the preferred 'houseboys' – from the neighbouring Natal colony. For a brief period, also, employers attempted to pay wages at rates substantially below pre-war and wartime levels, before being forced to give in to market pressures.

Importantly, the mines were also experiencing labour shortages after reopening in 1901 – this was aided, in part, by the mining houses' decision to further cut mine wages, which acted as a disincentive for black labour. As an interim solution, the Chamber of Mines arranged for the importation of thousands of Chinese indentured labourers to work on the mines. (See Chapter Three.)

Another Randlord-backed 'solution' – to the 'vociferous demands for cheap black labour'[31] – was the importation of white female domestic workers, through a sanctioned emigration programme. It was hoped that encouraging white British women to emigrate to South Africa would ease the growing demand for domestic servants, and that the women would gradually come to replace the black male 'houseboys' (who would then be available to work on the mines); finally, it was hoped that women would marry and settle down and 'contribute to the development of a stable and loyal British working class in the Transvaal'.[32]

In April 1902 a South African Expansion Commission (SAEC) was set up in London, in association with the existing British Women's Emigration Association (BWEA). A further branch of the SAEC was set up in Johannesburg, under Sir Percy Fitzpatrick. In 1903, the London-based SAEC became independent of the BWEA and was renamed the South African Colonisation Society. The Society handled applications from potential immigrants, and forwarded its selection of suitable domestic servants to the Transvaal. The Johannesburg branch considered applications from would-be employers and arranged for the placement of the immigrants.

Johannesburg's middle and upper classes embraced the scheme – over 1000 female domestic servants were placed between mid-1902 and 1905 – but there were too many flaws in its execution: firstly, the demand for white servants greatly exceeded the supply; secondly, the Society often found it difficult to secure candidates with the requisite specialist and general skills. In many instances, British domestic servants would refuse to consider positions in Johannesburg (despite being offered significantly higher wages) because it was an inherent requirement that each servant be willing and able to take on various duties.

Domestic service was also becoming less appealing to young British women, who were choosing industrial work and its relative independence. Even young women who made the journey to South Africa would often take the expedient and available escape route of simply getting married – leading to the Colonisation Society being referred to, by employers, as a 'matrimonial agency'. The greatest problem, however, arose when newly arrived white domestic workers realised that all the hard physical labour – the 'rough' work – could be (and was) delegated to black servants, in particular black males. In many wealthier households, white servants became domestic administrators.

The subject of sexual tension between white women – employees and employers – and black male domestic staff, was both suppressed and mythologised. Periodicals even issued guidelines for 'madams' on how to manage their staff to avoid any 'uncomfortable' situations:

'They [white female servants] should be civil and kind … but they should never allow any familiarity. They should not touch their [black male servants'] hands, or sit in a room where there are boys, or do anything whereby an insolent native may take liberties.'[33]

Despite this, there were a number of documented – and, at the time, shocking – cases of cross-colour love affairs in Johannesburg, including several liaisons initiated by white madams. The topic inspired Sol T Plaatje's 1921 essay 'The Mote and the Beam', in which he daringly described how a black male servant sponged his white mistress' back in her bathtub.

More commonly, however, the tension manifested itself in traditional gender – but not strictly sexual – stereotypes: some white women assumed a mother-like status with their black male employees; while others were abusive and showed little respect for their male workers' feelings, being classified as 'witches' (abathakathi).[34]

When depression hit Joburg between 1906 and 1908, white domestic workers were often the first to be dismissed – their services were far more dispensable than those of the black workers who performed essential tasks.

The worsening economic conditions had another consequence: the arrival of an alternative labour supply, in the form of black women from rural areas. The women's arrival was well timed for nervous white employers, who were caught up in the midst of a 'black peril' scare – what Charles Van Onselen (in New Babylon, New Nineveh) refers to as regular bouts of 'sexual hysteria', linked to accusations by white women that black men had, or had tried to, sexually molest them – or to fears that this would happen.

The black community initially resisted sending its wives, sisters and daughters into service; firstly, there was the (often valid) concern that black women entering into domestic work would be seduced by white men; secondly, black women also preferred work – legal or illegal – that offered more independence.

A good number, however, did take household positions – at the same high rates the male workers had commanded. Eager to cut costs, employers looked to a new labour source: juveniles. 'Piccanins' were young boys aged between 10 and 15, often sourced from the far north of South Africa, who were contracted to perform domestic chores. An officially sanctioned scheme to place 'piccanins' was established; when the Chinese indentured labour scheme fell into disfavour, it was hoped the 'piccanins' would provide a workable solution that would continue to force adult black men into the mines. In practice, the scheme proved difficult to manage and had largely been abandoned by 1908.

The cumulative presence of alternative domestic labour sources – black women, black juveniles, unemployed European domestic staff – combined with the continuing arrival of black men from the countryside and the decrease in the demand for servants (owing to the depression) ultimately achieved what white home-owners had been hoping for all along: a reduction in the wages of 'houseboys'. Between 1905 and 1908, cash incomes for this group dropped by 46 per cent.[35]

As rural settlements became increasingly unable to support extended families or communities (because of natural hazards such as drought, and political onessuch as the 1913 Land Act), greater numbers of black women continued to travel to the towns to seek work. This time, however, they were prepared to accept lower wages than their male counterparts.

At about the same time (in 1912), Joburg experienced its worst 'black peril' scare to date, following the serious sexual assault of a white woman by a gang of 'houseboys'. Black women gradually became the preferred domestic servants on the Rand – although Zulu 'houseboys' continued to be employed for decades to come, black males were largely relegated to the gardens... or the mines.

Between 1927 and 1939, the number of urban black women in Johannesburg more than doubled.[36]

After 1948, the apartheid government gradually sought to extend the permit restrictions (pass laws) applied to black men to black women. The effect of this was to galvanise black women into protest action, and marked the beginning of significant women's involvement in the fight against apartheid.

On 9 August 1956, 20 000 women staged a march on the Union Buildings in Pretoria, protesting specifically against the pass laws. The women left bundles of petitions (for the attention of the Prime Minister, Strijdom) containing more than 100 000 signatures, and stood silently outside the government building for 30 minutes, hands raised in salute. Among the protesters were hundreds of domestic workers – many of whom even brought along their white charges.

Joburg's Man-Made Forest

Saxonwald, 1902. Camp belonging to Major Ffennell prior to his building his home – now the Hope Convalescent Home. The view looks across what is now the Zoo and the lower part of Forest Town, to Hohenheim and Parktown Ridge towards Orange Grove.

Before 1886, Joburg would have been dominated by a mixture of indigenous grasses such as Loudetia simplex (common russet grass), Themeda triandra (red grass) and Trachypogon spicatus (giant spear grass), as well as indigenous trees such as Acacia caffra (common Hook–thorn) and Rhus leptodictya (Mountain karee).[37]

Today, only a few remaining sites – such as the Melville Koppies and the Klipriviersberg Reserve – preserve the city's original veld. The slow-growing indigenous trees proved unsuitable for the lumber demands of the city's housing and mining industries; and, one can conjecture, the superficially featureless grasslands appeared alien and unwelcoming to the settlements earliest European inhabitants.

Johannesburg's best-kept secret is the Brenthurst Gardens in Parktown – an astonishing 45 acres of breathtaking natural and structured gardens situated just below the Johannesburg General Hospital and above the M1 highway. Thousands upon thousands of motorists pass this spot every day, oblivious the 'Secret Garden' near by. The Gardens begin on Federation Road and stretch to the south-western border of Killarney. They include remnants of the original Sachsenwald forest in the form of towering eucalyptus trees over a hundred years old. The estate contains a mansion, which was built in 1906 and has been occupied by South Africa's wealthiest family, the Oppenheimers, since 1922.

The Gardens are tended by no less than 45 gardeners, and include a rose garden, a fragrance garden, the Venus garden (with a Pierre-Auguste Renoir statue – 'Vénus Victorieuse'), a stunning Japanese garden dominated by an 18-metre waterfall and a large vegetable garden. They also feature a topiary, a nursery and other remarkable statues.[38] The Gardens can be visitied by appointment, or as part of regular tours conducted by the Parktown and Westcliff Heritage Trust. For more information, contact (011) 646 4122 or go to www.brenthurstgardens.co.za.

Edouard Lippert's Sachsenwald plantation formed the centre of one of Joburg's largest and most important tree nurseries (there was another, larger, nursery in Turffontein, south of the city centre): it covered an area of about 1400 acres, and was planted with between two and three million trees – mostly exotic species of Australian eucalyptus and European pine, which grew rapidly in the South African climate and were ideal for use as timber props in the underground mining tunnels. Cypresses, oaks, poplars, maples, planes, elms and ash trees were also planted.

Within a decade, observers had already noted that the plantation of millions of imported species – such as the bluegum – had a detrimental effect on the region's water, as they desiccated the soil in which they grew[39]; it was even speculated that the plantations were linked to Joburg's 1897 drought. It would be decades before the true impact of such vast numbers of alien trees was understood (they altered the water table as well as the drainage and erosion capacity of the area), and nearly a century before comprehensive environmental legislation was implemented at state level.

The Sachsenwald Forest remained private property, and was a favoured recreation and riding spot – mainly for wealthier folk from the northern suburbs; access was strictly controlled. Nearby San Souci was also a regular weekend 'getaway' spot, and a swimming bath was constructed at the site in 1894, followed by a large hotel in 1897.

In 1908, the area between the forest and Parktown was developed into the suburb of Forest Town; with increased residential development, the forest dwindled.

During the First World War the plantation name was anglicised to 'Saxonwold'. It was gazetted as a township in 1924. Remnants of the forest can be seen at the Zoo Lake and in the grounds of the Joburg Zoo.

Beyond Parktown

In 1901 Parktown was incorporated into Johannesburg. Despite protests from some of the standholders, the Braamfontein Estate Company embarked on a new programme promoting growth in the suburb and looking to increase sales of land.

In 1902 smaller plots of land – about half an acre each – were developed for sale, with one of two set housing options designed by the partnership of Baker and Massey. Later that year, two blocks were converted to even smaller stands, to be used to provide housing for Eckstein's own employees as well as certain Rand Mine officials. This development was known as 'Eckstein's Compound', and also featured Baker-designed housing (although at substantially lower cost than on the larger stands).

At the same time, transport links to the suburb were revised and motor buses (paid for by the Company) were introduced to run between the estate and town, until such time as a new electric tram service was completed.

A new suburb was also proclaimed in the area adjacent to Parktown. It was originally called West Cliff (some spellings are given as 'West Cliffe' and 'Westcliffe')[40] and was advertised as offering 'extensive views'. The suburb contained as many impressive mansions – and residents – as Parktown; today, while much of original Parktown has been redeveloped or redefined by the encroaching city, Westcliff retains its status as the home of Joburg's old money – rivalled only by the nearby suburb of Houghton.

Only pockets of Victorian Parktown remain. In what would once have been the centre of the suburb, 56 houses were knocked down to build the Johannesburg College of Education (JCE) and the facing Pieter Roos Park. Additional houses were torn down in 1975 to accommodate the M1 North freeway – including much of Northwards' original gardens and orchards.

In the 1980s a number of modern office buildings (none over five stories, in keeping with the 'character' of the suburb) were established, as part of the 'flight' out of the CBD by businesses and professional practices.

Today, Parktown's once-grand mansions jostle for space between the highway, the sprawling hospital complex and a number of office park developments.

PLACES TO VISIT
The National Children's Theatre

(3 Junction Avenue, Parktown) is a wonderful little theatre situated opposite the entrance to the Wits College of Education. The National Children's Theatre Trust was formed in 1990 to take over the existing Youth Theatre, which uses both adult and child actors to perform favourites such as *Aladdin*, *Oliver* and *Charlotte's Web*. The Trust also runs a number of acting workshops for schoolchildren. A performance in this charming theatre is always likely to be a treat. For information, go to www.jyt.co.za or call (011) 484 1584/5.

PLACES TO VISIT
The Linder Auditorium

(27 St Andrews Road, Parktown) is the home of the Johannesburg Philharmonic Orchestra, and is renowned for its superb acoustics. A variety of concerts, choir festivals and dance performances are regularly held there. For more information call (011) 717 3223, or go to the Philharmonic Orchestra's website at www.jpo.co.za.

PLACES TO SEE
The Westcliff Hotel

(67 Jan Smuts Avenue) offers a very enjoyable high tea from its Polo Lounge. Even better than the sandwiches and petit fours, however, is the unrivalled view across the grounds of the Johannesburg Zoo and Military Museum. For information and bookings, go to www.westcliff.co.za or call (011) 481 6000.

Better Known as the Zoo

In July 1903, the firm of Wernher, Beit & Co. of London purchased 200 acres of freehold ground 'in the Braamfontein forest, Parktown, generally known as Sachsenwald', and presented the land to the inhabitants of Johannesburg the following month for use as a park, to be held 'in trust for the inhabitants of JHB for ever.'[41] The park was to be named after the late Hermann Eckstein, who had died suddenly a decade earlier, while in Germany.

The old lion enclosure

At the same time, Sir Percy Fitzpatrick suggested the establishment of a zoological garden. The nucleus of an animal collection (some brought back by Fitzpatrick from his hunting trips) was already kept on the grounds; it included one male lion, one male baboon, a female leopard, a pair of Rhesus monkeys, two Sable antelopes, a golden eagle, a genet, a pair of porcupines and a giraffe.

The grounds were developed over a number of years, starting with a limited number of enclosures (the first was for two young lions), later followed by a bandstand for live music. The tramway from town was extended to the gates, making the Zoo more accessible to Joburg's residents, and it was a popular family destination (even though public toilets were only built in 1916, and a waterborne sewerage system installed nearly two decades later).

In the late 1930s, camel and elephant rides were offered to visitors – in addition to the existing donkey and pony-cart rides; these and other animal rides, including on llamas and a zebra, continued to be popular until the late 1960s, when an elephant left its regular route and ran back to the Elephant House… with its cargo of children.

Today the Elephant House is used as a conference and function venue; many of the other early stone buildings are also still in use, though not as animal houses.

The Joburg Zoo was the first in South Africa to establish a system of open enclosures, starting with the moated lion's enclosure in 1921. Despite this apparent innovation, for many years plans for the animal houses were drawn up by the Town Engineers' Department and not zoologists; some of the remaining structures in use, such as the pit-like bear enclosures, testify to this.

The Zoo grounds were substantially redeveloped in the 1960s and 1970s, with changes made to the horticultural layout and the inclusion of more open, large enclosures with moats. Although most of the bluegum plantation (from the original Sachsenwald) had disappeared by 1927, some specimens are still visible on the Zoo grounds.

Zoo Story: Max the Gorilla

On a mid-winter morning in 1997, a householder in the suburb of Saxonwold surprised an armed man trying to break into his home and raised the alarm. The burglar fled along Jan Smuts Avenue with the police in pursuit and took refuge in the grounds of the Zoo. When he was cornered, he jumped over a wall into an enclosure that happened to house Max, the Zoo's 180-kilogram gorilla. Perceiving his partner Lisa to be under threat, Max grabbed hold of the robber and bit him, whereupon the man fired three shots from a .38 special, hitting Max in the shoulder and neck. The police, who had gathered on the viewing platform, returned fire, hitting the suspect in the groin.

Four policemen and two zookeepers then entered the night enclosure in an effort to evacuate the wounded man. Sergeant Percy Alberts managed to handcuff him – he was still full of fight – but as he and his men were withdrawing, the enraged gorilla attacked them. He threw Constable Amos Simelane on the ground and roughed him up a bit. Then he seized Constable Robert Tshabalala and bit him on the upper arm and buttocks. Finally, he dislocated Sergeant 'Rassie' Rasanele's arm. At this point one of the zookeepers managed to drive Max off by turning a fire extinguisher on him, and the men made good their escape.

The injured policemen and the suspect were taken to the Garden City Clinic. The Zoo's own veterinarians sedated Max and tried to treat him on the spot, but their X-ray equipment proved inadequate for the bulky frame of a Western Lowland gorilla and so he was conveyed under police escort to the Milpark Hospital. 'There were emotional scenes as the unconscious primate was gently placed on the back of the bakkie,' one paper reported. Indeed, there was an outpouring of tender concern from all quarters. Pictures showed Max lying on a

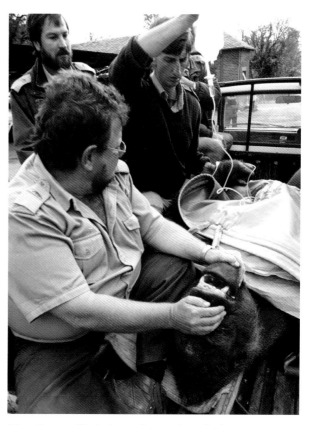

Max the gorilla being taken to hospital

stretcher under a blanket, with his head thrown back and his teeth bared, while a veterinarian tended to a drip. Another, burly, vet cradled Max's head, the fingers of one hand shielding his eyes, the others cupped under his chin. Perhaps it was this man who held Max's hand during the surgery to locate and remove the bullets. Some of Johannesburg's finest surgeons assisted in the procedure at no cost. On the admission form, Max's profession was given as 'Gorilla', his employer as the Johannesburg Zoo.
– From *A Portrait with Keys: Joburg and what-what* by Ivan Vladislavic (Umuzi)

• Max the gorilla died at the Joburg Zoo in May 2004 from complications owing to old age.

A view from the Zoo, 1914

Zoo Lake in the 1930s (top) and 1990s (bottom)

The Zoo Lake

Like the Zoo, the Zoo Lake was developed on the land donated by Eckstein's company in 1904. Land at the centre of the park was considered very marshy and, owing to runoff from the Jukskei River which flows through the Zoo and the park, in the early 1900s a man-made lake was dug as part of a municipal effort to provide employment for poor whites.

The Johannesburg City Council opened the lake in 1908 and rowing boats were introduced in 1911. There were apparently numerous drownings in the early years, but life-jackets are now compulsory. A fountain was built in 1937 to celebrate the coronation of King George VI and is known as the 'Coronation Fountain'. Red and green lights were used to illuminate the fountain, and the intensity of the water flow could be varied. In 1956, when Johannesburg was 70 years old, Margot Fonteyn danced *Swan Lake* at the Zoo Lake.

The Zoo and the Zoo Lake have always been open to all races and Indian families in particular used the facilities, even during the height of apartheid. Today over 20 000 people come to the Zoo Lake each weekend. Special events such as the 'Jazz on the Lake' concert (held in early spring) attract even larger crowds. Moyo, a popular African-themed restaurant chain, has opened in the Zoo Lake grounds and there are many other facilities at the park, including municipal swimming baths, bowling greens and an archery club.

While the Zoo Lake continues to be a family-friendly destination, visitors should be aware of occasional muggings and assault in the park – visiting as part of a group is recommended. The water in the lake is also usually very polluted.

PLACES TO VISIT

The **Johannesburg Zoo** – entrances are on Jan Smuts Avenue, on the corner of Lower Park Drive (for pedestrians), and on Erlswold Way (for motor vehicles) – is open seven days a week, between 09h00 and 17h00. It boasts over 2000 animals, including polar bears, elephants, lions, tigers, leopards, chimpanzees and gorillas, in some of the most innovative and interactive animal enclosures in the world.

The Zoo is an excellent family destination, and offers user-friendly facilities including a shuttle 'train', pushcart 'cars' for young children, a kiddies' amusement park, a petting zoo and a restaurant. For more information, go to www.joburgzoo.org.za or call (011) 646 2000.

Gay Joburg

By Shaun de Waal

Gay Pride march, Johannesburg, 1990s

Johannesburg is famous for having Africa's first lesbian and gay Pride parade. Kicked off by the late activist Simon Nkoli and the Gay and Lesbian Organisation of the Witwatersrand, Pride now celebrates the rights it helped win for lesbian and gay people, and is a favoured event on the annual gay calendar, with a multitude of satellite parties and other goings-on to bolster what is now seen as Pride Week.

Gay history in Johannesburg is hard to trace back further than about World War II, homosexuality having been illegal for so long, and many protagonists no longer with us. But projects such as Gala (Gay and Lesbian Memory in Action, formerly the Gay and Lesbian Archives) are dedicated to reconstructing and recording that history, and Gala offers a queer tour of Johannesburg that highlights key sites.

Among those sites is a luxurious house in the suburb of Forest Town, which in 1966 was raided by the police and led to a sort of gay panic in the press, then stricter legislation from the state, and finally the first nascent gay rights movement. The party was organised to celebrate the visit of an international model, and le tout fashionable gay Jo'burg (about 300 people, all white, and only one of them female) was invited to the party of the year.

After the police raided it, and arrested people for such crimes as wearing women's underwear, the state embarked on a programme to curb this great new threat to social stability. A Parliamentary Select Committee was set up to investigate the matter, and 'expert witnesses' reported such gems as the following: 'All true homosexuals drink excessively' and 'Uniform members of the police are known as "morons".

The resulting addition to the Sexual Offences Act declared that any acts 'calculated to stimulate sexual passion', committed by 'men at a party', were as illegal as sodomy and wearing women's underwear. A 'party' was defined as 'any occasion where there are more than two persons present'.

The law may have ended up being more repressive, but gay and lesbian people were galvanised to gather legal advice (from luminaries such as Arthur Chaskalson ...) and make representations to Parliament. This helped dispel some of the more bizarre myths. This legal reform movement was the start of the kinds of activism that culminated in the repeal of such laws after 1994, and ultimately in such legislation as the Civil Union Act of 2006, which allows gay and lesbian people the full rights of marriage.

Gay Pride march

Until relatively recently gay people had to carve out their own spaces in the interstices of public life, such as the bars (and a private club called 69) around Joubert Park in central Johannesburg during World War II. The adjoining army base was, unknown to the authorities, a source of many randy young men, and Joubert Park and surrounds became a favoured meeting place as well as one of the first areas of the city to have a notable number of gay residents.

By the 1960s, that distinction had passed to the inner city area of Hillbrow. Known as the most cosmopolitan part of the city, this 'Manhattan' of apartment blocks was what one resident describes as 'a very gay space'. Many of the gay-focused bars were in Hillbrow, and several survived for decades. One street in Hilbrow has now been named for Simon Nkoli – a bar he frequented is on that corner.

Other meeting places included the 'health clubs' of central Jo'burg, the London and the Atwater, which were straight by day and gay by night (for £5, one could rent a cubicle and sleep over). Certain bars, such as those of the Waldorf Hotel, His Majesty's Theatre, the New Library Hotel, and later the Carlton Centre, were known among gay people to be meeting places. The trend for coffee bars led to the opening of the popular Chiquita's in Rosebank, which catered for a largely gay clientele.

Such places were not openly gay but simply known by word of mouth to be gathering places for gay people. Specifically gay venues began to emerge in the late 1970s with the birth of disco. The Dungeon was the longest-running gay club, situated in a semi-industrial part of town; others such as Zipps (later Mrs Henderson's), Scants and Decodance followed suit. The block of gay clubs and bars that developed in the 1990s in Braamfontein, adjoining the University of the Witwatersrand, offered a thumpingly busy gay 'Heartland' for several years, but closed after drug arrests and conflict with city officials over zoning.

Nowadays the gay club scene seems to have moved to the salubrious northern suburbs, with Taboo in Sandton offering a swanky experience, and The Q Club doing likewise on certain weekend nights. Other venues such as The Risqué Lounge have also sprung up. The more bohemian suburb of Melville provides two popular gay bars, Statement and Oh! – the latter was even recommended by the *New York Times*. Capital, a music bar in Rosebank, hosts Playground, a 'womyn-only' evening on the last Saturday of every month.

Partygoers at such places are still largely white, despite the new South Africa's attempts to overcome racial divisions. Black gay men are, however, now a major part of the clientele of venues such as The Factory in Doornfontein. This sex club, which requires patrons to hand over their clothes at the entrance, is appropriately named for a venue situated among former and present factories near the sports stadium of Ellis Park.

For information about the gay tour of Johannesburg, go to www.gala.wits.ac.za or phone (011) 717 1063.

The Other Posh Suburb

The suburbs of Upper and Lower Houghton were originally part of the farm Klipfontein; in 1888, a portion of the farm was leased by WS Barrett, who planted some 250 000 bluegum trees there. His lease was taken over by the Houghton Estate Company – which announced its intention to prospect for gold on the land. Confident that the 'reef runs through the Houghton Estate', it sank shafts on both sides of what was later to become Munro Drive. The amount of gold obtained proved unpayable, however, and the land was taken over by the Johannesburg Consolidated Investment Company. Stands in Houghton went on sale as early as in 1901, when the South African War was at its height. According to a newspaper report, the suburb was laid out as a 'very high-class residential suburb with larger plots than usual'.[42] After the First World War, the mine shafts were filled in – including one at the bottom of Munro Drive – and residential building began in earnest.

Houghton got famous when Helen Suzman became a Member of Parliament for the Houghton constituency in 1953 and later split from the United Party to form the Progressive Party. For many years she was the sole parliamentary representative of this tiny liberal party, which bravely opposed apartheid. Suzman was honoured in 1978 with the UN Human Rights award. She visited political prisoners on Robben Island, including Nelson Mandela, and worked tirelessly for their release. In the 1990s, Houghton acquired another famous resident when Nelson Mandela moved into a house on Central Avenue.

Construction of Houghton Drive, 1939

Munro Drive under construction, 1919

PLACES TO SEE

Apart from the houses of famous South African politicians and statesmen, there are several sites worth seeing in Houghton. An Irish priest, the Rev. John Darragh, Rector of St Mary's Anglican Church, founded St John's College in 1898, in Eloff Street. The college moved several times before occupying its current site on Houghton Ridge, in 1907. Herbert Baker designed the key buildings and its central feature is a chapel that was built to commemorate ex-pupils and teachers who died during the First World War.[43] The chapel is a remarkable centrepiece and can be viewed on the schoolgrounds or from the street running past the school.

THE NORTHERN

'The old Transvaal earth has been smothered and the tiny spring flowers, that used to come up after the first rains, have wilted forever. Once the veld has been disturbed, they never come back.'

Juliet Marais Louw, *Wagon Tracks and Orchards*

In this chapter

☞ Iron Age versus Tuscanisation

☞ Johannesburg's Market Garden

☞ Peri-Urban Politics

☞ The Flight North

☞ Revolution in the Suburb

EXPANSION

Domestic worker with her young charge, walking past a security boom

Metropolis in the Veld

**Pink and white cosmos (originally from Mexico) growing
next to the highway, north of Johannesburg**

Some 28 km north of the city centre is the Lonehill Koppie, a 20-acre wildlife reserve with an 80-metre high boulder-strewn koppie at its centre – the rock-capped hill or 'tor formation' is made up of Archean Granite, and the stone dates back to some 3,2 billion years ago.

Hidden among the rocks and veld, and the numerous hyraxes or rock dassies, are the remains of the biggest Iron Age factory unearthed in Africa[1]. In the 1960s, three iron forges (dating back to about AD 1600, the same period as the forge at the Melville Koppies) were excavated by archaeologist Dr Revil Mason... only to be covered up again, to protect them from damage and decay, because of a lack of funding to develop the site.

The Lonehill Koppie – which, together with other nearby granite tors at Witkoppen and Norscot, was inhabited by Middle Stone Age hunters as far back as 30 000 years ago – was selected by Iron Age settlers because the area had an abundance of ferricrete, a concentration of iron salts in the soil. In addition to preserved tuyeres (bellows), the Lonehill site yielded a number of valuable clues about early iron production in South Africa, including a granite anvil and 'hammer stones', which were used to shape the metal.

The Koppie – which used to be called Bobbejaanskranz ('Baboon's Ridge') – fell between the Boer farmlands of Zevenfontein and Rietfontein, and was once quarried for granite by the government; these lands were consolidated as 'Lonehill' in 1934 when the area was purchased by Simon Notten, a Hollander who had married Anna Wierda, the daughter of Paul Kruger's favourite architect, Sytze Wierda. Notten also owned 100 acres of land a little to the south; when he sub-divided his stand, he created the present-day suburbs of Atholl and Wierda Valley.

Notten's son John moved to Lonehill in 1937. In 1970, the Notten family developed the space into a 'self-contained village', intended to preserve the Koppie, with plenty of 'parklands, bridle paths and open spaces'.[2] Unfortunately, suburban sprawl caught up with the settlement and today a number of houses in Lonehill encroach on the Koppie area.

A kilometre away from Lonehill, one of Africa's most significant Iron Age sites, is the mock-Tuscan entertainment complex of Montecasino. The site, which features a luxury hotel, a casino (1700 slot machines and 70 gaming tables), a movie theatre and a new stage theatre (the largest in Africa), was designed to resemble 'an old-world Tuscan hill-top village',[3] complete with fake ruined walls, and an indoor piazza with a painted sky. The development was named after a hill in Italy (Monte Cassino) which is home to a famous monastery. During the Second World War it was the site of a series of pitched battles that resulted in the death of over 70 000 soldiers.

The juxtaposition prompted Lindsay Bremner, former Chair of Architecture at the University of the Witwatersrand, to comment:

'The northern hills of Johannesburg are engulfed in a tide of Tuscan pastiche of absurd proportions. The developers of gated housing estates, casino complexes, hotels, shopping centers [sic] and office parks have somehow conspired to create an insatiable appetite for everything Italian, in particular Tuscan, amongst Johannesburg's affluent classes. These enclaves are surrounded by bristling fields of razor wire, electric fences, motorized gates, tracking devices, cordoned-off roads, sentries, patrols.'[4]

In a review of Clive Chipkin's excellent book, *Johannesburg Style*, which appeared in the American *Architectural Review*, the writer opined:

'With its rentier braggadocio and expanding infrastructure, Johannesburg was always a fertile breeding ground for new architecture and new ideas –

The interior of Monte Casino, Fourways

The Legend of Lonehill

During the late 19th and early 20th centuries, popular Afrikaner mythology held that if the large boulder at the top of the Lonehill Koppie could be dislodged, the English would be driven out of South Africa. Conversely, it was believed that if the same boulder fell, all the white settlers would leave South Africa.

👁 PLACES TO SEE

The **Lonehill Koppie** (with its entrance on Calderwood Road) is a reminder of what Johannesburg looked like before it was settled: rocky veld with small streams trickling through it, dotted with shrubs, small trees and knee-high grasses. Today, the Koppie's wildlife consists mostly of dassies and several bird species, but in the past the area was home to guinea fowl and porcupines – and even leopard (the last one was spotted in 1981). Visitors can climb to the top of the Koppie and enjoy the view, or picnic at the small dam, called the Lonehill Loch, around 200 m north of the Koppie, where there is a children's play park.[5] For more information, go to www.lra.org.za.

yet paradoxically it also embodied an essentially provincial, lower-middle class, philistine culture.'⁶

It is the latter quality that has, perhaps, emerged as the signature of Joburg's ever-expanding northern sprawl: in place of the ethnic or religious commonalities of many communities in the city's central, western, eastern and southern suburbs, the settlements of the north are united by neighbourhood watches, security-boomed suburbs, and patrolled housing estates.

In his book, Chipkin said: '[Johannesburg] felt like a place in some ways on the frontier of a new age and in other ways trammelled and contained by the frontier big-otry of the past. That is the essence of Johannesburg's heightened vulnerability, a glimpse of what it might be, contained by the limitations of what is.'⁷

The 'frontier' or settler mentality is echoed in what has been termed the 'fortress architecture' of the northern suburbs, typified by increasingly high perimeter walls topped with palisade fencing, razor wire, spikes, electric fencing... Family interactions, too, mimic the 'isolation of early settler societies'⁸ – by design, homes are created to draw the family into the house, and 'insulate and separate the family from direct experience of the wider social and cultural life in the city'.⁹

The (formal) northern suburbs have also continued to develop very much along racial lines, even after 1994 – which is to say, they are mostly white. Urban geographer and Johannesburg expert Keith Beavon went so far as to describe the new 'Johannesburg in the North' as being in real danger of becoming a neo-apartheid city.¹⁰

Joburg's Market Garden

The areas known today as Sandton and Randburg were settled by white farmers as early as the 1850s; the farms of Witkoppen, Rietfontein, Driefontein, Zandfontein and Cyferfontein were gradually subdivided, and later developed into the suburbs of Sandton. To the west, the farms of Klipfontein, Olievenhoutspoort, Boskop and the western portion of Driefontein became the town of Randburg.

Early images of Sandfontein (Zandfontein)

The farms' early inhabitants were a mix of Afrikaans-speakers together with German, Hollander (Dutch) and even Swiss immigrants. Famous early families included the Esterhuyzens, who owned Zandfontein (the homestead later became Stanley's Dairy, which supplied Sandton residents with fresh milk until the 1980s); the Heyneke family (who were related to the Esterhuyzens by mar-riage, and bought a portion of Zandfontein in the 1880s); the Ehlers family, who resided at Rietfontein (alongside what is Sunnyside Park today); Adolf and Elsa Wilhelmi, who came to the goldfields from Germany in 1891 and bought a portion of the farm Driefontein, opposite the present-day Field and Study Centre. Their daughter Freya married Max Weber, a qualified Swiss watchmaker who later achieved prominence as a geologist, donating many specimens to the Johannesburg Geological Museum.

Although small traces of alluvial gold were found in the Jukskei River in the 1850s, these early farmers generally led frugal lives – farming was often at a subsistence level, and infant and childhood mortality were common. In her history of Sandton, Jane Carruthers writes:

'Farms were few and scattered, and long distances even from the closest neighbours, meant that people were isolated from one another most of the time. … The first houses were primitive dwellings, usually with about three rooms, and built from mud bricks. Furniture was rudimentary, much of it constructed from local timber, although some families had treasured stinkwood or yellowwood kists and cabinets which they had brought with them from the Cape Colony. Antelope skins generally provided clothing and bedding. There was usually a kraal for livestock, a wagon-shed and a garden for fruit and vegetables.'[11]

The discovery of gold in the 1880s substantially increased property values, which in turn increased the subdivision of the farmlands – and provided a new market for the farms' fresh produce, one significantly closer than that of Pretoria, 50 km away.

At the outbreak of the South African War, many of the adult men in the area left to join the fighting – mostly on the side of the Boers. The farms were left to the women and children to work and manage. At intervals some of the men left their commandos to return home for short periods, for rest, provisions and fresh horses.[12] British units also periodically visited the homesteads for much the same reasons, and wives developed simple code systems to let their husbands know when it was safe to visit. To prevent Boer forces from re-provisioning, some of the homesteads and farmlands were burned.

A number of Afrikaner families were taken to the concentration camp at Turffontein, where they remained until after the war; male prisoners of war, including members of the Esterhuyzen and Heyneke families, were sent to camps in Ceylon (Sri Lanka).

After the war, many of the farming families returned to rebuild their homes and replant their fields. The Wilhelmi family settled on a different part of Driefontein and built a new home in 1906; today, this is the only remaining 'original' farmhouse in the Sandton area and is a national monument – although it is under threat from development.

After the war, an increased sense of security saw property values on the Rand increase, which led to the development of several new townships (suburbs) in the northern areas – Rivonia (in 1903), Athol and Parkmore (1904), and New Brighton and Sandown (1905).

Many of these suburbs were marketed as 'gentleman's estates', recreational country properties for Johannesburg's middle classes. Thomas Cullinan owned a 'shooting-box' stocked with game birds, called Rocklands (today the suburb of Woodmead). John Dale Lace bought a portion of the farm Boskop (or Boschkop) and converted the original farmhouse, built by the Labuschagne family, into a country home. Abe Bailey also invested in large tracts of land that he later developed through his SA Townships, Mining and Finance Corporation, which established Morningside (1932), Bryanston (1940) and Ferndale. In 1934 the Johannesburg Polo Club and the Rand Hunt joined forces to create the Inanda Club, where the hounds were kennelled. The hunting territory covered what is now Sandown, Wendywood, Buccleuch and Petervale.

In what would later become Randburg, a portion of Driefontein was renamed Bordeaux by owner Charles Rocher, after the French city from which his family had originated.

The north-west suburbs – today Randburg – developed as predominantly Afrikaans areas, while those in what would become Sandton were mostly English.

Craighall Park Hotel, 1906

Although most of the northern periphery could be considered middle class, there were certain areas, such as smallholdings in the vicinity of Ferndale, where the residents were categorised as low-income.

Craighall

In 1891 William Gray Rattray purchased a portion of the area known as Klipfontein No. 4 – a subdivision of the farm Boskop. Rattray named his portion Craighall, after his birthplace in Scotland; the land consisted of the modern suburbs of Craighall, Craighall Park and Blairgowrie. Rattray also owned an adjoining portion of the farm Driefontein. By special proclamation, Klipfontein was declared to be in the mining labour area while Driefontein was not. This caused innumerable headaches for Rattray each time he wanted to move farm labourers from one area to the other – as he had to obtain a special pass for the workers to enter the 'mining' land.

In addition to farming, Rattray dammed the Braamfontein Spruit to make Craighall Lake. In 1905 he started advertising the Craighall Park Hotel as an ideal recreational spot for city dwellers (at the time, Craighall was about an hour's journey from the city centre).

In 1902, and again in 1911, Rattray advertised that he was selling off plots of land in Craighall; it's not clear whether or not the sales were successful as the suburbs of Craighall and Craighall Park were only developed in the 1930s. They were incorporated into Johannesburg in 1938.[13] Rattray's dam silted up in the 1930s.

Farm Schools

Many of the Sandton farm children were home-schooled; those who attended formal schooling in town – the Wilhelmi children attended the German School in Edith Cavell Street in Hillbrow, for example – or in the suburbs of Fontainebleau or Rosebank, had to travel long distances each morning and evening on foot, by bicycle or on a cart.

The first school in Sandton was established on Rietfontein in 1903. Because the original building was situated close to the confluence of the Sand and Braamfontein spruits, it was sometimes impossible to attend class during the summer months when the rivers were full. In 1914 the school was moved to grounds in Rivonia; this school is still in existence as Rivonia Primary. Another small school building was established in the suburb of Parkmore, after Elsa Wilhelmi petitioned the school board. When the township of Parkmore was developed, a formal site was set aside for a primary school and Parkmore Primary – later Montrose Primary – opened in 1970.

A farm school for black children was established in Witkoppen in 1927, when the Mason family bequeathed a hectare of land in perpetuity to the 'African people of Witkoppen'. The school was managed by the Anglican Church for over 25 years, until the passing of the Bantu Education Act in 1955. Rather than hand the school over to the state, the Church decided to close the facility; the local black families, however, argued that they would rather have inferior education than none at all, and so the school remained open. Today the Witkoppen school caters mostly for disadvantaged children from the many informal settlements north of Sandton.

The Changing Shape of Joburg

Sandton in the early 1970s (left) and in the early 2000s (right)

In 1936 – the year of Johannesburg's Golden Jubilee – the city was home to an estimated 475 000 people; this figure was to double by the end of the next decade.

The Second World War had an important impact on the city: the absence of white males (who had gone into service) created employment gaps and opportunities for women and non-white workers; the slow-down of industrial production in Europe and North America also provoked a regional boom as South Africa, and particularly Johannesburg, manufactured goods for the war effort.

By the end of the War, the Witwatersrand was poised for a major shift. In the late 1940s, the region was producing 96 per cent of South Africa's gold; the country, in turn, was the source of about 40 per cent of the world's gold. The mines of the central Witwatersrand, lying largely within Joburg's metropolitan boundaries, were responsible for 34 per cent of this.[14]

Within the space of a generation, employment in the mining industry had dropped from 300 212 to 110 130. The city's total workforce, however, had risen to over a million people.[15]

Urban geographer Keith Beavon explains: 'The expansion in secondary industry coincided with declining output from the mines of the central Witwatersrand as the payable ores, which had been mined for some 70 years, were depleted. Not surprisingly, as secondary industry became more important it attracted and generated a surge of tertiary activity … .'[16] By the 1970s, the Witwatersrand had been transformed 'from what was primarily a mining region into a maturing metropolitan region'.[17]

By 1971, only one in 11 members of the region's labour force was still employed by the mining industry.[18] Increased employment in secondary and tertiary industries, combined with increased private ownership of automobiles, helped to extend the northward expansion of the 'suburbs'. ☞

The Peri-Urban Areas

In the early 1930s South Africa experienced the worst drought ever recorded on the sub-continent; at the same time, the country was going through the Great Depression – a slump that continued until the Gold Standard was abandoned in December 1932.

As crops failed and livestock died, impoverished country people – black and white – sought work, food and shelter in the towns; this was often referred to as 'the Second Great Trek'.

Many of these new migrants chose to settle on the northern periphery of Johannesburg, which was close enough to the city's employment opportunities, but free of restrictions on the types of dwellings that could be built, and the number of people who could live on any one property.[19]

By 1936, the 'unbridled developments on its northern boundary worried Johannesburg so much'[20] that a commission was appointed to investigate whether or not the city's boundaries should be expanded to incorporate these peripheral areas. Richard Feetham, the head of the commission, recommended that the city 'grow only in accordance with what its sewage system could handle'; on his recommendation, 'the areas of Craighall, Greymont, parts of Craighall Park, Linden, Illovo and what was to become Blairgowrie (in 1941) were included in the city area.'[21] The Sandton and Randburg suburbs were excluded, as it was thought it would prove too expensive – and place strain on municipal resources – to annex them.

In 1938 a further agency was established by the Minister of Health to investigate the 'health hazards of uncontrolled urban development' across South Africa. The Thornton Committee created a new local authority to administer a large area of the Transvaal: 23 000 km^2 were placed under the jurisdiction of the strangely named Peri-Urban Areas Health Board. A little over 1800 km^2 of this, in the more densely settled areas, were to be placed under local area committees, to be made up of residents.

The creation of the Board and the local area committees (LACs) was contentious, as all representatives appointed instead of elected. In particular, there was 'tension and dissatisfaction in the Sandton and Randburg areas'.[22]

By 1945, the Board had established three LACs in the north: the Northern Johannesburg LAC (including Hyde Park, Bryanston, Rivonia, Wendywood, Sandown and Athol); the North-eastern Johannesburg LAC (covering Kew, Lombardy East, Senderwood, Kelvin, Linbro Park and Buccleuch, as well as the township of Alexandra); and the North-western Johannesburg LAC (Blairgowrie, Ferndale and Fountainebleau).

In 1946, however, the arrest of a black labourer – by a Pretoria commissioner, in an area controlled by the Board – sparked intense debate about the Board's nature and very existence. For much of the year, the Board was declared *ultra vires* – not legally 'competent' – and ceased to function. In late 1947 new legislation was put into effect and the Board was reconstituted under a new chairman; residents, however, still resented this outside interference in local affairs and complained about paying taxes to a body on which they were not represented.

An additional aggravating factor was the fact that the Board gradually came to be dominated by the National Party, which had come to power in 1948. Sandton residents were, by and large, United Party supporters.[23]

The Board did, however, play an important role as Sandton in particular experienced tremendous growth during the 1950s, changing from an agrarian to a residential area. The only township in the area with a water supply was Bryanston, which bought the water in bulk from Johannesburg. In some suburbs, such as Illovo, water was delivered by tanker to individual households or collected in buckets from a central point. Steel shortages, a hangover from the War, led to delays in the installation of water mains but by 1955 most Sandton suburbs were integrated into a well-planned water scheme. The dependable water supply also made possible the installation of a water borne sewerage system.

Delta Park and Sewerage Treatment

The Klipspruit Sewerage Farm, to the south of Johannesburg, was only able to serve those parts of the city that fell to the south of the Witwatersrand watershed. Residents to the north had to rely on either French drains, or bucket systems – the buckets would be collected by horse- or mule-drawn sanitary carts in the dead of night, and their contents dumped into the Johannesburg sewers.

By the early 1930s the city's phenomenal growth prompted municipal bodies to establish new sewerage disposal works on the northern side of the watershed. 'Four sites were chosen in valleys that would allow gravity sewers to run from suburbs in the catchment areas of the rivers of the Witwatersrand. Names with classical connotations based on letters of the alphabet were chosen and were unconnected with any suburb so as not to diminish residential values in the vicinity.'[24] In the west, Antea Works took sewerage and industrial waste from Industria; Bruma (later developed into the Bruma Lake shopping complex) took domestic waste from the eastern suburbs; Houghton, Oaklands, Orchards, Norwood, Melrose and Illovo were served by sewerage works at Cydna (now the Melrose Bird Sanctuary). Delta was built to serve the suburbs of Parktown, Emmarentia, Auckland Park, Greenside, Parkhurst and Parkwood.

In 1959 the Northern Disposal Works, situated in Diepsloot, began to accept sewerage from Antea, Bruma, Cydna and Delta. In 1963 the Delta sewerage works stopped operating entirely; the land was given to the city's Parks and Recreation Department.

The main building at the Delta Park Sewerage Plant

Today, the converted sewerage works building – a beautiful Art Deco structure – houses the Delta Environmental Centre, situated within what is now known as Delta Park.

Randburg

In South Africa's 1953 elections the 'United' National Party (NP) won 94 of the 156 parliamentary seats – a clear victory, but not enough to secure the party the two-thirds majority it needed to change entrenched clauses of the Constitution (as the case of the disenfranchisement of black and coloured voters in the Cape Province, an action which had been challenged and overturned by the Supreme Court of Appeal).

Because of this, the National Party was quick to support the proposed establishment of a pro-Afrikaner municipality on the Reef prior to the general election of 1958.

There was already a relatively strong concentration of Afrikaans-speaking residents in the area covered by the North-western Johannesburg LAC. One of the most prominent political residents in that area was an Afrikaner named Robert Van Tonder, who lived in Ferndale. Van Tonder 'lived in fear that Ferndale would be annexed by Johannesburg',[25] an action he wanted to prevent for a number of reasons: firstly, he considered Johannesburg's Council to be 'communistic' in inclination; secondly he harboured dreams of nurturing an Afrikaner community with *'platteland'* values; thirdly, he was disappointed with the work of the Peri-Urban Board, which had not only failed to encourage the use of Afrikaans but had also exercised insufficient control (in his view) over the resident African communities in the region.

Van Tonder launched a campaign for the independent status of the suburbs under the North-western LAC. His petition received strong support, attracting over 1000 signatures within three days. Rather than present it to the Peri-Urban Board, where he knew it would get mired in internal politics, Van Tonder went directly to the Administrator, Dr William Nicol – after whom William Nicol Drive was named – known as the 'champion of the urban Afrikaner' (and a confirmed pro-German supporter during the War).

Nicol agreed with Van Tonder's proposal, and appointed a commission of enquiry to investigate granting autonomy to the North-western Johannesburg LAC, consisting of nine suburbs, with a white population of about 9000.

The new town was approved by the committee and, after returning an NP Member to Parliament in 1958, was formalised in July 1959. A competition was held in April of that year, to choose a name for the new municipality. Over 700 entries were received, with some of the suggestions including Wonderstad, Randstad, Mooirand, Banket and Uniekberg. The six entrants who had proposed the name of Randburg shared the £100 prize.[26]

Van Tonder remained on his smallholding in Randburg, founding the Boerestaat Party in 1986 (campaigning for the restoration of the old Boer republics). In 1999, suffering from very painful terminal cancer, he committed suicide there.

In the early 1960s Bryanston finally succeeded in separating from the other portions of the Northern Johannesburg LAC, forming its own Local Area. The remaining southern portion was renamed the Sandown Local Area.

Between 1956 and 1963, the number of townships in the greater Sandton area had doubled; during the same period, the Board (now renamed the Transvaal Board for the Development of Peri-Urban Areas) was also given the active task of developing every area under its control towards either autonomy or incorporation into an existing municipality.

In 1964 it was finally suggested that the three

◉ PLACES TO VISIT

Delta Park (with access at various points in Craighall Park and Victory Park) is a favourite spot for dog walks, Sunday church groups, short hikes and mountain biking. Visitors to the park should be aware that there have been a number of attacks there. It is best visited during the day, and in groups.

The Delta Environmental Centre (housed in the old sewerage works – access is on Road No. 3, Victory Park) provides regular courses and classes for schoolchildren and members of the community, teaching them about regional and general environmental issues. For more information, go to www.deltaenviro.org or call (011) 888 4831.

A house in Bryanston in the 1980s

remaining local areas – Bryanston, Sandown and North-eastern – combine to form one strong town.

At the same time, however, neighbouring municipalities (Bedfordview, Edenvale, Johannesburg and Randburg) had begun to regard the Board's well-developed and prosperous suburbs as desirable prizes. There were rumours that English-dominated Bryanston was the

The All Whites

During all the debates about 'taxation without representation', 'democracy' and the rights of people to control their own destiny, the lives of black residents in the northern peripheral suburbs were completely ignored.

The 1958 Nationalist victory saw pass-law regulations tightened; a curfew was imposed on black people from December 1958. Tara Hospital was forbidden to admit black casualty patients. Alexandra Township lost its Health Committee, and was taken over by the Peri-Urban Board, becoming totally state-controlled, with a tiny operating budget.

With the exception of Alexandra Township, Sandton did not have a large black population. Kensington B was the only black residential area, and by 1958 the Board had successfully forced these people to move elsewhere.

White suburban life, Randburg, 1980s

target of the predominantly Afrikaans-speaking Randburg, with which it shared a common boundary. More than anything else, this fear of being 'dismembered' brought the three local areas together. A report was commissioned, and indicated that the town would be successful.

The local government department, however, commissioned a full-scale inquiry before it would approve the matter. The Van der Spuy Commission was appointed in July 1965, and precipitated a rush of applications from other municipalities to incorporate part of the Peri-Urban Board's empire. Historian Jane Carruthers referred to this as the 'scramble' for northern Johannesburg.

The Van der Spuy Commission, which became known as the Greater Johannesburg Inquiry, lasted a year. It took a further year for the report (issued only in Afrikaans) to be completed.

In January 1968 a decision was announced: a new municipality was indeed to be formed from the three peri-urban local areas. A few boundary alterations were made: parts of the North-eastern Local Area would be incorporated into Johannesburg (Kew, Lyndhurst, Lombardy East and Lombardy West), into Edenvale (portions of Rietfontein), and into Bedfordview (Senderwood and Essexwold). Johannesburg took over most of the Board's Western Local Area – Northcliff Extension, Blackheath, Berario and Fairland. Roodepoort was granted the Panorama Agricultural Holdings, and Randburg got additional land on its western side.

THINGS TO DO

The **Mobiguide 'Talk Tour'** of Sandton takes visitors on a personal cellphone-guided tour through the 'richest square mile in Africa'. Starting at the Balalaika Hotel, once a favourite country getaway venue, tourists can dial specific numbers at each stop on the tour to receive information. For details, dial 083 227 1797.

The Mink and Manure Belt

From 1969 to 1979, the municipality of Sandton clung to its 'semi-rural' identity. Town planner Barry Bristow described the area as 'a town of 30 000 whites and 15 000 horses' – which statement explains why the region became known as the 'mink and manure belt'.

During the 1970s, the Sandton Town Council commissioned a report (the Milstein Report). It recommended that all the rivers and major hills and ridges be conserved, 'that a small game reserve be established in Gallo Manor, that an arboretum be created in Rivonia and that eight bird sanctuaries be established, including one specifically for waterfowl.'[27] The council supported all the recommendations, with the exception of the Gallo Manor reserve, and the preservation of the area's indigenous flora and natural beauty became a popular civic cause. Sandton's catchphrase became: 'Where the country meets the town'.

Increased urban growth together with high inflation and the unprecedented popularity of Sandton City (the shopping centre which opened in 1973) saw the 'initial ardour for a semi-rural lifestyle' start to wane.

In 1979, the Council formally ended Sandton's rural phase, and began to adopt a more positive – even aggressive – attitude to development. Almost all of the Milstein proposals were abandoned.

By the mid-1990s, the population of Sandton, which stood at 40 000 in 1969, had grown to over 150 000.

Mall Culture

The early 1960s saw the construction of the first decentralised shopping malls in Johannesburg – the Killarney Mall, built in 1961 by IW Schlesinger's son John, and the Southdale Mall, built in Robertsham in 1963.

In 1970 construction began on a massive new retail venture – Sandton City. When it opened in 1974, it

Sandton by night

offered 38 000 m² of floor space, making it the largest mall in Africa at the time.

The success of Sandton City saw the establishment of three additional malls in Sandton – in Benmore, Hyde Park and Bryanston. An open-air mall was established in the Randburg CBD. Shopping malls were also constructed in Bedfordview, Brixton, Blackheath and Cresta. In the suburb of Rosebank, two malls – the Rosebank Mall and The Firs – were established along the Oxford Road hub.

In 1978 South Africa's first 'supermall', Eastgate, was built, 'located at a major access and egress point of the new Witwatersrand freeway system linking the eastern suburbs of Johannesburg with the international airport in Kempton Park and with other East Rand towns, notably Germiston, Bedfordview, Edenvale, Boksburg and Benoni'.[28] By 1978, one third of all white shoppers were making their purchases in the suburban centres alone.[29]

The Flight North

Suburban office space followed a similar pattern of location to that of the malls.[30] As businesses evacuated the Johannesburg CBD, the cheaper rentals (at the time) and attractive 'lifestyle' elements of premises in the extended north saw the development of several significant business nodes in the greater northern periphery. By the 1990s, central Sandton had emerged as the premier business location of the greater Johannesburg area. With the exception of Standard Bank, FNB and ABSA, Sandton's business district is home to the headquarters of most of the country's leading financial services institutions. The Johannesburg Stock Exchange moved its premises from the western edge of the Joburg CBD to Sandton in 2000. The Sandton CBD is now referred to as 'Africa's richest square mile'.

Besides the development of many thousands of square metres of office space, central Sandton has also seen the development of ultra high-end residential space, particularly the Michelangelo Towers that crown the adjoining shopping malls of Sandton City and Nelson Mandela Square.

Linden – The Posh Afrikaner Suburb

The suburb of Linden was named after Johannes Jacobus Rabie van der Linde, a farmer who co-owned the south-western corner of Klipfontein together with Louw Geldenhuys.

In 1898 Van der Linde and Geldenhuys divided up the farm with a view to selling off the portions as lots, a procedure that had already made Geldenhuys a wealthy man with the sale of sections of Braamfontein.

The lots did not sell as quickly as Van der Linde had hoped, being so far out of town – some 8 km – and with access limited to three dirt tracks. It was not until the 1920s that that the land was finally consolidated into smallholdings.

The acidic clay in the area proved very fertile, and orchards soon flourished there. Some of the remaining fruit trees can be seen in the garden of a restaurant in 4th Avenue, Linden.

In addition to fruit farming, there was a large private retail dairy. In the 1950s, the farms gradually disappeared and wealthy Afrikaners moved in – resulting in the suburb being referred to as the 'Boere Houghton'.

Today, Linden has a mix of English and Afrikaans speakers; one of the suburb's most famous residents is Albertina Sisulu, wife of the late Walter Sisulu. The couple moved to Linden to be closer to Walter's doctors; Walter Sisulu died in his Linden home in 2003, at the age of 90.

Beyers Naudé

In 2001 DF Malan Drive – named after the apartheid politician – was renamed Beyers Naudé Drive, after the anti-apartheid cleric. A one-time member of the right-wing Afrikaaner Broederbond, Beyers Naudé was a Dutch Reformed Church minister who became increasingly critical of apartheid practices after the Sharpeville Massacre in 1961. Naudé publicly supported a World Council of Churches proclamation that rejected any theological basis for apartheid and was a founder member of the Christian Institute, an organisation established to unite Christians of all ethnic groups, denominations and languages in South Africa. His work with the Institute saw him lose his status as a minister of the Dutch Reformed Church and become increasingly ostracised by the Afrikaner community. He was later banned by the apartheid government.

In 1985 Naudé succeeded Archbishop Desmond Tutu as the secretary general of the South African

Beyers Naudé (at the back), Walter Sisulu and Govan Mbeki

Council of Churches; two years later, he was part of an Afrikaner delegation that met the ANC in Dakar, Senegal. In 1990, he was a member of the ANC's negotiating team which met with the National Party government.

Naudé received the Freedom of the City of Johannesburg in 2001; he died in Northcliff in September 2004, aged 89.

A Neo-Apartheid City in the Making? By Keith Beavon

As the incidence of crime in the suburbs increased dramatically in the 1990s so did the cost of securing property, thereby causing a shift towards smaller more easily protected premises, particularly for first-time white buyers. Consequently large numbers of cluster units, various forms of townhouses and other types of 'gash' (good address small house) accommodation mushroomed relative to the proverbial 'large house with large grounds and a pool' typical of the older areas in the northern suburbs. As the new 'lock-and-go' style of living has become more popular, the residential densities in small pockets of the north are now higher than ever before, although by northern hemisphere standards, or by the standards in black townships, they remain ridiculously low. Even so, the additional population in no way represents an increase comparable to that experienced in the sphere of retailing, service business and office space.

Although the only barrier to entering any residential area is price, in reality that alone creates a form of de facto apartheid. Of course there are a significant number of well-positioned and wealthy black people now living in many of the expensive northern suburbs. Yet the overwhelming majority of black people remain literally and figuratively on the margins, largely as a consequence of the cards dealt them in the apartheid years when they were growing up, seeking an education and searching for a good job. So, although there are no longer any racial barriers to where one might live, the northern 'wedge' and the suburbs adjacent to its western side remain overwhelmingly white. The anomaly is the poverty-stricken Alexandra township that has been a black ghetto almost since its founding in 1912.

The new black elite: the Dube family in Cedar Lake, 2004

• Keith Beavon is the author of *Johannesburg: the Making and Shaping of a City*. This extract is from the paper entitled 'Northern Johannesburg: part of the "rainbow" or neo-apartheid city in the making?'

Revolution in the Suburbs — Liliesleaf Farm

Liliesleaf was an old house that needed work and no one lived there. I moved in under the pretext that I was a houseboy or caretaker that would live there until my master took possession. I had taken the alias David Motsamayi, the name of one of my former clients. At the farm, I wore the simple blue overalls that were the uniform of the black male servant.
– Nelson Mandela, *Long Walk to Freedom*

In the early 1960s Nelson Mandela – known as the 'Black Pimpernel' for his ability to evade capture – was hiding from then apartheid authorities, posing as a gardener, cook and chauffeur, living in the servants' quarters on a smallholding in Johannesburg's semi-rural peripheral northern suburbs.

Mandela had moved to Liliesleaf Farm in Rivonia in October 1961; on paper, the house was owned by white artist and designer Arthur Goldreich – the purchase of the farm was paid for by the Communist Party, of which Goldreich was a member. He moved to Liliesleaf in December 1961, with his family, to provide cover for the farm's real purpose: to be the headquarters of the ANC's newly established armed wing, Umkhonto we Sizwe (the 'Spear of the Nation'), better known as MK.

In 1962 Mandela left South Africa for several months, travelling to a number of countries including Ethiopia, Tanganyika, Ghana, Sierra Leone and England. Shortly after his return to South Africa, he was arrested and charged with leaving the country without a passport and inciting workers to strike.

The ANC continued to operate from Liliesleaf Farm for nearly another year before the security

Surveillance photo of Liliesleaf Farm

police found out about the location from police agent Gerard Ludi, who had infiltrated ANC structures.

On 11 July 1963 dozens of armed policemen and several police dogs raided the property – disguised in a dry-cleaner's van – and arrested a dozen men, found sitting around a table discussing a document.

That document was the outline of Operation Mayibuye, the MK plan for guerrilla warfare in South Africa. The men in the room included Goldreich, Raymond Mhlaba, Lionel 'Rusty' Bernstein, Walter Sisulu, Bob Hepple, Andrew Mlangeni, Ahmed Kathrada and Dennis Goldberg. Significantly, not one weapon or explosive device was found on the property.

Police investigators inside Liliesleaf Farm, 1962

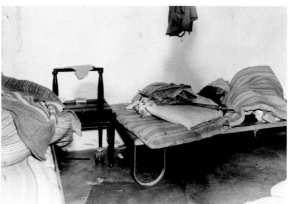

Inside Liliesleaf Farm, 1962

Mandela, who was already serving time on Robben Island but had been implicated in documents found at the farm, was brought to Pretoria for the trial – which famously became known as the Rivonia Treason Trial. Together with the other top MK members, Mandela was charged with sabotage, a crime carrying the death sentence.

Arthur Goldreich, as well as fellow communist Harold Wolpe and Natal Indian Congress members Mosie Moola and Abdulhay Jassat, managed to escape from Marshall Square prison – Goldreich disguised himself as a priest – and eventually fled the country for Swaziland and Botswana, before returning to Israel (where he had lived and fought during the 1948 Arab-Israeli War).

In June 1964 the judge handed down a sentence of life imprisonment for all the remaining accused.

Seven men were taken to Robben Island – Sisulu, Mhlaba, Govan Mbeki, Kathrada, Elias Motsoaledi, Mlangeni and Mandela. Bernstein, although he had helped draft the MK constitution, was found not guilty and discharged. Goldberg was the only white sentenced to life imprisonment, for which he was sent to Pretoria Central Prison. Most of the men served between 22 and 27 years; Mandela was the last one released, in February 1990.

When Mandela tried to locate Liliesleaf Farm

about 18 months after his release, the suburb had changed so much that it took some time before he was able to find and identify the property. Incredibly, the new owners, Veda and Helmut Schneider, had no idea of the property's history when they purchased their home in 1989.

In 2001 the Schneiders opened Liliesleaf as a luxury guesthouse and conference centre. In December of that year, a reunion of the Rivonia triallists was held, during which it was announced that a Liliesleaf Trust had been formed to return the house and outbuildings to their original state and to create a museum.

Approximately 60 per cent of the original buildings and outbuildings on the property still stand; the restoration project (which has included the purchase of surrounding land) has focused on returning the buildings to the state they would have been in the 1960s, using original brick and material.

During the course of excavations on the property, the foundations of the original outbuildings were uncovered; in 2006, several digs were also conducted in search of a gun that Mandela buried on the property shortly before his arrest.

Liliesleaf Farm is expected to officially open in late 2008. For more information, or to make bookings, go to www.liliesleaftrust.co.za.

TWIN CITY

Chapter Eleven

'I have watched you grow like fermented dough
and now that you overflow the bowl
I'm witness to the panic you have wrought.
You were born an afterthought on the by-paths of highways
and have lived like a foster child
whose wayward ways have broken hearts.'

Sipho Sepamla, 'The Soweto I Love' (1977)

In this chapter

☞ Klipspruit and Kliptown

☞ A 'Model Native Township'

☞ Mandela's Johannesburg

☞ Harsh Male Fortresses – Soweto's Hostels

☞ The Youth Rise Up

☞ Soweto After Dark

SOWETO

A woman trying on a wig, Maponya Mall. Photo by Jodi Bieber.

South Africa's Largest Township

**A peacekeeper watches over Soweto
before the country's first democratic elections, 1994**

Some time between Hitler's invasion of Poland in 1939 and the election of the National Party to government in 1948, Johannesburg's black population began to exceed that of its white residents.[1]

This would, perhaps, have come as something of a surprise to the city's various segregationist committees and lawmakers – in 1921, the Native Affairs Commission reported Joburg was 'a European area in which there is no place for the redundant Native.'[2] The following year, the Stallard Commission commented: 'Natives … should only be permitted within municipal areas in so far and for so long as their presence is demanded by the wants of the white population.'[3] Joburg proved a needy city; by 1948 it had close to half a million black inhabitants.[4]

For most of the 20th Century, Joburg's largest grouping of black townships – to the south-west of the city – was treated as an afterthought, developed as a series of temporary solutions for a permanent population the government persisted in treating as 'migrant' labour (and one which was expected to return to its respective designated 'homeland' once the work was done).

After 1948, the implementation of apartheid legislation saw Joburg's black residents almost entirely removed from the inner and central city, and its 'white' suburbs, and relocated to the growing number of loosely formalised black areas – the largest group of which would later come to be known as Soweto.

By the mid-1970s, Soweto's total population was estimated at between one and one-and-a-half million people – about twice the white population of municipal Johannesburg.[5]

Today, depending on who you ask, Soweto houses anywhere between one and four million residents. Official surveys state the population at just over a million;[6] urban developers say at least one-and-a-half million people commute from Soweto to Johannesburg each day; Soweto's residents tend to place stock in much higher 'unofficial' figures, of between three and four million.

This means between 43 and 65 per cent of greater Johannesburg lives in the 120 (or 65, or 150, or 100 – again, sources vary) square kilometres that make up Soweto's townships.

Soweto

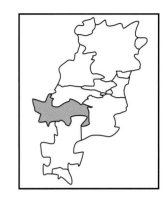

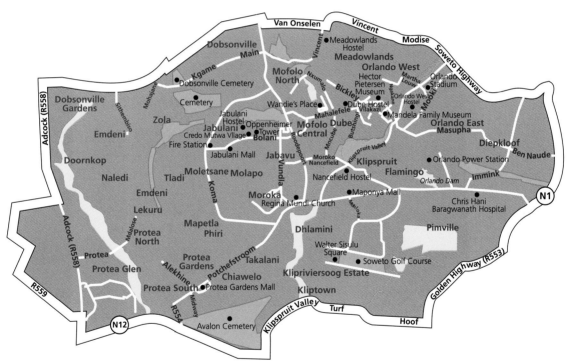

Van Onselen   Vincent   Modise

Dobsonville Main

Meadowlands Hostel

Meadowlands

Orlando West

Mofolo North

Dobsonville

Kgame

Dobsonville Cemetery

Hector Pietersen Museum

Orlando Stadium

Adcock (R558)

Dobsonville Gardens

Cemetery

Zola

Wandie's Place

Orlando West Hostel

Martha Louw

Emdeni

Jabulani Hostel

Jabulani

Oppenheimer Tower

Credo Mutwa Village

Bolani

Mahalefele

Dube Hostel

Vilakazi

Mofolo Dube Central

Mandela Family Museum

Orlando East

Masupha

Diepkloof

Doornkop

Fire Station

Jabulani Mall

Jabavu

Moroko Nancefield

Klipspruit

Ben Naude

Naledi

Tladi

Moletsane Molapo

Flamingo

Orlando Power Station

Immink

Emdeni

Nancefield Hostel

Orlando Dam

N1

Koma

Moroka

Maponya Mall

Lekuru

Regina Mundi Church

Chris Hani Baragwanath Hospital

Mapetla Phiri

Dhlamini

Pimville

Adcock (R558)

Protea North

Walter Sisulu Square

Protea

Protea Gardens

Potchefstroom

Takalani

Soweto Golf Course

Protea Glen

Alekhine

Chiawelo

Klipriviersoog Estate

Golden Highway (R553)

R559

Protea South

Protea Gardens Mall

Kliptown

R554

Midway

Klipspruit Valley

Turf

Hoof

N12

Avalon Cemetery

N

Klipspruit:
The story of an African (Sewerage) Farm

As late as the 19th Century, a favoured method for the urban disposal of human waste was to simply throw it out of the window – onto the streets, where it would (eventually) wash away to a nearby river or stream. It was considered polite to issue a warning cry of 'Gardee Loo' (from the French *gardez l'eau* or 'watch out for the water') before performing such ablutions.

Johannesburg, located more than 70 km from the nearest major river,[7] was without plumbing, water or niceties; as late as 1893, there were recorded complaints of toilet matter being thrown out of windows … without any warning to the people on the street outside.[8]

By 1887 sanitation had become such a big problem that Joburg's first governing body – the Digger's Committee – elected a separate Gezondheits Comité (health committee), also called the Sanitation Board. For nearly a decade, the Board effectively functioned as the settlement's only form of municipal government.

One of the Board's first tasks was to organise the nightly collection of sanitary pails, and the separate collection of slop (waste) water – which was usually stored in a tank at the back of each property.

Next the Board had to find suitable sites to deposit the waste. Four locations were initially proposed: near Ferreirastown; above the Braamfontein Cemetery; Barrett's Farm in Orange Grove; and at Wemmer Pan. White residents wasted no time in raising strenuous objections – although the latter two sites were used temporarily. And so the Board moved the nightsoil disposal sites and pumping stations (for the slop water) to where the residents couldn't complain: next to the three existing black settlements (the Malay Location, the Coolie Location and the Kaffir Location). One of the early sanitary depositing sites, built in 1896 on the farm Waterval, was later filled in and is today the suburb of Westbury.[9]

Despite the unpleasant nature of the work, the disposal of Joburg's waste was lucrative business, which meant that there were several parties competing for control of the sewers. The Town Council (elected in 1897) was elbowed out by the local national government; in 1898, Paul Kruger awarded a sanitation concession to E Mendelsohn (the same gentleman who developed the suburb of Hillbrow, and co-owned a local newspaper), giving him complete control of Joburg's sewers for two decades. This caused such an outcry that the concession was withdrawn, and it was not until after the South African War that the issue of sewerage was tackled again.

In 1903 formal control of sewering reverted to the Joburg Town Council, who planned to move the dumping sites from the west of the city to the south-west, on a portion of the farm Klipspruit. Again, adjacent landowners complained, but other events in the city (somewhat conveniently) overtook their objections: in March 1904 there was a suspected outbreak of bubonic plague in the Brickfields area (not surprisingly considered 'unsanitary', bordered by a refuse tip on one site and 'night soil' collecting sumps on the other).

Black inhabitants who had been evacuated from Brickfields were relocated at the Klipspruit 'health camp' – nearly 20 km from the city, and right next to the

Pipes for sedimentation tanks (with car showing scale), Klipspruit Sewerage Disposal, 1938

proposed new sewerage works; they were soon joined by more 'undesirables' – the AmaWasha black washerman (who washed, dried and ironed in Klipspruit for another 50 years).

A number of Klipspruit residents were housed in emergency shelters left over from the South African War – V-shaped corrugated iron huts, known as e'Tenki. Amazingly, many of these shelters were still in use a generation later, because no housing alternatives had been provided by any administration.

The new location was no more sanitary than its predecessor: in 1908, the Klipspruit Sewage Disposal Works was spreading 4,5 million litres of sewage over the land every day (the Works started receiving waste in 1907, but did not have a proper treatment plant until 1910).[10] As a result, the Klipspruit Location was plagued by flies, which bred in the nearby sludge; deaths from gastro-enteritis were higher in Klipspruit than anywhere else in Johannesburg; and infant mortality reached levels of close to 125 deaths per 1000 births.[11]

By 1920, the Town Council officially condemned the area of Klipspruit – because it was considered 'too squalid to be a residential area'.[12] Of course, nothing was done to improve the conditions, or offer suitable alternatives for the location's residents.

In 1934 a section of Klipspruit was renamed Pimville, in honour of Councillor James Howard Pim, and developed as a 'middle-class' black suburb.

Kliptown

The historically significant area of Kliptown consists of two proclaimed townships (Racecourse and Klipriviersoog Estate) neighbouring Klipspruit, and was the first urban area in Johannesburg to accommodate people of all races.[13] It was also one of the few urban areas in South Africa where non-whites could own land (although these properties were eventually appropriated by the West Rand Administration Board in the 1980s, turning landowners into tenants in their own homes).

Klipspruit River in flood, 1944

PLACES TO VISIT

In its heyday, the **Sans Souci** was host to South Africa's pre-eminent performers, such as Miriam Makeba, Kippie Moketzee and Dollar Brand (Abdullah Ibrahim). By the late 1990s, it had fallen into disuse and most of the original structure was disassembled by scavengers looking for corrugated metal for housing. The Kliptown Our Town Trust is working to restore the Sans Souci as a cinema and community arts centre. For more information, go to www.thesanssouci.org.

Kliptown's early community comprised a mix of blacks, Indians, coloureds and whites; it was a place where mixed marriages took place, where Chinese traders mixed with Jewish smouses (hawkers) – the predecessors of today's Metro Cash & Carry and Lubner's furniture stores.[14]

It was in Kliptown that, in the 1950s, Soweto's first movie house – the Sans Souci Bioscope – was erected, becoming an integral part of township life until the building was destroyed by fire in 1994.

It was in Kliptown, on June 26 1955, that a crowd of

over 3 000 people – including Nelson Mandela, Walter Sisulu, Helen Joseph and Father Trevor Huddleston – made their way through police cordons to gather on a dusty square, to sign a document that presented an alternative vision to the oppressive policies of apartheid. It was called the Freedom Charter.

'We, the People of South Africa, declare for all our country and the world to know:

That South Africa belongs to all who live in it, black and white, and that no government can justly claim authority unless it is based on the will of all the people;

That our people have been robbed of their birthright to land, liberty and peace by a form of government founded on injustice and inequality;

That our country will never be prosperous or free until all our people live in brotherhood, enjoying equal rights and opportunities;

That only a democratic state, based on the will of all the people, can secure to all their birthright without distinction of colour, race, sex or belief;

And therefore, we, the people of South Africa, black and white together, equals, countrymen and brothers adopt this Freedom Charter;

And we pledge ourselves to strive together, sparing neither strength nor courage, until the democratic changes here set out have been won.'[15]

The site – a dusty soccer field – was declared a National Heritage Site in 1997 – and has since been redeveloped and renamed the Walter Sisulu Square of Dedication, which officially opened in June 2005.

In June 2007 the city opened the Kliptown Open Air Museum on the west wing of the Square. The Open Air Museum tells the story of the people behind the drafting of the Charter.

Kliptown Today

Kliptown's business district bustles with traffic on a daily basis and is home to over 80 shops. Unfortunately the residential area – housing over 45 000 people – has been largely neglected. Some streets are not tarred, buildings are dilapidated and some areas, mostly Kliptown's informal settlements, are still without basic amenities like electricity. Unemployment is a significant problem, particularly in the informal settlements.

A Kliptown trust, working together with the Greater Johannesburg City Council, is in the process of revamping the area – which will include the construction of 1200 new social housing units; the upgrading or new development of an additional 5700 freehold units; rehabilitation of the Klipspruit River (which runs through Kliptown) and the sewer infrastructure; and refurbishment of the Kliptown rail station and additional transport links to and from the area.

The Kliptown renewal programme also involves the preservation of historical buildings in Kliptown, such as the houses of activists Charlotte Maxeke and Stanley Lollan, and artist Gerard Sekoto.[16]

Remembering the Freedom Charter during the apartheid years – a demonstrator marks the 30th anniversary of its signing, in 1985

The Walter Sisulu Square of Dedication

PLACES TO VISIT

The dusty soccer field that witnessed the birth of the Freedom Charter is now the striking **Walter Sisulu Square of Dedication** – home to the Kliptown Open Air Museum (which tells the story of the Freedom Charter through images, news clippings, art and song). The Museum is open to the public on Monday to Saturday from 10h00 to 17h00 and on Sunday from 10h00 to 16h30. Entrance is free. The Square is what developers call a 'mixed use' precinct: there are formal and informal trading areas, a monument, and an open theatre for 'community gatherings'; the most notable of these is the annual Soweto Festival (www.sowetofestival.co.za), held around Heritage Day in September. The four-star Holiday Inn Soweto (opened in November 2007) overlooks the Square, and offers 48 rooms, a restaurant and bar as well as conference facilities. For information on the hotel, call 0800 999 136.

A 'Model Native Township'

In 1930 the City Council bought land south-west of Klipspruit for the development of a new township. The site was chosen because of its proximity to a main railway line, a sewerage disposal works and a power station (although none of the early houses were electrified).

The new township was named Orlando, after the first chairman of the Native Affairs Committee, Counsellor Edwin Orlando Leake. Before construction started the council set up a competition, with a £500 prize, for the best layout for the new township. Entrants were instructed to avoid modelling the houses and landscape on the living quarters of the two existing townships. The first 300 houses were erected by October 1931.[17]

Punted as a posh residential area for Africans, the council advertised Orlando as a 'model native township' that was going to have a green belt, with parks and roads arranged to avoid any monotony in the landscape. The reality was that the houses in Orlando were all identical two-bedroom structures (later dubbed 'matchbox' houses because of their size) built in close proximity to

Undated photograph of Orlando

one another, with no indoor plumbing or electricity. For every 12 houses, there was one water pipe on the side-walk. The total floor space of two-thirds of the houses was approximately 40 m², the size of an average living room in a white middle-class home.

Squatters in Orlando, 1940s (far left) and James 'Sofasonke' Mpanza (left)

The launch of Orlando neatly 'coincided' with the subsequent evictions of black residents from the central-city slums, and many black people who were removed from New Doornfontein and Prospect Township took up rented housing in the new location.[18]

Although Orlando was considered the least crowded of the city's black areas (prior to 1940), each small house on average accommodated 5,94 people. The houses were also let in a semi-finished state.[19]

Orlando resident Nelson Botile described his family's new home: 'The walls were not plastered, they were rough, and the floor was just grass. It was not cemented. My father started plastering the house once we were inside. The houses had no taps. We didn't have sewage – we had what was called the bucket system and we had these people coming at night to remove the sanitation. The streets were not tarred and they had no names. The houses only had numbers.'

Most people resisted moving to Orlando because of the distance between the location and the city. Though the inner-city slums were overcrowded, people were closer to shops, banks and other basic amenities which weren't available in Orlando, and by 1936 only 12 000 people lived in the area.

The Housing Shortage

By 1939 the city's black population had grown to 244 000, with males outnumbering females by three to one. The Second World War led to the massive expansion of the local manufacturing industry, which was producing war materials and servicing local manufacturing requirements in the absence of European supplies.

Over 150 000 white men went to war against Germany, leaving a vacuum in the city's workforce. Black labourers who normally worked in the farming and mining industries were, for the first time, afforded better-paying jobs. Because of the demand for semi-skilled and unskilled labourers, the pass laws to restrict the flow of blacks into the urban areas were temporarily suspended. The result of this was a huge increase in the number of women and black families settling in the city.[20] Besides the lure of better-paying jobs, migrant workers were also attracted to the city by the false rumours that the Johannesburg municipality was giving black migrants plots of lands on which to build their own homes.

The new influx created a housing shortage. In 1945 the waiting list for houses in Orlando had risen from 143 (in 1939) to 16 000.[21]

During the War, construction of new houses in Orlando

Shacks in Moroka, 1940s

Squatters in Orlando, 1940s

❝❞ *'I was born, raised and still live in Orlando West. Although I grew up in the apartheid era and we faced a lot of hardships, there were a lot of things that were good about Soweto. To think that people like Bishop Tutu, Walter and Albertina Sisulu, and Winnie Mandela all lived there and still have houses there. I think this place is the home of many great people, not just in politics, but music and sport as well. I remember back in our day, we would go to places in Sophiatown to party and listen to great musicians like Hugh Masekela and Miriam Makeba. Oh, we would have so much fun, with everyone dancing and singing, and we used to dance when we were young, not like kids do today. Then, when we didn't go to Sophiatown, we would have stokvels. We still have them, you know, where every weekend we meet at someone's house and we just party; the better the food and the more booze you had, the longer people stayed and the more they bought. But the beautiful thing about it is that it wasn't just about drinking, that's how we helped each other grow; we were a real community.'*
– Mam' Christine Makgetha

virtually came to a standstill because the City Council claimed that resources were being allocated to the war effort. New arrivals to the city were forced to live as sub-tenants in the houses or backyards of Orlando residents.

While the council had previously condemned the overcrowded conditions in the urban slums and the Western and Eastern Native Townships, during the war it encouraged the practice in Orlando by issuing permits to residents who wanted to let space to sub-tenants. In Orlando it was not unusual to have two different sets of families crammed in one house or one family indoors while the other lived in a shack in the backyard.[22]

Squatter Settlements

By 1944 the overcrowding in Orlando had become critical and landlords were evicting their sub-tenants. With no place to go the homeless turned to populist leaders to solve their housing problems. The most infamous leader during this period was James 'Sofasonke' Mpanza. In March 1944 Mpanza led a group of squatters to build rudimentary shelters, made of hessian, canvas, maize stalks, flattened biscuit tins and bits of corrugated iron, on municipal land near what is today Orlando West.

It wasn't long after that Mpanza set up his own po-litical party – the Sofasonke (direct translation: 'we shall die together') Party – that acted as a municipal governing body that collected levies to keep the administration of the new informal settlement running.

The new informal settlement became known as Masakeng (the place of sacks), and within a month had a population of 20 000.

The developments forced the City Council to concede that they had a housing crisis in their midst. According to the Urban Areas Act of 1923 it was the municipality's responsibility to house urban Africans – so the council responded to the issue by erecting a temporary emergency camp made up of 4000 breeze-block shelters, 11,1 m² in size, with corrugated iron or asbestos roofs which were weighted down with stones. The area was dubbed Shantytown by its residents, who shared the few communal water taps, very basic health services and 73 pit latrines. The original shelters of Masakeng were demolished.

In January 1946 a second land invasion occurred in Orlando when a group of squatters, again led by Mpanza, moved into vacant houses that were allocated but not yet occupied by people on the official housing waiting list.

Shortly after that the council was yet again forced to provide housing for 2000 squatters from Pimville, lead by Abiel Ntoi. The squatters were allocated the same breeze-block shelters as Shantytown residents, on land south-west of Orlando East. The new site was named Jabavu.[23] John Tengo Jabavu was a journalist and activist who had founded South Africa's first black-owned and black-run newspaper; his son, Davidson Don Tengo Jabavu, was a prominent academic and political leader.

In 1947 the council provided additional land for 10 000 squatters from Pimville, Orlando and Alexandra, on an emergency camp south of Jabavu. This settlement would later be named Moroka, after Dr James Sebe Moroka who was ANC president during the 1952 Defiance Campaign.

By 1947 approximately 131 808 people were living in Jabavu, Moroka, Pimville and Orlando, all of which are suburbs of present-day Soweto.[24]

Orlando Today

The landscape of post-apartheid Orlando is a mixture of the original matchbox houses, contemporary single-storey houses, million-rand mansions and backyard structures.

When the apartheid government changed legislation in the 1980s and allowed blacks to buy their properties from the state, this led to a surge in housing renovations – referred to as extending – which is a popular fixture throughout Soweto.

Orlando is divided into Orlando East and Orlando West. Brian Mahlangu, real estate agent and managing editor of *Soweto Homes & Property*, says Orlando West is currently experiencing a property boom, with houses in the Vilakazi Street region going for as much as R1 million. Orlando West is cosidered one of Soweto's affluent areas and in the 1960s and 1970s was nick-named 'Beverly Hills' by Sowetans.

Orlando's population, like most of Greater Soweto, is a mixture of wealthy, middle-class and working-class Sowetans.

Besides historical sites, Orlando is also known for its restaurants. Locals and people from the northern suburbs hankering for a traditional African meal or *kasi* (slang for township) ambience, visit the two most popular places in the area: Nambitha Eatery and Sakhumzi Restaurant, also in Vilakazi Street.

On weekends both venues are packed to capacity and the sidewalks, which act as parking lots, are crammed with expensive sedans and 4x4s.

PLACES TO VISIT
Vilakazi Street is the place to go for traditional township fare. Try the following:
- **Sakhumzi Restaurant** is located at 6980 Vilakazi Street, Orlando West. For information, call (011) 536 1379 or go to www.sakhumzi.co.za.
- **The Nambitha Eatery** is situated at 6877 Vilakazi Street, Orlando West. For more information, call (011) 936 9128 or go to www.nambitha.biz.

Mandela's Johannesburg

Mandela in the office of Mandela and Tambo.
Photograph by Jurgen Schadeberg.

In 1941 Nelson Rolihlahla Mandela and his close relative Justice Bambilanga – both recently expelled from the University College of Fort Hare, for joining in student protests – used the proceeds from the sale of a cow ('borrowed' from their guardian, the Regent) to fund their escape from the Eastern Cape to Johannesburg.

Mandela admits his flight was mainly prompted by the desire to escape an arranged marriage; but, like many children growing up in rural South Africa, he had heard much about the city from migrant labourers who had worked in the mines, and was enthralled by Johannesburg's lights and glamorous billboards.[25]

After a brief stint as a night watchman at the Crown Mines (he was dismissed when it was found out he had run away from home and deceived the Regent), Mandela went looking for work at a real estate agency in town, where he met Walter

Sisulu, who would become his lifelong friend. Sisulu introduced Mandela to the law firm of Witkin, Sidelsky and Eidelman, where Mandela started his law articles while completing his bachelor's degree through the University of South Africa.

During this period, Mandela moved from George Goch Township (where he was staying with a cousin, Garlick Mbekeni) to Alexandra – first to the premises of the Anglican church on 8th Avenue, and then the house of the Xhoma family at 46 7th Avenue. He subsequently moved to the Witwatersrand Native Labour Association (WNLA) compound, to be closer to work in downtown Johannesburg.

While at the law offices, Mandela met Gaur Radebe, a well-known African Nation Congress (ANC) activist, and member of the South African Communist Party.[26] He began attending ANC meetings with Radebe, and joined his colleagues in a march in support of the Alexandra Bus Boycott.

'In Johannesburg, I had become a man of the city. I wore smart suits, I drove a colossal Oldsmobile and I knew my way around the back alleys of the city ... But in fact I remained a country boy at heart, and there was nothing that lifted my spirits as much as blue skies, the open veld and green grass.'
– Nelson Mandela, *Long Walk to Freedom.*

In 1943 Mandela registered for a post-graduate law degree (his LLB) at the University of the Witwatersrand; that same year, he joined the ANC. By 1944 Mandela had helped to found the ANC Youth League (ANCYL) together with Anton Lembede, Oliver Tambo and Walter Sisulu.

In July 1944 Mandela married Evelyn Mase, Walter Sisulu's cousin. In 1946 the couple, together with their son Thembikile, moved into a three-roomed house (without electricity) in Orlando, Soweto.

By 1947 Mandela had completed his articles and was elected to the executive of the Transvaal ANC; the following year he was appointed as the secretary of the ANCYL. He also failed to get his LLB, and left the university.

Mandela's involvement with the ANC became more prominent as the Youth League took control of the party; in 1949 he was elected to the executive of the ANC, and by 1951 he was president of the ANCYL.

By mid-1952, the ANC's Defiance Campaign, led by Mandela, saw him arrested under the Suppression of Communism Act. A crowd of black workers, Indian school children and white students

from Wits University marched through the streets in protest and gathered at the Johannesburg Magistrates Court in Fox Street to support Mandela and his co-accused.[27] In September, Mandela was given a suspended sentence and 'banned' (forbidden from attending meetings, talking to more than one person at a time, and leaving Johannesburg without permission) for six months. When his banning order expired in 1953, he was immediately banned for a further two years.

In August 1952 Mandela had set up his own law office; by December of that year, he had approached his good friend Oliver Tambo and the two lawyers set up South Africa's first black law firm in the Chancellor House building on Fox Street. Two years later, the Transvaal Law Society petitioned the High Court to have Mandela struck off the roll because of his participation in the Defiance Campaign. He was successfully defended (at no cost) by Walter Pollack, QC, and William Aaronsohn.

In 1955, after spending another short period in jail, Mandela returned home to find that his wife had moved out.

By 1956 Mandela was banned for a third time, this time for five years. The news depressed him as he felt he would be 'quarantined' to the '... same district, seeing the same streets, the same mine dumps on the horizon, the same sky'.[28] In that same year, Mandela and Tambo were arrested for High Treason, and were taken to the police station on Marshall Square. When they were released on bail, Mandela and Tambo renewed their practice. They represented women arrested for protesting against passes for women outside the Central Pass

Member of the crowd at Nelson Mandela's welcome-home rally at FNB Stadium, near Soweto

Office in downtown Johannesburg in Albert Street.[29]

In 1958 Mandela finalised his divorce from Evelyn and married Winnie Madikizela.

In 1960 the ANC itself was banned; Mandela was one of thousands detained during the country's first State of Emergency. As the struggle moved underground, Mandela's movements became more defiant – he burned his pass book, and ignored his banning orders to visit his son, Makgatho, who was ill, driving him back from the Transkei to receive surgery in Johannesburg.

In 1961 Mandela went underground; although he was acquitted in the first treason trial, he did not return home. Mandela moved around the country, visiting ANC leaders; he lived with a family in Market Street, Johannesburg; with activist Wolf Kodesh; in the servant's quarters of a doctor's house, where he pretended to be a gardener; and at a sugar plantation in Natal.

By mid-1961 the ANC formed its armed wing, Umkhonto We Sizwe, and Mandela moved to Liliesleaf Farm in Rivonia.

In 1962 Mandela was smuggled out of the country to attend a conference in Addis Ababa; he also flew to London and met labour and liberal party leaders. In August he was arrested at a roadblock in Natal and sentenced to five years for incitement to strike and leaving the country without a passport. He was held in Pretoria, then transferred to Robben Island. Following the raid on Liliesleaf Farm in 1963, Mandela and nine others were charged with sabotage and attempting to overthrow the state violently. Mandela was found guilty in 1964, and remained in prison (on Robben Island, then Pollsmoor Prison, then Victor Verster Prison) until February 1990.

On February 13, two days after his release from prison, Nelson Mandela was flown by helicopter to a 'Welcome Home' rally at the FNB Stadium near Soweto. Four years later, Mandela would become South Africa's first democratically elected president.

PLACES TO VISIT

The Mandela Family Museum (8115 Ngakane Street, Orlando) is Mandela's original house, where he moved with his first wife Evelyn Mase in 1946. When he married Winnie Madikizela in 1958, she joined him at his home. Politically active in her own right, Winnie was frequently arrested, and was also subject to various banning orders and house arrests, including being banished to the Free State in 1977. She returned to her Soweto home in 1986. In 1988 Winnie's unofficial bodyguards, known as the Mandela Football Club, kidnapped and murdered a young activist named Stompie Seipei; Winnie was later found guilty of kidnapping and of being an accessory to assault, but on appeal her sentence was reduced and then suspended. Winnie and Nelson Mandela separated in 1992 and divorced in 1996.

When Mandela was released from prison, he declined to stay in the new home Winnie had built during his incarceration, preferring to return to his original home. He was soon afterwards moved to a secret location (for security reasons), before eventually settling in his current residence in Houghton.

'I enjoyed relaxing at home, reading quietly, taking in the sweet and savoury smells emanating from pots boiling in the kitchen. But I was rarely home to enjoy these things.' – Nelson Mandela, *Long Walk to Freedom.*

In the mid-1990s Nelson Mandela handed the house over to the Soweto Heritage Trust; his ex-wife, however, refused to relinquish it and turned it into the Mandela Family Museum – at the site's inauguration, she even sold bottles of 'Mandela garden soil'. Many of the house's original fixtures have been lost – the Mandela house was petrol-bombed, and even set alight – but it contains an interesting collection of memorabilia.

The museum is open every day from 09h30 to 17h00. For more details, call (011) 936 7754.

Soweto Grows

Aerial view of Soweto pre-1960

By September 1946 the waiting list for municipal houses (for black people) had grown to 42 000.[31] That same year, the Union government had appointed the Fagan Commission to look into the problem of black people living in or near 'white' urban areas.

Contrary to the views of the earlier Stallard Commission, the Fagan report (published in 1948) held the opinion that the migration of black people into towns and cities was an 'economic phenomenon' that could be guided and regulated – but not halted or prevented. 'We, therefore, have to accept that there is a permanent urban Native population.'[32] The 1923 Urban Areas Act had outlined the creation of areas it referred to as 'native villages': urban spaces that would be allocated to 'educated' black residents, who would be offered freehold property rights.

Based on this concept, in 1946 the government had proposed a new 'elite' township between the areas of Orlando and Jabavu. Called Dube, it was to house between 6000 and 7000 residents in up to 1500 houses – each situated on stands of 464 m² (compared to stands as small as 37 m² in other areas).

When the City Council found that title deeds for the selected area contained a clause excluding black people from owning the land, the 'native village' model was simply amended to offer potential residents 99-year leases as an alternative. At the time, freehold rights still existed for African residents in some of the city's western suburbs (like Sophiatown); the prospect of leasehold was, therefore, less than appealing for the middle-class residents the Council had hoped to attract.

In 1950, Hendrik Verwoerd – the architect of grand apartheid – took the position of Minister of Native Affairs in the new Nationalist government. He promptly forbade freehold property rights to black people in white areas, and slashed Dube's proposed leasehold term to a maximum of 30 years, without the option of renewal (by the late 1960s, all leasehold rights were revoked entirely).

The model native village that had been planned for Dube was also reworked – and reduced (Verwoerd rejected the 'low-density' concept) to 330 plots of 464 m², 900 houses on 297 m² plots, and 780 more on even smaller pieces of land.

Some of the wealthier residents evicted from Sophiatown – those who had enough money to build their own houses – elected to settle in Dube when they moved, including former ANC president Dr Alfred Xuma; it became known as a 'glamorous' part of Soweto, but the structures were still a far cry from equivalent white housing in Joburg proper.

The rest of the area would be made up of houses constructed by the Council. But this did not stop Dube from becoming the middle-class African haven or 'native village' the council had envisaged.[33]

Dube residents were made up of shopkeepers, small businessmen, teachers, priests, police sergeants, nurses, factory workers with permanent jobs and good incomes, and clerks.[34]

Dube was soon identified as the most 'glamorous township' and the place of 'highbugs, 'tycoons' and 'social-ites' by working-class Sowetans, who also dubbed Dube as the place of 'excuse me's' because the intelligentsia who lived there were known to speak formal English most of the time.[35]

In 1954 – with the housing crisis as acute as ever, and the additional problem of increasing numbers of squatter camps around the Witwatersrand – Verwoerd designed a programme which would allow him to quickly move (relocate) communities and families, and identify who was (and was not) eligible for government housing. Called a 'site-and-ser-

PLACES OF INTEREST
Chris Hani Baragwanath Hospital
(known as 'Bara') is the largest hospital in the world, situated on 173 acres and with over 3000 beds.

The hospital (named after the Baragwanath family, who had owned land and opened a wayside inn in the area) was opened in 1942 to treat British military personnel who had been wounded, primarily in the Middle East, during the Second World War. In 1948, the South African government purchased the hospital for a million pounds, and designated it the official 'native' hospital. Today, it serves the entire community of Soweto as well as being a referral hospital for specialist cases from the rest of Africa. Bara trains approximately 60 per cent of medical students from the University of the Witwatersrand and is acknowledged as one of the finest training hospitals in the world.

PLACES TO SEE
Directly opposite the Chris Hani hospital complex is the recently upgraded **Bara taxi rank**, which handles up to 50 000 commuters a day. The taxi rank also hosts an informal traders' market.

PLACES TO SEE
The conical **Oppenheimer Tower** (built in 1957 to commemorate Sir Ernest's contribution – and modelled after one of the famous Zimbabwe ruins) provides a great vantage point from which tourists can see most of Soweto. Situated in Orlando East, near the Morris Isaacson School (where the 1976 uprising started), it's a regular feature on most guided tours of the area. An interesting note: In 2003, Anglo American again provided an interest-free loan to the Joburg Council – this time for the building of low-cost housing in the reclaimed Brickfields area next to Newtown.

Housing being built in Dube, 1954

succeeded in building permanent structures: between 1954 and 1965, over 45 000 houses were built,[38] many conforming with the NE 51/6 design – a special sub-economic housing prototype developed by the National Building Research Institute. The NE (Non-European) 51/6 was a basic four-roomed semi-detached unit with no bathroom or inside toilet; it was later replaced by the NE 51/9, which included a bathroom.

Home Loans

Predictably, very little in the way of funds was provided for the actual building of the houses required in the townships. In 1956, Will Carr, the head of Joburg's Non-European Affairs Department (NEAD) invited Sir Ernest Oppenheimer, head of Anglo American, to visit the temporary shelters of Shantytown and the Moroka Emergency Camp. Oppenheimer was appalled by the conditions, and by the middle of that year Anglo American, together with a conglomerate of other mining companies, agreed to provide the Council with a £3-million low-interest loan for the purpose of providing low-income housing in the townships.

Verwoerd made acceptance of the loan conditional on a portion of it being earmarked for building hostels – the single-sex barracks that would become a feature of

vice' scheme, the programme effectively provided sites only for eligible black residents – the homes were to be built at a later stage (funded through loans provided to the relevant authorities). The sites were provided with basic municipal services (at Verwoerd's suggestion, water outlets and toilet facilities were located 'at a rear corner of one stand, to supply these services also to the three other contiguous plots, "in keeping with the communal spirit of tribalism."')[36]

Site occupants were only permitted to erect a temporary shack at the back of the stand; the 'front section was to be kept clear for a formal house to be erected at a later date'.[37] It appears the 'formal' structure was intended to be built by the site's occupants, as resources allowed.

Against all odds, many of the residents actually

dislocated city life for unmarried or migrant African men.

Additional funds came from the Native Revenue Account – made up of profits from government-controlled beer halls – and the Native Services Levy Fund, which imposed a small tax on employers from 1953.

Building Soweto

The Bantu Building Workers Act, passed in 1951, made it a crime for a black person to perform skilled work in urban areas – except those designated by the government, such as the townships. While the Act's foremost intention was the protection of white workers' interests, it granted permission for blacks to be trained as artisans in the building industry (something previously reserved for whites only). The availability of skilled black labour in the townships gave rise to a development boom between 1954 and 1969. In that period 50 000 houses and 88 000 schools were built.[40] The following decade, however, construction infrastructure virtually ground to a halt as the government concentrated its efforts on providing houses in the homelands.

In 1978 black residents were allowed to obtain a 99-year leasehold title to their property; the new legislation also gave leaseholders the right to sell or renovate their property. At least 6000 Sowetan households did alterations on their houses between 1980 and 1983,[41] when urban blacks were finally allowed to buy their Council-owned homes (less than 3000 residents did so).

These developments did little to solve the increasing shortage of housing in Soweto – by 1981 there was a shortage of 35 000 homes in the area, and it was estimated that there was an average of seven people per house. The lack of accommodation led to a staggering increase in backyard shelters and informal settlements, a situation that persists to this day.

Since the early 2000s, a number of long-term Soweto residents have been given the title deeds to their homes – despite difficulties in unpacking traditional inheritance systems and frequent lack of documentation, in many Soweto suburbs this exercise has been a success. The provision of

PLACES TO VISIT

Alongside the Oppenheimer Tower is the fantastical **Credo Mutwa Cultural Village** (corner of Ntsane and Majoeng streets in Central Western Jabavu), created by artist, author and traditional healer Credo Mutwa in 1974 as a joint venture between the Joburg City Parks and Mutwa. The Village includes a number of large painted clay sculptures of human and animal figures depicting African culture and folklore. The buildings are constructed in a variety of African building styles. The Credo Mutwa Cultural Village is also known as Khayalendaba, or 'Place of Stories', and has always been associated with story-telling, rituals and ceremonies, plays and other cultural activities.

The Village has recently undergone a sensitive and comprehensive restoration, and is open seven days a week, from 07h30 to 16h00. Mighta Makhutle, the cultural officer at the village, is available to give tours of the site; he can be contacted on (011) 930 1813.

Figures at the Credo Mutwa Village

Hostels in Jabulani

affordable housing, however, remains unsolved: there is little land available in Soweto for development, current housing plans are inadequate for the city's growing population, and there are massive backlogs in low-cost housing allocation schemes.

Forced Removals

In 1951 the government announced that it would be clearing Joburg's Western Areas – declared whites-only suburbs in the 1930s – and relocating their African residents to the new townships of Meadowlands (next to Orlando West) and Diepkloof (east of Orlando East).

At the time, 90 per cent of the Western Areas – some 54 000 people – were black.

The national government bought land for the new townships from the Joburg Council, and placed it under the supposedly independent Natives Resettlement Board (NRB). The function of the NRB was to facilitate the eviction of Africans from Sophiatown, Newlands and Martindale to Meadowlands and later Diepkloof. The scheme was structured so that African property owners would sell their houses (in the Western Areas) to the NRB, who would in turn provide their future accommodation. Meadowland's residents would be allowed to 'own' their new

property … under Verwoerd's 30-year lease scheme.

Construction of the first houses in Meadowlands began in 1954; and in February 1955 the first 150 Sophiatown families were 'transferred' (accompanied by 86 military trucks and around 2000 policemen[42]) to their new homes. By October nearly 8000 people were set up in 2100 Meadowlands houses;[43] by the end of 1957 approximately 33 000 people had been relocated into the 7700 houses built under the NRB. In 1958 this was increased to over 9500 families; and 1400 single men were moved to the single-sex hostel in Diepkloof.[44]

The Western Areas were officially deemed to have been 'cleared'.

Harsh Male Fortresses

As early as 1903, the City of Johannesburg had started building municipal compounds for single African men working outside of the mining industry but deemed essential for certain menial tasks (street cleaning, refuse and night soil removal) within the city boundaries.[45]

Also 'permitted' to reside within the city limits were African domestic servants who lived on the premises of their white employers. When the numbers of white people living in flats (apartments) increased after the 1933 boom, so did the numbers of African servants living on the buildings' roofs (where the domestic quarters were usually located) – as well as other black tenants who would sub-let these already-small spaces. The city's medium- and high-rise rooftops became known as 'locations in the sky'[46].

In 1955 HF Verwoerd announced an amendment to the Natives (Urban Areas) Act – specifically aimed at these rooftop 'locations' – which would prohibit more than five African people from living on the premises of any apartment or office block and private residence.[47]

Based on the fiction that an 'urban Black population as such did not exist'[48] – whilst simultaneously conceding the necessary presence of just such a population – black housing was allocated in a calculatedly divisive manner

Residents of Nancefield Hostel eating lunch, 1991

(designed to inhibit any notion of permanent residence): by gender, by 'tribal group' and by marital status. Family dwellings were not allocated to unmarried persons (even single-parent households, including those who were widowed or divorced, were technically prohibited from registering for family units). Customary marriages were generally not accorded official recognition.

Unwed black males were required to take accommodation in new single-sex barracks – hostels – the first of which was built in the designated 'Nguni' township of Dube. Three additional hostels were completed in Meadowlands, Nancefield and Jabulani. By 1970 a total of ten hostels had been completed in and around Soweto, housing 38 095 people. Only one of these – in Orlando West – was for women.[49]

The hostels were single-storey grey buildings, built in monotonous rows. These 'harsh male fortresses'[50] offered little in the way of privacy, or comfort. The Diepkloof hostel was described as having 'only a few single rooms', with most of the hostel set up in 16-bed dormitory units. 'Beds were hollow brick boxes overlain with planks, and there were no cupboards or even pegs. Showers and washing facilities were all in one wing and the communal toilets had no partitions.'[51]

Life inside the male hostels was tough. There were reports of theft, prostitution (and the inevitable sexually transmitted infections) and unsanitary living conditions.

Because the hostels were also planned along ethnic lines, they also soon became associated with violence – internal (against non-aligned residents) and external (against outside communities). In 1957 the predominantly Zulu residents of the Dube hostel fatally attacked township residents who were attending a Sotho funeral. In August 1976, shortly after the June uprisings, clashes between Meadowlands hostel residents and the township youths resulted in the hostel being vacated.

In 1977, following severe flooding of several hundred homes in the Klipspruit valley south of Soweto, some 1200 homeless people were temporarily accommodated in the Meadowlands hostel. When no alternative accommodation for the families became available, they permanently occupied a section of the hostel and were later joined by other homeless Soweto families. The hostel would come to be known as Mzimhlope or 'Transit Camp'.[52]

In the late 1980s and early 1990s, hostel dwellers again assumed key roles in a new type of political violence

Khumalo Street, Thokoza, on the East Rand, August 1990. A girl leads her sister to safety as an impi, or regiment, of Inkatha-supporting Zulu warriors approaches during the Hostel Wars. Photo by Ken Oosterbroek. (Oosterbroek was killed here four years later).

– what the media simplified as clashes between Zulu and Xhosa speakers, an aggressive shorthand for the underlying conflict between two political parties: The Zulu-led Inkatha Freedom Party (IFP), which had waged a campaign in the hostels to enlarge its support base in Gauteng; and the Xhosa-dominated African National Congress.

Hostels were considered to have a 'propensity to brutal violence, due to a pervasive macho culture coupled to the absence of women and the constraining influence of family life.'[53] Hostels were the strongholds from which attacks could be planned and coordinated – and the fortresses to which residents could retreat when they were attacked in turn.

In the early 1990s the violence became particularly brutal in several East Rand hostels – with hundreds of people being killed in a matter of days; researchers started referring to the clashes as the 'Transvaal War' or the 'Hostel Wars'.

While reporters were able to understand the inherent forces (single-sex dwellings run along ethnic lines, poor living conditions, etc.) that shaped hostel dwellers into such implements of rage,[54] there was much about the hostel violence of this period that remained a mystery. Later evidence suggested (apartheid) state involvement in inciting some of the attacks – in an apparent attempt to destabilise the approaching democratisation of South Africa (in April 1994).

What Happened To Soweto's Hostels?
In the 1990s the National Department of Housing announced a R325-million Public Sector Hostels Redevelopment Programme, promising to change the character of Gauteng hostels from seedy, overcrowded single-sex dormitories to less congested, self-contained low-cost family units.

By 2002 only Jabulani, Mapetla and Nancefield hostels in Soweto had been listed as upgraded. The improvements, though, were not what some residents had envisioned – the structures had remained more or less unchanged – and were more of a 'paint and patch' job. The Provincial Housing Department conceded the programme had not gone according to plan, and the same year development on hostels in Meadowlands, Dobsonville, Orlando West and Dube began – with a focus on making actual structural changes to the buildings. The exercise was, however, criticised for its high costs – running to R40 000 a unit, compared with the R16 500 allocated for an RDP house.

In addition to the construction and refurbishment, the Housing Department has also had to find alternative accommodation for residents who were displaced during the process and in some cases were made homeless (because the alterations decreased the number of people the hostels can accommodate).

The programme was developed on the basis that the expenditure would be recouped from the rental charges, which are as little as R30 to R40 a month, but collection of rents has been erratic and most residents admit that they have not paid their rents since moving back into the new buildings.

These financial obstacles have not stopped the project from moving forward. In March 2003 the Johannesburg Social housing announced a R68-million redevelopment initiative for the City Deep hostel, which is due for completion in 2008. The new hostel will be made up of 800 one- to three-bedroom units that will house the current residents of City Deep.

Soweto's renovated hostels are now home to an assortment of people from unemployed single mothers and elderly migrant workers (most of whom know no life other than that of the hostel) to semi-skilled workers who own houses outside of Johannesburg and use the hostel as an urban base.[55]

> *'There was a time during the 70s and 80s when there was a lot of trouble here between black people. You had Zulu people working with the Afrikaners, and they went around killing other black people. They would come down from the hostels and randomly go into people's houses and kill them, especially the men and boys. They didn't care who you were; if you weren't one of them they would kill you. They had knives, machetes and other weapons. When we heard the commotion outside, all we could do was hide in our houses and pray that they didn't attack us. I lost a few of my friends that way; and I remember one day they went and killed my next-door neighbours, we were just lucky they didn't come to our house as well. It was terrible, because they had no reason to kill all those helpless people. Just thinking about it hurts so much, and brings back painful memories.'*
>
> – Mam' Angelina Mlakeng

Soweto's Tribal Zones

Apartheid's separate development policies did not just reject the idea of a permanent black urban population – it was official 'policy' that 'the flow of blacks to the cities would be reversed in the mid 1970s',[56] as the 'temporary sojourners' returned to their respective homelands. In line with this flawed thinking, Soweto had been divided into ethnic zones in the 1950s.

The policy meant that people were allocated houses in their ethnic regions, children attended schools of their ethnic origin, and businesses only traded in their particular ethnic zone.

The areas were divided as follows: Dlamini, Dube, Seaoane, Zola, Zondi, Jabulani, Emdeni and White City for isiZulu and isiXhosa (Nguni) speakers; Chiawelo for xiTsonga and tshiVenda speakers; Naledi, Mapetla, Tladi, Moletsane and Phiri for seSotho and seTswana speakers.

HF Verwoerd stated: '... those who belong together naturally want to live near one another, and the policy of ethnic grouping will lead to the development of an intensified community spirit.' [57]

Soweto Rises Up

June 1976, Soweto. Old cars are used as roadblocks

'We should not give the Natives any academic education. If we do, who is going to do the manual labour in the community?' – JN le Roux, National Party politician, 1945

In 1953, the apartheid government passed the Bantu Education Act – establishing a Black Education Department whose role was to compile a curriculum that 'suited the nature and requirements of the black people'; subjects like mathematics and science were de-emphasised (if they were taught at all) in favour of 'practical' lessons – such as domestic and agricultural skills.

Six years later, the Extension of University Education Act prohibited black students from studying at white universities, making provision instead for a number of black 'tribal' colleges.

In the June 1957 issue of the journal Liberation, *Nelson Mandela wrote of these institutions:*

'… the education they will give will not be directed towards the unleashing of the creative potentialities of the people but towards preparing them for perpetual mental and spiritual servitude to the whites.'

It was not only the content of Bantu Education that was to be substandard: black school facilities were also totally inadequate – a situation that was intensified by a government ban on the building and operation of new black secondary schools.[61] Between 1962 and 1971 no new secondary schools were built at all in Soweto – resources were, instead, concentrated on developments in the 'homelands'.

The net result of such practices was that schools in Soweto (and elsewhere) were hopelessly oversubscribed – some classes contained over 100 students, and teachers were often forced to teach two shifts each day.[62]

Between 1970 and 1975 the number of black secondary school children across the country grew dramatically from 122 489 to 318 568. In Soweto 40 new secondary schools were built between 1972 and 1976, and enrolments increased to nearly 35 000 teenagers.[63]

The growth of secondary schooling introduced 'a new youth subculture in Soweto – a new collective identity.'[64] Soweto already had a number of youth gangs, made up of primary school leavers who had been unable to find work; these gangs were localised and extremely territorial, fighting amongst themselves and focused on survival and petty pleasures. Such groups 'often lacked any wider political consciousness, and were unresponsive to the black consciousness ideas that were taking root in other sectors of Soweto's black population.'[65] Initially, these gangs targeted secondary school pupils, in particular the girls; but the students 'responded with mass resistance and retaliation, which further reinforced their collective consciousness and solidarity.'[66]

In 1975 the government decided to reduce the number of school years from 13 to 12; the Grade 8 (Standard 6) class was cut and pupils from Standard 5 were graduated straight to secondary school. This had serious implications for the already overcrowded schools: in 1976 there were 257 505 pupils enrolled in Form 1 (the first year of secondary school) at high schools; the available schools could only accommodate 38 000 students.

All of these factors contributed to simmering tensions among students, teachers and parents. The issue that made everything boil over was a decree from the Bantu Education Department that, from 1976, Afrikaans would be used as a medium of instruction in half the school subjects. By June, as mid-year exams approached, the students took action.

At the height of the day
Youth Rage spilled all over the place
unleashing its own energy
confounding the moment
exploding the lie
take away
*   your teachings*
take away
*   your promises*
take away
*   your hope*
take away
*   your language*

Give me this day myself...

I shall learn myself anew
I shall read myself from trees
I shall glean myself from all others
I shall wean myself from you ...
– Sipho Sepamla

THINGS TO DO

Most tours of Soweto will include visits to the major struggle sites – including the Hector Pieterson Museum, the houses of Nelson Mandela and Archbishop Desmond Tutu, and the Regina Mundi Catholic Church. If you're visiting Joburg, your hotel or guesthouse should be able to recommend a good tour operator to you. You can also contact Vhupo Tours (www.vhupo-tours.com) on (011) 936 0411 and Soweto.co.za (use the same web address to see their site) on (011) 326 1700. For an online map showing Soweto's struggle 'routes', go to www.sowetouprisings.com.

PLACES TO VISIT
Regina Mundi Catholic Church (at
1149 Khumalo Street Moroka) – Soweto's largest Catholic church was used to house political rallies that were banned in most of Greater Soweto and was also where protestors from the 1976 uprisings found refuge from police bullets. Most tours to Soweto include a trip to Regina Mundi Church but independent trips to the church are available. For more information call (011) 986 2646.

PLACES TO SEE
The Hector Pieterson Memorial
Museum (Kumalo Street, Orlando West) is

situated just a few blocks from where Hector was killed. The Museum features moving photographic and video displays dedicated to the 1976 student uprising, and there is a memorial in the courtyard outside. The Hector Pieterson Museum is open Mondays to Saturdays from 10h00 to 17h00, and Sundays from 10h00 to 16h00. For information, call (011) 536 0611.

On 16 June a peaceful protest march was planned by the Action Committee of the Soweto Students' Representative Council (SSRC). Students from Naledi High and Morris Isaacson were to march from their respective schools, picking up other students on the way before meeting at a central point from where they would proceed to the Orlando Stadium. In the end, there were 11 columns of students making their way towards the stadium; along the way, a number of minor skirmishes with police were avoided – student leader Tsietsi Mashinini climbed on to a tractor to appeal to the crowd for calm. 'We have just received a report that the police are coming. Don't taunt them, don't do anything to them. Be cool and calm. We are not fighting,' he said.

By the time the students reached what is now Hector Peterson Square, close to Orlando High School, the police were waiting. The students, holding placards and singing 'Nkosi Sikelel' iAfrica, began to taunt the police. In response, a policeman lobbed what is believed to have been a teargas canister into the crowd. According to an eyewitness, reporter Sophie Tema from *The World*, the students became angry and began throwing rocks at the police. Without warning, one of the white policemen drew his revolver, pointed it and fired. 'A single shot rang out. There was a split second's silence and pandemonium broke out. Children screamed. More shots were fired. At least four students fell and others ran screaming in all directions.'[67] The first casualties were 15-year-old Hastings Ndlovu and 13-year-old Hector Pieterson.

The shootings sparked off days of rioting, and hundreds of deaths.[68] Government administration buildings – particularly those of the West Rand Administration Board (WRAB) – were set alight; a white WRAB official was pulled out of his car and beaten to death. Near Regina Mundi Church in Orlando and the Esso garage in Chiawelo, more students were killed.

As students were stopped by police in one area, they moved their protest action to others. Fires burned into the night. By 9 p.m. the police started moving their armoured cars, known as Hippos, into Soweto.

By the morning of 17 June, 1500 police armed with Sten guns, automatic rifles, and hand machine carbines had taken up strategic positions in Soweto. 'Helicopters flew overhead. The army was on standby. The police force had never developed methods of crowd control other than the use of live bullets. The police shot at people indiscriminately and casualties were even higher than the day before.'[69]

In Johannesburg, white students from Wits University marched through the city centre to protest against the killing of black schoolchildren; as they marched through the streets, they were joined by many black workers.

The protest action spread to neighbouring townships, then the whole country.

In the days following June 16, violent riots spread across Soweto and the country.

Burying The Dead
By Ismail Farouk

In the aftermath of the June 1976 uprisings, a mass burial was planned for those who lost their lives. An application for a mass burial was made to the Johannesburg Chief Magistrate – the application was denied. Further attempts to list the dead were foiled by the police as bereaved families were denied access to the bodies of their loved ones. Anti-apartheid activist Dr Nthato Motlana suggested a symbolic service be held to commemorate the dead; a symbolic funeral service was conducted for Hector Pieterson at the Regina Mundi Church – every year since then, a special service is held at the church to commemorate the events of June 16 1976, followed by a procession to the Avalon Cemetery.[70] Avalon Cemetery is one of the largest cemeteries in South Africa and is the final resting place of many political and cultural activists. The cemetery is about 170 ha in size and is managed by the City of Johannesburg's City Parks division. At the entrance to the cemetery, a memorial with the words, 'Never Never Again' inscribed on it pays tribute to those who lost their lives in the Soweto uprisings of 1976.

With more than 200 funerals occurring each weekend, Avalon Cemetery is facing severe pressure. The death rate is increasing by ten per cent per year. Cremation is not considered appropriate for most people so City Parks are encouraging families to consider the 'second burial' option, where several members of a family are buried in the same grave. Compounding the problem is the AIDS pandemic. With more than 6,5 million of the country's 47 million people infected with HIV, demand for space is increasing. Every weekend, convoys of buses carrying mourners bring the Old Potchefstroom Road to a standstill. This has resulted in special traffic marshals being deployed to deal with the traffic congestion every weekend.

A teenager in Daveyton, near Johannesburg

A Township By Any Other Name

Up until 1963, the patchwork of townships – Moroka, Pimville, Klipspruit, Orlando East, Dube, Mofolo North and South, Central West Jabavu, Molape and Moletsane – still had no name. The grouping was referred to as the South Western Bantu Townships or Matchbox City, a reference to the identical brick houses that dominated the landscape.

In 1959 the City Council's Department of Non-European Affairs announced a competition to give the area a name.

Some of the names put forward were: Goldella, Sothuni (a combination of the words 'Sotho' and 'Nguni'), Dumuzweni (a Zulu word meaning: 'famous all around the world'), KwaMpanza ('the place of Mpanza'), Kwantu ('place of the Ntu or Bantu'), Oppenheimerville (for his generous housing loan) and Partheid Townships, to name a few. A committee finally decided, for the purposes of pronunciation and neutrality on Soweto.[59] When the name was announced, in April 1963, the *Rand Daily Mail* commented on the 'perspective bias that characterised the township more by its geographic location (in relationship to white) Johannesburg than by a sense of its own place'[60].

Gangsters and Sub-Cultures of Soweto
By Thomas Thale

Despite its squalor, Soweto has, over the generations, produced a vibrant youth culture, which betrays a strong American influence.

In their speech, dress, music and outlook, Sowetans exude a sense of urban sophistication. Indeed, Sowetans pride themselves on being trendsetters. With its cosmopolitan outlook, Soweto has also spawned many youth sub-cultures.

Soweto youths categorise themselves in terms of class, dress and speech. Perhaps the most conspicuous trendsetters at the moment are the so-called '*mabujwa*' – a corruption of the word 'bourgeois', meaning classy. This category refers to fashion-conscious youths who go to extreme lengths to look good. The *bujwa* ladies wear tight-fitting, often coloured, jeans or pedal-pushers with high-heeled shoes. The guys also wear tight-fitting pants and designer vests to reveal their muscles.

Then there are the 'clevers' – generally streetwise and more hardened youths, who dismiss the *bujwa* as sissies. Their brimmed hats called 'spotties', Dickies pants and All Star sneakers distinguish the current generations of 'clevers'.

Like other ghettoes the world over, Soweto has created many generations of gangsters, known as *'magintsa'* in township parlance. These are rather shady characters that keep irregular hours, drive flashy cars and have distinguished criminal careers.

Urban slickness has been a part of Soweto culture from its beginnings. In the 1950s, residents who had been relocated to Soweto from the freehold areas displayed their urban sophistication by speaking *flaaitaal*, a mixture of Afrikaans with indigenous languages. Those who had been in Soweto for a while developed *is'camtho*, a local lingo that drew on indigenous languages. These languages have now evolved into *tsotsitaal*, a universal language among urban youth.

In his book, *BoTsotsi*, Clive Glaser traces the emergence of youth sub-cultures and gangsterism in Soweto to the 1930s.

The term *tsotsi* (thief), as Glaser demonstrates, started off as a reference to a pair of narrow-bottomed trousers, but later changed from a dress style to refer to delinquent youth, some of whom belonged to gangs. Soweto's early gangsters, like the Otto Town of Orlando, the Apaches and the Berlins from Orlando East, the Black Swines of White City, the Torch Gang of Orlando, started off by engaging only in misdemeanours like gambling and pick-pocketing before venturing into more serious crimes like train robbery, and becoming violent. Some tended to idolise screen gangsters and wreaked havoc in communities as they became more and more brutal.

Since the 1950s, Soweto gangsters have been involved in skirmishes and sometimes-serious warfare with school-going youths. Scholars have taken it upon themselves to defend their schoolmates against gang harassment, abduction and rape. As early as 1959, the Apaches of Orlando were involved in running battles with students from Morris Isaacson High School. There have been eruptions of violence between gangsters and scholars at irregular intervals ever since.

(Originally published on www.joburg.org.za)

PLACES TO VISIT

Started as an illegal shebeen in 1981, **Wandie's Place** (618 Makhalamele Street, Dube) has become one of Soweto's best-known eating and drinking spots, for locals and tourists alike – although there are days when the latter appear to outnumber the former. Owner Wandie Ntaba has recently added a boutique hotel adjacent to the tavern. For more information, go to www.wandies.co.za or call (011) 326 1700.

Soweto After Dark

In 1938 the four-decade prohibition was lifted on blacks consuming or trading in any form of alcohol – the lifting was partially to encourage black people to drink traditional sorghum beer, but only in the sterile and tightly regulated municipal beer halls which were frequented by unskilled black labourers. Urban blacks were barred by law from drinking wines, spirits, malts and other beers (considered 'white man's liquor').

By the 1950s 'white liquor' was being sold illegally in private homes, called shebeens, throughout Soweto. Unlike the beerhalls, shebeens were deemed socially acceptable, especially for women, and entrance was free.

At night, homes would turn into all-night drinking clubs, usually run by 'shebeen queens', often characterised as brazen single or divorced women.

The trade of so-called 'white liquor' was particularly popular in exclusive middle-class shebeens, where the atmosphere resembled that of a social club and attracted a clientele that included teachers, writers, social workers and doctors.[71]

This was in stark contrast to some of the shebeens run in the poorer parts of the township, which were frequented by *'lala vuka* drinkers' (those who would drink until they passed out) and where heady homemade brews were sold.[72]

PLACES TO VISIT

• For a **Shebeen Tour** of Soweto, contact Jimmy's Face to Face Tours on (011) 331 6108/6132 or Soweto.co.za on 011 326 1700.

• **The Rock** was established in Rockville in 1998. This hang-out spot is just off Old Potchefstroom Road between the Regina Mundi Church and the Soweto Cricket Oval. The venue consists of a large bar area, private lounge area, dance floor and roof deck which has spectacular views of Soweto. There is ample parking with security. Live jazz sessions take place regularly and the restaurant serves wholesome traditional township cuisine.

• **The Backroom** in Pimville (Shop 20, Pimville Square) has a bar and jazz lounge, and upmarket restaurant offering a buffet menu that is a mix of classic *kasi* (location) and western cuisine. Open until late, from Tuesday to Sunday. For information, call (011) 938 9388.

THINGS TO DO

The **Soweto Beer Festival** takes place in October each year in Mofolo – the venue has been upgraded to accommodate the 80 000+ people who visit over the course of the five-day event. For details go to www.sowetobeerfestival.co.za.

Midnight police raids happened frequently and would result in the confiscation of all alcohol on the premises or the immediate arrest of the shebeen queen and her clientele. Sometimes the police would pour out all the liquor into the streets but this rarely deterred other shebeens from operating. In fact, shebeen owners developed clever ways of outwitting the law and protecting their customers.

In 1962 the 'white liquor' law was repealed, but it was still illegal for blacks to trade in alcohol; this prohibition was eventually lifted in 1983 when 86 residential sites in Soweto were rezoned for business purposes so liquor could be sold on the premises while permitting the owner to live there. By that stage, Soweto had around 4000 shebeens.[73]

Though shebeens were an integral part of Soweto nightlife, the disco scene provided alternative entertainment in the 1980s. Following the lifting of restrictions on black business practices in the 1970s, Soweto came alive. Nightclubs like the double-storey Pelican Club in Orlando, Club 707 in Orlando West, and Club 2000, between Moletsane and Mapetla, became popular dance spots.[74]

Shebeens are still a popular social venue for many Sowetans and, as part of the growing tourist industry, shebeen tours have become a regular part of the itinerary. While there are still many shebeens that operate from private homes, nightclubs, lounges and taverns have burgeoned over the last 15 years in various pockets of Soweto.

The Mall Boom

When the trade restrictions (governing how many businesses and the types of businesses Africans could own) were abolished in the 1970s, Soweto went through an economic resurgence. Black businessmen were no longer limited to businesses like fish fryers, butcheries, bakeries, milk shops, fruit-and-vegetable stalls and undertaker services.[75] Within five years Soweto's landscape changed as new grocery shops, dry cleaners, liquor stores, service stations and fast-food outlets were erected throughout the township.

During this time prominent Soweto businessman, Richard Maponya started the first Soweto General Motors franchise, until they disinvested following the 1976 riots.

The informal sector which, during the restriction period, had been limited to selling primarily meat, cups of hot tea and coffee, and vetkoek, branched out and sold everything from cigarettes, washing powder, fresh fruit and vegetables to cosmetics.

Spaza shops (informal shops in private residences)

Girls shopping with their mom inside Maponya Mall

mushroomed all around Soweto, as everyone tried to take advantage of the new economic opportunities.

A number of neighbourhood shopping centres were developed in the 1980s around the township but it was not until 1994 that Soweto had its first major shopping complex: the Dobsonville Shopping Centre. In 2005 the Protea Gardens Mall, in Protea Gardens, opened its doors, followed by the Bara Mall in Diepkloof, adjacent to Chris Hani Baragwanath Hospital and taxi rank; in 2006, the Jabulani Mall was opened in Jabulani.

In September 2007, Richard Maponya opened Soweto's first 'mega mall': the impressive Maponya Mall (on Old Potchefstroom Road) – the 60 000 m² retail development had been a dream of Maponya's since buying the land in the 1980s. 'When I wanted to open a shopping mall in the township 20 years ago,' Maponya remarked at the opening, 'I was reminded by the powers-that-be at the time that I was a temporary sojourner in the city of Johannesburg. But I never tired to keep on knocking on doors to get permission to build my dream.'

'I'm only in my thirties, but I've seen quite a lot of change here. I was born in Orlando East, and even though I don't live at home anymore, I'm here every weekend and building a house in the area. Soweto is the best place to be: if you want to have a good time, you'll always find something happening either at a street corner or at someone's house. This is the only place I know where I can walk into just about anyone's home and they will welcome me. We're a big family and there's a great sense of community here. And the fact that we have museums, soccer stadiums, two malls and people like me are building houses here, I'd like to think that we're growing and Soweto is no longer a place people stay away from. My mother always says to me 'sivela kude' (we've come a long way), and we're still going on, trying to improve ourselves and our community.'
– Themba Masote, businessman

LENASIA

'It must not be forgotten that the Indian people are sons and daughters of a country with a proud and cultured heritage. Their ancient motherland is the bearer of a tradition of civilisation as old as any in the world.
Never, either in India or South Africa, have Indians willingly submitted to laws and practices which brand them as inferior, or curtail their liberties.'

The Indian People in South Africa: Facts About the Ghetto Act (pamphlet published by the South African Communist Party, June 1946)

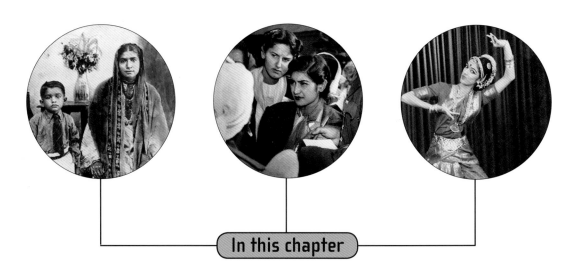

In this chapter

☞ Resistance to the Ghetto Act

☞ New Suburb, 'Happy Future'?

☞ History on Foot: A Walking Tour of Lenasia

☞ Places of Worship

☞ Ahmed Kathrada's House

☞ Tolstoy Farm

Temple in Lenasia during Diwali

Resistance and Defiance

**Monty (GM) Naicker addresses anti-'Ghetto Act' crowd during a
hartal or strike demonstration, Durban, 13 June 1946**

*'The major part of the Indian community …
came to South Africa between 1860 and 1911 as
indentured farm labour to serve as field hands and
mill operatives in the sugar and other agricultural
plantations of Natal … Most of the initial migrants
were drawn from what is today Tamil Nadu and
Andhra Pradesh with some from eastern Uttar
Pradesh and Bihar.'[1] After 1880, a second wave
of Indians arrived (mainly traders from Gujarat).
They were known as 'passenger Indians', because
they paid their own fares on passenger steamships
bound for South Africa.*

*Despite offers of repatriation, most of the
indentured Indians decided to remain in South
Africa once their contracts were completed; many
made their way from Natal up to the goldfields of
the Transvaal, particularly to Johannesburg (about
15 per cent of South Africa's Indian community
today lives in Gauteng). The practice of Islam had
been unbanned in 1804, and Hindus and Muslims
'generally coexisted peacefully and assisted in
common goals and objectives'.[2]*

*It would take a full century, from the time of
the first Indian arrivals, before Indians in South
Africa were granted the status of full citizens –
subject, of course, 'to the same discrimination as
the rest of the black people of South Africa.'[3]*

*In 1946, the government announced the
introduction of the Asiatic Land Tenure and
Indian Representation Bill – restricting the rights
of Indians to own or occupy land; and providing
for a separate Indian voter's role. The South
African Indian Congress (SAIC) mobilised the
entire Indian community in opposition to the
Bill, and sent delegations to India, Britain
and the United States.*

Lenasia

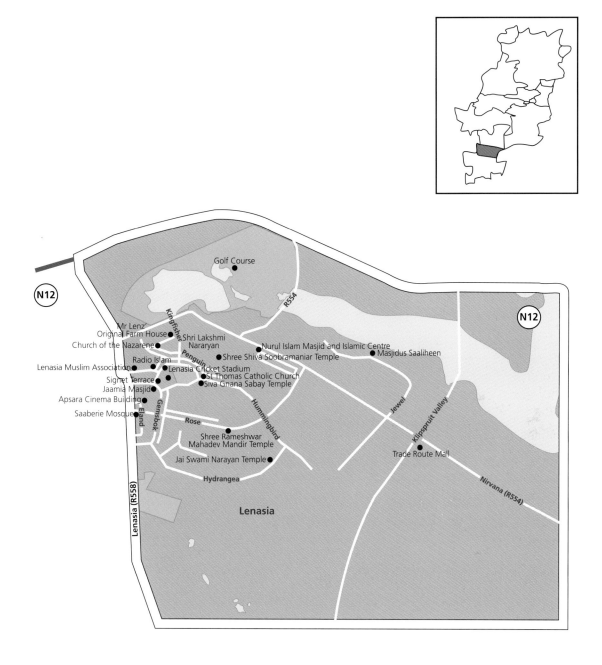

- Golf Course
- N12
- R554
- N12
- Kingfisher
- Mr Lenz'
- Original Farm House
- Shri Lakshmi Nararyan
- Church of the Nazarene
- Nurul Islam Masjid and Islamic Centre
- Masjidus Saaliheen
- Penguin
- Shree Shiva Soobramaniar Temple
- Radio Islam
- Lenasia Muslim Association
- Lenasia Cricket Stadium
- Signet Terrace
- St Thomas Catholic Church
- Jaamia Masjid
- Siva Gnana Sabay Temple
- Apsara Cinema Building
- Gemsbok
- Saaberie Mosque
- Eland
- Hummingbird
- Jewel
- Klipspruit Valley
- Rose
- Shree Rameshwar Mahadev Mandir Temple
- Trade Route Mall
- Jai Swami Narayan Temple
- Lenasia (R558)
- Hydrangea
- Nirvana (R554)
- Lenasia

An old family portrait

The Indian government, in turn, sent a formal request to the United Nations (UN) that the treatment of Indians in South Africa be considered by the General Assembly at its next session, and used the 'South African problem' as an argument to oppose South Africa's request to annex the territory of South West Africa (the annexation request was rejected, and the organisation adopted a resolution 'that the treatment of Indians should be in conformity with the relevant provisions of the United Nations Charter'[4]). The Indian presentation was aided by a multi-racial delegation from South Africa that included Dr AB Xuma, President of the African National Congress (ANC).

The Natal and Transvaal Indian congresses set up passive resistance councils (PRCs) to the 'Ghetto Bill' – agreeing that, immediately after the Bill became law, resisters would defy it by occupying municipal land at the corner of Gale Street and Umbilo Road in Durban. In June 1946, hundreds of passive resisters were violently beaten and as-saulted by white 'hooligans'; by the end of the month, the government arrested the first group of resisters, including the regional Congress leaders Dr GM Naicker (Natal) and Dr Yusuf Dadoo (Transvaal). The resistance movement was joined by theologians, students, doctors, lawyers, workers, farmers, housewives and traders; more importantly, it had a profound effect on the development of co-operation between the SAIC, the ANC and the African People's Organisation. 'No less than 15 Africans and 47 Coloured people joined the Indian resistance in an exceptional demonstration of solidarity.'[5]

In turn, Indians supported 'African' struggles; the Transvaal PRC organised relief for striking black miners in August 1946 and Dr Dadoo (who was also chairman of the Joburg District of the Communist Party) was again arrested (one of three Indian PRC members), for inciting the strike.

Indian Congress leaders also sought support from whites; a Council for Asiatic Rights was formed in Johannesburg to support the passive resistance movement, writing letters to the press and publishing information pamphlets about the Indian cause.

The 'Ghetto Bill' proved impossible to enforce; and the mutual support of the Indian and African congresses – together with success at the UN – encouraged continued cooperation between the groups. The National Party, elected to power in 1948, became so concerned by this that it promised 'drastic action against Indians who incite the Non-European races against the Europeans.'[6]

In June 1952 the ANC, the SAIC and the Coloured People's Congress launched a non-violent 'Campaign of Defiance against Unjust Laws', during which 8000 people of all races were imprisoned. It marked 'the first large-scale, multi-racial political mobilisation against apartheid laws under a common leadership'.[7]

'New Suburb With a Happy Future'

In 1956 the apartheid government passed the infamous Group Areas Act, assigning separate residential areas to different races. Three years earlier, planners had decided that Johannesburg's Indian area should be removed to near the Lenz military base, some 35 km from the city centre. The area was named 'Lenasia' (most likely from 'Lenz' and 'Asia').

Opposition to the Act, and to forced relocation, was strong. White officials responded with laughable attempts to 'sell' the benefits of their new township, as in this an official promotional pamphlet from the time, which read:

'… the vast majority of Indians remained a landless community, forced to live as tenants of often unscrupulous, rack-renting landlords.

The Group Areas Act, much maligned though it is, changed all that. Under its provisions, Indian group areas are constantly being proclaimed – providing Indians with the living space they need in or near centres where they make their living in any number. For the Indians of Johannesburg – many of whom have had to live for years in semi-slum tenements – the new residential area at Lenasia, seventeen miles from the city, will provide the solution to all their housing problems.'[8]

Dr Dadoo (who was born in Fietas) had strong words for those Indians who accepted the group areas proclamation, calling them 'timid, faint-hearted people who panic and, like a drowning man, clutch at any straw.' In August 1956 he issued a statement, saying: 'We must not go to Lenasia or any other group areas set aside for our people. We must forge a strong bond of solidarity between landlords and tenants in the common struggle for existence, by calling upon Indian landlords to cease charging goodwill money and exorbitant rents.'[9]

In the end, the community's solidarity was gradually worn away through the government's forced removals programmes – and through underhand tactics such as moving Indian schools to Lenasia, forcing parents to send their children on a 70-km round-trip daily commute… or give in, and move to their 'designated area'.

Anti-apartheid campaigners being arrested, August 1952. Facing the camera are Sakina Nathee (centre left), Amina Cachalia (centre right) and Aletta Nonyane (extreme right). Photo by Jurgen Schadeberg.

Although the Group Areas Act was nullified in 1991, Lenasia remains home to Johannesburg's largest Indian community; the suburb (nearly large enough to be a town in its own right) has three radio stations, and its own website: www.lenzinfo.org.za.

Perhaps it is because Lenasia is a relatively young suburb – at a little over 50 years old – that relatively little published work exists about its foundations, its communities and its development… Why write about 'history' when the past still exists in the memories and stories of many people still alive today? But there also has to be another reason for the dearth of documentation: the move to Lenasia was far from a happy one. The birth of the new area represented the death of areas like Fietas, where vibrant, diverse and successful Indian communities had lived, traded and grown for decades.

Because of its distance from 'town', Lenasia also

A diverse community lives in Lenasia. From left: anti-apartheid protestor; a decorated chariot, with Ganesha at the top and Shiva in the centre; Muslims protest against US involvement in the Middle East

remains largely unknown and unexplored by Joburg's non-Indian residents. Even if a tourist (domestic or otherwise) were to stumble across Lenasia's streets, the neat lines and prosaic street names reveal almost nothing about the community that lives there – a community that has developed its own names, not reflected on any map, for different areas and different housing developments.

This chapter offers the reader a long 'itinerary' – as this is the best way to understand the diverse and under-recorded aspects of this incredible 'township'. Hopefully, this section will inspire readers to visit Lenasia rather than just read about it.

For a number of reasons, this chapter covers only Lenasia and not Lenasia South. Although Lenasia South (referred to as 'Daxina' by locals) is worth a visit for its many beautiful temples, these are not signed and so require an adventurous disposition. Lenasia South hosts the annual Shiva Yatra procession, when all the temples in Lenasia prepare a Shiva chariot and people dressed in white walk from temple to temple. The event, however is badly advertised and it is difficult to find out the exact

date of the event unless you live in Lenasia and see it advertised.

The guide that follows is divided into two 'parts'. The first is a recommended walking tour of central Lenasia, through the old residential areas. The second part is a recommended drive that looks at other places of importance in the history or community of Lenasia, but are too far apart to be included in the walk.

A Walking History

This walk takes about two and a half hours. The ideal time to begin is at about half past nine on a Saturday or Sunday morning, finishing off with a traditional meal for lunch. We recommend walking in small groups – don't do the walk on your own – and during daylight hours.
Start: Signet Terrace shopping complex, corner Robin and Gemsbok streets, Lenasia Extension 1. The walk begins and ends in a safe residential area. Signet Terrace provides secure parking, free of charge. There is a nearby taxi rank if you wish

to take public transport. Begin your walk by facing the monumental Jaamia Masjid, and step out of the parking lot via the exit to your right.

Jaamia Masjid (on your right) is one of Lenasia's biggest mosques, funded by a single family from Johannesburg. If you happen to stand in front of the mosque during a call to prayer, you will see the parking space in front of the mosque filling up within minutes – and you will hear, coming from at least three Lenasia mosques, a call amplified by loudspeakers and sung with a distinct voice. The area around the mosque was named 'the dust bowl' by locals since red earth blew from this area towards the CBD before Signet Terrace was build in 2005.

Turn right into Guinea Fowl Street, walk on for about 100 m and turn left into Cuckoo Avenue. After a few steps you will see Link Street to your right. Before turning right into Link Street, walk along Cuckoo Avenue until you spot two signboards. On your right you will see the Lenasia Muslim Association; on the opposite side of the road, the home of Radio Islam.

The Lenasia Muslim Association (LMA) was founded in 1962 – early on, considering that Lenasia was only established in 1956. In the early 1960s Lenasia consisted of the so-called 'old camp' (next to the train station), providing provisional shelter for 50 families, and new government housing in Extensions 1, 2 and 3, where prefabricated houses had been erected unconnected to electricity, the sewage system or any paved roads.

The LMA began its activities with a small *madrasah* (religious school) for 30 children. There was one teacher, earning R30 per month. Today the LMA employs some 170 teachers and runs a *madrasah* programme for more than 3000 children, with two nursery schools, five schools and three educational centres.

The LMA pioneered *madrasah* teaching material in English as its teachers quickly realised that students in Lenasia came from various linguistic backgrounds (Gu-jarati, Urdu, Arabic…) and were seldom proficient in the languages of their forefathers. The LMA's English teaching material is today used not only in South Africa but also in English-speaking countries all over the world. The use of English as a medium of explanation made Islam – and Hinduism – accessible to wider audiences in South Africa. Radio Islam, opposite the LMA headquarters, also conducts broadcasting in English.

Radio in Lenasia

Lenasia has three radio stations catering to the diverse community. Radio Islam (MW 1548, www.radioislam.org.za) is probably the smallest of the three, and began broadcasting in 1997. The station initially ran into difficulties over the question of whether female radio presenters would be permitted on air. After a controversial court case the station was given a conditional licence, but was requested to include female presenters for at least three hours per day. Today the station offers a diverse programme with a strong emphasis on Islamic topics. To reach listeners beyond its MW range, Radio Islam is available as a live stream on the Internet.

The second radio station in Lenasia is Channel Islam (www.ciinetwork.net/broadcasting). This station, which is based in Gemsbok Street (where this walk starts), went on air in October 2000. It was established by a team of four people, including two Lenasians: Ashraf Ali Seedat and Essop Patel. Channel Islam is produced in Lenasia, but has digital satellite coverage in 55 countries. The station can be received over the whole of Africa, and most of Europe and the Middle East. It advertises itself as the first English-medium global Islamic broadcaster.

The third radio station in Lenasia, East Wave Radio (FM 92.2), has a broader target audience. As a community station for Lenasia and its surrounding areas, East Wave Radio tries to produce a diverse programme with special slots for children, Bollywood and classical Indian music, religious programmes and programmes in various Indian languages.

Left and right: traditional dancers. In the centre: a Hindu wedding ceremony.

Take Link Street, cross Hummingbird Avenue and go left at the T-junction, into Sunbird Avenue. The remarkably inventive architecture along the streets is characteristic of this area of Lenasia. Turn right into Sparrow Avenue before the Corner Shop and stop when you reach the junction with Penguin Avenue.

At the corner of Sparrow and Penguin avenues you can see the Church of the Nazarene. This protestant church is the oldest Christian church in Lenasia, funded by American missionaries in the early 1960s. Unusual – and therefore widely discussed in Lenasia – was the fact that the missionaries funded not only this church building but also the living quarters for the resident priest.

Continue on Sparrow Avenue. Opposite the park, look to your left for the house set back behind a front yard with a palm tree.

Before Lenasia was built the land in the area belonged to a Mr Lenz, who sold it when it was decided that South African Indians would be settled there. The South African Indian communities in Johannesburg had fought against initial plans to be resettled in the suburb of Robertsham. It is ironic that Lenasia, which is much further away from town, became the new township location. Mr Lenz moved out before Lenasia was built and no one in Lenasia

remembers him personally. Yet his farmhouse still stands at 32 Sparrow Avenue.

In the early years of Lenasia the farmhouse was sold to the Ajoodha family. This large family – Mr Ajoodha, his two official wives and one unofficial wife, and his 26 children – moved into the farmhouse, buying a large plot of land on both sides of it in the process.

The Ajoodha family were known for their inventive business spirit. In the early days of Lenasia they ran a business collecting bottles, and bones for glue production. Up and down the roads of Lenasia they drove a horse-drawn cart, exchanging bones for oranges. Some of the many Ajoodha children were inventive too. Old Lenasians remember them charging their peers an entrance fee to the swimming pool in their garden. For a long time this swimming pool was the only one in Lenasia – and prized as not everybody dared to swim in the water at the quarry right at the end of Hummingbird Avenue. Until the 1970s, the well of Mr Lenz's farm could be found in front of the house, in the small park across the street.

Turn right, walk across the park to get on to Penguin Avenue, and go left.

Penguin Avenue is a good example of Lenasia's religious diversity. A short way from the Church of the

Learners from the Nurul-Islam nursery and pre-school

Nazarene, on the opposite site of the street, is a small neighbourhood mosque, the Masjidus Salaam (note the loudspeakers under the roof). A further four houses down the road you will find the Sanathan Ved Dharma Sastha, a temple devoted to Hinduism (as the name states). Unfortunately it is often closed – but if it happens to be open for a function, speak to a member of the community and ask if you can be shown into the temple, which is situated in the left portion of the building. The temple is frequented mainly by Lenasians whose ancestors were Hindi speaking.

When Lenasia was initially constructed, people settled according to their wealth – and not based on markers of identity such as religious, ethnic or language affiliation. Families of Gujarati, Urdu, Hindi, Tamil and Telegu origin all lived side by side. Neither were Muslims, Hindus or Christians segregated through apartheid town planning. Penguin Avenue was part of the high-end market, a freehold area where land was bought and individual houses were built by the owners.

Walk down Penguin Avenue – passing Lenasia Secondary School on your left – and turn left into Kingfisher Street for a short detour. Approximately 50 m into Kingfisher Street you can visit the impressive Shri Lakshmi Narayan Temple.

The Shri Lakshmi Nararyan Temple was founded in 1972 and reconstructed in 2001. It is a Hindu temple frequented mainly by Lenasians who are of Gujarati origin. You are welcome to enter the temple, which is open daily. The community celebrates many of the Hindu festivals (see www.lym.org.za for a calendar of events). If you decide to enter the temple, please leave your shoes at the bottom of the stairs leading to the temple entrance. You may ring the brass bell hanging over the entrance to request the presence of the temple's gods and goddesses. Do not directly turn your back towards the *murties* (Hindu statues of gods and goddesses) when you exit the temple, as this is considered impolite.

On exiting the temple, turn right. Further down Kingfisher Street is another Hindu temple (most often closed) and the Lenasia Music School, where students are instructed in classical Indian instruments such as the tabla and the sitar.

To continue the tour, turn left into Penguin Avenue. Turn left again at Primary Street, walking on the right-hand side of the street to reach the Lenasia Model Primary School. Through the fence you can see the impressive golden Dome of the Nurul Islam Mosque in the distance.

Schooling in Lenasia

The early growth of Lenasia is related largely to the school policy under apartheid. In the 1960s children of South African Indian heritage were forced to attend the high school that had recently been opened in Lenasia (located where Signet Terrace is today). All inner city schools for 'Indian' students had been closed, and other schools denied 'Indian' pupils access. As a consequence, many families decided to move to Lenasia despite the distance to town and the less than ideal infrastructure and transport.

Today a surprising number of black students attends classes in this former Indian township. Most of them do not live in Lenasia. They come from surrounding areas

Nelson Mandela is welcomed in Lenasia.

A Zulu dancer and a Hindu danceer perform at an ANC rally.

where local schools, by comparison, are considered to be of a lower standard. The influx of black students into Lenasia has not, however, translated into greater learner diversity within classrooms. With increasing wealth and a strong community focus on education, many Lenasians now send their children to the local private – and often very costly – schools.

Adjoining the premises of the Lenasia Model Primary School is the Lenz Shree Siva Soobramaniar Temple. You can enter the temple via a small red gate, or walk around the corner to the main entrance.

At first the area now known as Lenasia had only the house of Mr Lenz, a train station and, next to it, several vacant army barracks. In 1955 to 1956 the first 50 families were moved into the vacated military barracks, where families had to create private space using sheets. Among the first settlers were a number of waiters who had frequented a temple in Newclare.

Initially the new settlers celebrated Hindu festivals at the army barracks, locally termed the 'old camp'. They later transferred the *murtis* of the Newclare temple to the private house of Harry Singh (in Extension 1), but soon saw the need for a temple in Lenasia. In the early 1960s a committee was formed, and grounds for a temple were purchased in Heron Street. Bricks for £15 000 were

ordered on loan – when the brick factory requested payment several years later, there was a crisis as no funds were available.

It took the joint effort of the community to overcome this first crisis. With donations of money, building materials and many volunteeer hands, the temple was erected between 1968 and 1970.

The Shree Siva Soobramaniar Temple was designed by Ray Poonin, a local teacher and architect who, like Nithia Moodleya who did the woodwork, worked for free. The statues in the temple were ordered from Mr Ricrotri, an Italian sculptor from Pretoria who supplied many temples in Gauteng with statues, working from pictures of gods and goddesses the various Hindu communities supplied him with. The temple is a beautiful and simple haven – thus far succeeding in resisting community pressures to get 'flashier'.

The *murtis* of several gods and goddesses can be seen in the temple. The resident priest, Kumaran, explains that it was initially planned to be devoted to Lord Murugan[10], the god of war and the patron deity of Tamils. It is in his honour that the *Kavadi*[11] festival is held at the temple every year. Currently, however, the temple's chief god is Shiva, whose *murti* is given central position and whose *vahana*[12] or mount, the bull Nandi, lies outside the temple. Shiva's wife, Parvati, is depicted to the right of

Beauty contest in Lenasia, 1985

Shiva while their son Ganesh[13], the elephant-headed god, sits to his left.

If you look inside the temple you will find pictures of Sathya Sai Baba, to the left, and Shirdi Sai Baba to the right. On Thursdays, a group of Sai Baba followers come to the temple for their prayers. It is characteristic of Hindu temples to be inclusive, and pictures of living spiritual leaders and avatars (incarnations of Hindu gods or goddesses) are often featured. When visiting the temple, do not miss the beautifully decorated tree on the right side, where the goddess Mariamman[14] is worshipped.

For more information on the temple, and on upcoming festivals, go to www.lenzshree.co.za.

Should you wish to take a short break here, you may ask to use the toilet facilities at the temple.

Step out of the main gate, proceeding right along Primary Street again, and turn right into Albatross Street. Continue on Albatross Street until you reach Hummingbird Avenue. Turn right. In the distance you will see another Hindu temple.

The first part of Lenasia covered on this walk is locally termed the 'Township', referring to the early freehold residential area. While this area attracted the better-off families who had the means to purchase land, most of Lenasia followed a different settlement pattern – occupying government buildings marketed as 'affordable housing'.

On Hummingbird Avenue, you will see the features of what the locals call 'Rainbow Valley' (look at houses 210, 222, 223, 243 and 244). Houses in Rainbow Valley came in six slight variations, all with a characteristic chimney in the front. Plots were comparatively large, at 50 by 100 feet, and the houses were painted in a variety of colours, earning the area its name. The design of the houses came from Port Elizabeth, where a similar settlement had been erected previously. Inhabitants of Rainbow Valley paid monthly instalments towards the purchase of their house and plot. In the initial settlement pattern, Rainbow Valley houses bordered on vacant plots that were later sold as freehold areas.

Continue walking down Hummingbird Avenue until you see the St Thomas Catholic Church on your left.

The St Thomas Catholic Church on Hummingbird Avenue is using Indian cultural elements as a way of making young people aware of their cultural heritage. While some Lenasians, especially of Tamil origin, have been Christians for as long as remembered family history goes, other Lenasians converted more recently. Among newly converted

Two Hours on Sundays...

In 1958, Reggie Vandeyar mobilised Lenasia residents in a protest against the all-white general elections. He subsequently joined MK (Umkhonto we Sizwe, the armed wing of the ANC). Arrested in 1963, he was beaten and tortured, sentenced to ten years on Robben Island and thereafter banned for ten years. On returning from Robben Island, he lived in Lenasia under house arrest. The only exemption from his house arrest was that he was allowed to visit the Shree Siva Soobramaniar Temple for 'two hours on Sundays'. Soon after his banning order expired in 1983, he became vice-president of the Transvaal Indian Congress.

Christians it is common to encounter the belief that all cultural aspects of Indian origin should be abandoned, for fear of syncretism (the mixing of religions). The rejection of Indian cultural aspects may encompass traditional clothing, decorative items and sometimes even Indian cooking.

Recently, however, churches in Lenasia have begun to reclaim elements of Indian cultural heritage. While some converts are sceptical about what they regard as too fine a line between religion and culture, others see the incorporation of Indian cultural traditions as resulting in worshipful jubilation enmeshed with celebratory elements. Some of the churches have experimented by integrating Indian dance into the Liturgical Mass. The special services, which happen a few times a year, include lamps, garlanding, incense, a *Garba* dance[15], and Indian traditional musical instruments. This 'enculturation' has been supported by the Archdiocese of Johannesburg, as a promotion of cultural diversity.

Walk across the road to the Siva Gnana Sabay Temple. The entrance is to the left, on Robin Avenue.

The Siva Gnana Sabay Temple, or simply the 'Siva Koil',[16] is a Hindu temple that is frequented mainly by South Africans of Tamil origin. You may enter the temple compound to look at the beautiful statues.

Continue walking along Robin Avenue, and you'll see the Cricket Stadium of Lenasia.

The Cricket Stadium of Lenasia has not only been the location of many exciting matches, but has also hosted funfairs and political rallies.

Its largest functions were held on 18 March 1990, when 15 000 people came to listen to Walter Sisulu, and on 18 November 1990, when an even larger crowd came to listen to Nelson Mandela. In his speech, Mandela described how Lenasia had grown tremendously while he had been imprisoned and stated that he was 'proud that from the inhumanity of apartheid … emerged communities with beautiful homes and gardens, and colourful churches, temples and mosques'.[17]

Sisulu appealed to the solidarity of discrimination,

The Tricameral Parliament

In the early 1980s, a parliamentary committee tabled a report encouraging the creation of a Tricameral Parliament – to include limited representation for coloured and Indian people, but excluding black people. In November 1983 a referendum was held for white voters to ascertain their wishes on the matter; 70 per cent of them voted in favour of the 'reforms'. (Many white South Africans who were opposed to apartheid registered to vote for the first time, to say no to the tricameral system.) The new Parliament was inaugurated in 1985, despite the low turnout of coloured and Indian voters (in 1984, the Indian 'Parliament' elections achieved a poll of just 16,2 per cent – and the Muslim Judicial Council declared the elections to be *haraam*, judicially forbidden). The Indian Assembly was known as the House of Delegates; the coloured Assembly, the House of Representatives. (The white Parliament was the House of Assembly.)

Boycott and protest action against the tricameral elections drew swift and fierce reprisals from the state.

the 'common experience of inequality, poverty, race discrimination, humiliation, exploitation and violence', stating that South Africans of Indian origin were 'no less South African'[18] than he was. He also paid tribute to two MK soldiers from Lenasia: Prakash Napier and Yusuf Akhalwaya. They died on 11 December 1989 while planting a bomb near Park Station in Johannesburg. Prakash Napier had received military training in the Soviet Union a year before the accident, and both men had been involved in a number of sabotage actions targeting railway and business properties.

Lenasia, unlike many other settlements with South

An injured protestor is carried away after an encounter with the police. The poster in the background reads: 'Don't be a Ja-Baas. Don't Vote'.

Being There

'This particular day, we knew that there were these Tricameral elections taking place. What I remember was getting up very early and driving around with my friends to the various polling stations; the biggest polling station was at the Civic Centre. We went to someone's house in the morning and people were planning what we were going to do. Then we went to a flat just outside the shopping centre. The group was made up of varsity students, school-going pupils, a lot of Coloured lighties (young men) from Eldorado Park, and lots of community people. Word got around through the existing left political structures. We stood outside with our placards, and the cops kept coming; harassing us and chasing us away. When we moved away, we moved to the old Union Grocery Stores, behind Apsara Cinema. I remember a few guys from the group turning a cops' car on

its hood in a matter of seconds. Later, people were coming from work to join the demonstrations. There were very few who did vote, but they bussed people in from old-age homes and from the poorer areas to let them vote. At around this time, the demonstrations got a lot more heated; we were a lot more vocal. Some started stoning the Caspirs. Those guys started shooting tear-gas and they fired rubber bullets at us from a big shot-box. The area there at the top shops resembled a war-zone; Caspirs moving up and down, shooting, people running all over the show. Uncle Wayne got a shot on his face with a sjambok trying to help a pregnant woman hide in the fish and chip shop's fridge with the others. That's about all I remember. But we were very proud to see Indian people standing up.'

– Dale Abrahams, university student

Typical houses in 'old' Lenasia

Africans of Indian origin, largely supported the ANC. Solidarity with black South Africans clearly dominated over the attitude of the 'apartheid collaborator' required by the Tricameral Parliament.

Turn left into Link Road and walk straight across the small park, following the avenue of trees. Continue into the same direction along Hawk Street. Turn left into Vulture Avenue.

Initially the streets of Lenasia, unpaved as they were, were numbered. For example, Hawk Street used to be 4th Street. The numbers of the streets in Rainbow Valley repeated themselves in the township avenues, which led to much confusion. It was therefore suggested that residents propose names for their streets. Given the cultural diversity of Lenasia's residents and their preference for memorable names with religious connotations, the initial participatory plan led to quarrels and had to be abandoned. Without further consultation, Lenasia received 'neutral' street names. Township and Rainbow Valley roads were given bird names, while the lower income areas, Greyville and Thomsville, got flower names. One suspects that the residents of Vulture Avenue were not altogether pleased with their new street name.

Turn into the first street to your right, Impala Street. On your right is the impressive Saaberrie Mosque.

Walking along Impala Street you will see the ladies' entrance to the Saaberie Mosque, the first mosque built in Lenasia. This mosque is one of the few in Lenasia with facilities for women. Saaberie Masjid has been rebuilt,

as the original building was not well constructed.

The architect of today's Saaberie Masjid also built the Nurul Islam Masjid, the large mosque with the golden dome you may have spotted driving into Lenasia or earlier on the walk. He received a prize for the design of the Saaberie Masjid, a difficult architectural task as the mosque had to include not only ladies' facilities but also five classrooms on its very small plot.

Around the corner you will see the main entrance to the mosque, which is frequented mainly by Memons.[19] If you have ever wondered what the words of the call to prayer mean, you will find a large signboard with an English translation of the Arabic words to the left of the entrance.

Take a break. If, at this point in the walk, you require some refreshment, turn into the Saaberie Shopping Arcades, where you'll find a bakery and excellent Italian ice cream. If you need a little retail therapy, you can also look for a sari.

To continue the walk, cross Rose Avenue and continue along Impala Street, into the formerly less-affluent areas of Lenasia. When you reach Greyville Primary School, turn right into Anemone Avenue and immediately left again into Gardenia Avenue. Walk along Gardenia Avenue until you reach Lilac Street on your right.

At the corner of Lilac and Gardenia streets, you will be able to see the design of the original Greyville government houses. These houses were substantially smaller than those in Rainbow Valley and were originally painted grey. They had a kitchen, a lounge-cum-dining area and two bedrooms. The Greyville houses also had their toilets in the backyard, a feature most residents changed as soon as they had the means to do so.

A few metres further down, on Geranium Street, you will again have the opportunity to compare types of houses – the left side belonged to the low-income area named Thomsville, while the right side of the street had the much larger Greyville houses.

Thomsville houses were also called the 'two-room houses' as they had a kitchen and one bedroom. They were rented and only recently were residents – many of whom had been living there for decades – permitted to purchase their homes.

Built as a temporary settlement, the Thomsville houses remained a permanent feature of Lenasia. Geranium Avenue and the next street, Gladioli Avenue, are locally termed Jump Street and Electric Avenue. This re-naming mocked the absence of streetlights in the area[20] while referring to the famous 1983 song by Reggae musician Eddy Grant, whose political, anti-apartheid lyrics (including the Johannesburg song 'Gimme Hope Jo'anna') were very popular.

Thomsville residents fought many battles for better living conditions, including access to sewage, electricity and water. During apartheid Lenasia's schools were forbidden to take in 'coloured' or 'black' children – yet many of the children of mixed heritage who were growing up in Thomsville were classified as 'coloured' rather than 'Indian'. As a result they could not attend the local schools. A group of Lenasia teachers got together, forming the initiative 'The Time to Learn'. They wrote applications for the children to be reclassified as 'Indian', teaching them in their spare time at the community hall of the Via Christy Church in Flamingo Street.

Turn to your right and walk into Geranium Avenue. Turn left at Camelia Avenue. Walk until you reach Gemsbok Street after the park to your left. If you would like to complete your walk now, turn right and walk along Gemsbok Street until you reach Signet Terrace.

If, on the other hand, you feel peckish – and if you are curious to see Lenasia's CBD – turn right into Gemsbok Avenue and immediately left again into Anemone Avenue. Walk to the end of Anemone Avenue and turn right into Eland Street. To your left on Eland Street, you will see the Civic Centre.

Shopping

The earliest shop in Lenasia was located right where you left the bazaar area, as you entered the square. Khan's Shop, as Lenasians remember, stocked everything one could need, but the owner wasn't always community-minded. Essential goods such as candles became more expensive at weekends, when Lenasians did not travel to town and had no other means of purchasing the items.

Today Lenasia's CBD is flourishing. Walk around Grand Place for some exceptional sari and kurtha shops (Sauda Boutique, for example – ask to be shown bangles in their special back room), or venture into the specialist hookah shop (Grand Place 2). If you are interested in Bollywood, try Global Music (Gemsbok Street Stand 1827, Shop No. 2, Morgan Builders Centre) and peek into Lotus Puja. Next door you can shop for a small *murti* of a Hindu god or goddess. Try Laxmi's for spices (enter Concorde Place from Gemsbok Street at Ajoodha's bottle store) or alternatively try the spice shop at Signet Terrace.

Eating Out in Lenasia

Most eateries in Lenasia cater for western food (see Gemsbok Street for any of the common chains), as Lenasians usually eat Indian food at home, and at social gatherings and religious functions. It is therefore rather common for people to get an Indian take-away to be eaten at home – while eating 'out' usually means eating western food.

Local home-cooked specialities such as apple curry cannot be ordered in any of the restaurants in Lenasia, but you can have a quick bite at the Taste of India (Anemone Street) or try a bunny chow – a South African

Biryani for 800 People[21]

4 kg ginger

2 kg garlic

200 kg mutton (cut 6 pieces from each 500 g of meat)

50 kg rice

32 kg masoor

80 g saffron (8 tolas)

2 kg chilli powder (red)

2 kg crushed chillies (red)

500 g whole green chillies

360 g elachi

250 g turmeric (use sparingly of this quantity and use egg yellow to obtain richer colour)

500 g jeera

250 g shah-jeera

250 g tuj

20 kg ghee (use sparingly; if mutton is fatty, less will be needed)

20 ℓ oil

1½ ℓ lemon juice (or vinegar, or ½ vinegar and ½ lemon)

40 × 500 ml yoghurt

12–16 doz eggs

25 kg potatoes

20 kg onions

1 kg fine salt (use only as much as is required)

6 kg coarse salt (for rice and meat)

Method:
Marinate meat with spices and fried onion. At the bottom of the cooking pot put only oil, layering your meat, masoor, eggs, etc. on top before finally adding the rice. Place lumps of all the ghee called for in the recipe over top of rice. Seal the pot with a double layer of foil before closing the lid. This is easier and more economical than the old-fashioned flour and cloth seal.

Indian dish consisting of a loaf of bread with the inside scooped out and filled with mutton or bean curry. Alternatively, you can have a decent sit-down Indian meal at the Pride of Indian Cuisine (Eland Street). For truly excellent vegetarian food, try Shayona (Eland Street) and do not miss out on their sweetmeat selection. Both the thali and the dosa are exceptionally good.

Lenasians are also famous for mass cooking, which is required at any large gathering where food is to be served. Whether at religious functions or for private parties, local women are experienced and skilled at cooking for several hundred people at a time.

At Manilal Ratanji & Co (corner Anemone and Eland streets) you can find huge pots and ingredients for mass cooking, alongside a selection of devotional goods.

Walk along Eland Street, cross Rose Avenue and continue onto Station Street. Walk along the shopfronts until you see the Universal Church of the Kingdom of God to your right (located in the former Apsara Cinema hall). Turn right after the church into the pedestrian area, and have a look at the street market. Walk straight on for several hundred metres until you reach a large square used as a parking lot. Opposite this you will see the Jaamia Masjid. Behind the mosque you will find Signet Terrace, where this walk started.

Driving Lenasia

Drive into Lenasia on the R554, coming either from the Golden Highway (N10) or the N12 Eldorado Park/ Lenasia offramp.

Lenasia got its own shopping mall in 2004 – the Trade Route Mall. You may start or end your visit here with a Bollywood movie at the cinema and a glimpse into some Indian clothing boutiques. Do not expect exotic eateries; be prepared for the usual chains. (for more information go to www.traderoute.co.za.)

Follow the R554 (Nirvana Drive) and turn left into

Extension 13 Heliodor Street at the traffic lights. Drive until Heliodor Street becomes Jewel Street. On your right will be the impressive Masjidus Saaliheen.

Music and Politics at the Barn

Opposite the Masjidus Saaliheen is a plot where a farm building stands. Behind the building there used to be a large barn, the former centre of cultural life in Lenasia. In the early years of Lenasia, when most of the mosques and temples with their adjoining community halls were not yet built, there was a shortage of venues. Before the Civic Centre was built, the Jasmine Hall at the old post office and the Barn were the only two places that could be hired for social functions.

The Barn used to be a legendary meeting point for Lenasia's youth where, on Saturdays and Sundays, live music was played and impromptu 'boot bars' compensated for the fact that no alcohol was served at the Barn.

In the spring of 1977 nearly 100 schoolchildren, teachers and adults were arrested at the barn when they held a gathering in solidarity with Soweto students protesting against apartheid policy. How the police learned about the meeting is unclear, but the feeling of security and freedom previously enjoyed at the Barn became a thing of the past.

Detained students were held for three days at John Voster Square and parents gathered in a large crowd outside the police station.

Return to the R554 (Nirvana Drive East) and turn left into Rose Avenue. Turn right into Giraffe Avenue. Follow the bend until you reach the Nurul Islam Masjid.

The Nurul Islam Masjid and Islamic Centre (on Nyala Avenue) was built with initial funding of US$200 000 from the Rabitat al-Alam al-Islami of Makkah. It was the first time in South Africa that an Islamic Centre had been officially sponsored from Makkah. The foundation stone of the centre was laid on 16 May 1975, by Dr Inamullah Khan and Abdul Muhsin. Since then, Nurul Islam (the

A fast-food chain in Lenasia in the 1980s

Light of Islam) has been financially supported by the community, and especially by the Lorgat family.

The centre comprises the beautiful golden-domed masjid, a multi-purpose octagonal hall, a convention hall, an education centre, *madrasah* facilities for boys and girls, a library, a research centre, and a printing press. In addition, the mosque runs a private co-educational school, which is famous for its academic achievements. Visitors are welcome to enter the compound of the mosque and wander among the palm trees.

Continue along Giraffe into Nyala Avenue. Return to Rose Avenue, where you turn right. Continue on Rose Avenue until you reach the corner of Willow Street.

Ahmed Kathrada on trial in 1952
(back row, second from the right,
next to ANC president Dr James Moroka)

Ahmed Kathrada after his release in 1989

The Shree Rameshwar Mahadev Mandir Temple in Rose Avenue is a large Shiva temple frequented mainly by South Africans of Gujarati origin. The community places a high emphasis on vernacular language proficiency and some of the prayers at this temple are held in Gujarati. Among young people in Lenasia this temple is known for its splendid religious functions. At Diwali the temple hosts the largest fireworks; and on Shiva Ratri the biggest bonfire. Large functions and prayers are advertised on the signboard facing Rose Avenue.

Turn right into Willow Street, and look to your right at No. 92.

A Hero's House

Ahmed Mohammed 'Kathy' Kathrada was born in the town of Schweizer Reineke, moving to Johannesburg for his schooling (as he could not be admitted to the white or black schools in his area). At the age of 16, he gave up his schooling to work full time in the Johannesburg offices of the Passive Resistance Council. Kathrada later became secretary general of the Transvaal Indian Youth Congress, and repeatedly came into contact with resistance leaders such as Nelson Mandela and Walter Sisulu as the alliance between

Indian and African congresses grew. Between 1952 and 1964, Kathrada was to join Mandela and Sisulu three times on the dock: after the 1952 Defiance Campaign; during first treason trial of 1956 to 1961; and again at the Rivonia Trial of 1963 to 1964, when they were sentenced to life imprisonment.

In 1989 Kathrada was released from Pollsmoor Prison, after serving 25 years.

Upon his release, Kathrada initially stayed with his brother at 92 Willow Street in Lenasia; he described how, within 15 minutes of his arrival, the news had travelled the whole of Lenasia, with and many well-wishers arriving over the next hours.[22] Many Lenasians who had been active in the ANC remember the large crowd in front of the house; and the reception arranged at the small park in Willow Street, where several thousand people gathered on the evening of 15 October 1989.

Turn right into Protea and take the fifth right (crossing Rose Avenue) into Hydrangea Avenue. On your left you will see the Jai Swaminarayan Temple.

The Jai Swaminarayan Temple is probably the most impressive temple in Lenasia – and the youngest (it was inaugurated in 2004). Swami Narayan followers began to meet in Lenasia around 1974, at a family home in Albatross Street. In the 1990s they acquired and converted the building of a Dutch Reformed Church in Mayfair for their community purposes.

With a tremendous financial effort, the small community of approximately 400 devotees managed to raise R7 million to build this temple. Devotees are generally expected to pledge five to ten per cent of their earnings for the upkeep of the temple.

The temple is usually open to the public between 07h00 and 12h00, and from 16h00 to 20h00. The resident priest is from India and speaks almost no English. He lives on the grounds of the temple, as do the four Indian cooks who work in the temple kitchen to the left of the compound. The temple offers food catering for large functions and produces sweetmeats for Shayona, the local eatery in Eland Street, as a means of income.

Unlike other Hindu temples in Lenasia, this temple emphasises a particular guru. The founder of this religious branch within Hinduism was Lord Swaminarayan (1781–1830), whose fifth incarnation, Pramukh Swami Maharaj, inaugurated this temple in 2004, at a spectacular function visited by over 20 000 Hindus.

Continue on Hydrangea Avenue and take the sixth left into Gemsbok Street. Take the second left into Lenasia Drive. Continue in the direction of Lenasia South. Midway between Lenasia and Lenasia South/Daxina lies Lawley Station. Immediately before reaching Lawley Station, follow the sign indicating 'Lawley' with a train symbol next to it, turning right at the four-way crossing.

Cross the railway tracks at the stop sign and follow this road – paved with red bricks – for 500 m, until you see the old Corobrik factory to your right as well as a farm house in the distance. Before you reach the Corobrik factory, turn left into the first dirt road and follow this road for 1,5

km. At first the road goes slightly uphill, then turns downhill in a bend where you can spot overgrown brick dunes to your left. Cross a dirt road at the bottom of the hill and turn right at the forthcoming fork. To your left you can now see the brick foundation of a farmhouse originally build by Hermann Kallenbach, in about 1920. This is Tolstoy Farm.

Tolstoy Farm began on 30 May 1910, as the Transvaal Satyagraha base where Gandhi and his followers settled, forming a commune practising non-violent resistance. Within six months three large corrugated iron sheds had been erected, to serve as men's quarters and women's quarters and to host a school, offices and a workshop.

At the height of the movement in 1912, about forty young men, two or three old men, five women and twenty to thirty children, of whom four or five were girls, lived at the farm.[23] Hermann Kallenbach, who joined the movement and provided the funding for the location (a farm of 1100 acres) ran a carpentry school and taught sandal-making on the premises. Gandhi initiated a school for the resident children, where Gujarati, Tamil, Telegu and Hindi were taught.

The foundations you can see today are of a farmhouse originally built by Hermann Kallenbach in about 1920. The building was restored by the Transvaal Gandhi Centenary Council (TGCC) in the 1980s, but unfortunately was badly vandalised afterwards. The now-visible reinforced foundation was built in 1997. The peppercorn trees near the foundation were planted in the 1920s, and today surround an outdoor auditorium build by TGCC in the 1980s.

In 1910 the farm had approximately 1000 fruit trees including peaches, apricots, figs, almonds and walnuts as well as eucalyptus and wattle trees, watered by two small springs. Today, except for the occasional fruit tree, there is nothing left to reveal the former farm.

ALEXANDRA

Chapter Thirteen

'And Alexandra,
My beginning was knotted to you,
Just like you knot my destiny.
You throb in my inside silences
You are silent in my heart-beat that's loud to me.'

Mongane Wally Serote

In this chapter

☞ • Alex-on-the Jukskei

☞ • The Alexandra Bus Boycott

☞ • Hostel Takeover

☞ • Saving Alex

☞ • Street Justice

☞ • Alex Society

DARK CITY

Children playing soccer in front of a hostel in Alexandra

A River Runs Through It

The Jukskei River runs through Alex – the West Bank is visible on the left, the East Bank on the right of the river.

Alexandra – Alex, as it's known – bears the scars of over a century of human struggle. Its bustling, pockmarked landscape is testimony to decades of political battles, shifting communities, and the economics of daily survival.

Alex's close proximity to upmarket Sandton (just four kilometres away) and the north has meant access to jobs and income ... and a demand for housing that has always far exceeded the supply. Between 350 000 and 400 000 people reside in Alex, in an area covering the equivalent of about 20 city blocks; there are an estimated 34 000 shacks, jostling for space with brick structures, hostels and apartment blocks. Poet Kgafela oa Magogodi described Alex as a place where 'the shacks are as crammed as a mouth full of teeth that seem to squeeze each other off the jawline.'[1] For decades, Alex was known as 'dark city' – because many of its residents had no access to electricity, and there was no street lighting.

Alex hosts a community that is diverse, vibrant ... and easily ignited; the township was a hotspot of resistance during the apartheid decades. More recently, in May 2008, Alex saw the flare-up of violent anti-foreigner pogroms.

Alex is divided into three distinct areas: Old Alex, or the West Bank (west of the Jukskei River, which runs through the township – this is the poorest area, with the largest density of shacks); the mostly middle-class East Bank, with freestanding brick houses; and the recently developed Far East Bank, including the Tsutsumani Village, developed to provide housing during the All Africa Games in 1999.

Alexandra

Far East Bank

Tsutsumani

Far East Bank

Lombardy

N3

East Bank Oval

East Bank

Florence Moposho

14th
13th
12th
11th
10th
9th
8th
7th
6th
5th
4th
2nd
1st

John Brand

Alexandra

Richard Baloyi
Alexandra Police Station
Alexandra Stadium
Alexsan Kopano Centre
Freedom Square
15th
16th
17th
18th
19th

Impala

East Bank Municipal Clinic

Vincent Tshabalala

River Park

Mandela Yard Interpretation Centre
Women's Hostel (Helen Joseph)
Fourth Ave Municipal Clinic
Reverend Sam Buti
Alexandra's People Centre
St Hubert Catholic Church
Watt
Alfred Nzo
Alexandra Municipal Clinic
13th
14th
Josias Madzunya
3rd
3rd Avenue Children's Library
Men's Hostel
6th
Wynberg Magistrate's Court
Josias Madzunya
Wynberg
Police Station
Alexandra Health Clinic
Arkwright

Pretoria Main

N

The Tsutsumani Village, Far East Bank

Alexandra was established in 1904, named after the wife of 'a Mr Papenfus' – in contemporary histories of the settlement, there are two commonly cited contenders for this title: HB Papenfus, a some-time Member of Parliament; and S Papenfus, who received the concession as the first market master of Johannesburg, in 1887. It's unclear why confusion exists between the two Papenfuses – old photos and early histories of Alex clearly name Mr Stephen Papenfus, and not HB, as the founder.

Papenfus installed his cook, Hey Nxele Mbanjwa and his wife Eva, in the heart of Alexandra, where they 'built themselves a mud hut [which] acted as a donkey refreshment station for carts carrying Papenfus' milk from his farm in Midrand to Johannesburg'.[2] The Mbanjwa's daughter, Annie, married a thatcher named Phumuza Twala and had ten children – when Annie died, in 2003 at the age of 99, thousands of Alex residents attended her funeral. One of Annie's sons, Linda Twala, is one of Alex's most prominent philanthropists and entrepreneurs.[3]

Papenfus originally hoped to develop Alexandra into a desirable white residential township, but it proved too far from the city centre and he began offering the land to black buyers.

In 1912 the area was proclaimed a Native Township. Established before the passing of the 1913 Land Act, it became one of the few urban areas where black people could own land, and freehold stands were offered to 'natives and coloured persons only' on easy terms. Until well into the 1950s, residents did not require passes or permits to stay in Alexandra – although they were required to work in Johannesburg.[4]

By 1916, a Health Committee (under jurisdiction of the Transvaal Province – Alexandra fell outside of Joburg's municipal boundaries) was established to manage the fast-growing settlement; unusually, the Committee, although chaired by a white man, had an

HB Papenfus   **S Papenfus**

Shacks in Alex, 1912

A sign indicating land for sale in Alex, 1914

elected local black majority membership until 1929.

Because of the poverty of its residents, Alex's Health Committee had little access to funds or resources, and was limited in its powers to manage or develop infrastructure in the settlement. Despite this, Alex's population continued to grow – from between 8000 and 10 000 people in 1932, to an estimated 45 000 to 50 000 in 1940, and nearly double that number by the late 1940s.[5]

During the same period, the 'problem' of black urbanisation became a focus for local, provincial and national government structures – provoking the slum clearance laws in the 1930s. In Johannesburg 'officials were additionally concerned with several freehold townships situated to the west and north of the city, where Africans had the legal right to own property'.[6] Alex was considered an uncontrolled 'black spot', its proximity to the white suburbs giving further cause for concern.

In 1942 Deneys Reitz, then Minister of Native Affairs, commented that Alexandra was 'a running sore of evil and a place where the King's Writ runs with difficulty. All the toughs and roughs and criminals congregate there.'[7] During the Second World War, Alex was even, inexplicably, painted as 'a main Nazi propaganda and plotting centre'.[8]

Between 1935 and 1945 the (white) North Eastern Districts Protection League (NEDPL) actively campaigned to have the township of Alexandra permanently removed. The movement succeeded to the point that, by 1942,

the Joburg City Council voted in agreement of Alex's removal – if the provincial and Union government each agreed to contribute a third of the cost of the removal.

The Alexandra Standholders' Protection and Vigilance Association (ASPVA), an association of property owners in the township, raised several objections, including submitting evidence that the NEDPL 'consisted "mainly of land-owners and land speculators who hold property adjoining Alexandra Township" who would benefit by opening up the area for European settlement'.[9] Other residents' organisations that joined in protest included the Alexandra Ratepayers Association and the Alexandra

A street scene from Alex in the 1940s

Joint Committee, under Daniel Reginald Koza (who later formed the African Democratic Party).

In the end, the high cost of removing the township – estimated then at over £3 million – particularly during wartime when the state's resources were allocated to its military, and Alex's valuable labour pool (despised by but essential to the white communities in the north) meant that the settlement was given a temporary reprieve.

Alexandra later fell under the administration of the Peri-Urban Health Board. After the National Party victory in 1948, these functions were directed by the Department of Native Affairs under HF Verwoerd. Verwoerd's strategies were 'to reduce the population, to control movement into the area, and to expropriate freehold property'.[10] In the decades that followed, government attempted to implement its divisive strategies in varied ways, often succeeding in relocating pockets of residents (usually to other townships) in the short term, but making little difference in the longer term.

VISITING ALEX

Alex is often left off tourist itineraries in favour of Soweto – but it's becoming an increasingly popular 'authentic township' destination for local and domestic visitors. Because of Alex's relatively small size (just 7,6 km², compared to Soweto's 100 to 150 km²) and proximity to the hotels and access roads of Sandton, it's also an easy location to explore in under a day.

We recommend that all visits to Alex are done so with an accredited tour guide – crime is a problem in some parts of the township; roads are bumpy and potholed; and the dense residential structures make it difficult to navigate through certain parts of Alex. To find a tour guide (most guides will arrange a pick-up in Sandton), go the official Alex Tourism website at www.alextourism.co.za and click on the telephone icon for further details.

The yard and room Mandela rented from the Xhoma family on 7th Avenue, Alexandra. The area opposite the room has now been developed into the Mandela Yard Interpretation Centre (below).

PLACES TO SEE

The striking **Mandela Yard Interpretation Centre** (hopefully completed by the time this book is printed), on the corner of 7th Avenue and Hofmeyer Street, is planned as a tourist site and community hub – housing a tourism office, restaurant and retail outlets, and an exhibition that documents Alex's history and development over the past century.

For more information, contact Alexandra Tourism (www.alextourism.co.za) or the Gauteng Tourism Authority (www.gauteng.net).

Front view of the Interpretation Centre under construction

Being There

Life in Alexandra was exhilarating and precarious. Its atmosphere was alive, its spirit adventurous, its people resourceful. Although the township did boast some handsome buildings, it could fairly be described as a slum, living testimony to the neglect of the authorities. The roads were unpaved and dirty, and filled with hungry, undernourished children scampering around half-naked. The air was thick with the smoke of coal fires in tin braziers and stoves. A single water tap served several houses. Pools of stinking, stagnant water full of maggots collected by the side of the road. Alexandra was known as the 'Dark City' for its complete absence of electricity. Walking home at night was perilous, for there were no lights, the silence pierced by yells, laughter and occasional gunfire.
– Nelson Mandela, describing Alex in the 1940s in *Long Walk to Freedom* (1994)

March 1957 – the 'longest walk to work', during the bus boycott

'Azikhwelwa' – We Will Not Ride

Land rights were not the only issues Alex's residents protested over. Transport was a key issue for the township's resource-poor labour pool, who had to travel to white areas or the CBD. Private transport ownership was virtually nonexistent, and there were no trains running nearby Alex; as a result, commuters relied on crowded and poorly managed bus services to travel to and from work.

In the 1940s, Alex residents took part in four bus boycotts – forcing bus companies to reduce commuter fares by a penny and stifling further attempts to raise bus fares.

By the mid-1940s, the Public Utility Transport Company (PUTCO) had been formed by amalgamating several smaller transport companies; when PUTCO was given permission to increase its fares by one penny (25 per cent) in January 1957, it sparked a three-month boycott that started in Alex and soon spread to neighbouring townships, even as far as Pretoria, as residents joined the boycott in solidarity. Similar (though shorter) boycotts were implemented in the Eastern Cape and Free State.

Within a few days, some 60 000 people were walking tens of kilometres to work each day, through the heat and heavy rains of the Highveld summer. Despite ongoing harassment – police would stop and search boycotters for no reason, or puncture the tyres of bicycles; white

The Molete Family

A remarkable set of pictures shows the family of Mr Johannes Molete at their home in Alex, between 1949 and 1974. Captions are from the original photographs, courtesy of Museum Africa.

1949: First house built in 16th Avenue by Mr Johannes Molete – the next house was built of bricks.

Alex in the 1960s

motorists would drive through puddles to splash workers as they walked[11] – the boycotters remained resolute. In addition to restoring the old fares, residents also demanded an increase in the number of buses on the routes (to eliminate the very long queues that were common) and the erection of shelters at bus stops.

Later in January 1957, workers also began boycotting municipal beer halls; 'profits from beer-halls made up an important part of the Native Revenue Account responsible for township amenities and this action was regarded as a threat to municipal finance. The Non-European Affairs Department toured the townships in loudspeaker vans appealing to residents not to associate beer-halls with the Bus Boycott. Their efforts failed.'[12]

By April 1957, negotiations between boycott leaders, PUTCO representatives and the Chamber of Commerce reached a settlement of sorts, whereby the Chamber agreed to temporarily subsidise the transport services; by the middle of April, full bus services were running again. Two months later the government passed the Native Services Levy Act, which required employers to make a monthly transport subsidy payment to a fund.

The 1957 bus boycott provided impetus for the South Africa Congress of Trade Unions' (SACTU) £1-a-Day Campaign in the 1950s and 1960s, which fought for a minimum wage of a pound a day for all workers.

1966/67: Mr Johannes Molete and his son-in-law, Mr W Mabunda, at the home of the former in 16th Avenue, Alexandra. The bucket is for milking cows.

1974: Mr and Mrs J Molete, at their home in 16th Avenue

Hostel Takeover

Washing lines inside the women's hostel

In the early 1960s, the government announced its plans to rebuild Alex as a 'hostel city'. Family accommodation was to be eliminated, and 25 single-sex hostels, each housing about 2500 people, were to be built. The freehold rights of 2000 black property owners were abolished in 1963,[13] and thousands of residents were forcibly 'resettled'. Between 1958 and 1973, some 56 000 people were moved from Alex to Soweto, and a further 15 000 to Tembisa on the East Rand.[14] Not all Alex's residents were to be resettled, explains urban specialist Pauline Morris: 'Men and women employed in areas to the north of Johannesburg, those living in "servants' quarters" at the top of blocks of flats and on the premises of their employees in the suburbs would, it was stated, also be moved to the hostels.

'"Qualified" families living in Alexandra would have to move to other townships which served the area where the head of the household was employed. Persons who still owned property would be given the opportunity to buy plots in the homelands.'[15]

Ultimately, only three hostels were constructed: two for men, and one for women. The first hostel – M1, better known as Madala hostel – was completed in 1971; the second (M2 or Nobuhle hostel) was completed in 1972. The women's hostel (Helen Joseph) was only completed in 1981, long after the hostel plan had been shelved.

Children playing on an abandoned car inside the women's hostel

Strong local opposition – such as the Residents' Interim Committee, established by Reverend Sam Buti in 1974 – 'mobilised popular support for resistance to the removals and called for the development of family accommodation'.[16] Resettlement (of displaced people) and construction (of the hostels) also proved too expensive to finance.

By the late 1970s, following the 1976 riots and their violent aftermath, the government adopted a 'softer approach towards urban blacks',[17] including token recognition of their permanence through the 'temporary cessation of evictions, removals and expropriations in Alexandra';[18] the introduction of a 99-year lease (which would be introduced in Alex once the remaining 300-odd freehold properties had been expropriated!); and the announcement that Alex would be replanned for family housing.

In the early 1990s, during the approach to the country's first democratic elections, violence flared up between the residents of the two men's hostels – ostensibly between supporters of the Zulu Inkhata Freedom Party (IFP) and the African National Congress (ANC). Some 10 000 people were displaced from their homes by the fighting, and the area around the hostels became known as 'Beirut'. Under the Alexandra Renewal Project (ARP), the hostels are earmarked for redevelopment into one-, two- and three-bedroomed family units.

Saving Alex

An unlikely friendship played a crucial role in saving Alex from demolition – and rezoning as a hostel-only zone …

In the late 1970s, a 'Save Alex' campaign was initiated by Dutch Reform Church (DRC) minister, Reverend Sam Buti, who formed the Alexandra Liaison Committee together with other community leaders such as Linda Twala, teacher Leepile Taunyane (who later became the Premier Soccer League Life President), town clerk Mr Arthur Magerman, and Daniel Khoza.

At that time, the apartheid government's Minister of Co-operation and Development was Dr Piet Koornhof. Buti and Koornhof knew each other through their fathers – both DRC ministers in the Free State. Buti also spoke Afrikaans, and approached Koornhof to speak on Alex's behalf. After lengthy negotiations, the message came back: 'Alexandra gaan bly.' (Alexandra will remain.)

In 1983 it was officially announced that Alex was to be given its own town council. Buti later became Alex's mayor, but subsequently resigned – his role was interpreted by many as siding with the apartheid government.

In 1980 Minister Koornhof announced a new 'Master Plan' for Alex – the grand plan proposed seven suburbs; a central business area with supermarkets, shops, offices and administrative buildings; primary schools for each area together with three high schools and technical schools; a complex of light industries and community factories; and the development of sports complexes, parks, and a dam in the Jukskei River valley.[19]

The plan would be implemented over a five-year period, costing R25 million (in 1981 prices) per year.

Riot police in Alex, 1986

A car burns in the centre of Alex, February 1986.

To effect the plan, all properties in Alex would be acquired, and existing houses demolished; residents who 'qualified' would be 'moved into shared houses, refurbished buses and a disused TB hospital'[20] as temporary accommodation during the development. Not surprisingly, the plan was opposed by standholders, who refused to give up their land, and residents who had no desire to be moved from their homes – even 'temporarily' – without suitable alternative accommodation.

By early 1982, redevelopment of the township was delayed by lack of finance; less than 30 of the proposed 1300 houses (to be built each year of the plan) had been completed. By 1984,

Riot Police in Alex, 1986

only one small area (about five per cent of Alexandra) – now known as the East Bank – had been developed, with about 260 houses.[21]

In 1985 the Master Plan ground to a halt as political violence swept across South Africa – a State of Emergency was declared by the government in 36 magisterial districts; this gave the police and army additional power to ban organisations and detain people, and prohibit

media coverage of the protests. In June 1986 a State of Emergency was declared across the whole country.

In October 1986, police teargassed mourners after a funeral (for a youth, Michael Diradeng, allegedly killed by a security guard); the township went up in flames – between 19 and 40 people were killed over a six-day period, and individuals believed to be 'enemies of the government' were targeted and attacked, their houses bombed and set alight.

In response to the ongoing State of Emergency, the government embarked on a new Urban Renewal Plan for Alex, hoping to 'win the hearts and minds' of residents by developing the area – and, at the same time, harshly repressing protestors.

In 1987, five leading Alexandra activists, all members of the United Democratic Front (UDF) – an anti-apartheid organisation formed in 1983 – were arrested and put on trial for treason. The five accused were acquitted in April 1989. A further eight activists were also arrested and put on trial – known as the Alexandra Eight, or the Zwane Trial for its chief accused, Ashwell Zwane. These eight were also acquitted.

A funeral in Alex in 1986 (with the yellow, green and black flag in the colours of the then-banned ANC). Mourners wear T-shirts commemorating the 'Alexandra Massacre'.

Alex in 1988

Street Justice

In the absence of any effective state management in the 1970s and 1980s, residents of Alexandra developed their own committees – each street committee was able to elect two representatives to an executive committee known as the Alexandra Action Committee (AAC), which was headed by Moses Mayekiso, General Secretary of the Metal and Allied Workers Union (and who was one of the five residents put on trial for treason in 1987).

The AAC addressed issues such as unemployment, harassment by police, the high cost of transport, education, housing and sewerage, and the displacement of other residents through the demolition of their shacks. The committee also organised consumer boycotts – against businesses in Alex – and changed Alex's street names: 'Instead of names like Roosevelt and Hofmeyer, they rechristened streets after MK (short for the ANC military wing Umkhonto we Sizwe), Steve Biko, Nelson Mandela, Joe Slovo (South African Communist Party chief), Robert Sobukwe (the late leader of the Pan African Congress), Bazooka and ANC president Oliver Tambo.'[22]

Alex's street committees also meted out 'people's justice'; writer Steven Mufson reported, in 1988, that the action committee was dealing with 'four to five cases a day … ranging from settling marital problems to prose-cuting "tsotsis" or gangsters'. Allegations of witchcraft and tribalism were also heard. It is not clear exactly what punishments were meted out to guilty parties.

The detailed records kept by the AAC were later used by the state as evidence in the treason trial against Mayekiso and his colleagues.

Mufson also reported that, in mid-1986, the South African police mistook memos from the Alexandra Arts Centre (AAC) for the Alexandra Action Committee (also AAC), and 'arrested a butcher, who kept a piano in his butcher's shop so he could practise when business was slow'.[23]

Between July 1987 and October 1991, the number of people moving into Alex increased substantially – the number of shacks increased from 7352 to 20 000;[24] in some instances people were so desperate for land and living space that shacks were erected overnight on roads being prepared for paving.[25] The Urban Renewal Programme failed to take this migration into account, 'nor was suitable alternative land made available to accommodate those who were displaced'.[26] It was during this period that a new area known as the East Bank was constructed. However, '[n]ew infrastructure was insufficient to cater for the demands of the population, proper maintenance was difficult and infrastructure quickly deteriorated. By the end of 1990 the programme was abandoned.'[27]

A house on 1st Avenue, Alexandra

Alex Society

Together with historical ownership rights, Alex's physical and geographical divisions – tin shack versus brick house, West Bank or East Bank – create a 'strong sense of social stratification'[28] within the township, with the clearest divisions running not necessarily along tribal lines, but between 'old' and 'new' residents.

'Old' Alex residents are those who owned the township's original freehold properties 'and the backyard shacks that over time occupied the yards'.[29] The 'new' residents are those who have settled on 'inappropriate' land: riverbanks and tributaries of the Jukskei; in school-yards; and on road reserves. Some of the 'new' settlements have been in place for over 20 years; more recent additions include shack areas known to house immigrants from neighbouring countries such as Zimbabwe and Malawi – one such settlement is known as 'Mountain View' because it is built on a slight hill.

Thousands of shacks have also been built right up to the banks of the Jukskei River – which regularly floods, washing away shacks and possessions when it breaks its banks.

In 2001 thousands of Alex residents were forcibly

⊙ **PLACES TO SEE**

One of the most important community initiatives to emerge to fill the vacuum created by the state's failures was that of the **Alexsan** (Alex/ Sandton) **Kopano Centre** – created in 1986, with the centre officially opened in February 1992.

The centre runs a number of its own projects such as a library, career guidance counselling offices, computer studios and training programmes, and provides a base for many service organisations operating in Alex such as the Alex Satellite Clinic; ALXFM Community Radio; Alex Chamber of Commerce; LifeLine (telephone counselling services); Kelly Permanent and Temporary Employment Agency; and Electricity, Rates and Pension pay points.

For more information, go to www.alexsan-kopano.org.za or call (011) 882 0673/1142.

removed from alongside the Jukskei after an outbreak of cholera and the discovery of cholera bacteria in the river water. Shacks were demolished by an army of municipal workers dressed in red overalls (known as the Red Ants), and 4500 families were relocated. The move was incredibly unpopular, with many residents saying it reminded them of apartheid-era forced removals. The government insisted the relocations were prompted by health concerns, adding that, unlike the previous regime, it had found alternative accommodation for displaced families … in Diepsloot informal settlement, some 30 km away.

In 2001, the government launched the Alexandra Renewal Project (ARP) as part of its Integrated Sustainable Rural Development and Urban Renewal Programme. The estimated budget for the ARP, at the time, was R1,3 billion over an eight-year period. Although the renewal process has not been problem-free, remarkable successes have been achieved – you can view updates and virtual tours of the ARP's projects at the website www.alexandra.co.za.

Mountain View

Shacks alongside the Jukskei

A shack falling into the swollen Jukskei River during a flood

❝❞ Being there

There has been a lot of development in Alex, to the extent that now there is nowhere you can stand and see the boundaries of it. If you take a drive along its boundaries, even going to the airport, you will see that there are so many people still building and expanding this township. Most of the houses have electricity and running water, you will see that some people are even building big modern houses. But there are a lot of places that are still very dirty and poor, and it will take some time to make things better. But for the people at least there are more schools, clinics and more businesses are opening up as well – there haven't always been shopping malls here, but now we have. One of the main taxi ranks is also in Alex, which means that we get more people coming through Alex, which is always good for business.

– Paul Sibiya, shop owner

Red Ants

New housing built through the Alexandra Renewal Project

A view of the Far East Bank in Alexandra

305

THE INFORMAL

'The government was like the man who has a cornfield which is invaded by birds. He chases the birds from one part of the field and they alight in another part of the field. We squatters are the birds. The government sends its policemen to chase us away and we move off and occupy another spot. We shall see whether it is the farmer or the birds who get tired first.'

Oriel Monongoaha[1]

In this chapter

☞ Joburg's Early Squatter Movement

☞ Supply and Demand: Patterns of Informal Living

☞ Peri-urban Areas: Diepsloot, Kliptown, Orange Farm, Weiler's Farm, Zandspruit and Ivory Park

☞ Sustainable Settlements

SETTLEMENTS

Road construction in Diepsloot, February 2004

Informal Joburg

There are urban slum areas in every city. In the third world – and those countries straddling third and first-world status – there is an added residential dimension: informal settlements, distinct from inner-city slums and other low-income areas. Locals usually develop their own, more candid, labels: in Brazil, they are known as favelas (named after a hardy plant with thorny leaves); in Argentina villas miseria – literally, 'Miseryvilles'. Mexico has ciudades perdidas (lost cities); Desmond Dekker famously sang about Jamaica's 'shanty towns'. In Serbia, these urban slums are called kartonsko naselje ('cardboard settlement'); the Turks call them Gecekondu ('land overnight').

In South Africa, they are commonly known as squatter camps – many of the settlements are on private land, hence the 'squatting'.

Two-thirds of Africa's urban population live in informal settlements, often without access to water, electricity and other basic services; in sub-Saharan Africa, this figure is as high as 78 per cent.[2]

The demand for low-income housing in Johannesburg has always exceeded the availability: the settlement's earliest 'slums' were those of Brickfields, inhabited by poor whites as early as 1887; and the 'locations', for black, coloured and Indian residents, established at much the same time – before the various governments' systematic programmes of forced removals and restricted land ownership created societies of people without homes.

In the latter half of the 1940s, a formal squatter movement arose in Johannesburg in response to the continued lack of housing and increased political disenfranchisement. From 1944 until the end of the decade, somewhere between 63 000 to 92 500 black people settled in squatter camps across the city. The movements were led by charismatic men of the time and had a combination of social and political goals in mind. The first was led by James Mpanza, a man with a controversial place in South African history. A convicted murderer who was not above colluding with tenants to create a homeless populace, he led 250 households to invade a piece of open land between the Orlando Town Hall and the railway line.[3] The households set up a series of shelters made from hessian sacks and whatever else could be scavenged (hence one of its names 'Masakeng' or 'the place of sacks').

Within a few months, the 250 households were joined by a further 20 000 people who are been turned out of their rooms and backyards.

Initially, the City of Johannesburg wanted to prosecute and remove the squatters; until it realised it had nowhere else to put them. At that point plans were made to temporarily accommodate the squatters in barracks made from breeze blocks. The accommodation was built with the caveat that the squatters should not allow any more people to move into the settlement. Such a demand was clearly unenforceable and what followed was part farce and part tragedy as people settled and were displaced, in a repeating and ridiculous cycle. The authorities would build shelters for the existing squatters; then more people would come along and either take over the new housing – or locate themselves on new land, and wait for housing to be allocated. The authorities would then force them off the land … and the squatters would simply find somewhere else to settle.

Informal Settlements

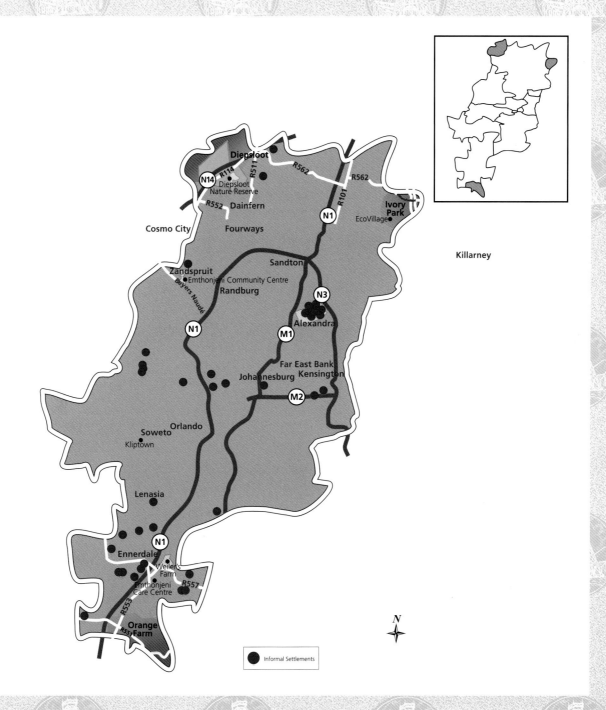

Diepsloot

N14 R114 R511 R562
Diepsloot
Nature Reserve R562
R552 Dainfern
Cosmo City Fourways R101 N1

Ivory
Park
EcoVillage

Killarney

Sandton
Zandspruit
Emthonjeni Community Centre
Beyers Naudé Randburg N3

N1 Alexandra
M1
Far East Bank
Johannesburg Kensington
M2

Orlando
Soweto
Kliptown

Lenasia

N1
Ennerdale
Weiler's
Farm
Emthonjeni R557
Care Centre
R553
R551 Orange
Farm

N

● Informal Settlements

Squatters in Orlando, 1940s

Informal dwellings in Zamimpilo Settlement

It would seem the 'birds' Oriel Monongoaha referred to proved, over the next few years, to have the greater stamina. What followed between 1945 and 1947 is a story of squatting, internal strife amongst the political leadership of the movement and the rise of informal settlements all over Soweto – and further attempts at settlement all around the city, including Lombardy East, Alexandra and Alberton. Realising that the present strategy was not working, the local authorities set up

'emergency camps' that provided services to households which met certain criteria (these often had more to do with just wanting to decrease the size of the settlement then anything else). People were allowed to move and settle in these emergency camps, which charged the residents a small fee. This was also a way of breaking the squatter leaders' power, by destroying their followings and annexing their income streams. Without strong leadership, the mass movement of the squatters slowed down and the government breathed a sigh of relief as the flood of people slowed to a comparative trickle.

In 1947 the government made a further token stab at housing the black population by building 6788 units over a four-year period, all of which were in outlying areas of the city.

Black urban communities were sites of communal cohesion, which often resulted in political and social rebellion. Informal settlements, in particular, with their roots in the squatter movements of the previous few years, were seen by the regime of the time, as encouraging 'an attitude ... of contempt for authority and for constitutional methods in favour of direct action, however illegal and violent, coupled with growing political, and national consciousness ...'[4] Many anti-apartheid factions were born amongst the noise, dust and discontent of these settlements.

The status quo between government and informal dwellers seems for the most part to have been maintained until the passing of the Prevention of Illegal Squatting Act of 1952, which, as its name implies, was intended to prevent the establishment of any further informal settlements.[5] The Act and its implementation meant that new migrants, and people achieving maturity and wishing to strike out on their own, were offered the choice between becoming a backyard sub-tenant, a resident of the single-sex (and increasingly violent) same-sex hostels, or settling on a peri-urban farm. At the same time increased emphasis on influx control and the consistent 'repatriation' of black South Africans to the 'Bantustans' or Homelands meant that freedom of movement for the majority was severely curtailed. From the mid-1950s until the mid-1970s housing was mainly constructed in the Homelands. By the 1960s a moratorium was effectively placed on building houses for the black population in the cities, Johannesburg included, and the earlier pattern of backyard densification and peri-urban settlement continued. Expenditure on housing for the urban black population was cut by almost 80 per cent from R14,5 million to R2,7 million between 1969 and 1976.[6] In addition, close attention by the authorities to what was happening on open land and within the townships meant that there were very limited options for land invasions and the development of informal settlements in Johannesburg.[7]

It was only in the 1980s – particularly with the abolition of the influx control laws – that the number of freestanding informal settlements reappeared on the Johannesburg landscape, and it was a swift and significant return.[8] At first, sites saw trickles of settlers finding space and building informal dwellings; within a few years, both the number and the size of the settlements increased. Although the newly developing informal settlements were occasionally raided by the minions of the dying regime, for the most part they were left alone until suitable legislation and by-law regulations could be developed and implemented. These came in the form of the offer of site-and-service schemes in other parts of Johannesburg. In a move that had echoes of an earlier battle between government and squatters, informal dwellers were offered land in other parts of Johannesburg with basic services – if they would agree to not allowing any more shacks into their settlements. The first of these site-and-service relocations was to Orange Farm, in the far south of Johannesburg.

By the early 1990s, there was a significant informal settlement sector in Johannesburg (and within the greater region of what was at the time the Transvaal Province), constituting 43 per cent of the black population. Interestingly, at the time 85 per cent of informal dwellings/shacks were to be found in the backyards of formal homes in the

black townships. The remaining 15 per cent constituted shacks in free-standing settlements, the vast majority located adjacent to formal townships on what were 'buffer zones', close to the industrial areas. The previous image of informal dwellers as migrants from rural and homeland areas no longer held true for Johannesburg, as many of the informal dwellers had been born and raised in the greater Johannesburg region. Their move into informal settlements was not a question of urbanisation but often a question of space and the limited capacity of township backyards, and members of households who had become unemployed moved to the informal settlements in the hope of finding a job and better living conditions for their families.

Conversely, peri-urban farms that had been deserted by their owners (and had significant black populations living on them) became attractive to urban dwellers, who had been living in crowded and uncomfortable conditions in backyards in the townships. It was estimated that the average township home housed 13 people and that anywhere between 84 000 and 540 000 units were needed in the city. It would then seem reasonable that households would move out of the overcrowded and squalid conditions of the townships in the hope of finding better and less crowded and far cheaper (if any) rentals on the urban periphery. Since informal dwellers were, and remain, the lowest-paid sector of society, finding cheaper accommodation within Johannesburg was a serious consideration for these households.

A further contributing factor to the increase in homelessness and informal settlements was owing to the nature of the housing market in South Africa. Prime land in Johannesburg had been designated as being available only for white occupation and ownership since the early 1930s, and the pattern was artificially maintained until the end of apartheid in 1994. Even when government agreed to allow a privatised housing market in black-designated areas, the supply did not meet or suit the demand and most of the property was out of the reach of the majority. By 1985,

29 per cent of households living in the Greater Witwatersrand area could not make any contribution to housing, let alone afford a privately constructed home in one of the better suburbs of Johannesburg's black townships.

By the mid-1990s, free-standing informal settlements on the periphery of Johannesburg were significant features of the cityscape.

The informal settlements were not, however, uncomplicated places to live and in the early and mid-1990s displayed a great deal of political upheaval. Although the settlements had been relatively calm when compared to the same period in the Johannesburg townships, by the 1990s factional politics had become a feature as violence erupted both over political differences and limited resources. Political organisations such as the Mass Democratic Movement and the ANC used the issue of squatting as a rallying point particularly in the lead-up to the first democratic election in 1994.

In the years that followed, the general patterns of informality became entrenched in Johannesburg; this was due to several factors. Following the first democratic election, Johannesburg's municipal structures were changed to reflect the new inclusive democracy; where there had previously been municipal structures to deal with each of the four 'race' groups, now only one was needed. At the same time the city's very geography needed to be examined and changed in order to incorporate sections of the city that had previously either been ignored or neglected. The same restructuring processes were taking place at national and provincial levels, which meant

Aerial view of Diepsloot

that the city and the country were in a state of suspended animation, without new laws, regulations or policies to actually address the lack of adequate shelter for millions of South Africans.

Today's Informal Settlements

The precise number of informal settlements is contentious, and grows and shrinks according to the seasons, government interventions and essentially who is counting them. A fair estimate would be to say that there are between 120 and 200 informal settlements in Johannesburg, housing somewhere in the region of between 200 000 to 250 000 households, or about three quarters of a million people.[9] The vast majority of the settlements have households whose members are extremely poor and on average earn less than R1500 a month. They house the most marginal and vulnerable members of South African society. There are also a significant proportion of foreign nationals, refugees and illegal migrants who cannot find alternative accommodation. The largest informal settlements house tens of thousands of people, whilst the smallest consist of a few shacks forlornly grouped together. Informal settlements also often adjoin existing townships or formal settlements so that some areas have both a formal and informal component. Some of the city's informal settlements also fall outside of the city's limits, but their residents work and transact within the city itself – and so the boundaries become blurred.

In 1998 the government passed the Prevention of Illegal Eviction Act, which repealed the Prevention of Illegal Squatting Act and made it illegal to evict any tenant or resident who has occupied a piece of land or property for more than 24 hours, unless an alternative location can be found.

Diepsloot, situated halfway between Johannesburg and Pretoria, first saw a number of families settle in the area in 1993. Households looking for employment in either of the two cities, but with nowhere to stay, settled in the open veld. New households joined the settlement both voluntarily and through government using Diepsloot as a re-settlement area for households from other settlements and townships. One of the biggest removals was the transfer of people from Alexandra Township who had been living on the banks of the Jukskei River in 2000. When a cholera epidemic broke out the local authorities removed the affected households and 'settled' them in Diepsloot. The move caused a great deal of misery for the relocated tenants. 'We have been dumped here,' remarked a relocated resident from Alexandra. 'Now I regard myself as a bad example to my children. I sleep with my husband in front of my children. I was made to leave my house in Alexandra, where I had a bigger stand and a better shack. Now we are made to drink filthy water, which is not even tested because they say it is expensive to conduct tests.'[10]

The number of people in Diepsloot now totals almost 60 000 with significant numbers living in backyard shacks. The community is one of the poorest in Johannesburg with few services and little infrastructure. There is one clinic in the settlement with the closest (public) hospital being 63 km away. One toilet is shared by 20 families (with an estimate of between 3,9 and 4,6 people per family) and owing to low levels of electrification in the settlement air pollution (from cooking and heating fuel sources) is high. The rest of the statistics for the areas are equally distressing with 57 per cent of youth not attending school. The majority of residents live at what the World Bank defines as the absolute poverty level of less than one dollar a day.

Kliptown, July 2007

The area is well known for epitomising the contrast between the rich and the poor in Johannesburg. Diepsloot is located virtually right next door to the Dainfern gated community, one of the most elite, expensive and prestigious housing estates in Johannesburg and host to the wealthy of the city. It is certainly a comparison worth making when trying to understand South African society. Close to the settlement is the Diepkloof Nature Reserve, a state-protected nature park that hosts a wide variety of bird species and some lovely day walks. As for the informal settlement itself, it provides scenes of daily informal life and the myriad activities that constitute its dynamics. Pavements of the main roads are used for a whole lot of informal activities such as car washing, taxi ranks, vegetable and fruit markets, and stalls given over to street hair and beauty salons.

Kliptown, in Soweto, is one of Johannesburg's oldest neighbourhoods, and has seen wave upon wave of migrants settle in the area. The population is now at about 45 000, most of whom live in a wide variety of shacks and informal dwellings. One writer described Kliptown as an area where 'tin shanties litter the backyards of the more formal brick housing, rows of chemical toilets stand outside homes, and the untarred roads run with streams of filthy water'. It is an area of serious poverty,

A hair salon in Orange Farm

where some 60 per cent of the population are unemployed and almost half the community records no monthly income at all. The result is a population of informal dwellers – 85 per cent of people in Kliptown live in just under 9000 shacks, with a tiny percentage living in the 100 formal houses built by the municipality. The area is poorly lit at night with an average of two lights for the 3000 shacks, communal mobile toilets with a ratio 200 for every 12 000 people and communal taps from which most residents get their water. There are no formal educational facilities such as primary and secondary schools, except for informal crèches in two areas. The area lacks any form of recreational facilities and most of the children play in the streets. Government facilities are also extremely limited – there is only one clinic in Kliptown and the nearest hospital is located at least 15 km to 20 km away, whilst the closest police station and fire station is about 3 km to 5 km away.

Orange Farm is one of the biggest and most marginalised of the informal settlements in Johannesburg, some 60 km away from the centre of Johannesburg. It is home to 350 000 people and is characterised by the City of Johannesburg as, 'an isolated area that has been a "dumping" ground for low-income housing'.[11]

It was initially established in 1989 as a site-and-service scheme for squatters from Soweto, Meyerton, Evaton and as far afield as the Free State, and grew into the largest free-standing informal settlement in South Africa. The informal settlement has a number of issues, including the poverty of its residents with over 60 per cent of households living below the poverty line of R840 per month and the vast majority of residents living in shacks and other informal dwellings. Unemployment rates are high (at almost 90 per cent) and many households subsist on piece-work and odd jobs in order to try and feed themselves and their households. The settlement is further afflicted with a high HIV/AIDS prevalence – at one time suspected as being almost 80 per cent of the population. Only two-thirds of the community have electricity and none have running water. Due to the lack of waterborne sewers and running water, as well as limited refuse collection, gastro-intestinal disease and parasitic infestations are rife. The high HIV/AIDS rate in Orange Farm means that there are a large number of child-headed households, who are left to fend for themselves in this hostile environment.

Owing to the impoverished nature of the community and the size of the settlement there are a large number of NGOs active in the area. The Ma'Afrika Tikkun (a Jewish Development Organisation – www.maafrikatikkun.org.za) Community Centre Project provides care, training and counselling for households that have been or are affected by HIV/AIDS. It also co-ordinates activities with the multitude of NGOs, community-based organisations and aid organisations working in the settlement. Emthonjeni Care Centre (www.emthonjeni.org) is another vital NGO in Orange Farm. The Centre has a full-time nurse and a part-time doctor as well as a dedicated team of counsellors and volunteers. The Centre provides education and healthcare to people in the area suffering from HIV/AIDS and its associated ailments. It also acts as a base from which meals are distributed and home visits by trained counsellors are co-ordinated. Other initiatives have included the building of a day-care centre, which houses a pre-school, an office, kitchen, sanitary facilities, two big classrooms and a rest area for 60 children from the surrounding settlement.

There is also the community garden project in which six schools use their fields to grow vegetables to feed the students, staff and their households, with any leftovers being sold and the money reinvested in the project.[12] The settlement has not only used low-tech methods to improve itself but has also partnered with the Council for Scientific and Industrial Research (CSIR) and the City of Johannesburg's Department of Economic Development to create an ICT Hub. The aim of the Hub, housed in the Orange Farm Cultural Centre, is to ensure that Orange Farm's residents are computer literate. Internet connectivity is provided to the Centre by local firm Internet Solutions, who tested their wireless Internet and Voice Over Internet Protocols (VOIP) in Orange Farm[13] as well as providing IT teacher training.[14]

Weiler's Farm, in the south of Johannesburg and quite close to Orange Farm, was originally established in the 1960s when the Weiler brothers who owned and farmed the land allowed their labourers to settle on the farm and build shacks for themselves and their families. In later years the property held a small diamond mine that proved not to be particularly successful and, by 1985 when the owners retired to more pleasant climes, the settlement had over 70 families. Within two years 1100 shacks had been built on the previous farmland. Currently there are about 3500 households living in the settlement. The majority of residents live far below the breadline and, due to the distance from the Johannesburg CBD, find it difficult and expensive to find work. The settlement has no refuse removal and consistently suffers from illegal dumping from factories and small businesses. The problem of solid waste is compounded by the lack of sewers and there is no piped water into the area. It would seem that while Orange Farm is going from strength to strength its neighbour is facing increasing poverty and desolation. Weiler's Farm does unfortunately represent some of the worst ravages of poverty and lack of infrastructure and decent housing.

Aside from the contrast between Weiler's Farm and to Orange Farm, it also has some interesting projects. Among them is the growth of Islam in the settlement, to the point that Weiler's Farm now has a mosque, madras and residence for a full-time cleric. It is also home to another fascinating piece of architecture, a kindergarten designed and constructed by 21 students from the Technical University of Graz. The building had to be constructed utilising cheap materials and skills that were available either within the team or the surrounding community so that the local community could reproduce the building if so desired. The end result was a kindergarten that was user friendly and fitted in with the environment, whilst supplying a healthy and innovative space for the children to learn and play in.

Zandspruit in the north-western part of Johannesburg, 30 km from the city centre and located just next to the Beyers Naudé arterial route and the Zandspruit River, houses over 5240 poor households. The origins of the settlement rest in the pre-1994 period, when workers on the surrounding small plots and market garden farms in the area needed labourers to work on their land. Many of these households were made up of Zimbabweans, who were only joined by South Africans and Mozambicans after the first democratic elections. When government announced its intention to provide housing for all poor South Africans Zandspruit became a location of choice for a number of rural migrants and within a few years housed almost 50 000 people. The original community of foreign nationals and migrants managed to live in peace in the first few years, but with increasing competition for resources in the area tensions have exploded. South African residents argue that the Zimbabweans are violent and brutal and are responsible for the crime in Zandspruit while the Zimbabweans reckon that the hatred they experience from locals has more to do with the fact that

A panorama of the Eco Village in Ivory Park

they are more skilled than the local population and are thus more often (although this is a relative term) employed than their South African neighbours. Tension has erupted in violence and, in 2001, 100 shacks belonging to Zimbabweans were set alight and gutted and a further 124 were looted and vandalised.[15]

The news is not all doom and gloom. Government has recognised the desperate needs in the area and has committed to building housing and putting in services. There are also a number of community and private-sector projects in the settlement. The largest one is the Emthonjeni Community Centre (www.emthonjeni.com) funded by Umbono, the corporate social investment arm of PriceWaterhouseCoopers (PWC). The Centre provides a créche, after-school care for learners, peri-natal education and a skills development programme. There is also the Zandspruit Plangi Project, where women use traditional dying skills (known as *plangi*) to manufacture cushions, bags and tablecloths that are sold at the Centre; a jewellery-making business in the informal settlement where the goods are sold locally to tourists and exported overseas; and a youth dance group called PHYCS – they provide tourists with a guided walking tour through the settlement followed by a show and dinner.

Ivory Park (about 10 km north of Midrand, in Joburg's far north) was a planned informal settlement established in 1990 – on land adjacent to the then-designated 'coloured' area of Rabie Ridge – by the Transvaal Provincial Administration, to deal with the overflow of people from

nearby Tembisa as well as Alexandra and other settlements. By 2004 it was estimated that Ivory Park housed up to 80 per cent of the Midrand area's residents[16] – as many as 200 000 people[17] – on less than 10 per cent of the area's land.

Significant local government and corporate investment has seen Ivory Park transformed from 'an informal settlement replete with shacks to a place where residents boast of decent, formal houses'.[18] The lighting and naming of 1126 streets was announced in late 2006, and almost all the roads in Ivory Park have now been tarred.

The Lord Khanyile Multi-Purpose Community Centre (MPCC), launched in 2006, provides residents with access to basic service centres – like community development workers, the Department of Home Affairs, Joburg Water and the City of Joburg – and free Internet services. A youth centre, Ubuntu Centre for the Aged, a revenue pay point, the Ivory Park Library and a community hall are all located in the Lord Khanyile MPCC precinct.

One of the most remarkable projects in Ivory Park is its growing Eco Village, a development that includes an organic produce market, waste recycling co-operatives, a business and community centre, and residential housing built using eco-friendly principles and materials.

Living in an Informal Settlement

Informal settlements are notorious for their unpleasant and rather unsanitary conditions. Some settlements, as mentioned earlier, have a relatively long history and have

Getting to Know Informal Settlements

Informal settlements around the world have their own vocabularies used by the residents and the people involved with their upgrading and development. They also give some insight into the kind of life that is led by the majority of the residents. The following terms are used in infromal settlements around Joburg:

Chibhanzi – slang word for money, often used for illegal transactions in informal settlements, e.g. money that is paid for the services of a prostitute

Housing/land mafia – a group of people or an individual (known as a 'shacklord') who maintains control of an informal settlement, and gives permission for a household to build/sell/buy a shack in an area. Generally a 'registration' fee is charged for people to settle (about R50), and they then pay a monthly amount – which is defined as 'rent' but is actually protection money.

Impimpi – refers to a police informant, generally means the person is untrustworthy

Kaaps – a mixture of English, Afrikaans and Xhosa used in the informal settlements and townships

Kleinhuisie – literally means tiny houses but generally means an outside toilet or port-a-loo, the most common form of toilet in informal settlements

Makoya – refers to 'the real McCoy', the genuine article

Makwerekwere – a slang word and very derogatory term, with xenophobic connotations for African foreigners, many of whom live in informal settlements

Moola – a general term for money

S'camtho – language of the youth and the streets; very closely associated with Kwaito music and Loxion Culture

Shack farming – putting up shacks and encouraging the growth and settlement of informal dwellers, often done by private landowners looking for a quick profit or by land mafias

Skorokoro – also known as a 'skedonk', is a car that is old, dilapidated, and damaged, often used as a form of public transport in informal settlements

Spaza – an informal township or informal settlement shop that sells a wide variety of goods

Tokoloshe – a malevolent spirit in local folklore that is responsible for a wide variety of mischief and mayhem

Tsotsi – criminal or thug

A sign outside a Spaza shop in Zamimpilo informal settlement near Riverlea

achieved some legal status, which they are able to use to demand the satisfaction of a series of rights. Unfortunately until the services are in place and the shacks are upgraded to small government-issue (RDP) homes the situation in the settlements remains unhygienic and more than awful. One account of an informal settlement next to Soweto describes '…corrugated iron shacks, broken toilets and shower stalls, garbage piling up, and even an open trench of raw sewage spilling across most of the settlement. The settlement is located near towering masses of mine dumps – the cast off material from decades of gold mining – the debris of which blasts through the area on any windy day'.[19]

The areas are unsafe from a number of perspectives: informal settlements are often located on sites that are geologically unsafe (dolomite); close to mine dumps (filled with cyanide and other poisonous chemicals); land fills (with their accompanying rats); or on floodplains. The end result is that informal dwellers are constantly at risk from their environment.

Elvis Dube's unusual shack in Ivory Park

Unfortunately it is not just the environment that threatens informal dwellers' lives. Lack of running water, sewerage, electricity and housing all play their part, as well as high levels of crime and violence. The lack of services and infrastructure results in a wide variety of illnesses and early deaths. Waterborne diseases like cholera and diarrhoea have a devastating effect on the elderly and very young, and the use of wood and coal for heating and cooking means that rates of respiratory disease such as lung cancer and asthma are much higher in these communities. Poor housing, made of corrugated iron, wood and whatever other scraps are available, with no electrical power has meant that these areas are prone to fires, which ravage informal settlements leaving many homeless, injured and bereaved. One informal resident was quoted as saying, 'The thing that scares me most is fire. If the surrounding shacks catch fire, this is where we will die because there is no way we will be able to escape.'[20]

Poverty and low employment levels mean that many households lack money to buy basic supplies and hunger and malnutrition are constant visitors.

Violent crime in informal settlements seems to be a constant fact of life, and murder, rape and assault statistics are higher in Johannesburg's informal settlements than in the rest of the city. The situation is made worse by households having relatively little to spend on security and the protection of their families and goods. There are also fewer police in these areas and policing is less effective owing to the density of the shacks and the difficulties associated with patrolling and pursuing suspects through small, badly lit alleyways.

Since they are generally built on peripheral land or on any 'unused' open space, this land is either owned by private landowners or by government and, as such, the rights of the owners also demand protection. Property owners demand the right to utilise their land in whatever manner they feel is appropriate and argue that squatters devalue their land and limit its possible uses; informal communities argue that they literally have nowhere else to go. Unhappy (white) landowners living in proximity to newly established informal settlements are known as NIMBYs – Not In My Back Yard. The eviction debate rages as both sides feel their rights are consistently being infringed.

One of the key problems with informal settlements is the matter of improving people's lives and situations; the constant risks, threats and disasters that infest people's lives make such improvement difficult. The effects of illness, poor education and consistent loss are not conducive to alleviating poverty and ensuring that households have the ability to improve their lives. In an education study in one of Johannesburg's largest informal settlements, learners were quoted as saying, '… sometimes I don't have money to go to school. I stay at home.' The ramifications of such a statement are huge.[21]

The Future of Informal Settlements in Johannesburg

The South African state, the provincial government and Johannesburg's local authorities have been and continue to be deeply concerned about the number of people living in informal settlements in Johannesburg and the conditions in which they are living. Since 1994 the plight

Cosmo City

One of the largest public-private partnership projects addressing the shortage of housing in Johannesburg is the 1200-hectare Cosmo City development, near Kya Sands in the north of Johannesburg. Cosmo City emerged out of the urgent need to accommodate the informal settlers of Zevenfontein and Riverbend, who had been illegally occupying privately owned land in Joburg's north-west. The City of Johannesburg, together with the Gauteng Department of Housing, acquired the land to create a mixed-use, integrated housing development with 5000 fully subsidised units (for households earning less than R1500 per month); 3000 partially subsidised units (for households earning over R1500 but below R3500); 3300 fully bonded houses which are to be sold on the open market; and 1000 apartments for rent.[24]

Cosmo City, November 2007

of the informal settlements and the lack of adequate housing has been a priority for all spheres of government. High placed rhetoric about 'We are all one human force, inexorably drawn to the ideal that until all are without shackles of poverty, none of us is free'[22] and a Constitutional commitment to '... provide adequate and affordable housing' to all South Africans has to some degree found its way into National Housing Policy. In addition it is estimated that by 2010 there will be between 101 940 to 144 725 new households in Johannesburg, each one earning less than R3500 a month, which means that there are likely to be more informal dwellers in the future.[23] Taking both the national stance and the local conditions into account has meant that there has been a great deal of policy-making on informal settlements, with initial commitments to their eradication in Johannesburg by 2007 and then, when (in 2006) almost 200 informal settlements were counted in the city, a new commitment to rid the city of informal settlements by 2014.

The city is not short of policies, strategies and plans that outline how this target is to be achieved. The City's Integrated Development Plan (IDP) as well as the Jo'burg 2030, the Johannesburg Housing Master Plan, are a few amongst a range of other policies that argue not only for improved housing for the poor but, in keeping with international thinking, want to create 'Sustainable Human Settlements'. The Sustainable Human Settlement Approach is intended to provide economic, social and political opportunities for poor households as well as appropriate housing. The programmes include *in situ* upgrading, which allows, where possible, for informal-settlement households to get a formal house and basic services in the same area where they are currently living or as close to it as possible. Alternatively, where the land is privately owned or is considered dangerous for some reason, informal dwellers are relocated to housing in another part of the city or province (this can be up to 60 km away).

The reality is that the programmes on the ground reflect an urban environment of stark monotony, with rows of 'matchbox' houses of dubious quality, interspersed by dusty streets, far from the bright lights of the city and much that it has to offer. Government has realised the urgency of resolving this issue and is seeking to redress the problems through a range of inclusive housing policies.

Joburg: What Happens Next

For the first time in human history, more people live in cities than in rural areas. In the next 25 years, it is predicted, two-thirds of the world's population will be living in cities.

Urban areas tend to be labelled according to their size and importance: a 'metropolis' (with a minimum population of 500 000 people) is considered to perform 'an important commercial, cultural and political function for its region or even the whole country'[1]; while a 'global city' is a metropolis 'whose political, cultural and commercial influence extends across the entire globe',[2] for example Tokyo, London or New York. A 'megacity', on the other hand, is defined by the single factor of population size, determined by the United Nations to be over 10 million inhabitants. In recent years, a new category has been developed: that of the 'hypercity', with over 20 million inhabitants. Hypercities include Delhi, Mexico City, Mumbai, New York City, Sao Paolo, Seoul and Tokyo.

To accommodate their massive and growing populations, our cities don't just expand outwards – they grow inwards, and upwards; the rich measure their wealth based on how much space they own, while the poor huddle closer in increasingly cramped quarters.

To the far north and east of Johannesburg, 30 km from the city centre, settlements like Diepsloot and Ivory Park nudge the boundaries of neighbouring Tshwane and Ekurhuleni. There are plans to develop 180 hectares of disused municipal land lying between Diepsloot and the upper-income housing estate of Dainfern, for housing, retail and public facilities.

The Soweto Golf Course, in Pimville, is in the process of being relocated so that the land can be used for housing. This is partly to accommodate informal settlements in Kliptown. The new golf course, however, will also accommodate Soweto's first 'golf estate'.

In the inner city – where, says Phil Harrison, Joburg's Executive Director for Development Planning and Urban Management, the residential population is expected to double in the next decade. Some 20 000 housing units (out of a proposed total of 50 000 – 75 000) will be earmarked for low-income residents in Hillbrow and the surrounding areas. Urban regeneration initiatives will also see the upgrading of public space over 200 city blocks in Yeoville, Berea and Hillbrow; the work will include paving, landscaping, street lighting, street furniture, improvements to five public parks, storm-water inlets, litter bins and public toilets.

The boom in property prices over the past decade has contributed to other challenges in the middle-income housing market – as development continues unabated in the city's central suburbs and northern reaches, higher-density housing projects are placing increasing strain on Johannesburg's resources and services.

Urban planners face a daunting task as they try not only to house the poor and accommodate the demands of the rich, but also to navigate the impenetrable maze of legislation, by-laws and improvement strategies that impact on greater Johannesburg. National, provincial and municipal interests frequently overlap – which, more often than not, results in duplication or omission rather than a combined effort.

Despite the hurdles of bureaucracy – and the cynicism of Joburg's residents – many of the strategies and developments are working. Improvements to pockets of the inner city and the central business district have yielded cleaner, safer streets and unexpectedly desirable residences. Heritage projects, such as Constitution Hill on the border of Hillbrow, are visually and politically remarkable. Low-income housing developments such as Brickfields in Newtown have proved both practical and aesthetically acceptable.

The largest project to date, the multi-billion-rand Gautrain,[3] appears to be on schedule (if over budget); once completed, the Gautrain will link Johannesburg, the city of Tshwane and OR Tambo International Airport. High-speed commuter train services will operate 18 hours a day, travelling a minimum of six trips between the two cities. Seven Gautrain stations are under construction in Johannesburg (at Park Station, Rosebank, Sandton, Marlboro, Midrand, Rhodesfield and OR Tambo International Airport), with high-density residential, commercial and community facilities planned within walking distance of each station precinct.

A Gautrain bus link will provide transport between the stations and their surrounding suburbs, and this service will be integrated with a bus rapid transit (BRT) network. Initial BRT routes will include a north–south corridor running from Soweto to Sunninghill, and an east–west link from Alexandra to Randburg.

The transport hub of Park Station will also be redeveloped, to create an international transit and shopping centre that will integrate all modes of transport – the Gautrain, trains, minibus taxis and buses). In a separate project, Stretford Station in Orange Farm will be the subject of a plan to attract the private sector to the area and improve the local economy.

Several large private developments, too, are taking place in and around Johannesburg. Chemical services company AECI is selling off or developing portions of its land in Modderfontein (the site of Joburg's old dynamite factory, now conveniently close to the airport and the Gautrain route). The existing Conservation Park is being spared, but the site already includes yet another golf course (there are already more than 35 golf courses in Johannesburg and its surrounds).

Between Buccleuch and Midrand, the development of Waterfall City is being billed as the largest privately owned property venture in South Africa. (It is owned by the Mia family, who originally purchased the property in the name of a company because the Asiatic Land Tenure Act prevented property ownership by an Indian individual.) Plans for the 2 200-hectare estate include a golf course, residential units and a cemetery.

In Soweto, the Joburg Property Company[4] is involved in the first billion-rand investment into a black township: the Orlando Ekhaya Project will see the conversion of the disused Orlando Power Station into a mixed-use waterfront mall development, to include 700 middle-income houses and an Extreme Heights Adventure Centre. The latter will convert the 200-metre cooling towers into the only indoor bungee jump in the world.

Despite the tendency of the passage of time to encourage nostalgia and reminiscence, Johannesburg is not a city easily given to sentiment about its history. While the trappings have changed and the mines have moved west, the city today remains much the same strange settlement it has always been. There are too many people, not enough houses; and when it rains – the big, gusty thunderstorms of summer – the roads get badly potholed.

We, the city's inhabitants, are survivors, entrepreneurs, dealers and trailblazers. We are also aggressive, greedy, mercenary and callous; and our crime is more often violent than petty.

A hundred years ago, families were being murdered in the veldt while out on a Sunday walk, and mothers were reported to have been assaulted while lying next to their infants. In this way, then, we are the same as those who came before us. We are afraid, but we will stay. We are bound by the promise of change, the potential for greatness, the certainty of streets washed clean by the same thunderstorms, illuminated by lightning. And we will make history.

Endnotes

Chapter One

1 Davidson, CF, 1965. 'The mode and origin of banket orebodies'. Institute of Mining and Metallurgy, London. Cited by HE Frimmel, Earth Science Reviews 70, 2005.
2 The Origin of Gold in South Africa, J Kirk et al. From an article published in American Scientist, November – December 2003.
3 Ibid.
4 Muntean J, 'The rush to uncover gold's origins'. www.agiweb.org/geotimes/apr06/feature_GoldOrigins.html
5 The Vredefort Dome Conservancy at. www.tvdc.co.za
6 Dyer, B cited by Margulis, L and Brynes, L, 1999 in 'Rock not always a hard place'. Whole Earth, Fall 1999.
7 Rickard, TA. 'The Primitive Smelting of Iron'. American Journal of Archaeology Vol 43, No 1 (Jan–Mar 1939), pp 85–101.
8 Holl, cited by Stanley B. Alpern. 'Did they or didn't they invent it? Iron in sub-Saharan Africa'. History in Africa, Vol 32, 2005.
9 Schmidt cited by Stanley B. Alpern. Did they or didn't they invent it? Iron in sub-Saharan Africa.
10 Mason RJ, 1971. Prehistoric Man at Melville Koppies Johannesburg. University of the Witwatersrand Press.
11 Ibid.
12 Alpern, SB, 2005. 'Did they or didn't they invent it? Iron in sub-Saharan Africa'. History in Africa, Vol 32, 2005.
13 City of Johannesburg website at www.joburg.org.za
14 Johannesburg City Parks at www.jhbcityparks.com
15 These languages form part the Bantu languages group – the group covers over 400 diverse ethnic groups across Africa, from Cameroon to South Africa. The 'Sotho-Tswana' languages are distinctly different (in language root) from Nguni languages – isiZulu, isiXhosa, siSwati – although both are considered Bantu languages. Sesotho sa Leboa dialects include Sepedi.
16 Pula: Botswana Journal of African Studies. Online at http://archive.lib.msu.edu/DMC/African%20Journals/pdfs/PULA/pula015001/pula015001004.pdf
17 Nguni languages include isiZulu, isiXhosa and Siswati. They have a different root from that of the Sotho-Tswana languages.
18 Makhura, J, 'The Pre-Colonial History of Mpumalanga Societies until the 19th Century'. www.mpumalanga.gov.za/HeritageManuscript/4%20Precolonial.pdf
19 South African History online at www.sahistory.org.za
20 The amaManala branch also exists, as the smaller of the 'Southern' amaNdebele. Each branch has its own king.
21 Makhura, J, 'The Pre-Colonial History of Mpumalanga Societies until the 19th Century'.
22 Ibid.
23 Delius, P and Cope, R, 'Hard Fought Frontiers: Mpumalanga 1845–1883'. www.mpumalanga.gov.za/HeritageManuscript/5%20HFF.finaldoc.pdf
24 Ibid.
25 Grant, G and Flinn, T, 1992. Watershed Town: The History of the Johannesburg City Engineer's Department. Johannesburg City Council.
26 Ibid.
27 Delius, P and Cope, R, 'Hard Fought Frontiers: Mpumalanga 1845–1883'. www.mpumalanga.gov.za/HeritageManuscript/5%20HFF.finaldoc.pdf
28 Ibid.

Chapter Two

1 One talent is equal to approximately 34 kg.
2 Department of Arts of Africa, Oceania, and the Americas, Metropolitan Museum of Arts, New York. 'The Trans-Saharan Gold Trade, 7th–14th Century'. www.metmuseum.org
3 Rosenthal, E, 1970. Gold! Gold! Gold! Macmillan.
4 Ibid.
5 Ibid.
6 Ibid.
7 Newberry, JS. The Genesis and Distribution of Gold. Cited by Rosenthal, E in Gold! Gold! Gold!
8 Master, S, 2003. 'Louis de Launay and the Debate on the Origin of the Witwatersrand Gold (1896 – 1903): What Has Changed in a Hundred Years?' Wits Economic Geology Research Institute, Information Circular No. 375. Http://web.wits.ac.za/Academic/Science/GeoSciences/Research/egri/circulars.htm Accessed 8 June 2008.
9 Rosenthal, E, 1970. Gold! Gold! Gold! Macmillan.
10 City of Johannesburg website at www.joburg.org.za
11 Macmillan, A (ed.). The Golden City. WH&L Collingridge Ltd.

Chapter three

1 Bosman, HC, cited in Van Onselen, C, 2001. New Babylon, New Nineveh. Jonathan Ball Publishers.
2 Rosenthal, E, 1970. Gold! Gold! Gold! Macmillan; City of Johannesburg website at www.joburg.org.za
3 Oats, GT, 1966. 'They Assisted at the Birth of a City'. Africana Notes and News, September 1966, Vol. 17 No. 3.
4 Ibid.
5 City of Johannesburg website.
6 Grant, G and Flinn, T, 1992. Watershed Town. City of Johannesburg.
7 Based on original article by Irwin Manoim, courtesy of City of Johannesburg website.
8 City of Johannesburg website.
9 Grant, G and Flinn, T. Watershed Town.
10 Johannesburg – One Hundred Years. 1986. Chris Van Rensburg Publications.
11 Davie, L. City of Johannesburg website.
12 Meiring, H. Early Johannesburg. Cited by Neil Fraser on City of Johannesburg website.
13 Johannesburg Stock Exchange website at www.jse.co.za

14   Van Onselen, C, 2001. New Babylon, New Nineveh. Jonathan Ball Publishers. Note that the historian Luli Callinicos gives a different date for the formation of the Chamber of Mines.
15   Rosenthal, E. Gold! Gold! Gold!
16   Van Onselen, C. New Babylon, New Nineveh.
17   Neil Fraser at www.joburg.org.za/citichat/2005/may23_citichat.stm
18   Cited on the Rand Club's websit at www.randclub.co.za
a20   Ibid.
21   Van Onselen, C. New Babylon, New Nineveh.
22   Ibid
23   Ibid.
24   Ibid.
25   Van Onselen, C. New Babylon, New Nineveh; Rubin, MW. The Jewish Community of Johannesburg 1886–1939. Masters Thesis, University of Pretoria.
26   Jochelson, K. 2001, Colour of Disease: Syphilis and Racism in South Africa, 1880–1950. Palgrave Macmillan.
27   Van Onselen, C. New Babylon, New Nineveh; Jochelson, K. Colour of Disease: Syphilis and Racism in South Africa, 1880–1950.
28   Rubin, MW. The Jewish Community of Johannesburg 1886–1939.
29   Van Onselen, C. New Babylon, New Nineveh.
30   Jochelson, K. Colour of Disease: Syphilis and Racism in South Africa, 1880–1950.
31   Van Onselen, C. New Babylon, New Nineveh.
32   SA History Online at www.sahistory.org.za
33   Callinicos, L, Gold and Workers at South African History Online at www.sahistory.org.za.
34   Cited by Van Onselen, C in The Small Matter of a Horse: The Life of 'Nongoloza' Mathebula, 1867–1948 Protea Boekehuis.
35   Based on Van Onselen, C in The Small Matter of a Horse: The Life of 'Nongoloza' Mathebula, 1867–1948 Protea Boekehuis; Steinberg, J, 2004. 'Nongoloza's Children'. Centre for the Study of Violence and Reconciliation.

Chapter Four

1   Holland, H and Roberts, A, eds 2003. From Jo'burg to Jozi: Stories about Africa's infamous city. Penguin Books.
2   Rosenthal, E, 1970. Gold! Gold! Gold! The Macmillan Company.
3   Bell, FG and Stacey, TR, 2003. The influence of subsidence on planning and development in Johannesburg, South Africa.
4   Cited in Earthweek, September 2003. www.earthweek.com
5   Cited by Rosenthal, E, 1970.
6   Rosenthal, E, 1972. Meet Me At The Carlton. Howard B Timmins.
7   Ibid.
8   Telford, p. 92
9   WS Churchill, Frontiers and Wars. Harmondsworth (1972), p. 570, cited in Chipkin, C, 1993. Johannesburg Style: Architecture and Society 1880s – 1960s. David Philip Publishers.

10   From articles at City of Johannesburg website (www.joburg.org.za) and www.amethyst.co.za/JhbLandmarks
11   City of Johannesburg website at www.joburg.org.za
12   Telford, AA, 1969. Johannesburg: some sketches of the golden metropolis. Books of Africa.
13   www.kairoscomotion.org/2005march/candle_form.html
14   Ibid.
15   Ibid.
16   Ibid.
17   Ibid.
18   The Standard Bank in Johannesburg, issued by Standard Bank Heritage Department
19   Picton-Seymour, D, 1989. Historical Buildings in South Africa. Struikhof Publishers.
20   Telford, AA, 1969.
21   Ibid.
22   Davie, L, 2002. Jo'burg, the 24-hour city. City of Johannesburg website at www.joburg.org.za
23   Davie, L, 2008. Great shops in Joburg. City of Johannesburg website at www.joburg.org.za
24   Chipkin, C, 1993. Johannesburg Style: Architecture and Society 1880s – 1960s. David Philip Publishers.
25   Palestrant, E, 1986. Johannesburg One Hundred. AD Donker.
26   Alhadeff, V, 1986. A Newspaper History of South Africa. Nelson.
27   Palestrant, E, 1986.
28   Zeederberg, H, 1972. Golden Days. Van Riebeeck.
29   Beavon, K, 2004. Johannesburg: The Making and Shaping of the City. University of South Africa Press.
30   Ibid.
31   Johannesburg One Hundred Years. Chris van Rensburg Publications (1986).
32   Palestrant, E, 1986.
33   Palestrant, E, 1986.
34   Picton-Seymour, D, 1989.
35   Palestrant, E, 1986.
36   Chipkin, C, 1993.
37   African National Congress website at www.anc.org.za
38   Davie, L, 2006. Dorkay House hangs on. City of Johannesburg website at www.joburg.org.za
39   Alhadeff, V, 1986.
40   African National Congress website, www.anc.org.za/un/marof01.html
41   Dlamini, N, 2004. Joburg police station banishes apartheid blues on City of Johannesburg website at www.joburg.org.za
42   Beavon, K, 2004.
43   Ibid.
44   Davies, L, 2007. Wits turns 85 today. Joburg City Website at www.joburg.org.za
45   Ibid.

Chapter Five

1   Cited by Beavon, K, 2004, Johannesburg: The Making and Shaping of the City. University of South Africa Press.
2   Macmillan, A (ed), The Golden City. WH&L Collingridge.
3   Cited by Neil Fraser on the JDA website at www.jda.org.za

4   Van Onselen, C, 2001. New Babylon, New Nineveh. Jonathan Ball Publishers.
5   Sani, G, 1992. History of the Italians in South Africa 1489–1989. Zonderwater Block.
6   Davie, L. City of Johannesburg website at www.joburg.org.za
7   Ibid.
8   Hellman, E, 1948. Rooiyard: A Sociological Study of an Urban Native Slum Yard, Rhodes-Livingstone Papers No. 13, Oxford University Press, available at www.swarthmore.edu/SocSci/tburke1/8bsyllabus/rooiyard.html
9   City of Johannesburg website at www.joburg.org.za and SA Astronomical Society at www.saao.ac.za
10 Smith, A, 1971. Johannesburg Street Names. Juta & Company.
11 Ibid.

Chapter Six

1   From The Star, 10 February 1890, cited by Neame, LE in City Built on Gold.
2   Fourie, J, 2006. The South African Poor White Problem in the Early 20th Century. University of Stellenbosch.
3   Lewis, 1973. Cited by Fourie, J, 2006.
4   Beavon, K, 2004. Johannesburg: The Making and Shaping of the City. University of South Africa Press.
5   Brink, E, cited by Fraser, N, on CitiChat, at www.joburg.org.za.
6   Van Onselen, C, 2001. New Babylon, New Nineveh. Jonathan Ball Publishers. Note that the historian Luli Callinicos gives a different date for the formation of the Chamber of Mines.
7   Feinstein 2005, cited by Fourie, J, 2006.
8   South African History Online at www.sahistory.org.za.
9   Ibid.
10 Ibid.
11 Ibid.
12 Cartwright. The Dynamite Company. Cited by Davies, L, at www.joburg.org.za.
13 Survey cited by Grant, G, and Flinn, T, 1992. Watershed Town: The History of the Johannesburg City Engineer's Department. Johannesburg City Council.
14 Ibid.
15 Callinicos, L. South African History Online at www.sahistory.org.za.
16 The Golden City PLEASE SUPPLY INFO.
17 Paulsen, MA. The Malay Community Of Gauteng: Syncretism, Beliefs, Customs and Development. Rand Afrikaans University. 0-etd.uj.ac.za.raulib.rau.ac.za/theses/available/etd-05252005-115424/restricted/CHAP3TO6.pdf
18 South African History Online at www.sahistory.org.za.
19 Fraser, N, CitiChat, at www.joburg.org.za.
20 South African History Online at www.sahistory.org.za.
21 South African History Online at www.sahistory.org.za.
22 Chetty, K, 1996. Gandhi: Mahatma in The Making. University of Durban-Westville. Available at http://scnc.udw.ac.za/doc/TEXTS/kc/kctext.html.
23 Ibid.
24 Fraser, N, CitiChat, at www.joburg.org.za.
25 From www.southafrica.info.
26 Gandhi, M, cited at www.nvpf.org/np/english/workadayforpeace/briefhistory.pdf.
27 South African History Online at www.sahistory.org.za.
28 City of Johannesburg website, at www.joburg.co.za.

29 South African History Online at www.sahistory.org.za.
30 Davie, L, at www.joburg.co.za.
31 Plaatje, ST, 1916. Native Life in South Africa.
32 Callinicos, L. South African History Online at www.sahistory.org.za.
33 Grant, G, and Flinn, T, 1992. Watershed Town.
34 South African History Online at www.sahistory.org.za.
35 'Toby Street Blues'. Time magazine 21 February 1955. Available at www.time.com/time/magazine/article/0,9171,892971,00.html.
36 Grant, G and Flinn, T, 1992.
37 Joburg city website at www.joburg.org.za.
38 South African History Online at www.sahistory.org.za.
39 Ibid.
40 Mattera, D, cited on South African History Online at www.sahistory.org.za.
41 Smith, A, 1971. Johannesburg Street Names. Juta.

Chapter Seven

1   United Nations table on Urban Agglomerations. Figures cited are for 2005.
2   Chipkin, C, cited by Grobbelaar, KM, 2004. A Cultural Centre for the Foreign Community, Hillbrow. University of Pretoria, at upetd.up.ac.za/thesis/submitted/etd-05302005-152858/unrestricted/00front.pdf
3   Cited by Beavon, K, 2004. Johannesburg: The Making and Shaping of the City. University of South Africa.
4   Chipkin, C, 1993. Johannesburg Style. David Philip Publishers.
5   Davie, L, on City of Johannesburg, at www.joburg.org.za
6   Beavon, K, 2004.
7   Ibid.
8   Ibid.
9   Ibid.
10 Ibid.
11 Ibid.
12 Madondo, B, 2007. Hot Type – Icons, Artists and God-figurines. Picador Africa.
13 Smith, A, 1971. Johannesburg's Street Names. Juta & Company.
14 Ibid.
15 'Diamond Cut Diamond', Time magazine, 29 February 1932.
16 Dodd, A. Sunday Times, cited on http://www.barrybester.com/voortrekkers.htm
17 Smith, A, 1971.

Chapter Eight

1   Johannesburg: One Hundred Years. Chris van Rensburg Publications (1986).
2   Beavon, K, 2004. Johannesburg: The Making and Shaping of the City. University of South Africa.
3   Macmillan, A, ed, The Golden City. WH & L Collingridge.
4   Davie, L. City of Johannesburg website at www.joburg.org.za
5   Shorten, JR, 1970. The Johannesburg Saga. Cape & Transvaal Printers Limited.
6   The Star newspaper, 1924.
7   Collings, J, 1987. Gold Under Their Hooves. A history of the Johannesburg Turf Club 1887–1987. Chris van Rensburg Publications.
8   Johannesburg: One Hundred Years. Chris van Rensburg Publications (1986).

9 Davie, L. City of Johannesburg website at www.joburg.org.za
10 Collings, J, 1987.
11 Davie, L. City of Johannesburg website at www.joburg.org.za
12 Davie, L. City of Johannesburg website at www.joburg.org.za, citing: Smith, A, 1971. Johannesburg Street Names. Juta. Meiring, H. Early Johannesburg, its buildings and its people. Human & Rousseau.
13 From notes by Dennis Adams, member of the Parktown & Westcliff Heritage Trust; and www.booysenshotel.co.za/history.html
14 Smith, A, 1971. Johannesburg Street Names. Juta.
15 Musiker, N and Musiker, R, 1999. A Concise Historical Dictionary of Greater Johannesburg. Francolin.
16 Ibid.
17 Interview: Jose da Cunha, owner of Parreirinha Restaurant Bar and Beer Garden.
18 Musiker, N and Musiker, R, 1999.
19 Smith, A, 1971.
20 Davie, L. City of Johannesburg website at www.joburg.org.za
21 Musiker, N and Musiker, R, 1999.
22 Davie, L. City of Johannesburg website at www.joburg.org.za
23 Smith, A, 1971.
24 Ibid.
25 Davie, L. City of Johannesburg website at www.joburg.org.za
26 South African History Online at www.sahistory.org.za
27 Ibid.
28 www.kaizerchiefs.com
29 Davie, L. City of Johannesburg website at www.joburg.org.za

Chapter Nine

1 Beavon, K, 2004. Johannesburg: The Making and Shaping of the City. University of South Africa.
2 From Cartwright, AP, The Corner House, cited by Shorten, JR, 1970. The Johannesburg Saga. Cape & Transvaal Printers Limited.
3 Shorten, JR, 1970.
4 The Parktown and Westcliff Urban Walk 1982. Parktown and Westcliff Heritage Trust.
5 Monograph No. 25, Parktown and Westcliff Heritage Trust.
6 Monograph No. 16 by Nola Green. Parktown and Westcliff Heritage Trust
7 Pakenham, T, 1979. The Boer War. Jonathan Ball Publishers.
8 Ibid.
9 Parktown and Westcliff Heritage Trust website at www.parktownheritage.co.za
10 Monograph No. 16, Parktown and Westcliff Heritage Trust.
11 Monograph No. 12 by David Syme-Grant. Parktown and Westcliff Heritage Trust.
12 Welsh, F, 1998. A History of South Africa. Harper Collins.
13 Blainey, cited by Van Onselen, C, 2001. New Babylon, New Nineveh. Jonathan Ball Publishers.
14 Pakenham, T, 1979.
15 Salisbury, cited by Welsh, 1998.
16 Welsh, F, 1998.
17 Neame, LE, 1968 City Built on Gold. Central News Agency.
18 Monograph No. 17 by Flo Bird. Parktown and Westcliff Heritage Trust.
19 Ibid.

20 Oxford Dictionary of National Biography, at www.oxforddnb.com/public/themes/93/93711.html
21 Monograph No. 17 by Flo Bird. Parktown and Westcliff Heritage Trust.
22 The Parktown and Westcliff Urban Walk 1982. Parktown and Westcliff Heritage Trust.
23 Monograph No. 7 by Dennis Radford. Parktown and Westcliff Heritage Trust.
24 Mchunu, M. The Advent of the 'Kitchen Suit': Understanding Zulu Male Initiation. At www.uwc.ac.za/arts/gendervisuality/mchunu.doc
25 1911 Edition of Encyclopaedia Brittanica. Entry under Johannesburg. Available at www.1911encyclopedia.org
26 Census cited by Van Onselen, C, 2001.
27 Van Onselen, C, 2001.
28 Domestic Service in Parktown's Heyday by Daphne Saul. Parktown and Westcliff Heritage Trust.
29 Van Onselen, C, 2001.
30 Ibid.
31 Ibid.
32 Ibid.
33 Article from Imperial Colonist, included in Callinicos, L. Working Life (1987); cited by Mchunu. M.
34 Mchunu, M.
35 Van Onselen, C, 2001.
36 Callinicos, L, cited on South African History Online at www.sahistory.org.za
37 www.ceroi.net/reports/johannesburg/csoe/html/nonjava/Conservation/natural/introduction.htm
38 Davie, L. Brenthurst, Joburg's breathtaking secret garden. City of Johannesburg website www.joburg.org.za and Brenthurst Gardens website www.brenthurstgardens.co.za
39 Smith, A, 1971. Johannesburg Street Names. Juta.
40 Smith, A, 1971. Johannesburg Street Names. Juta.
41 Shorten, JR, 1970.
42 Smith, A, 1971. Johannesburg Street Names. Juta.
43 Telford, A. Johannesburg: Some Sketches of the Golden Metropolis.

Chapter Ten

1 Clarke, J, 2002. Coming Back to Earth: South Africa's Changing Environment. Jacana.
2 Lonehill residents' website, at www.lonehill.za.com
3 Montecasino website, at www.montecasino.co.za
4 From the President's Medals website, at www.presidentsmedals.com/Projectdetails.aspx?student_id=0&proj_id=1042&year=2002#.
5 Davie, L. City of Johannesburg website at www.joburg.org.za
6 Slessor, C, 1995. 'Johannesburg Style: Architecture and Society, 1880s–1960s. Book reviews. The Architectural Review. March 1995
7 Chipkin, C, 1993. Johannesburg Style: Architecture and Society, 1880s–1960s. David Philllips.
8 Czeglédy, AP, 2003. 'Villas of the Highveld'. Emerging Johannesburg – Perspectives in the Post-Apartheid City. Routledge.
9 Ibid.
10 Beavon, K, 2000. 'Northern Johannesburg: part of the 'rainbow' or neo-apartheid city in the making?' At www.arts.uwa.edu.au/MotsPluriels/MP1300kb.html

11 Carruthers, J. 1993. Sandton: The Making of a Town. Celt Books.
12 Marais Louw, J, 1976. Wagon Wheels and Orchards – Early Days in Sandton. AD Donker.
13 From the report 'Significance of the road reserve situated adjacent to erven 163, 168 and 169 North Road and Beaufort Avenue Craighall Park', compiled by Jean Beater for the Craigpark Residents' Association.
14 Scott, cited by Beavon, K, 2004. Johannesburg: The Making and Shaping of the City. University of South Africa.
15 Beavon, K, 2004.
16 Ibid.
17 Ibid.
18 Beavon, K, 1997. Johannesburg: A city and metropolitan area in transformation. At www.unu.edu/unupress/ unupbooks/uu26ue/uu26ue0g.htm
19 Carruthers, J, 1993.
20 Ibid.
21 Carruthers, J. ND. From Sewage Sludge to Pleasant Park: The Story of the Delta Disposal Works, 1934 to 1963. On Delta Park website: www.deltaenviro.org
22 Carruthers, J, 1993.
23 Ibid.
24 Carruthers, J, ND. From Sewage Sludge to Pleasant Park.
25 Carruthers, J, 1993.
26 From www.amethyst.co.za, original source cited as Randburg Sun. 7 September 2001.
27 Carruthers, J, 1993.
28 Cited by Beavon, K, 2004.
29 Beavon, K, 2000.
30 Ibid.

Chapter Eleven

1 Beavon, K, 2004. Johannesburg: The Making and Shaping of the City. University of South Africa and South African History Online at www.sahistory.org.za
2 Native Affairs Commission. Cited by Beavon, K, 2004.
3 Stallard Commission, 1922. Cited by Beavon, K, 2004.
4 Beavon, K, 2004.
5 Beavon, K, 1997. Johannesburg: A city and metropolitan area in transformation. Available at www.unu.edu/unupress/ unupbooks/uu26ue/uu26ue0g.htm
6 Census 2001, from City of Johannesburg website at www.joburg.org.za
7 Haarhoff, J, Juuti, P and Maki, H. A short comparative history of wells and toilets in South Africa and Finland. Available at www.td-sa.net/files/article-23-file_2.pdf
8 Grant, G and Flinn, T, 1992. Watershed Town. Published by the City of Johannesburg.
9 Ibid.
10 Ibid.
11 Beavon, K, 2004.
12 City of Johannesburg website at www.joburg.org.za
13 From an article by the Kliptown Our Town Trust, available at www.criaasadc.org/pdf/Kliptown_article.pdf
14 City of Johannesburg website.
15 The Freedom Charter, from www.anc.org.za
16 Davie, L, 2005 and 2006. Articles on Kliptown on City of Johannesburg website, at www.joburg.org.za
17 Bonner, P and Segal, L, 1998. Soweto – A History. Based on the video documentary Soweto: A History. Maskew Miller Longman

18 Beavon, K, 2004.
19 Bonner, P and Segal, L, 1998.
20 Beavon, K, 1997.
21 Bonner, P and Segal, L, 1998.
22 Beavon, K, 2004.
23 Beavon, K, 2004 and City of Johannesburg website.
24 Beavon, K, 2004 and Mandy, N, 1984. A City Divided: Johannesburg & Soweto. Macmillan
25 Sampson, A, 1999. Mandela. Harper Collins.
26 Ibid.
27 Ibid.
28 Ibid.
29 Ibid.
30 From www.chrishanibaragwanathhospital.co.za
31 Beavon, K, 2004.
32 Cited by Beavon, K, 2004.
33 Beavon, K, 2004.
34 Gprodnov, V, 1989. Soweto: Life and Struggles of South African Township. Firebird.
35 Bonner, P and Segal, L, 1998.
36 Evans, I, 1997. Bureaucracy and Race: Native Administration in South Africa. Berkely: University of California Press available at http://ark.cdlib.org/ark:/13030/ft2n39n7f2/
37 Beavon, K, 2004.
38 Evans, I, 1997.
39 South African History Online.
40 Mandy, N, 1984.
41 Ibid.
42 Ibid.
43 Ibid.
44 Ibid.
45 Ibid.
46 Ibid.
47 Ibid.
48 Ellen Hellman, cited by Pohlandt-McCormick, H, 2000. '"I Saw a Nightmare . . .": Violence and the Construction of Memory' (Soweto, June 16, 1976). History and Theory 39 (4), 23–44 doi:10.1111/0018-2656.00144
49 Morris, P, 1980. Soweto: A study. Transvaal Region of the Urban Foundation. Perskor.
50 Beavon, K, 2004.
51 Grant, G and Flinn, T, 1992.
52 Tomlinson, R, et al, 2003. Emerging Johannesburg: A Perspective on the Post-apartheid City. And Morris, P. (1980).
53 Segal, L, Simpson, G, and Vogelman, L, 1990. 'Why the townships turned into war zones', in The Star, 19 August 1990. Cited by Simpson, G, at http://www.csvr.org.za/ papers/papjack.htm#note24
54 Simpson, G, http://www.csvr.org.za/papers/papjack. htm#note24
55 Thale, T, 2003. Articles for City of Johannesburg website at www.joburg.org.za
56 Grant, G and Flinn, T, 1992.
57 Bonner, P and Segal, L, 1998.
58 Ibid.
59 Ibid.
60 Pohlandt-McCormick, H, 2000.
61 Bonner, P on South African History Online at www.sahistory.org.za
62 Ibid.

63   South African History Online.
64   Bonner, P on South African History Online.
65   Ibid.
66   Ibid.
67   Brooks, A and Brickhill, J, 1980. Whirlwind before the storm. London International Defence & Aid Fund for Southern Africa.
68   Bonner, P on South African History Online.
69   South African History Online.
70   Mashabela, H, 1987. A People on the Boil, Reflections on Soweto. Skotaville Publishers.
71   City of Johannesburg website.
72   Beavon, K, 2004.
73   Bonner, P and Segal, L, 1998.
74   Mandy, N, 1984.
75   Bonner, P and Segal, L, 1998.
76   Beavon, K, 2004.

Chapter Twelve

1   Website of the High Commission of India to South Africa, at www.indiainsouthafrica.com
2   Cajee, ZA, 2003. 'Islamic History & Civilisation in South Africa: The Impact of Colonialism, Apartheid, and Democracy (1652–2004)'.
3   Website of the High Commission of India to South Africa.
4   South African History Online, at www.sahistory.org.za
5   Ibid.
6   Ibid.
7   Michigan State University, African Studies Centre. 'Overcoming Apartheid, Building Democracy', at http://overcomingapartheid.msu.edu/multimedia.php?id=8
8   'Lenasia: The New Surburb with a Happy Future', pamphlet issued by the apartheid authorities to convince Indian people to move into the new 'Indian' area of Lenasia.
9   Dadoo, Y, 1956. Statement on the Proclamation of Group Areas in Johannesburg. New Age, Cape Town, 23 August 1956.
10   Lord Murugan is considered to be the elder brother of Ganesh. He led an army against the demon lord, Surapadman. Murugan is also termed Shanmukha, meaning 'six faces' – as he was created by uniting six children born of the ashes of an arrow aimed at Shiva.
11   Tamils faced with danger may take a vow to offer Lord Murugan a kavadi if spared an anticipated calamity. The kavadi is a sacrifice decorated and carried on people's shoulders in a procession. Devotees may struggle to carry the sacrifice and some emphasise their devotion by adorning themselves with body piercings – some even pulling chariots of Lord Murugan by attaching ropes to the hooks of their piercings. During the ceremony some devotees enter into a trance, a supreme state of devotion in which the god enters the body of the devotee.
12   A good way of identifying a statue when in doubt is to look at the vehicle (vahana – mount) on which the god or goddess rides. Shiva's vehicle is the bull Nandi, while Ganesh rides on a rat or mouse. Durga rides a lion or tiger, Krishna's vehicle is a garuda and Lord Muruga rides on a peacock. When you approach a temple the vehicle awaiting its master outside the front door will allow you to identify the main god or goddess inside the temple.
13   Ganesh, the elephant-headed god, is worshipped as the lord of beginnings and as the lord who can bring about or remove obstacles. He is honoured at the start of any ritual, any day and any letter. Often, as at the Shri Lakshmi Narayan Temple, he guards the doors of buildings. Ganesh received his elephant head from Shiva (his father), to whom he denied access to Parvati (his mother) upon being instructed to guard her chambers. Shiva, not recognising his son, battled with Ganesh, whom he beheaded. When Parvati threatened to destroy heaven and earth on hearing that Shiva had killed their son, Shiva offered to put the head of the first living being he encountered onto his son's head.
14   Mariamman is the main South Indian mother-goddess, associated with Durga and Parvati. Her relation to the syringa tree stems from a legend describing a drought and a measles outbreak that followed. Mariamman, disguised as a lady dressed in yellow clothes, carried a pot of fermented mealie-meal and some syringa leaves to cure the sick. South Africans of Tamil origin honour Mariamman every year during the 'porridge prayers', and by worshipping the divine mother at shrines and trees such as the tree at the Shree Siva Soobramaniar Temple.
15   Gujarat was during the 9th Century divided into four regions – Saurashtra, Kachchh, Aanarta and Laat. Garba dances originated in the north (Saurashtra and Aanarta). The dance forms of Gujarat are performed in two circles (men and women) moving in clockwise and anti-clockwise directions, with two sticks (dandiyas) held in their hands that are clapped rhythmically with changing partners. Originally Garba was performed only by females and originally the dance was performed in reverence to the goddess Ambaji (a local form of Durga, the mother goddess).
16   The Tamil word for temple is 'koil', while north Indian languages refer to the temple as 'mandir'.
17   Vadi, I, 2004. Images of ANC Politics in Lenasia. Published by the ANC Lenasia Branch, p. 25.
18   Ibid, p.29.
19   Memons come originally from Gujarat and follow the Hanafi school of Sunni Islam. Many Memons, like many Hindu Gujeratis, became businessmen after a serious drought in Gujarat led to migration. Since the 19th Century, Memon communities can be found throughout the Indian Ocean basin.
20   Electric Avenue in Brixton was the first electrified shopping area in London. It was built in the 1880s.
21   Mayat, Z, 2006 (1961). Indian Delights: a book on Indian cookery. Women's Cultural Group, Durban, p. 18.
22   Kathrada, A, 2004. Memoirs. Zebra Press, p. 332.
23   Meer, F (ed.), 1995. The South African Gandhi: An Abstract of the Speeches and writings of MK Gandhi 1893–1914. Madiba Publishers and Gandhi Memorial Committee.
24   Itzkin, E, 2000. Gandhi's Johannesburg: Birthplace of Satyagraha. University of the Witwatersrand.

Chapter Thirteen

1   Kgafela oa Magogodi, 'A Town Like Alex', Mail & Guardian. 1 November 2002.
2   City of Johannesburg Website, cited at www.southafrica.info
3   Davie, L, 2003. 'Linda Twala, Alex's philanthropist'. 22 September 2003 at www.joburg.org.za

4   Nauright, J, 1998. 'The Mecca of Native Scum' and 'a running sore of evil': white Johannesburg and the Alexandra Township removal debate, 1935–1945. Klio 38, 1998 at www.unisa.ac.za/default.asp?Cmd=ViewContent&ContentlD=1263
5   Ibid.
6   Ibid.
7   Cited by Nauright, J, 1998.
8   Ibid.
9   Ibid.
10   Morris, P, 2000. 'Alexandra Township – A History, Lessons for Urban Renewal and Some Challenges For Planners'. At www.alexandra.co.za/downloads/xtra_morris_history_2000.pdf
11   From ANC official website (http://www.anc.org.za/ancdocs/history/congress/sactu/organsta05.html) cited by SA History Online at www.sahistory.org.za
12   Ibid.
13   Mufson, S, 1988. 'Alex: From Showdown to Showcase?' APF Reporter Volume 11, Number 3 at www.aliciapatterson.org/APF1103/Mufson/Mufson.html
14   Wilson, M. 'Alexandra Township and the Alexsan Kopano Resource Centre: Background Report', at http://link.wits.ac.za/papers/unesco-alex-bkg.pdf
15   Morris, P, 2000. 'Alexandra Township – A History, Lessons for Urban Renewal and Some Challenges For Planners', at www.aliciapatterson.org/APF1103/Mufson/Mufson.html
16   Ibid.
17   Ibid.
18   Ibid.
19   Ibid.
20   Ibid.
21   Ibid.
22   Mufson, S, 1988.
23   Ibid.
24   Wilson, M. 'Alexandra Township and The Alexsan Kopano Resource Centre: Background Report', at http://link.wits.ac.za/papers/unesco-alex-bkg.pdf
25   Morris, P, 2000, cited by Wilson, M.
26   Alexandra Renewal Project at www.alexandra.co.za
27   Ibid.
28   Ibid.
29   Ibid.

Chapter Fourteen

1   Cited by Beavon, K, 2004. Johannesburg: The Making and Shaping of the City. University of South Africa Press.
2   UN-Habitat report, cited at www.citymayors.com/society/urban_africa.html
3   Beavon, K, 2004.
4   SAHO. 2005: at 'The Squatter Movement, Egoli, A History of Black Johannesburg, Urbanization and Housing in South Africa's largest city', at www.sahistory.org.za
5   Stevens, L and Rule, S, n.d.: 'Moving to an Informal Settlement: The Gauteng Experience', Gauteng Department of Housing and Land Affairs.
6   Crankshaw, O, 1993. 'Squatting, Apartheid and Urbanisation on the Southern Witwatersrand', African Affairs, Vol. 92, No. 366, pp. 31–51.

7   Sapire, H, 1992. 'Politics and Protest in shack settlements of the Pretoria-Witwatersrand-Vereeniging Region, South Africa, 1980–1990', Journal of Southern African Studies, Vol. 18, No. 3, Special Issue: Political Violence in Southern Africa, pp. 670–697.
8   Crankshaw, O, 1993. 'Squatting, Apartheid and Urbanisation on the Southern Witwatersrand', African Affairs, Vol. 92, No. 366, pp.31–51.
9   Dlamini N, 2005. 'Housing Plan looks at Homeless Blues', City of Johannesburg website at www. joburg.org.za/2005/jul/jul113_housing.stm
10   Thale, T, 2002. 'The mayor's delegates visit the people of Diepsloot', on City of Johannesburg website at www.joburg.org.za/june_2002/shacklands.stm
11   City of Johannesburg, n.d. 'Region 11: Ennerdale/Orange Farm', at www.joburg.org.za/unicity/region12.stm
12   Majola B, 'Orange Farm launches self-help gardens', 31 January 2003 at www.joburg.org.za/ ORANGE FARM LAUNCHES SELF-HELP GARDENS.htm
13   Abraham, A. 'Orange Farm gets connected', 12 July 2005, www.southafrica.info/ess_info
14   Internet Solutions Trains Teachers in IT Skills, 08 February 2006, www.is.co.za/news/general/Internet+Solutions+Trains+Teachers+in+IT+Skills.htm
15   ka'Nkosi S, 'Matter of life or death in the enemy's camp', Sunday Times, 28 October 2001.
16   Van Zyl, I, 2004. 'Midrand's blend of ebony and ivory', Sabinet Online at www.sabinet.co.za
17   Cited by Nel, T, 2002. 'Estimated population of 196 000' at www.joburgnews.co.za/june_2002/ivory_park.stm
18   Dlamini N, 2002. 'More houses finished in Ivory Park', 1 February 2008, at http://www.joburg.org.za/content/view/2129/168/
19   Beasse Kirk. 2004: The Power to Change, University of Alberta Express, 7 July 2004, wwwexpressnews.ualberta.ca/article.cfm?id=5928
20   Mangxamba, S. 'Johannesburg to transform informal settlements', Mail and Guardian, 19 August 2004.
21   Evangelides, B, 2004. 'Life Stories of Achievers in Informal Settlements in Gauteng'. Unpublished mini-dissertation, Masters of Education, Rand Afrikaans University.
22   Sisulu, L (Minister of Housing), 2006. 'Partnerships between government and slum/shack dwellers' federations'. Address at FEDUP's Annual Conference May 2006.
23   Huchzermeyer, M, Baumann, T, and Mohamed, S, 2004. 'Background Report 3: Informal Settlement Practice in South Africa's Metropolitan Cities', Study into the Support of Informal Settlements, National Department of Housing, Pretoria.
24   'Cosmo City: a place to call home'. 25 July 2005, at www.southafrica.info/ess_info/sa_glance/social_delivery/cosmo-130505.htm

Index